D1715108

Pragmatism

PRAGMATISM
From Progressivism to Postmodernism

EDITED BY
Robert Hollinger
&
David Depew

Westport, Connecticut
London

Library of Congress Cataloging-in-Publication Data

Pragmatism : from progressivism to postmodernism / edited by Robert
  Hollinger and David Depew.
      p. cm.
    Includes bibliographical references and index.
    ISBN 0–275–94882–X (alk. paper)
    1. Pragmatism—History. 2. Positivism—History.
    3. Postmodernism—History. I. Hollinger, Robert. II. Depew, David
J.
    B944.P72P73   1995
    144'.3—dc20   94–22657

British Library Cataloguing in Publication Data is available.

Library of Congress Catalog Card Number: 94–22657
ISBN: 0–275–94882–X

First published in 1995

Praeger Publishers, 88 Post Road West, Westport, CT 06881
An imprint of Greenwood Publishing Group, Inc.

Printed in the United States of America

The paper used in this book complies with the
Permanent Paper Standard issued by the National
Information Standards Organization (Z39.48–1984).

10 9 8 7 6 5 4 3 2 1

Copyright Acknowledgments

The editors and publisher gratefully acknowledge permission to quote from the following sources:

Lewis Mumford: Public Intellectual, edited by Thomas P. Hughes and Agatha C. Hughes. Copyright © 1990 by Oxford University Press, Inc. Reprinted by permission.

Lewis Mumford, *Technics and Civilization*. New York: Harcourt, Brace, & World, 1962. Excerpts from *Technics and Civilization* copyright 1934 by Harcourt Brace & Company and renewed 1961 by Lewis Mumford, reprinted by permission of the publisher and by permission of Routledge.

Isaac Nevo, "Continuing Empiricist Epistemology: Holistic Aspects in James's Pragmatism," *The Monist* 75 (October 1992): 458–76. Copyright © 1992, THE MONIST, La Salle, Illinois 61301. Reprinted by permission.

Ralph W. Sleeper, "Vanishing Frontiers in American Philosophy: Two Dogmas of Idealism," in *Frontiers in American Philosophy*, edited by Robert W. Burch and Herman J. Saatkamp (College Station, TX: Texas A&M Press), 47–57.

Cornel West, "Theory, Pragmatisms, and Politics," in *Consequences of Theory*, edited by Jonathan Arac and Barbara Johnson (Baltimore, MD: The Johns Hopkins University Press), 22–38.

Richard Rorty, *Consequences of Pragmatism*. Minneapolis: University of Minnesota Press, 1982. Copyright © 1982 by the University of Minnesota.

Richard Rorty, *Contingency, Irony, and Solidarity*. Cambridge: Cambridge University Press, 1989. Reprinted with the permission of Cambridge University Press.

Thomas McCarthy, "Private Irony and Public Decency: Richard Rorty's New Pragmatism," *Critical Inquiry* 16 (Spring 1990): 355–70. Reprinted with the permission of The University of Chicago Press.

Richard Rorty, "Truth and Freedom: A Reply to Thomas McCarthy," *Critical Inquiry* 16 (Spring 1990): 633–43. Reprinted with the permission of The University of Chicago Press.

Thomas McCarthy, "Ironist Theory as Vocation: A Response to Rorty's Reply," *Critical Inquiry* 16 (Spring 1990): 644–55. Reprinted with the permission of The University of Chicago Press.

Richard Rorty, "Philosophy as Science, as Metaphor, and as Politics," in *The Institution of Philosophy*, edited by A. Cohen and M. Dascal (La Salle, IL: Open Court, 1989), 13–34. Reprinted with the permission of Open Court and the author.

In memory of Konstantin "Konnie" Kolenda
and Ralph W. Sleeper

Contents

Acknowledgments

The editors wish to thank the contributors to this volume for their cooperation and patience. We would also like to thank Mr. Peter Coveney of Greenwood Publishing Group, who has been most helpful and cooperative.

David Depew would like to thank the Department of Philosophy of California State University, Fullerton, for financial and staff assistance, especially Elaine Weidener. Bob Hollinger would like to thank Edna Wiser and Marge Langloss of the I.S.U. Philosophy Department for secretarial assistance. We would both like to give special thanks to David A. Hollinger, Giles Gunn, and Joseph Margolis for support and advice.

The remote origins of this volume lay in the Twentieth CSUF Philosophy Symposium on Philosophy and American Culture held at California State University, Fullerton, March 8–10, 1990. We thank the members of the Departments of Philosophy and American Studies, and students in both departments, who planned the conference, and those who participated in it. We also thank the CSUF Departmental Associations Council (DAC) and the California State Lottery, which funded this event.

Two of our contributors—friends as well as colleagues—have recently passed away: "Konnie" Kolenda and Ralph Sleeper. We dedicate this volume to their memories, as a token of our appreciation for their work in American Philosophy, and our respect and affection for them as colleagues, friends, and human beings.

General Introduction

David Depew and Robert Hollinger

Pragmatism has become popular again. It has become so popular, in fact, that everyone seems to know what it is. In keeping with pragmatism's antiessentialist spirit, however, we should recognize that from its earliest days pragmatism has meant many things to many people. Only a year after William James's influential 1907 lectures on pragmatism, Arthur O. Lovejoy was able to discriminate thirteen distinct meanings for the term.[1] Since then, every subsequent rebirth of pragmatism has generated more views about it. Indeed, having been given new currency by Richard Rorty, the term *pragmatism* is now being bandied about in so many ways that Lovejoy, were he alive today, would be cast into paroxysms of *Schadenfreude*.

We say *Schadenfreude* because Lovejoy regarded pragmatism's dissemination of meaning as *ipso facto* a condemnation of it. Like other professionalizing philosophers, Lovejoy believed that if philosophy was to make as much progress as science, it would have to trade in sober, unambiguous, technical meanings. By contrast, the editors of this volume, and many of the intellectual historians and historically sensitive philosophers who have contributed to it, are not as sour as Lovejoy was about plural meanings. On the contrary, we are generally in sympathy with pragmatism's tendency to let a thousand semantic flowers bloom. But for this very reason most of us do not believe that taking a pragmatic view of history grants to one's present interests or one's prospective hopes unlimited license to reshape the past, especially the past of one's own intellectual filiation. If pragmatism's present condition is to be properly assessed and if its future prospects are to be realized, no good will come from retrospectively prescribing to diverse people living in diverse times what they must have meant.

It is simply not pragmatic to believe that there is a pragmatism that rides serenely over these differing circumstances.

If the arguments of pragmatists, and the consequences they draw from them, have differed wildly, it is nonetheless true that pragmatists share a number of characteristic attitudes, which they explicate, justify, and commend in different ways. Pragmatists have a suspicious attitude, for example, toward the epistemological and ontological problems that have virtually defined the philosophical tradition, which have made of skepticism a constantly looming threat. Accordingly, it is important to recognize that when they claim that ideas derive their meaning, and even get their truth, wholly from their utility in guiding behavior, pragmatists do not wish to cast doubt on our ability to know things. For pragmatists, meaning, truth, and knowledge are not scarce. On the contrary, they are ubiquitous. This is because pragmatists are viscerally convinced that overly objectivistic, or "foundationalist," epistemological criteria are, by their very unfulfillability, the main cause of the skeptical temptations into which philosophers regularly fall. Pragmatists say that such criteria are incoherent and irrelevant. No reasonable person has any cause to be disappointed if it turns out that their conditions cannot be met.

One way to defend this intuition is to stress the primacy of action over contemplation in the cognitive efforts of humans. This is another characteristically pragmatic attitude. If *praxis* is primary, knowledge abounds whenever and wherever people cooperatively do and make things. Only to isolated, passive thumb-suckers does it seems hard to come by. For this reason, pragmatists deny that philosophical contemplation can furnish a separate kind of knowledge above and beyond what we learn as inquiring animals situated in an interactive cultural environment. They also affirm that ordinary people are capable of running their own lives, and improving the lives of others, because the cognitively rich skills and experience they come to possess can never be eclipsed by the arcane *gnosis* of this or that priestly caste. In stressing the primacy of *praxis* over *theoria*, accordingly, pragmatism shows itself to be more than an epistemological stance. It is also an attitude about values and purposes. The epistemic permissiveness of the pragmatic tradition, and the active, this-worldly, democratic perspective from which pragmatism speaks, is intended to blunt the moral, social, and political passivity, cynicism, even nihilism, that seem so often to accompany epistemic cramp. It is intended to unleash a sense of freedom, autonomy, novelty, and progress. If there is any respect in which pragmatism is a characteristically American doctrine, this is it. Indeed, following its career in America is a good way of investigating how knowledge and power have been intertwined in this country throughout the twentieth century.

From this perspective the history of American pragmatism can usefully be divided into three periods. In the first period, classical pragmatism became linked to the diffuse social and political movements known as progressivism. This link was formed, on the epistemological side, by what John Dewey called "the influence of Darwinism on philosophy." On the assumption that evolutionary theory shows mind to be a collection of adaptive traits, which enable humans to get around in the world, pragmatists as different as James, George Herbert Mead, and Dewey conceived of personal development as adaptive behavior within a cultural environment, and of social, political, and economic reform as ameliorative human ecology. In this way, pragmatism helped America pass from unregulated forms of capitalism to more regulated versions.

A second phase of American pragmatism began when sophisticated advocates of logical positivism or logical empiricist views about philosophy, scientific method, and social engineering began arriving in America in flight from Nazi tyranny in the late 1930s and early 1940s. Positivists like Rudolf Carnap and American pragmatists like Charles Morris felt immediately that they had much in common. Pragmatists agreed, for example, that their own notion of meaning as the "cash value" of an idea was a crude first approximation to the positivists' "verificationist" theory of meaning, according to which a proposition that cannot possibly be judged true or false has no clear meaning. In the course of clarifying this notion, Carnap, and after him W.V.O Quine, took what they both described as a pragmatic turn. No amount of information can determine which of the many conceptual and theoretical frameworks we use to interpret our experience is better or truer apart from our purposes and problems. The proof of conceptual schemes is entirely in the pudding. They are to be judged pragmatically.

In both of these phases, pragmatists took a commendatory view of the natural sciences, the experimentalism of which contrasted vividly with the priestly ideal of knowledge as passive contemplation. At the same time, the pragmatists' positive attitude toward the benefits of scientific method in an experimentalist culture pointed to an ambiguity that has dogged them from the outset. Do pragmatists, and progressives, advocate enhanced participatory democracy or technocratic social engineering? Are they populists or elitists? To this disputed question the authors in this volume repeatedly return. The issue had already been raised in the 1920s, when Randolph Bourne, a former disciple of Dewey, Lewis Mumford, and others, adopted a more critical stance toward capitalist democracy than most pragmatists, as well as a more highly aestheticized sense of the lifeworld, and, from this perspective, attacked Dewey's "pragmatic acquiescence" to "Wilson's War." In this matter, Dewey was not without ways of defending himself. When he gave ground, moreover, it was generally by moving toward Bourne's and Mumford's values. Yet, to Dewey's dismay, the positivists' infusion of markedly scientist attitudes into the pragmatic tradition subsequently tilted pragmatism's sense of itself toward the technocratic and away from the communal and the aesthetic. In an atmosphere dominated by World War II, the Cold War, the emergence of a national security state, the ascendancy of managerial capitalism, and consumerist conceptions of the good life, behaviorist views about human motives were combined with ideas about how capitalistic economics could be rationalized in ways that displaced the public-minded, participatory ideals of earlier progressive pragmatists, and put in

their place versions of liberalism that stressed the wider scope of personal freedom and private pursuits that would be made possible when experts were left
free to manage public affairs, and the economy, for others. Positivized and
scientized pragmatism played a role in this shift by declaring, often in the name
of pragmatism itself, the notion that ''an end of ideology'' had by the 1950s
been reached in America.

In recent decades, things have changed dramatically. Beginning in the 1960s,
a cultural reaction against fetishized scientific and technocratic worldviews, and
new attraction to aestheticizing, expressive, and participatory conceptions of the
lifeworld, began to take shape. This sea-change was doubtless triggered by widespread recognition that enormous power had been flowing to technocrats
throughout the century, and that science, when linked to power in that way, was
at least as often a force for ill as for good. That is an idea that would scarcely
have crossed the brows of most nineteenth-century progressives, including
Dewey. This cultural shift stimulated and was in turn intensified by a widespread
revolt against positivist philosophy of science by students of many disciplines.
Thomas Kuhn's *The Structure of Scientific Revolutions* (1962, 1970) was an
important catalyst of this revolt. Kuhn argued that scientific theories do not
organize data in ways that are any more, or any less, rational than political
ideologies, religious beliefs, and aesthetic movements, and therefore that those
who would strongly demarcate the rationality of science from the alleged irrationalism of these other dimensions of life were misguided. Against this background a third, and quite distinctive, moment in pragmatism's career began to
find a voice. Pragmatism began to disentangle itself from positivism, scientism,
and technologism, and to link itself with the humanities.

A key event was the publication in 1979 of Richard Rorty's *Philosophy and
the Mirror of Nature*. In it, and in subsequent volumes such as *Consequences
of Pragmatism* (1982) and *Contingency, Irony, and Solidarity* (1989), Rorty, an
analytic philosopher who had edited a canonical anthology on *The Linguistic
Turn* (1967), chided his professional colleagues for too often remaining enslaved
to Platonic dreams of finding the one true ''language'' in which nature was
presumably written, and of having the arrogance to impose the preferred language on all ''first-order'' inquirers. Rorty argued that in point of fact analytic
philosophy's successful pursuit of the ''meaning of meaning'' leads to an even
more thoroughgoing pragmatism than Quine and his disciples had suspected, in
which scientific ways of interpreting experience cannot be privileged over those
of artists and poets, and in which the transcendance of scientism implies the
transcendance of philosophy itself. Appearing in the garb of a latter-day Deweyan public intellectual, Rorty has gone on to proclaim that the death of philosophy carries with it cultural consequences as large as those that once
accompanied the displacement of theology from the centrality it once enjoyed.
A postempiricist, postphilosophical, and in these respects postmodern, society
will certainly affirm the promises of liberal democracy. Each person will be free
to reinvent himself or herself. Postmodern pragmatists are convinced, however,

that the full scope for self-creation, self-interpretation, and self-expression will be granted only when liberalism has liberated itself from the earnest appeals to human nature and natural rights that bewitched our founding fathers, and from the religious conceptions of the human condition that modern philosophy both displaced and at the same time preserved. According to Rorty, universalist, essentialist ideas like these fall into the "mind as mirror of nature" fallacy. Just as scientific essentialism "blocks the road of inquiry" by constraining world descriptions, so "the right and the good" cherished by ethicists are too aprioristic to allow Rorty's thousand flowers to bloom.

In this atmosphere, philosophers who had remained true to pragmatism after it lost its earlier ascendancy have gained a new hearing. Some of their voices can be heard in this volume. Moreover, many analytic philosophers, such as Nelson Goodman, Hilary Putnam, Donald Davidson, and Joseph Margolis have acknowledged, sometimes under Rorty's prodding, the pragmatic genealogy and purport of much of their work, while at the same time refusing to follow Rorty in abandoning the philosophical tradition altogether. For Rorty himself, however, disentangling the pragmatic tradition from the cultural primacy of science signals that literary humanists, long on the defensive in the heyday of positivized culture, will henceforth be pragmatism's primary audience, champions, and developers. In this spirit, Rorty, as well as literary and social critics like Richard Pourier, Stanley Fish, Giles Gunn, and Cornel West, all of whom think of themselves as pragmatists, have provided creative new readings of James, Dewey, and other pragmatist heroes, in which they appear as prophets of a culture in which scientific theories will be treated exactly like other texts, and in which texts will be freely constructed and deconstructed from the perspective of active interpreters rather than in terms of supposedly invariant, essentialist intentions that authors impose on supine readers.

This is not to suggest that neopragmatist readings of pragmatism's past have always been received with equanimity. Many of the contributors to this volume, for example, believe that the great figures of classical pragmatism cannot plausibly be construed as harbingers of postmodernity, whose pragmatic impulses just happened to be contingently constrained by a naive belief in science. Nor is it necessary to believe that the classical positivists shared in anything remotely like the kind of scientism to which the positivists and their pragmatic acolytes gave widespread currency in the middle decades of this century. If postmodern pragmatists do not always recognize this, that is because their efforts are better interpreted as a revolt against positivized pragmatism of the middle decades of the twentieth century than as an accurate account of what we have called progressive pragmatism. Postmodern pragmatism bears the scars of that revolt. Indeed, Rorty himself seems merely to invert, rather than fully to transcend, the positivist scale of values when he suggests that public affairs are best left in the hands of technocratic managers, so that the rest of us can get on with the important business of pursuing the private happiness that material well-being makes possible. Is that the sort of politics, we may ask, that postmodern pragmatism portends? If so, does it not thereby move even further away from Dewey's participatory politics than positivized pragmatism by combining cultural elitism with deep contentment about leaving the culture of expertise in charge of the public sphere? Alternatively, are there forms of postmodern pragmatism that transcend, rather than merely invert, the science-humanities dichotomy? Does the "prophetic pragmatism" of Cornel West, for example, which stresses recovery of the cultural past as a means of communal action, and which has a positive attitude toward the religious traditions that have bound us to one another, count as such a transcendance? Will exploring new forms of pragmatism lead to a deeper recovery of James, Mead, and Dewey, and of the participatory side of the progressive heritage than those we have seen so far? This volume comes up against these questions. But it leaves their answers to others.

NOTE

1. Arthur O. Lovejoy, "The Thirteen Pragmatisms," *Journal of Philosophy* 5 (1908): 36–39.

Part I

Pragmatists and Progressives

Introduction

David Depew

The quirky genius Charles Sanders Peirce first explored the pragmatist conception of meaning in meetings of a Metaphysical Club at Harvard in the 1870s, which William James also attended. In order to make any of our ideas clear, Peirce claimed, all we have do is "consider what effects that might conceivably have practical bearings we conceive the object of our conception to have." Those consequences, either as "conduct to be recommended or experiences to be expected," are what the idea *means*.[1] Peirce's use of the term *pragmatic* to describe this notion of meaning was inspired by Kant's.[2] Kant held that in fields like biology, history, and politics we cannot help but orient our thought and behavior by acting "as if" certain functional or purposive notions ("x is there *in order to* do y") are true, even though they seem to clash with the laws of mechanistic physics. For Kant, the validity of such "regulative" ideas is predicated on how they orient our conduct in making further inquiries and in deciding what to do, rather than on whether they give us accurate theoretical representations of the world. Hence such ideas are pragmatic (from the Greek verb *prattein*, to act).

The sphere to which Kant assigns pragmatic ideas largely coincides with what was left of the old purposive or teleological Aristotelian worldview, from which Kant could not bear entirely to part after modern science had mechanized the world-picture. Peirce realized, however, that since James Clerk Maxwell, Ludwig Boltzmann, Josiah Willard Gibbs, and Charles Darwin, science itself had been changing. A second scientific revolution was revealing a much less deterministic and mechanistic world than the one portrayed by Newton, Laplace, and Kant.[3] It was a processive and unfinished world, shot through with chance, contingency, and seat-of-the-pants adaptations, yielding its contours, therefore, to statistical and probabilistic forms of reasoning. Peirce concluded that in such a world *all* our ideas must be pragmatic in something like Kant's sense. In an inherently changing world, the determinacy of which shapes up mostly behind us, ideas guide us from one point in inquiry to another. Because the world itself, however, and not just our ideas about it, is in process, our changing ideas can point toward objects, or be objective, rather than merely calling attention to the contrast between our mutable subjectivity and a reality that is assumed to be invariant, as Kant had it.

This conviction undergirded Peirce's problem-centered model of thinking, according to which belief is the temporary cessation of genuine puzzlement and doubt through successful inquiry, "a demi-cadence," as he put it, "in the symphony of our intellectual life."[4] Peirce went on to argue that in an inherently changing world the only reliable, because corrigible, way of "fixing belief" and of guiding behavior so that it correctly anticipates the changing flow of events is the experimental method of modern science. This method allows knowledge to change while still distinguishing it from mere belief, a point that overturned nearly the entire philosophical tradition. In this spirit, Peirce applied the pragmatic criterion of meaning to the concept of truth by defining it as a Kantian regulative ideal. We sort out what is known from what we merely opine, and move more surely toward an objectively correct account of things, by regarding truth as a property of a hypothetical, contrary-to-fact state of affairs in the indefinite future when unconstrained inquiry would have produced universal agreement on the basis of total information.

Although he was attracted to Peirce's processive view of reality and to the pragmatic criterion of meaning, James believed that Peirce's restriction of the effects of our ideas on our conduct to what might eventually emerge from "laboratory habits of mind" tended to ratify the long-standing prejudices of metaphysicians and natural scientists against the lived world of cultural experience, and so to draw the wrong lessons from the discovery of an inherently processive world, of knowledge that is revisable, and of the pragmatic criterion of meaning. For his part, James thought we live within the bonds of a profoundly useful, but indefinitely reinterpretable cultural inheritance, which comes up against the bounds of sense only at the edges. Because there are so many good ways of describing one's experience and acting reasonably in the face of it, Peirce's conception of inquiry settling around a single world-version seemed to James wrong-headedly to retain relics of the changeless world-picture that Peirce did so much to overthrow. From James's humanistic perspective, Peirce was simply putting experimental scientists instead of armchair metaphysicians in charge of the drive toward what is objectively, and unpragmatically, true, even if he did it hypothetically and counterfactually.

In order to undercut this tendency, James narrowed the gap Peirce posited between meaning and truth. For James any idea that has a favorable effect on conduct and the coherence of one's life is not only meaningful, but true. Peirce was so appalled by contentions like this, which began to gain currency of the sort that, in his mind, attended ideas that "fall into literary clutches," that he ceased calling his own philosophy pragmatism. Dubbing it "pragmaticism" instead—a term he acerbically but wittily said was "so ugly it will be safe from kidnappers"—Peirce relinquished control over the notion of pragmatism.[5] It can still be reasonably asked whether he should have done so. For the resulting subjectification of pragmatism obscured Peirce's profound revision of what objectivism means. In a "community of discourse" divided between pragmatists of a "humanist" stripe and "realists" who clung to the old foundationalism, Peirce went willingly, if obscurely, into the realist camp.

Much of what James was insisting on represented the resolution of his personal struggle with depression and its philosophical counterpart, determinism. However, as David Hollinger suggests in an influential essay reprinted (with an updated postscript) in this volume, James's motives for insisting that "true" means "what is good in the way of belief"[6] cannot come fully into focus until he is lifted out of his personal, and his hothouse familial, situation, and shown to be up to his neck in a constellation of ideas, concerns, and attitudes characteristic of a particular subculture or class. The general object of James's thinking, writing, and lecturing was to stiffen the spine of genteel postpuritans like himself, asking them to preserve their high-mindedness in the face of the collapse of the transcendent worldview to which idealists like his friend Josiah Royce were still precariously clinging. It was from this perspective, as George Cotkin shows, that James's stress on the strenuous life, so redolent of what we today find comical about Theodore Roosevelt, was typical of a generation of protomodernists who were trying to preserve the moralistic individualism they inherited from Emerson in a world in which Emerson's metaphysical comforts were simply unavailable, and in which there was no corresponding guarantee that all was right in the social and political domain. A good deal of the progressive movement was bound up with impulses like these. For all was not in fact well in society. Unconstrained capitalism, chaotic immigration, and imperialism had destroyed the craftsman-farmer economy and *ethos* in which the nation's ideological self-conception and institutional practices had hitherto been deeply rooted, as well as the Protestant monopoly on spiritual matters.

James's philosophizing was unabashedly psychologistic. His version of pragmatism, that is to say, was an inference from his attempt, in *Principles of Psychology*, to revise and radicalize the tradition of British psychological empiricism by denying that there is any rock-bottom stratum of experience into which everything else can be resolved, analyzed, or elementally sundered. Replacing the atomistic and mechanistic analysis characteristic of the first scientific revolution with a holistic, probabilistic, field theory of the mind, James affirmed that consciousness is a "blooming, buzzing confusion." We can never get a spectator's view, but are constrained to make our way through what John McDermott has called "streams of experience" by trial and error.[7] In this task, one ought to be as cautious as possible by reinterpreting rather than outright rejecting one's cultural inheritance. "New truth," James wrote in *Pragmatism* (1907) "is always a go-between, a smoother-over of transitions. It marries old opinion to new fact as ever to show a minimum of jolt, a maximum of continuity."[8] This contention had some real consequences. Whereas the resolutive mode of analysis that had characterized empiricism from Locke to Hume to Mill had made it hard to believe that sensory data could ever rationally justify such things as religious belief, James judged that "humanism," and even religious experience, could be pragmatically verified.

If James's pragmatism was built on his psychology, it is no less true that James's psychology was based on an up-to-date biological conception of mind as a product of natural selection. "Taking a purely naturalistic view of the matter," James wrote, "it seems reasonable to suppose that, unless consciousness served some useful purpose, it would not have been superadded to life."[9] James was being Darwinian when he stated "that new modes of thought and conceptual innovations spring up in the mind as spontaneous mental variations. We come to accept them as representations of the environment only if they continue to meet the test of survival."[10] He reasoned that any adaptation that yields a capacity for reacting creatively to various environmental contingencies will, *ceteris paribus*, be more valuable than one that dictates only fixed reactions to relatively stereotyped occasions. On this score, the human mind is a highly valuable cognitive and conative adaptation. Its spontaneity allows creative responses to the contingencies and indeterminacies of experience by way of complex and creative versions of the world that guide and shape further experience. From this perspective, mind is not a passive recorder of the environment, as it is in classical empiricism, but an active determiner of a person's possibilities in an open world, "a fighter for ends" in James's fine phrase.

Peirce was a help to James in making a philosophy of this biocentric psychology not only because of his doubt-inquiry-belief model of mental activity, but because he too placed great emphasis on the evolutionary grounding of his theory of inquiry. "A persuasive article on pragmatism," Peirce wrote, "should show on evolutionary and other grounds that intellect is an adaptive character."[11] For his part, Dewey was even more committed than Peirce or James to deploying an adaptationist theory of meaning to arrive at redescriptions of experience. At the same time, Dewey did not believe that an adaptationist theory of mind allows each of us to count as true whatever helps us get up in the morning. Rather, what Dewey called "the influence of Darwinism on philosophy" should lead us to favor a range of redescriptions of experience in which individual life is characterized as social, and in which social life is described in interactive and cooperative terms that foster ongoing projects of social reconstruction through communal experimental inquiry and democratic decision making.[12]

This shift from individual reinterpretation to collective reconstruction is what Dewey meant when he remarked, in an autobiographical sketch far more insightful than most instances of this self-serving genre, that James did not "fully

and consistently realize . . . the return to a biological conception of the *psyche*"
that he was primarily responsible for reintroducing to a post-Darwinian world.[13]
What Dewey means to return to is an Aristotelian understanding of mind and
other psychological traits as organic functions rather than subjective experiences.
By focusing on humans as social animals, Darwinian adaptationism, as Dewey
understood it,[14] provided a way of articulating a new Aristotelian naturalism, in
which, in an open, unfinished Peircean world, humans appear as problem-solving
animals, and their linguistically mediated social environment seems as natural
to them as water to fish.

Neither in his early idealist nor his subsequent naturalistic stages did Dewey
believe that experience is an onslaught of information flowing before, around,
and behind relatively isolated egos, on which each of us struggles to impose
order and predictability, as empiricists both classical and "radical" are prone
to suggest. Rather, for Dewey experience comes to us in evolved, generic patterns, patterns that are recognized and further shaped by our activities as social
animals. Dewey, that is to say, removed what he somewhat unfairly took to be
the phenomenalist veil from James toward a more object-centered naturalism
and a more biologized psychology. For this reason, Dewey was far less sympathetic than James to merely private expressions (whether religious or humanistic) of metaphysical or aesthetic comfort, or to Emersonian self-assertions,
even of a polite and genteel Nietzchean cast. Cooperative democratic experience
in political, economic, educational, and even private spheres was for Dewey to
replace the comforts of religion. It was to be their transcendence and fulfillment.
In the Hegelian *argot* of Dewey's philosophical youth, it was to be their *Aufhebung*.

Dewey's adaptationism has both a critical and a reconstructive side. On the
critical side, it cuts off any foundationalist appeals to transcendent entities and
principles, and hence to the traditional primacy of *theoria* over *praxis* and
techne. It turns Aristotle's psychology on its head. As Sidney Hook was perhaps
the first to see, for Dewey, as well as for Marx, the ideal of pure theoretical
contemplation is a reflex of societies in which power is granted and legitimated
precisely in proportion to the degree to which one is free from the honest toil
and craftsmanly interaction with the world out of which experimental science,
technology, and industry arose.[15] The world of work and experimental method,
suppressed by aristocratic politics, is to be liberated and rationally transformed
by democratic culture, and hence by a philosophy that assimilates theoretical to
practical and productive reason.

The reason Dewey alleges for this reversal of cognitive interests and values
is biological. The mind is adaptive, and adaptations are, by their very nature,
referentially tied to the particular environmental conditions and needs that shape
them. "If organic adaptations are due simply to constant variation and the elimination of those variations which are harmful in the struggle for existence,"
Dewey writes in "The Influence of Darwinism on Philosophy," "interest shifts
from the wholesale essence back of special changes to the question of how

special changes serve and defeat concrete purposes.''[16] This means that outside of their relevance to a real problem-solving situation, or what Dewey calls ''inquiry,'' ideas lose their meaning. Transcendental illusions, that is to say, will accompany thinking outside of a real problematic context and not just, as Kant thought, thinking beyond the bounds of empirical sensibility. In the naturalistic space secured by evolutionary psychology and epistemology, the problems of philosophy are not to be ''dropped,'' but ''reconstructed'' by translating them into a fruitful vocabulary for social reform. For Dewey, ideas are tools or instruments of adaptation, like organs. That is why he called his philosophy *instrumentalism*. Instrumentalism bids us to analyze and reform our beliefs and values in the biosocial and adaptational terms under which, in Dewey's view, they can alone be effective, true, or meaningful. ''Desires and interests produce consequences only when the activities in which they are expressed take effect in the environment by interacting with physical conditions,'' he wrote. ''The missing link in the chain of knowledge that terminates in grounded valuation propositions is the biological.''[17]

In Dewey's reconstructed philosophy, socially cooperative persons living in a democratic society will necessarily become more highly individuated and autonomous than the isolated and merely reflective egos of class-stratified societies, whose alienation is imaged by traditional epistemology-centered philosophies, in which private Cartesian egos inspect little more than the field of their own consciousness. Both early and late, Dewey took it as a postulate that ''It is through association that man has acquired his individuality and it is through association that he exercises it.''[18] This conviction expressed themes that Dewey had absorbed deeply in his Hegelian youth. Hegel had argued that it was the destiny of modernity to secularize the Judaeo-Christian conviction of the infinite worth of the person. That would mean providing concrete institutional conditions—legal, economic, and political—for the mutual recognition of individuals in society. Meditating profoundly on the aftermath of the French Revolution, Hegel argued that mutual recognition, and so individuation itself, could occur only in and through the bonds of a strong social *ethos*. Throughout the nineteenth century, Hegel's best disciples tried with more or less success to disengage this vision from their master's short-sighted belief that the required bonds are those of an inherited monarchy rationalized and stabilized by a well-educated and well-oiled bureaucracy. The point of Dewey's practice-centered reconstruction in philosophy was always to preserve and deepen the Hegelian theory of individuation through socialization by identifying participatory, if also representative, democracy, already planted in the rich soil of American culture, as the medium in and through which the idealists' ''identity of subject and object'' was to be achieved.

Dewey never changed his mind about this theory of persons and the conditions necessary for their flourishing. Convinced, however, that idealist versions of democratic Hegelianism could never successfully face or solve the real problems of modern life—Dewey had in mind figures like T. H. Green in Britain and Royce in America, as well as his old patrons and mentors William Torrey Harris and George Sylvester Morris—Dewey made a decisive switch in the mid-1890s from an idealist to a naturalistic interpretive matrix. If Dewey often appears as a modern Aristotle that is because he was contesting Hegel's claim to have updated and completed Aristotle by making Aristotle more idealistic. Like Marx, Dewey was claiming instead that Aristotle's biocentric psychology and his view of human flourishing as essentially social, could be developed only by taking Aristotle's basic contentions in a more consistently naturalistic direction.[19] This could be done with the help of Darwinian rather than Aristotelian biology.

Dewey's shift to naturalism took place in the context of his engagement in the distinctive sort of populist progressivism that flourished in the Midwest at the end of the nineteenth century. In 1894, just as he was prying himself loose from the Social Gospel Christianity and idealist philosophy that had thus far served to focus both his professional and reformist efforts, Dewey left the University of Michigan to serve as chairman of the Philosophy Department at the new University of Chicago, to whose founding president, William Rainey Harper, he had been recommended by James Hayden Tufts. Tufts, who had been Harper's student at Yale, had already begun to work closely with Dewey at Michigan. In turn, Dewey brought George Herbert Mead, a third member of their emerging research group, from Michigan. All three came from New England Congregationalist backgrounds and from German or German-oriented educations. As James Campbell shows in the paper he has contributed to this volume, all three of them were post-Hegelian communitarians, and all three were devoted to the project of naturalizing that inheritance.

For the Chicago philosophers, Hegelian naturalism and democratic communitarianism could triumph only if the primacy of practice over theory as the site at which intelligence is paradigmatically exercised could be philosophically defended. Professional philosophers would be convinced of that only with difficulty. If it was possible to convince them at all, they would have to be shown that the philosophical problems of logic, epistemology, and metaphysics can best be resolved from a praxical rather than a purely intellectualistic point of view. By 1903, Dewey and his students had turned out an impressive piece of cooperative philosophical work aimed at demonstrating precisely this. The idea of *Studies in Logical Theory* was to portray logic as a tool of discovery, mediating between problematic situation and problem-solving response. Dewey and other contributors argued that if philosophers resisted this idea they must necessarily regard logical form as externally imposed on alien, sensuous matter. Hegel had long before criticized Kant on this very point. More recently, Dewey had criticized Green for making the same error. In this way, the Chicago philosophers now asserted that a practical logic of discovery, in which matter and form are fused and refused through problem-solving innovation, would better account for the quality of necessity that had traditionally and rightly been ascribed to logic than any theory in which contingency enters through a theoretical gap between empirical content and logical framework. (The neo-Kantian Hermann Lötze was the whipping boy in much of *Studies*, but the point had wider resonance.)

Most professional philosophers remained incredulous. When he visited the United States, Bertrand Russell, for example, was scathingly dismissive of it. The late Ralph Sleeper, on the other hand, has been well disposed to the theory expressed in *Studies in Logical Theory* even on strictly philosophical grounds. In *The Necessity of Pragmatism*, Sleeper suggests that what he calls the "dogmas of idealism" (in an address to the American Philosophical Association reprinted in this volume) can be overcome only on these terms.[20] However that may be, it was not only technical philosophical issues that Dewey, Tufts, and Mead were working to solve at Chicago. Direct social engagement was a no less prominent part of their program. Arriving just as the smoke was clearing from the Pullman strike, Dewey and his colleagues entered into an alliance with the progressive Chicago Civic Federation, a group of businessmen shaken by the specter of class warfare, who sought to mediate this and other strikes. Soon they found themselves working with Jane Addams at Hull House. Dewey's experimental or laboratory school at the University of Chicago, in which Alice Dewey played a leading role, was leavened with Addams's ideas about social work, while Addams soon learned to talk about her settlement work in a Deweyesque idiom.[21]

This circle gained the trust of the liberal business elite in part because its members did not espouse a theory of inevitable class conflict. On the contrary, their experience, direct or indirect, with German politics, social theory, and post-Hegelian philosophy bid them to translate the cooperative attitudes they had brought from their liberal Protestant backgrounds into a theory of class harmony facilitated by complex mediations between voluntary associations, including labor unions.[22] After Dewey moved to Columbia University in New York in 1904, this vision was harder to keep in mind, and even more difficult to project to others. New York had a different political climate from Chicago. It also had a different intellectual culture, in which theories of class harmony were not likely to get much of a hearing among those on the left, whether liberals or Marxists.[23] It was in this context that Dewey's Hegelian philosophy began to be dismembered by romantic aestheticists on the one side and scientist technocrats on the other.

As Casey Blake's *Beloved Community* demonstrates, and as his essay in this volume illustrates, Randolph Bourne, Lewis Mumford, and other members of the "Young America" movement were struggling with the same problems as the Hegelians: the fate of craftsmanship in a world of industrial production and mass consumption, and how to strengthen the communitarian context in which individuals and democracy can alone flourish.[24] Their critique of capitalism and political liberalism was mounted in this context. The Young Americans did not work, however, within the neo-Hegelian conceptual matrix in which the various aspects of Dewey's philosophy were woven together. Trying to return to or preserve the remnants of the aesthetic and ethical "golden day" of pre-machine craftsmanship more than to preserve it by cancelling it and transcending it in good Hegelian fashion (*Aufhebung*), as Dewey was trying to do, Mumford and other Young Americans were quick to bristle at the scientism and technologism they saw as an excrescence on Dewey's communitarianism. When Dewey appeared to collude with the state in World War I, Bourne and Mumford denounced his "technological acquiescence," as if Dewey had betrayed his true self. In responding, Dewey did not bother to make the conceptual matrix in which his thoughts about modernity and modernization were nurtured very explicit. For as his naturalized version of Hegelianian communitarianism found its voice, the language in which it was born was relegated to an inarticulate background, like an old, embarrassing relative, especially after he moved to New York. In the absence of any very strong protestations to the contrary, however, the very features of Dewey's thought that were vices to Dewey's formers friends were then taken as virtues by people who really did advocate technocracy and social engineering. In sum, if Dewey's reconstructed philosophy has ever since been fractured into two seemingly incompatible halves, it is in part because the post-Hegelian philosophical framework outside of which Dewey's ideas make little coherent sense was no longer available.

It is, in any event, misleading to portray Dewey as an advocate of "social engineering." As Larry Hickman shows in *John Dewey's Pragmatic Technology*, as well as in his contribution to this volume, Dewey may have used technologistic and social engineering buzzwords, but he used them to name something quite different in spirit, something that cannot be articulated properly outside of the suppressed Aristotelian-Hegelian vocabulary in which they were thought out.[25] Dewey's approach contrasts with positivist instrumentalism, where tools are "applied" by experts to facilitate externally defined ends in an objectified, rather than participatory, world. In a reversal of Aristotle's epistemic hierarchy, Dewey assigns *techne* primacy over *praxis*, and *praxis* over *theoria*, not because a set of technically skilled experts can run a society better than an educated citizenry, but because, for natural, socially cooperative beings living in a world that affords no certain knowledge of immutable things, *techne* is the matrix in which and out of which the very intelligibility of the experienced world is constituted. "Active, productive skill," writes Hickman, "is for Dewey at center stage because it includes and informs both the theoretical and the practical whenever and wherever they are effective."[26] This vision depends on a broad conception of *techne* and technology, in which tool-use, including language, creates habits that open up new ends. "Dewey did not treat tools and instruments as value-neutral," writes Hickman, "but rather as teeming with values and potentialities that form the basis for intelligent selection of ends-in-view."[27]

Richard Rorty's well-known essay "Dewey's Metaphysics" is a latter-day manifestation of the idea that Dewey's philosophy is fractured.[28] Rorty believes that Dewey's misguided attempt to make metaphysics out of his biocentrically

reconstructed philosophy in *Experience and Nature* (1926) constrains, even con-
tradicts, what is genuinely pragmatic about his work. In saying this, Rorty proposes to help himself to the destructive, antifoundationalist half of Dewey's
argument and to drop the reconstructive part. Accordingly, Rorty would like to
think that while evolutionary theory may have provided Dewey with an occasion
for criticizing the primacy of *theoria*, it does not provide any philosophical
foundation to the pragmatism that it stimulated. Rorty's essay is significant because in separating the ''good Dewey'' from the ''bad Dewey,'' as he puts it,
Rorty lays the antifoundationalist foundations for his own brand of neopragmatism. In liberating Dewey from what Rorty sees as an ill-conceived desire to
provide metaphysical backing for his biocentric naturalism, and to ask everybody to speak the language he commends, Rorty is preparing to articulate and
commend, as he does in his subsequent writings, a voluntaristic and nominalistic
aestheticism closer in spirit to Bourne than to Dewey or *a fortiori* to the positivized and technologized Dewey that Rorty rightly rejects.

In order to drive this point home, Rorty certainly finds Dewey's weakest
point: his belated attempt to turn his reconstructed philosophy into a reconstructed metaphysical system. ''For most of his life,'' Rorty writes, Dewey
''wanted to write a metaphysical system.''[29] In *Experience and Nature*, accordingly, Dewey presents his biocentric pragmatism as leading to a ''first philosophy'' in which, like Aristotle, certain scientific facts are supposed to ground
Dewey's values and policy recommendations because the facts in question are
rooted in the nature of things. Rorty plausibly claims that Dewey succeeds,
however, merely in ''blowing up notions like 'transaction' and 'situation' until
they sounded as mysterious as 'prime matter' and 'thing in itself.' ''[30] From
Rorty's point of view, it was Dewey's vain belief that he could reconstruct
philosophy, instead of rejecting it as the incurably foundationalist enterprise that
it is, that caused him to overplay his hand. The only way, in Rorty's view, to
resist the temptation to make naturalism produce, commend, and justify one's
values and one's preferred language for describing and guiding experience is to
resist the genre of writing called philosophy. Dewey's metaphysical ambition
was, for Rorty, the return of the Hegelian repressed.

It is unclear, however, whether Rorty can so blithely separate the ''bad
Dewey'' from the ''good Dewey,'' or take as much comfort as he does in the
fact that Dewey acknowledged, after the failure of *Experience and Nature*, that
he was ''dumb'' not to have written instead a book entitled *Experience and
Culture*.[31] For even if Dewey recanted his regression to philosophical foundationalism, it is far from clear that he would have moved appreciably closer to
Rorty's own brand of pragmatism. A putative *Experience and Culture* would
have been no less biologically grounded than the book Dewey did write, no less
committed to Dewey's thick, organismically rooted conception of experience.
For, even if they are not recast in a pseudo-metaphysical way, Dewey's antifoundationalism is inseparably tied to his adaptationism. Dewey could not, for
example, have told the story he tells about *theoria*, *praxis*, and *techne* without

these arguments, as Rorty suggests he would have been well advised to do.[32] These categories are what makes the story move. Dewey would probably say, in fact, that if you take his biosocial adaptationism away you are more likely to regress to James's cryptosubjectivism than to advance toward Rorty's antifoundationalism. (Put otherwise, Rorty's pragmatism is more plausibly construed as a linguistic restatement of James than of Dewey, as several authors in this collection suggest. The idea that fragments of the field of experience are made meaningful by the invention and deployment of ever more novel "vocabularies," all of which, from serious scientific theories to novels, plays, and poems, have *prima facie* equal epistemic status, sounds a more Jamesian than Deweyan note. Peirce, for his part, would have surmised that in both cases we see what happens when ideas fall into "literary clutches.")

Even if Rorty succeeds in prying Dewey loose from what he wants evolutionary theory to do, however, it is unlikely that the continuity of the classical pragmatic tradition will thereupon come into any better focus. In spite of the differences between them to which we have been calling attention, one is still entitled to think that what binds together the Kantian pragmatism of Peirce, the Humean-Millean pragmatism of James, and the Hegelian pragmatism of the Chicago School is their distinctive commitment to the primacy of the mode of inquiry or problem solving, conducted from a position within the flow of experience, over the mode of resolutive analysis and construction from a perspective external to it, together with the efforts that all these thinkers made to ground the primacy of inquiry in certain biological facts about humans that had been made available by the rise of evolutionary theory. Yet this is just the story Rorty's account of pragmatism resists.

It is true that classical pragmatism is more of a patchwork *bricolage* than Dewey makes it appear when he told a typically teleological Aristotelian-Hegelian story about it in "The Development of American Pragmatism," and that Rorty's voluntaristic interpretive canons, according to which the past becomes coherent and directional mostly because of someone's sheer effort to make it look that way, are well calculated to bring out its constructed character.[33] Rorty might readily see how James coopted Mill and Peirce to create a pragmatic tradition after his own heart, and how he recruited Dewey and his colleagues by recognizing what he called "the Chicago School" as pragmatic comrades-in-arms. Much to Dewey's surprise, James, in reviewing *Studies in Logical Theory*, enthused that "The Chicago School has formed a view of the world, both theoretical and practical, which is so simple, massive, and positive that in spite of the fact that many parts of it yet need to be worked out, it deserves the title of a new system of philosophy."[34] By 1907, when he was composing the *Preface* to his Lowell lectures on pragmatism, James was even saying that "John Dewey's *Studies in Logical Theory* are the foundations" of pragmatism. One can only surmise that in downplaying differences between himself and the Chicago philosphers, James was actually cobbling together a pragmatic tradition in which it became obscure who was riding on whose coattails.[35]

At the same time, Rorty's repulsion from the scientistic elements he sees in the early pragmatists leads him to toss aside evidence that in its own time and place pragmatism's enemies, as well as pragmatists themselves, identified their movement in precisely the biocentric way I have been describing. One of Lovejoy's thirteen definitions of pragmatism is that it is the belief that knowledge consists of "those general propositions . . . which have in past experience proved biologically servicable to those who have lived by them."[36] Royce, who knew James better than anyone, characterized pragmatism as "the effort of the live creature to adapt himself to his natural world. Ideals and beliefs are, in a word, organic functions."[37] Dewey's colleague Frederick Woodbridge, to whose nagging challenges about Aristotelian metaphysics *Experience and Nature* was a response, spoke of pragmatism as "the biological account of knowledge."[38] Woodbridge says of the pragmatists, "Their motives have been mainly the difficulties which have arisen from the Kantian philosophy in its development into transcendentalism, and the desire to extend the category of evolution to embrace the whole of reality, knowledge included."[39]

So construed, pragmatists were arguing against philosophers who identified themselves as realists. Leaving aside the rapidly decaying idealist tradition, if you were not a pragmatist in those days you were willy-nilly a realist of one sort or another. As Daniel Wilson has shown, what was at stake in the protracted quarrels between realists and pragmatists that virtually defined American philosophy from the 1910 to about 1940 was nothing less than the status of philosophy as a respectable profession in a rapidly professionizing academy.[40] Realists of every stripe—whether they were adherents of the "Scottish philosophy" or "common sense realism" that was the basis of American collegiate instruction almost until the end of the nineteenth century, or "new realists" like Ralph Barton Perry, or "critical realists" like Roy Wood Sellars and Woodbridge—were uniformly devoted to defending the notion that philosophy is in a position to dictate epistemological criteria and an unrevisable, *a priori* ontology to the sciences, and to culture as a whole.[41] Opposing that view is what the antifoundationalism of the classical pragmatists amounted to. According to the classical pragmatists however, to undercut the opposing camp it was not necessary to add to antirealism about *philosophical* (metaphysical) theories what we now call, in a quite different intellectual milieu, antirealism about *scientific* theories. All that the classical pragmatists were asserting was that experimental methods, and the inherently revisable knowledge that was turned up by their means, were powerful enough to overturn cherished philosophical methods and presuppositions, and that this fact could be properly appreciated only when the contemplative stance of traditional philosophy was replaced with an actional conception of the knowing, experimenting, cooperating subject.

In this spirit, James says "Not one of the pragmatists is skeptical; not one doubts our ultimate ability to penetrate theoretically to the very core of reality."[42] Dewey, meanwhile, responded to the new realists' belief that pragmatists are insufficiently cured idealists, still caught in an "egocentric predicament" within the circle of their own ideas, by declaring that he was "frankly realistic in acknowledging that certain brute existences . . . set every problem for reflection and hence serve as tests of its otherwise merely speculative results."[43] Noting that new realists liked to portray themselves as on the side of the plain man when they spoke of his "naive realism" about sense objects, Dewey retorted that realists were not nearly naive enough. They assumed wrongly that the plain man's primary relationship to sensory objects is a contemplative gaze. The genuine article, however, refers to things by connecting them up as objects of his or her practical and productive interests. Ordinary persons, in scrutinizing their perceptions, do not regard them as objects of knowledge, but as sources of evidence. "While perceptions are the sole ultimate data," Dewey wrote "the sole media of inference to all natural objects and processes . . . we do not, in any intelligible or verifiable sense, *know* them. Rather, we know . . . things . . . *with* or *by* them. . . . Their nature as evidence, as signs, entirely overshadows their natural status, that of being simply natural events."[44] Later, Dewey resisted protestations by critical realists like Sellars and Woodbridge that they could be as naturalistic and as evolutionary as Dewey while affirming at the same time the autonomy of philosophy's questions about the nature of mind, knowledge, and ultimate reality, and the validity of philosopher's reflective, as opposed to experimental, methods of answering these questions. Maintaining that a truly adaptationist theory of mind must rule out contemplative picturing of the world as it is "in itself" as a meaningless irrelevancy to an organism's dealings with its environment, Dewey resisted these claims. He would no doubt have regarded Sellars's statement that he "could never accept the tendency of the Chicago School to a social consciousness" as evidence in his favor.[45]

To report what the classical pragmatists held, and were acknowledged by their opponents to hold, is not, of course, to say that they were right to hold it. Perhaps pragmatism could, as Rorty suggests, become truer to itself only by evolving away from the uncritical beliefs about science held by its early partisans. There the matter stood, however, at the end of the 1930s, when the unstable, and rather provincial, equilibrium between pragmatists and realists was disturbed by the coming of logical positivism. That, however, is another story.

NOTES

1. Charles Sanders Peirce, "Pragmatic and Pragmatism" (1902), in *Pragmatism: The Classic Writings*, ed. H. Standish Thayer (Indianapolis: Hackett, 1982), 79–100. See C. S. Peirce, "How to Make Our Ideas Clear" (1878), in Thayer, *Pragmatism*, 79–100.
2. Peirce, "Pragmatic and Pragmatism," 49. See also John Dewey, "The Development of American Pragmatism" (1931), in Thayer, *Pragmatism*, 23–40.
3. For accounts of the probability revolution, see Ian Hacking, *The Emergence of Probability* (Cambridge: Cambridge University Press, 1975); Ian Hacking, *The Taming of Chance* (Cambridge: Cambridge University Press, 1990); G. Gigerenzer, Z. Swijtink, T. Porter, L. Daston, J. Beatty, and L. Krueger, *The Empire of Chance: How Probability Changed Science and Everyday Life* (Cambridge: Cambridge University Press, 1989); L. Krueger, L. Daston, and M. Heidelberger, *The Prob-

abilistic Revolution, 2 vols. (Cambridge, Mass.: MIT Press, 1987); T. M. Porter, *The Rise of Statistical Thinking* (Princeton, N.J.: Princeton University Press, 1986).

4. Peirce, "How to Make Our Ideas Clear," 85.

5. Peirce, "What Pragmatism Is," in Thayer, *Pragmatism*, 105. Peirce blames F.S.C. Schiller rather than James for turning pragmatism into humanism. That is presumably because James's position was in fact more sophisticated, as well as because Peirce and James were bound by ties of friendship and mutual support. See William James, "What Pragmatism Means," in *Pragmatism*, ed. Bruce Kuklick (Indianapolis: Hackett, 1981), 32–33.

6. James, "What Pragmatism Means," 37.

7. John J. McDermott, *Streams of Experience* (Amherst: University of Massachusetts Press, 1986).

8. James, "What Pragmatism Means," p. 31.

9. William James, *North American Review* 121 (1875), 201, quoted in Robert Richards, *Darwin and the Emergence of Evolutionary Theories of Mind and Behavior* (Chicago: University of Chicago Press, 1988), 433.

10. Quoted in Richards, *Darwin*, 427.

11. Peirce, "Why I Am a Pragmatist," quoted in Philip Weiner, *Evolution and the Founders of Pragmatism* (Cambridge, Mass.: Harvard University Press, 1949).

12. Dewey's commitment to participatory democracy is documented in Robert Westbrook, *John Dewey and American Democracy* (Ithaca, N.Y.: Cornell University Press, 1991).

13. John Dewey, "From Absolutism to Experimentalism," in *Contemporary American Philosophy*, ed. G. P. Adams and W. Montague (New York: MacMillan, 1930), vol. 2, 24.

14. Dewey's Darwinism is rather idiosyncratic. His clearest statements are in book reviews and essays that he wrote in the crucial mid-1890s, especially "Review of Ward's *Psychic Factors in Civilization*," in *Early Works, 1882–1898*, ed. Jo Ann Boydston (Carbondale: Southern Illinois University Press 1989), vol. 4; and "Evolution and Ethics," in *Early Works*, vol. 5. Dewey, along with James, James Mark Baldwin, Lester Frank Ward, and others, were what I will call progressive Darwinians. Progressive Darwinians opposed Social Darwinism by denying that Social Darwinism was based on good Darwinism. Dewey is also opposed to something he calls "Weismannism in its extreme form." By this Dewey did not mean to deny August Waismann's refutation of acquired characteristics, and hence his refutation of Lamarckism. He meant to deny only that there is any legitimate inference from Waismann's refutation to the idea that organisms are passive pawns of a cut-throat environment that predetermines every move they make if, like a capitalist entrepreneur, they are to survive at all. In breaking this alleged inference, Dewey concedes that it is indeed the fittest who survive, but asserts that fitness requires the ability to anticipate future contingencies. "If one is fitted simply to the present," he writes in "Evolution and Ethics," fitness includes "the ability which enables organisms to adjust themselves without too much loss to sudden and unexpected changes in the environment," so that what is fit today can be fit tomorrow as well. Thus, even where it works on hard inheritance, natural selection will select for the problem-solving capacities that Dewey calls "intelligence." Dewey defines intelligence as the ability of organisms to anticipate the consequences of their behavior and to guide that behavior toward useful ends by amending their environment. "Intelligence," Dewey writes, "is indirection, checking the natural direct action, and taking a circuitous course." So construed, intelligence is not a push-pull mechanism, but an anticipatory capability that happens to be highly developed in humans, but is well-nigh universal among organisms to one degree or another. Dewey's picture is that natural selection begins from the spontaneous activities of organisms, creates over time capacities for niche-specific problem solving, and then gets adaptationist leverage by leaving the particular exercise of those capacities to intelligent action and cultural learning. A cycle is thereby set up in which the advantages of Lamarckism are combined with the explanatory power of Darwinism without violating Waissmann's strictures against the inheritance of acquired characteristics. A prominent part of this cycle is that there is selection pressure for sociality itself, since sociality is the medium in which learning can be an effective adaptation. Thus, the fact that the human environment is "now a social

one,'' Dewey writes, means that human fitness includes ''reference to social adaptation'' and co-operation.

I believe that Dewey continued to maintain this view throughout his life. Indeed, he took it so much for granted that he never bothered to defend it, or to show how it related to fast-moving changes in evolutionary science itself, contenting himself instead with drawing out large implications of ideas that brought less and less credit to their author.

15. It was Sidney Hook who first made this connection between Marx and Dewey in *The Metaphysics of Pragmatism* (Chicago: Open Court, 1927).

16. John Dewey, ''The Influence of Darwinism on Philosophy,'' in Dewey, *The Influence of Darwinism on Philosophy and Other Essays* (New York: Henry Holt, 1910).

17. John Dewey, ''Theory of Valuation,'' in *International Encyclopedia of the Unified Sciences* II: 4. (Chicago: University of Chicago Press, 1939), 63.

18. Quoted in Westbrook, *John Dewey and American Democracy*, 433–34.

19. On this topic, see David J. Depew, ''The *Polis* Transfigured: Aristotle's *Politics* and Marx's *Critique of Hegel's Philosophy of Right*,'' in *Marx and Aristotle: Nineteenth Century Social Thought and Classical Antiquity*, ed. G. E. McCarthy (Lanham, Maryland: Rowman and Littlefield, 1992), 37–73.

20. Ralph W. Sleeper, *The Necessity of Pragmatism* (New Haven, Conn.: Yale University Press, 1986).

21. On Dewey and Addams, consult Westbrook, *John Dewey and American Democracy*, and Andrew Feffer, *The Chicago Pragmatists* (Ithaca, N.Y.: Cornell University Press, 1993).

22. This account is closer to Feffer's account than to Westbrook's.

23. Radical intellectuals who recognize Dewey as a kindred spirit were, and still are, sometimes puzzled by his steadfastly dismissive attitude toward the Marxist tradition. They would do well to bear in mind that the Chicago School, as it was soon called, did not believe that class conflict went so deep, especially in a democratic society, that conflict models of social reality and revolutionary programs were necessary to alleviate it. As Blake suggests, it is no less misleading to think of Dewey as a liberal. Dewey's antiauthoritarianism is not a reflection of the liberal tradition's conception of freedom, but of his reworking of democratic republican tradition by means of Hegelian categories and themes. For Dewey, freedom does not consist of freedom to enter and exit markets as one pleases, or to vote for public officers in accord with one's self-interest, or to prefer a private conception of one's good to a conception of oneself as sustaining the public good.

24. Casey Nelson Blake, *Beloved Community: The Cultural Criticism of Randolph Bourne, Van Wyck Brooks, Waldo Frank, and Lewis Mumford* (Chapel Hill: University of North Carolina Press, 1990).

25. Larry Hickman, *John Dewey's Pragmatic Technology* (Bloomington: Indiana University Press, 1990).

26. Ibid., 18.

27. Ibid., 13.

28. Richard Rorty, ''Dewey's Metaphysics,'' in Rorty, *Consequences of Pragmatism* (Minneapolis: University of Minnesota Press, 1982).

29. Ibid., 73.

30. Ibid., 84.

31. Dewey said this in a letter to Arthur Bentley. See Rorty, ''Dewey's Metaphysics,'' 72, 85; Westbrook, *John Dewey and American Democracy*, 95–96.

32. Rorty, ''Dewey's Metaphysics,'' 72–89.

33. Dewey, ''The Development of American Pragmatism,'' 23–40.

34. William James, ''The Chicago School,'' in James, *Collected Essays and Reviews* (Cambridge, Mass.: Harvard University Press, 1906), 445–47.

35. Bruce Kuklick, *Churchmen and Philosophers* (New Haven, Conn.: Yale University Press, 1977), especially when read in conjunction with his study of the glory years of the Harvard Phi-

losophy Department, *The Rise of American Philosophy* (New Haven, Conn.: Yale University Press, 1977), shows just how different the religious and philosophical genealogies of James and the Chicago philosophers actually were. While James breathed the ambiance of the Unitarian wing of Congregationism, and philosophically tried to reform British Empiricism, Dewey, Mead, and Tufts came out of Trinitarian Congregationalism, which used Kant, Hegel, and Schelling as philosophical handmaidens. It was their naturalization of this idealist inheritance that united the Chicago School, as something like it had united Feuerbach and Young Hegelians like Marx in the Germany of the 1830s and 1840s.

36. Arthur O. Lovejoy, "The Thirteen Pragmatisms," *Journal of Philosophy* 5 (8) (1908): 38; reprinted in A. Rorty, ed., *Pragmatism* (New York: Doubleday, 1966), 340.

37. Josiah Royce, "The Problem of Truth," (1908), in *Basic Writings of Josiah Royce*, ed. J. McDermott, vol. 2 (Chicago: University of Chicago Press, 1980), 684.

38. Frederick W. Woodbridge, *Mind and Nature* (New York: Columbia University Press, 1940), 69. See also John Herman Randall, "Epilogue: The Nature of Naturalism," in *Naturalism and the Human Spirit*, ed. Y. H. Krikorian (New York: Columbia University Press, 1944), 378. Randall writes: "Both [Morris] Cohen and Woodbridge were keen critics of the excesses of the genetic method of the evolutionary enthusiasts. They have transmitted their suspicion to their students. Mr. Dewey's evolutionism, especially when under the influence of G. H. Mead, has put much more emphasis on various types of genetic analysis, though he would in fact pretty much agree with the specific criticisms [of Mead] advanced by Woodbridge."

39. Woodbridge, *Mind and Nature*, 791.

40. Daniel J. Wilson, *Science, Community and the Transformation of American Philosophy, 1860–1930* (Chicago: University of Chicago Press, 1990).

41. I have argued elsewhere that ordinary language philosophy, or "linguistic analysis," (which is not to be confused with the kind of analysis practiced by the logical atomists or logical positivists) was a linguistic restatement of common sense realism, the wide diffusion of which in the United States in the period after Quine's attack on the analytic-synthetic distinction was prompted, in my view, by the keen desire of professional philosophers to protect their autonomous status. See David J. Depew, "American Philosophy in the Twentieth Century," in *Encyclopedia of United States History in the Twentieth Century*, ed. S. Kutler, *et al.* (New York: Simon and Schuster, in press).

42. William James, MS, published in R. B. Perry, *The Thought and Character of William James* (Boston: Little, Brown, 1936), vol. 2, 478–80; reprinted in Thayer, *Pragmatism*, 132.

43. John Dewey, "The Short Cut to Realism Examined," *Journal of Philosophy* 7 (1910): 553–57.

44. Ibid.

45. R. W. Sellars, "Realism, Naturalism, and Humanism," in *Contemporary American Philosophy*, ed. G. P. Adams and W. Montague, vol. 2, 274. See Randall Auxier's essay in this volume for a view different from the one expressed here, in which pragmatists are said to be committed to an evolutionary (processive) metaphysics. I do not believe this view does sufficient justice to the Realist-Pragmatist divide that more than anything defined the meanings of these terms roughly from 1910–1940.

1

The Problem of Pragmatism in American History: A Look Back and a Look Ahead

David A. Hollinger

We will not understand pragmatism as an episode in American history so long as pragmatism is either stretched to cover all of America or confined to those of its formulations sufficiently fruitful philosophically to have found places in the history of Western philosophy. In the first instance, the tradition of Peirce, James, and Dewey is flattened into a style of thought characterized by voluntarism, practicality, moralism, relativism, an eye toward the future, a preference for action over contemplation, and other traits of the same degree of generality. Each of the traits commonly attributed to pragmatism can indeed be found at some level in the writings of one or more of the leading pragmatists. And, even if we now gasp ritualistically at the thought of attributing these traits to Americans ''in general,'' there is no reason to doubt that these traits were among the intellectual ideals of a good many of the rank-and-file Yankees with whom scholars once tried to link James and his cerebral colleagues. Yet the obligation to characterize the pragmatists as representatives of America inhibits exploration of the relationship between the pragmatist philosophers and the more specific segments—chronological and social—of America in which the writings of the pragmatists appeared and demonstrably functioned. In the second instance—the confining of pragmatism to its philosophic contributions—the tradition is sharpened into a highly distinctive theory of meaning and truth to which the writings of other modern philosophers can be contrasted. Often this theory is projected as an ideal type toward which the pragmatists strived, but which they failed to fully articulate. In this view, the task of the scholar is to fill in the holes in the formulations of the pragmatists in order to complete and clarify their arguments. Even when the pragmatic theory of meaning and truth is made the subject of more authentically historical studies, in which the actual development of the ideas of one or more of the pragmatists is reconstructed, the mission of the scholar can be achieved with little attention to the constituency won among Americans by the work of the pragmatists.

The recognition that the intellectuals who rallied to pragmatism were preoccupied with the place of science in modern life is the point at which to begin an assessment of pragmatism's role in the lives of Americans who cared about it. The writings on meaning, truth, goodness, and other basic philosophical issues on account of which Peirce, James, and Dewey became known as pragmatists were the apex of a larger intellectual edifice constructed by these three men and their followers in response not only to the great epistemological and metaphysical questions of post-Kantian thought, but also to the desire for a way of life consistent with what they and their contemporaries variously perceived as the implications of modern science. Peirce, James, and Dewey were conspicuous leaders, among Americans, in the efforts of Western intellectuals to find and articulate such a way of life. That these efforts were so widespread as to constitute the framework for much of European and American intellectual history in the late nineteenth and early twentieth centuries is well known, as are the facts that ways of life as well as epistemologies were felt to be at issue and that the pragmatists were among America's most listened-to participants in this enterprise. Yet these aspects of the scene deserve more attention in the interpretation of pragmatism than historians have accorded them, for they largely define the specific setting in which Peirce, James, and Dewey gained constituencies beyond philosophy, were perceived as part of a single tradition, and thus functioned as related presences in the history of the United States.

Viewed in this setting, the pragmatists emerge as reflectors of, and powerful agents for, a distinctive cluster of assertions and hopes about how modern culture could be integrated and energized. The particular elements in this cluster were often articulated singly and in relation to other ideas by other moralists of the period, including some critical of pragmatism, but the combination of elements found in the writings of the pragmatists and their popularizers was nowhere else advanced more persistently and with more notice from educated Americans. Since the basic texts of Peirce, James, and Dewey were the raw materials out of which the pragmatic tradition was forged, I will use these texts as the basis of my account of the combination of elements peculiar to the pragmatists.

One element in this combination was a sense of the role of scientific method in a universe of change and uncertainty. The pragmatists were more concerned than were many of their contemporaries with the integrity and durability of *inquiry*, on the one hand, and the tentativeness, fallibility, and incompleteness of *knowledge* on the other. While they sometimes compared the body of existing knowledge favorably to the smaller amount available in the past, and while they often noted the superior reliability of empirically supported propositions over other propositions, the pragmatists were never among the leading celebrants of knowledge's solidity, vastness, and stability. It was rather to what they called the "spirit" of science, or its "method" and "attitude" that they looked for a foundation stable enough to support a modern culture. Knowledge was transient, and as such was another aspect of the universe of change through the experience of which the attitude of inquiry was, in itself, the most reliable single guide. Some of the pragmatists were more eager than others to see the knowledge available at a given historical moment applied vigorously to social, religious, and political life, but the priority of method as a cultural commitment was projected vividly in the works of Peirce, James, Dewey, and a host of followers.

This projection is easiest to illustrate in the case of Dewey, who was forever insisting that if only people could become scientific in the way they went about things, the potential for human fulfillment would be liberated from the bondage of a sterile, repressive, outrageously long-lived antiquity. "The future of our civilization depends upon the widening spread and deepening hold of the scientific habit of mind."[1] This assertion of Dewey's became a favorite epigram among his admirers[2] and expressed accurately, if blandly, the methodological emphasis of his thought. This emphasis was so tightly bound up with skepticism about the adequacy of existing and yet-to-be-discovered knowledge that Dewey's prescribed "scientific attitude" was defined *in terms of* a principled openness toward, and an enthusiastic search for, new and temporarily valid knowledge in a universe of constant change.[3] Willingness to accept and act upon the facts at hand would not satisfy Dewey as it had satisfied the many Victorian moralists eager to make people obey facts; Dewey's devotion was to the process of investigation itself.

So, too, was James's. The claim of some scientists to have virtually completed their task inspired James's proudest scorn; "our ignorance," he said, is "a sea."[4] His legendary assaults on the pretensions of science turned the supposed ideals of the scientific endeavor against the arrogance of contemporary scientists: James piously and passionately reminded them of the "scientific" imperative to inquire further, to remain critical of past findings, to remain free from dogmatism.[5] If. T. H. Huxley, as has often been observed, turned the tables on established Christianity by claiming for Darwinian science a Protestant morality more strict than that of the church, so, too, did James turn the tables on the established science of Huxley's generation by claiming for psychical research an ideal of free inquiry more unflinching and open-minded than that of Huxley and W. K. Clifford. Scholars have made much of James's defense of religiously conventional and scientifically unorthodox beliefs, such as the conceivable reality of spirits; what needs more emphasis is what James did and did not do with such beliefs. He supported no movement to protect such beliefs from science; instead, he instituted what he regarded as a scientific investigation of the evidence on which these beliefs were supposedly founded.[6] While James developed a reputation as a hostile critic of the worldviews of many contemporary apologists for science, he also gained a reputation as a striking exemplar of the ideals of scientific inquiry.[7]

Peirce was more inclined than either James or Dewey to suspect that the object of knowledge was, technically speaking, finite,[8] but he too depicted inquiry as virtually endless and its results as unavoidably fallible. He could be as eloquent as James on "the paucity of scientific knowledge"[9] and on the sentiment expressed in his own, often quoted injunction, "Do not block the way of inquiry."[10] Peirce was unusual—even in an age of extravagant "scientism"—in the extremity and singularity with which he identified goodness and progress with science, and he was among the first admirers of science to focus this adulation explicitly on the community of investigators and on the common methodological commitments that enabled members of this community to correct both each other and the stock of propositions they took to be true.[11] It was in direct response to Peirce's vision of an eternally self-correcting community of inquiry that Royce "solved" *The Problem of Christianity* by urging the church to model itself on the scientific community.[12]

Yet it would be misleading to imply that Peirce's vision of the scientific community and its moral functions was widely noted beyond a few departments of philosophy; he was, by virtue of his great creativity and prolonged neglect, the Melville of American philosophy. The aspects of his work that did function decisively in the discourse of his generation and of the one immediately following his death in 1914 were those singled out by James and Dewey, particularly the aspect James in 1898 dubbed the "principle" of pragmatism.[13] This principle—to the much disputed substance of which we must now attend—connoted in all its formulations a willingness to treat knowledge as temporal and to treat method as both primary and enduring.

To take account of the practical consequences an object might have is the way to form a clear idea of it, Peirce had said in 1878 in "How to Make Our Ideas Clear." In what was to become the classic illustration of the pragmatic theory of meaning, Peirce analyzed in terms of this maxim the calling of a thing "hard." To be hard, a thing must be able to resist scratching by other substances; such "effects" constitute the "whole conception" of hardness. "There is absolutely no difference between a hard thing and a soft thing so long as they are not brought to the test," said Peirce, insisting, in effect, that the "qualities" often said to inhere in objects be translated into the behavior the objects manifest in relation to other objects.[14] The uncertainty of Peirce specialists even today about just what Peirce was trying to say[15]—what consequences were "practical," for example, and was the maxim a general one or designed only for science?—need not deflect us from identifying the essential freight that this proposal of Peirce's was made to carry in the development of the pragmatist movement once James launched it in 1898.[16]

To that movement no paper was more central than James's "What Pragmatism Means," in which he presented "Peirce's principle" as the basis for an entire philosophy. That philosophy was to be more scientific in outlook, James alleged, than philosophies, as a class of intellectual constructions, tended to be. Pragmatism's predecessors and rivals were too committed to one particular set or another of "results" of inquiry, such as the conclusion that the world is made up of "Energy" or that it is all contained within "the Absolute." Such philosophies employed merely "verbal solutions," reasoned from "fixed principles," built "closed systems," and fell victim to "dogma, artificiality, and the pretence of finality in truth." Pragmatism stood for less and was capable of doing more; it carried less baggage, was more autonomous, and was open to more possibilities. The pragmatic method of tracing the consequences of ideas operated in the manner of a hotel corridor—a metaphor James adopted from his Italian follower, Giovanni Papini—through which one might pass in order to get in and out of rooms representing a virtual infinity of intellectual activities.[17]

When James moved to the explicit statement of a theory of truth, he began with the observation that to modern science "laws" were at best "approximations," too numerous and too subject to "rival formulations" to enable us to view any of them as "absolutely a transcript of reality." Theories "may from some point of view be useful" by summarizing old facts and leading us to new ones. It was to this analysis of scientific knowledge that James connected the theory of truth he attributed to himself, to the British pragmatist F. C. S. Schiller, and to Dewey and his Chicago disciples. Truth in any realm was an "idea that will carry us prosperously from any one part of our experience to any other part, linking things satisfactorily, working securely, simplifying, saving labor; [it] is true for just so much, true in so far forth, true *instrumentally*." Such sentences put James on the defensive with other philosophers, so he spent much time during his last years trying to elaborate and defend "this pragmatist talk about truths in the plural, about their utility and satisfactoriness, about the success with which they 'work,' etc."[18] Yet in all these disputes, including those involving Dewey and other pragmatists after James's death in 1910, one thing was never in doubt: whatever else the pragmatist theory of truth entailed, it carried with it the sense that truth was a condition that happened to an idea through the course of events as experienced and analyzed by human beings. This temporality of truth was basic even to the less publicized depiction by Peirce of truth as a "fated" opinion, as something that a community of investigators would eventually agree upon.[19] What was rejected everywhere in the movement was the notion of truth as "a stagnant property inherent in" an idea, apart from the process of its emergence in history and from its possession by human beings interacting contingently with each other and with the larger natural world.[20]

That this social and physical world was responsive to human purpose was a second conviction advanced by the pragmatist tradition. If one basic element in this tradition was a belief that inquiry itself could stabilize and sustain a culture for which truths could be only tentative and plural, another was the sense that inquiry could change the world. Not that the world altogether lacked resistance to human imagination and will; but neither was the world's structure so hard-and-fast as to force human purpose into headlong retreat with each new discovery of science. In contrast to the moralists who hailed or lamented the scientific enterprise as the exploration of a one-way street, down which orders for belief and conduct came from "nature," the pragmatic tradition carried a faith in inquiry's reconstructive capabilities in the most rigorous of the sciences and in everyday life.

This faith is consistent with the pragmatic approach to truth as a form of utility, but is not entailed by it. Ideas, in this view, are instruments that not only can become true by doing their job in inquiry, but can also transform the environment to which they are applied. This effect takes place most obviously in the improvement of medical and industrial techniques, but the effect was held by Dewey and his followers to operate throughout experience even at the cognitive level, in the knowing relation itself. For Dewey, the entire knowing process is a manipulative one in which inquirers seek to rearrange to their satisfaction whatever components of a given situation stimulated inquiry.[21] Peirce's account of inquiry as a response to doubt has sometimes been taken to imply a transformative role for inquiry, but Peirce drew back from such implications, and he was in any event no agent of their popularization. Dewey did the most to identify this reconstructive vision with pragmatism, while trying over a period of several decades to clarify what he meant by it.

In precisely what sense does inquiry "change" the various "situations" it is led to confront? How do we evaluate the claims to utility that may be advanced on behalf of various reconstructive solutions? It is a striking feature of the history of pragmatism that Dewey's most detailed answer to these questions appeared only in 1938, long after his more vague and question-begging pronouncements had helped win for his reconstructionist vision a following greater than it has enjoyed during the more than forty years since he did his best to justify it philosophically.[22] Persons attracted to the vision were all along held in tow by a few prominent, easily apprehended assertions of Dewey's; the world, Dewey reassured his public, has been proven by the growth of science and invention to be sufficiently amenable to human ends to warrant yet more experimentation with it, particularly its previously neglected social and moral dimensions. Here the connection between pragmatism and early-twentieth-century reform[23] was at its closest, but Dewey's social engineering was only one example of pragmatism's confidence in the responsiveness of nature to human purpose. This confidence was equally hard to miss in James's "voluntarism."

James focused on the vitality of will versus outside forces in determining the life of the individual, but he also addressed the effect of human purpose on the universe outside the self. Not only did his formidable work in psychology assist vitally in the demolition of the passive mind of the British empirical tradition;[24] James's most popular essays continually asserted that "will" was an authentic force in the world. James was particularly reassuring about the role of purpose in the inquiries carried out by scientists; the phenomena of nature would ultimately decide an issue, but all the more decisively if scientists brought to their investigation—critically, to be sure—their own most intense hopes for a given outcome.[25]

The advancement of human purpose in the world through inquiry was not to be limited to professional scientists or even to philosophers. It was a mission and a fulfillment open to virtually anyone. The pragmatist tradition consisted also in this third basic element: the sense that inquiry was accessible on meaningful levels by the rank-and-file membership of an educated, democratic society. The pragmatists did not insist that all forms of inquiry were accessible to everyone, nor did they deny that inquiry was subject to a division of labor according to which people were sometimes dependent upon the expertise of others. Inquiry was a continuum of investigatory, reconstructive endeavors exemplified above all by the work of Galileo and his scientific successors, but available for practice in appropriate contexts by any citizen capable of assimilating its spirit.

Dewey translated so many of life's activities—humble and exalted—into the terms of inquiry that Bertrand Russell once accused him of being unable to distinguish between the work of a scientist and that of a bricklayer.[26] Dewey did seek to distinguish between the controlled, reflective, experimental inquiry characteristic of specialists and the common-sense thinking of everyman, but even then he insisted on their similarity and urged a program of public education to render common sense more effective by closing the gap between it and experimental science. James, too, emphasized the continuity between the intellectual life of the average soul, on the one hand, and James's own vocation as a scientist and philosopher on the other. Always an acerbic critic of the elitist pretensions of academic professionals, James urged the laity to take on the most demanding intellectual problems it could, and to adopt in their pursuit the pragmatic method long practiced without hoopla in the laboratory and now characteristic of the best philosophers.[27]

No index of the accessibility of inquiry was more dramatic than its availability to people wanting answers to ethical questions. Not only were social scientists encouraged to extend to the social realm the search for facts pioneered by practitioners of the physical sciences; persons of any station confronting issues in politics and morals were encouraged to face them "scientifically." The continuum of inquiry as depicted by Dewey, and less explicitly by James, included ethical choices as well as the explanation of physical and social phenomena;[28] the pragmatic tradition was proverbially reluctant to make what were, to other philosophic traditions, all-too-clear distinctions between the good and the true, between value and fact. This reluctance stimulated a vast polemical literature, in which critics generally insisted that the formulations of pragmatists begged the standard philosophical questions while the pragmatists, especially Dewey, argued that these questions, as traditionally conceived, were simply outdated. Although Dewey made a determined, and increasingly technical, effort to perform his own philosophical analysis of ethical judgment in terms of "inquiry," his work also served to reinforce a feeling James had first inspired in admirers of pragmatism that many of philosophy's standard questions were irrelevant. These admirers might cheer Dewey along as he fought his learned opposition, but they knew that a *little* philosophy—provided it was, like their own, the right philosophy—was enough. The active life of inquiry, it was clear, needed to wait upon no guidelines from the cloistered men who sat and talked about "is" and "ought."

The pragmatists' combination of senses of what the possibilities were for a modern, scientific culture seems at first glance very general indeed. Yet it was specific enough to distinguish pragmatism from a number of other, highly visible signposts even within the intellectual neighborhood populated by enthusiasts about science and its cultural contributions. Pragmatism's antielitist bias distinguished it, for example, from the program for behaviorist research and social reorganization popularized by John B. Watson,[29] whose understanding of how the human mind worked was both similar to Dewey's and loudly applauded by many followers of both James and Dewey. Socialism, too, was offered frequently in the name of science, and it attracted some pragmatists when the latter were led to think of socialism as appropriately experimental and democratic,[30] but the pragmatist tradition's emphasis on the continuity of inquiry cut against the grain of class-based, revolutionary socialism. Russell's "A Free Man's Worship"—one of the most widely cited testaments of the 1910s and 1920s— celebrated an ascetic's renunciation of human hope in the face of a hard, hostile, science-discovered world.[31] Sinclair Lewis's *Arrowsmith* was built around the precious unattainability, by any but the most superhuman of heroes, of the scientific idea.[32] Nobel physicist Robert A. Millikan's *Science and the New Civilization* assured the nation's Babbitts that their conservative social values were in no way threatened by scientific knowledge or inquiry.[33] Innumerable industrialists, engineers, and medical professionals filled popular and learned magazines with adulation of past and future technological progress, without hinting that the imperatives of inquiry itself might come to occupy the spiritual landscape once supervised by the Christian church.[34] The imposing bulk and permanence of existing knowledge was incandescently hailed, and mastery of its detailed contents earnestly prescribed, by a multitude of publicists and spokesmen for scientific societies.[35] Oliver Wendell Holmes, Jr., linked adulation of scientific method with serene acquiescence in the often cruel operations of an unresponsive world.[36]

The pragmatist tradition that distinguished itself in this context, and that was yet more distinctive when contrasted to outlooks skeptical of science, was constituted by more than the careers of Peirce, James, and Dewey. Until now I have made attributions to this tradition exclusively on the basis of the most extensively absorbed texts of these three men because these texts provided the adhesive to make pragmatism a tradition: from these texts the less original pragmatists drew inspiration, and to these texts educated Americans went when they wanted to confront "pragmatism." But the tradition is manifest not exclusively in these classical texts; it is found also in the writings of those who sought to summarize, elaborate upon, defend, and sympathetically analyze the contributions of the three masters. Such writings, indeed, were instrumental in establishing the canon of pragmatist classics and in sustaining a particular sense of what was common to thinkers as diverse as Peirce, James, and Dewey.[37] Attention to such writings can confirm or correct an impression of where pragmatism's center of gravity was located as pragmatism went beyond its great texts and as it transcended departments of philosophy.

If, for example, Joseph Ratner's introduction to the Modern Library Giant of 1939, *Intelligence in the Modern World: John Dewey's Philosophy*, were difficult to assimilate into what is here characterized as the pragmatist tradition, one would want to quickly revise that characterization. Ratner's 241-page introduction serves as both an attempted summary of Dewey's thought and a polemical assertion of that thought's correctness. The essay has never been taken seriously as a contribution to the philosophical refinement of pragmatism, as have the works of C. I. Lewis and George Herbert Mead, for example.[38] Nor should it so be taken. Yet it is a crucial historical document as a representative reading of Dewey and as, in turn, an agent of this reading's dissemination. So widely circulated was this book that yellowing, pencil-annotated copies can be found today in used bookstores far from Chicago and Columbia in some of the remotest areas of the United States.

Galileo's discovery of a "*general* method, available and adaptable for use by all . . . no matter what the area," is for Ratner, as for Dewey, the central moment in history. For three centuries this discovery was taken advantage of only by a handful of people, mostly those practicing the physical sciences. Resistance by philosophers to the Galilean general method of experimental inquiry is "as bad a case of cultural lag as one could ever hope to come across." At last, Dewey has come along to lay out the implications of Galileo's breakthrough for "philosophy" in the most comprehensive sense of the term, including our understanding of and prescriptions for everyday life. In so doing, Dewey has performed for the modern world the tasks performed for the ancient world by the great Athenian philosophers, explains Ratner. Much of Ratner's time, therefore, goes into demonstrating how "the two greatest of Dewey's contemporaries," Russell and Alfred North Whitehead, despite their eagerness to take account of scientific knowledge and method, remain mired in prescientific ways of thinking: they have not fully substituted the Galilean experimental attitude for the ancient "quest for certainty." They have even failed to see how fleeting a presence our current knowledge is: Russell, for example, took Newtonian physics as given in 1914 and in 1927 took Einsteinian physics as given.[39]

Ratner's Dewey is fully consistent with the outlook of the two most prolific and popularly read interpreters of pragmatism, Horace M. Kallen and Sidney Hook.[40] Kallen and Hook have long been recognized as elaborators, respectively, of James's more individualistic, unsystematic approach to the vocation of inquiry and of Dewey's more social and organized approach. Yet the careers of Kallen and Hook illustrate how difficult the problem of pragmatism looks when it is addressed in American history rather than in Western philosophy. Both of these writers were trained as philosophers by their respective masters, and both addressed some of the same technical questions involving "truth" and "meaning" that their mentors did. Yet what Kallen and Hook wrote about these questions did not make a lasting mark on the course of philosophical argument; hence, their writings are not, as are C. I. Lewis's and Mead's, given detailed and sober treatment in philosophers' histories of pragmatism. One need find no fault whatever with these histories to observe that Kallen and Hook, in their exceptionally long careers as self-defined ''pragmatists,'' are fundamentally constitutive of pragmatism as a presence in America. The ideas attributed above to the founders of pragmatism are easily found in the writings of Kallen and Hook, often offered from forums of culturally strategic importance. Kallen wrote the article on pragmatism for the *Encyclopedia of the Social Sciences*—a monument in so many ways to the ideals of pragmatists—where he performed the standard equation of pragmatism with science and democracy.[41]

No one has ever mistaken Herbert Croly for a philosopher, nor the *New Republic* for a journal of philosophy. Yet Croly and his magazine have been routinely denoted as ''pragmatist'' for years, as have been Croly's *New Republic* associates, Walter Weyl and Walter Lippmann. The sense in which these three men were pragmatists is left implicit in Charles Forcey's meticulous and extremely helpful monograph on the trio, *The Crossroads of Liberalism*, in which the appellation is regularly applied.[42] Yet the intellectual portraits that Forcey constructs do, indeed, make Croly, Lippmann, and Weyl unambiguous participants in the pragmatist tradition as I have characterized it. The writings of the three confirm the impression left by Forcey. Lippmann's influential *Drift and Mastery*, for example, was a vehicle for precisely the combination of hopes and aspirations found in the classic texts of the pragmatist philosophers.[43]

Lippmann later soured on all three themes in this combination, but the tradition was carried on by other publicists and academics of various affiliations, including historians Frederick Barry and James Harvey Robinson, Senator Paul H. Douglas, and the popular radio personality and lecturer Lyman Bryson.[44] Bryson, who wrote a number of *Drift-and-Mastery*-like books of cultural criticism, taught at Columbia Teachers College, where colleagues of his had institutionalized the pragmatist tradition in the early 1920s. There some 35,000 teachers were trained by William Heard Kilpatrick, a devoted if vulgarizing disciple of Dewey who relentlessly emphasized ''method over content.''[45]

The pragmatist tradition, then, was considerably more concentrated in structure and constituency than have been the general tendencies—practicality, voluntarism, moralism, flexibility, openness—one or more of which have often been used to characterize James Madison, Benjamin Franklin, or John Winthrop as pragmatists. If the tradition was amorphous compared to the clearly defined philosophical work that forms the tradition's most easily identified core, this larger tradition was nevertheless more specific and concrete than the stereotypical American traits that informed some of the work of the pragmatists and motivated some Americans to identify themselves with pragmatism. Pragmatism became a tradition in the discourse of American intellectuals as the work of James, initially, then of Dewey and to some extent of Peirce, was perceived to constitute a rudimentary ''philosophy of life'' providing a coherent orientation toward the ill-defined but undoubtedly massive and consequential entity these intellectuals called "science."

So considered, pragmatism had a lot to offer, including the supremely important fact that it did not try to offer too much. It was so spare that one could believe in it while entertaining a whole range of other beliefs, ancient and modern, idiosyncratic and conventional. Hadn't Papini said pragmatism was not so much a philosophy as a way of doing without one?[46] There was something to this, even if only because people sympathetic to pragmatism so much enjoyed quoting it. Critics also quoted it, voicing thereby what was eventually to become the standard critique of pragmatism: that pragmatism was too shallow to accomplish anything and that its adherents had mistaken vacancy for liberation. But liberating it undoubtedly did feel to many American intellectuals. Pragmatism demanded very few commitments at a time when the need to have "a philosophy" was still felt by people who were sensitive to the risk of being burned by too large and too long a hold on beliefs of greater scope. Hadn't the Darwinian revolution shown how rapidly our assumptions about the world could change? And hadn't the increasingly discredited efforts of some thinkers to build out of "evolution" a comprehensive system now confirmed the danger of taking a philosophy too far? Wasn't the urban, industrial order of 1910 more different from American life in 1860 than the latter had been from life in 1810? Pragmatism promised a small but versatile supply of insights with which to prepare oneself for an existence in which more changes were no doubt on the way.

If the inevitability of change was to be successfully faced by society as a whole, a philosophy of limited scope was surely needed by the class of managers and bureaucrats assigned the task of supervising American public affairs. It can scarcely be a coincidence that the age in which pragmatism became popular was also the age in which American intellectuals were unprecedentedly engaged by the managerial ideal.[47] Fully consistent with this ideal was the elevation of "bold, persistent experimention" to the level of a principle in the rhetoric of the New Deal.[48] Spare as pragmatism was, it was fleshy enough to support this much admired principle, to sustain an optimistic perspective on science, and to reinforce certain of the least contested, most familiar, and most security-providing ideals in American culture.

One such ideal concerned "action." By closing the gap between thinking and doing, pragmatism preferred action to passivity wherever the choice presented itself. Method was emphasized over bodies of knowledge, and whatever potential for stasis knowledge might have was undercut by repeated reminders of its temporality. Humanity's relation to the universe was depicted in terms of the purposive action people might employ to affect their fate. The activity of inquiry was something confined not to a few—with the rest of the world passively looking on—but opened to as many persons as could meet the challenge of performing it.

Pragmatism was also "democratic." Not only was its method announced as widely accessible and as an engine of improvement; the very practice of that method was supposed to be open, undogmatic, tolerant, self-corrective, and thus an easily recognized extension of the standard liberal ideology articulated by Mill and cherished by so many late-nineteenth-century Americans. Pragmatism was also "moralistic," "voluntaristic," and "practical." It is no great trick to go on down the list, finding these dispositions in the writings of the pragmatists and their popularizers *as these writings specifically advance* the cluster of ideas by means of which pragmatism became a presence in American intellectual life. What needs to be emphasized is that these dispositions had a function in pragmatism other than to provide the terms for supererogatory rhetoric and to be crudely mirrored in a theory of meaning and truth: these dispositions were focused and put to use by pragmatism's capabilities as an orientation toward science at the level of "philosophy of life."

This emphasis need not prevent the recognition that theories of meaning and of truth can be important to large numbers of people and that the pragmatic theory was indeed a source of pragmatism's appeal. When James said that truth was no "stagnant property," but something that happened to ideas in the course of a particular sequence of events, one did not have to be a philosopher to take an interest in the issue. That meanings, truths, and goods were somehow functions of relationships, and not absolutes written into the structure of being, was of course an arresting concept. But the power of such concepts to obtain and keep widespread attention derived in part from the context in which they were advanced. This is to say that pragmatism's answers to philosophical questions, in the narrow sense of the term, gained interest and plausibility among nonphilosophers because these answers were, like "democracy" and "action," built into a "philosophy" in the broad, Emersonian sense, and one that was equipped with an apparently viable orientation toward science.

Pragmatism as a presence in the discourse of American intellectuals consisted essentially of three interpenetrating layers: a theory of meaning and truth that served to flag the movement, a cluster of assertions and hopes about the basis for culture in an age of science, and a range of general images stereotypical of American life. Pragmatism no doubt meant many things to different people, and enabled people to cope with a variety of concerns; yet it is of this three-layered structure that we are justified in thinking when we refer to the pragmatist tradition as manifest in the first half of the twentieth century.

To so regard pragmatism is not to insist that the historical significance of Peirce, James, or Dewey is exhausted by each one's participation in pragmatism. Much of what Peirce wrote about "signs" and what James wrote about the psychology of religion, for example, has flourished well outside of this tradition and can claim attention philosophically as well as historically. Nor does this view of pragmatism insist that, with its decline in popularity during the 1940s and after, the pragmatic themes in the writings of "the three" were rendered so anachronistic as to mock the efforts of more recent thinkers to learn something from them. Few American philosophers can claim to be more vividly contemporary than Richard Rorty, for example, who addresses and appreciates

Dewey from a perspective that Croly would find hard to recognize.[49] If pragmatism has a future, it will probably look very different from its past, and the two may not even share a name.

To bring the problem of pragmatism in American history down to a question of what pragmatism did for two generations of intellectuals may seem a narrow construction of the problem. Yet this modesty enables a more authentic pragmatism to come more clearly into view. The relations between this pragmatism and both the history of philosophy and the history of the United States are then more easily identified. If "pragmatic" ideas about meaning, truth, and goodness were latent in those parts of American culture discovered by Alexis de Tocqueville and explored by Louis Hartz and Daniel J. Boorstin,[50] these ideas remained mute and inglorious until explicitly developed by certain members of a particular, science-preoccupied generation of intellectuals. These ideas, moreover, did not become part of the public culture of the United States until spread by these same intellectuals and their immediate successors. The pragmatic theory of meaning and truth could not come into being until it was rendered in specific language, and it could not become a cultural possession until that language was taught to people with a will to use it. Since this language was worked out and popularized by late-nineteenth and early-twentieth-century American intellectuals, it is in the discourse of these intellectuals that the problem of pragmatism primarily resides. The pragmatism found in that discourse performed a number of political, philosophic, and religious acts that historians have only begun to assess. Not the least of these acts was the persuading of a great many people that pragmatism was an emblem for America.

POSTSCRIPT 1995: A LOOK AHEAD

Historians should know better than to look ahead. The article of 1980, reprinted above, offered one sentence about the future of pragmatism, and it soon proved to be more wrong than right. "If pragmatism has a future, it will probably look very different from its past, and the two may not even share a name." Fourteen years later pragmatism's name is invoked in a host of contexts, mostly by people who claim to be inspired by the classical pragmatists, and who see themselves as reaffirming doctrines inherited from them. Today's pragmatists, found as often in our faculties of law,[51] English,[52] history,[53] sociology,[54] and religion[55] as in our departments of philosophy, are less inclined than were their predecessors to identify science as a basis for culture, but these pragmatists of our own time are too directly engaged with the texts of Peirce, James, and Dewey to vindicate my prediction that pragmatism's future would look "very different" from its past. One could debate in detail, to be sure, the degree of difference between the old pragmatism and the new, but I prefer to concede that my conjecture about the future was mistaken.

This concession helps to clear a space in which I can respond with more confidence to the editors' request that I look ahead. I will do so historiograph-

ically. I want to suggest that an interesting question for some future historian
will be this: How and why did so many American intellectuals of the 1980s and
1990s come to believe that "pragmatism" was a desirable label for their ideas,
and why were these intellectuals eager to establish connections between themselves and Peirce, James, and Dewey? I will not try to answer this question
here, but I want to point out that this inquiry is very close to the one I attempted
for the first half of the twentieth century in my article of 1980. Behind this
question in regard to both epochs is my presumption that pragmatism is a construction, rather than a natural affinity between the ideas, texts, and careers said
to be involved in it. Its character is not to be taken for granted, but to be
explained historically.

The "old" pragmatism was built in the context of intense concern about the
cultural promise of science. This pragmatism, as I have tried to show, was
propelled by three basic assertions: that inquiry itself is a discipline that could
stabilize and sustain a modern, "scientific" culture for which truths could be
only tentative and plural; that the social and physical world is responsive to
human purpose; and that inquiry is an activity open to the rank-and-file members
of an educated, democratic society. These assertions bonded very easily with
the two phenomena most often flagged by the term, "pragmatism": a) the theories of meaning, truth, and goodness contributed to philosophy by Peirce,
James, and Dewey; and b) the impatience with principles, privilege, stasis, and
tradition stereotypically attributed to Americans in general. Hence, if we want
to assess the character of pragmatism as a broad movement among American
intellectuals from the 1910s through the 1940s, we would do well to see this
movement as more than a response in peculiarly American terms to some of the
classical issues in philosophy; this movement was also a specific response to
contemporary uncertainties and yearnings about science's cultural capabilities.
One could easily break down this movement into a "philosophy" and the "cultural motives" people had for appreciating it. I have intentionally blurred this
conventional distinction in order to emphasize what made pragmatism into so
powerful a movement: the sense that the philosophy of pragmatism itself directly
embodied, rather than merely served, a culture geared to science.

Selected utterances of Peirce, James, and Dewey were the raw materials out
of which pragmatism was constructed and maintained during the era stretching
from the 1910s through the 1940s. So it is today, but the favored passages are
not always the same, the work they are made to do is sometimes different, and
the rival persuasions against which they are invoked vary considerably. The
self-consciousness with which some of today's pragmatists construct a "pragmatic tradition" suitable to present purposes is perhaps the most striking point
of contrast between the contemporary discourse about pragmatism and that of
only forty years ago. Discussions of American pragmatism as late as midcentury
still conveyed a belief that there existed in history a genuine pragmatic tradition
that could be discovered, assessed, and critically renewed. Today, some of pragmatism's most prominent champions are quick to admit that they are all but

making it up: they are designating as pragmatists those past thinkers with whom they feel the most affinity. An example of this approach to the study of pragmatism is Cornel West's *The American Evasion of Philosophy*, which includes Lionel Trilling, C. Wright Mills, W. E. B. Dubois, and Reinhold Niebuhr— along with many of the usual suspects—within a "genealogy" of pragmatism offered candidly, if somewhat immodestly, as a series of antecedents to West himself.[56] One need not find fault with West in order to identify his work as a salient source for some future historical study of how pragmatism was constructed in the 1980s and 1990s.

Such a study is likely to concentrate on two concerns felt by many American intellectuals in the wake of post-1968 French thought popular in the United States. One concern has to do with democracy as a political ideal, and the other with knowledge as a goal of inquiry. Although it was easy to discern antiauthoritarian elements in the work of Foucault, Lyotard, and Derrida, just where democracy came in was not always apparent. But pragmatism, especially as associated with Dewey and his followers, was at least forthright in trying to vindicate and promote democracy.[57] Pragmatism was also understood to combine a strong sensitivity to the contingent, constructed character of knowledge with a gut sense that the objects of knowledge were capable of putting up at least some resistance to human constructions.[58] Although the newly popular French thinkers could, again, be read as sharing this suspicion that knowledge was more than the will-to-power, their emphasis was surely on the latter. Pragmatism, whatever else it might be construed to be, was at the very least a charter to critically update these old Englightenment ideals in relation to the experiences and sensitivities that had, by the end of the twentieth century, given credibility to postmodernist critiques.

NOTES

1. John Dewey, "Science as Subject-Matter and as Method," *Science* 36 (January 28, 1910): 127.

2. It is quoted without specific citation, for example, as the epigram to Leo E. Saidla and Warren E. Gibbs, eds., *Science and the Scientific Mind* (New York: Mcgraw Hill, 1930).

3. John Dewey, *The Influence of Darwin on Philosophy and Other Essays in Contemporary Thought* (New York: Henry Holt, 1910), 8–9, 19, 55–57, 70–72; John Dewey, *Reconstruction in Philosophy* (New York: Holt, 1920), 40, 54, 60–61, 67, 175–77; John Dewey, *The Quest for Certainty: A Study of the Relation of Knowledge and Action* (New York: Putnam, 1929), 99–101, 192–94, 228, 251, 296; John Dewey, *A Common Faith* (New Haven, Conn.: Yale University Press, 1934), 26, 32–33, 39.

4. William James, *The Will to Believe and Other Essays in Popular Philosophy* (New York: Holt, 1897), 54.

5. Ibid., x, xii–xiii, 7–10, 14, 18–19, 53–54, 323–27.

6. Ibid., 299–327.

7. Walter Lippmann, "An Open Mind: William James," *Everybody's Magazine*, 23 (December 1910): 800–801; Robert H. Lowie, "Science," in *Civilization in the United States: An Inquiry by Thirty Americans*, ed. Harold E. Stearns (New York: Henry Holt, 1922), 152–53; T. V. Smith, "The

Scientific Way of Life with William James as Guide,'' in T. V. Smith, *The Philosophic Way of Life* (New York, 1934), 69–110.

8. For an interesting discussion of this problem in Peirce, see Nicholas Rescher, *Peirce's Philosophy of Science: Critical Studies in His Philosophy of Induction and Scientific Method* (South Bend, Ind.: University of Notre Dame Press, 1978), 19–39.

9. Charles Sanders Peirce, *Collected Papers of Charles Sanders Peirce*, ed. Charles Hartshorne, Paul Weiss, and Arthur W. Burks (8 vols., Cambridge, Mass.: Harvard University Press, 1931–1958), 1.116–20.

10. This is emphatically stated in ibid., 1.135.

11. Ibid., 5.311. This aspect of Peirce has been helpfully called to the attention of historians by R. Jackson Wilson's essay, ''Charles Sanders Peirce: The Community of Inquiry,'' in R. Jackson Wilson, *In Quest of Community: Social Philosophy in the United States, 1860–1920* (New York: Oxford University Press, 1968), 32–59. See also Jakob Liszka, ''Community in C. S. Peirce: Science as a Means and as an End,'' *Transactions of the Charles S. Peirce Society*, 14 (Fall 1978): 305–21.

12. Josiah Royce, *The Problem of Christianity*, ed. John E. Smith (New York, 1968), 404–05. Peirce's direct influence on this crucial work of Royce's is clarified by Bruce Kuklick, *Josiah Royce: An Intellectual Biography* (Indianapolis: Hackett, 1972), esp. 214–15, 235.

13. William James, ''Philosophical Conceptions and Practical Results,'' in William James, *Collected Essays and Reviews* (New York: Holt, 1920), 406–37, esp. 410.

14. Peirce, *Collected Papers*, 5.403.

15. According to H. S. Thayer, Peirce's maxim ''is probably the unclearest recommendation for how to make our ideas clear in the history of philosophy.'' Thayer, *Meaning and Action: A Critical History of Pragmatism* (Indianapolis: Bobbs-Merrill, 1968), 87. See also Charles Morris, *Pragmatic Movement in American Philosophy* (New York: Braziller, 1970), 20–23; John E. Smith, *Purpose and Thought: The Meaning of Pragmatism* (New Haven, Conn.: Yale University Press, 1978), 18–32, 35; Elizabeth Flower and Murray G. Murphey, *A History of Philosophy in America* (2 vols., New York: G. P. Putnam, 1977), vol. 2, 590.

16. For a useful chronology of the development of pragmatism as a movement and a sketch of steps antecedent to this development, see Max H. Fisch, ''American Pragmatism Before and After 1898,'' *American Philosophy from Edwards to Quine*, ed. Robert W. Shahan and Kenneth R. Merrill (Norman: University of Oklahoma Press, 1977), 78–110.

17. William James, *Pragmatism: A New Name for Some Old Ways of Thinking* (New York: Longmans 1907), 48, 51–54.

18. Ibid., 55–58, 67, 197–236.

19. Less publicized among nonphilosophers, this depiction is very much the stuff of debate among philosophers assessing the pragmatists. Peirce's relevant texts include *Collected Papers*, 5.407, 565.

20. James, *Pragmatism*, 201. See also William James, *The Meaning of Truth: A Sequel to ''Pragmatism''* (New York: Longmans, 1909), v–vi. For help in sorting out the various versions of the pragmatic theory of truth, see Gertrude Ezorsky, ''Pragmatic Theory of Truth,'' in *Encyclopedia of Philosophy*, ed. Paul Edwards (8 vols., New York: Macmillan, 1967), vol. 6, 427–30; H. Standish Thayer, ''Introduction'' in James, *The Meaning of Truth* (Cambridge, 1975), xi–xlvi; Smith, *Purpose and Thought*, 32–33, 50–77.

21. John Dewey, ''The Need for a Recovery of Philosophy,'' in John Dewey et al., *Creative Intelligence: Essays in the Pragmatic Attitude* (New York: Holt, 1917), 48–50; Dewey, *Reconstruction in Philosophy*, 112–13, 121–22, 177; Dewey, *Quest for Certainty*, 3, 24–25, 85–86, 103–5, 204–5.

22. John Dewey, *Logic: The Theory of Inquiry* (New York: Macmillan, 1938). How differently the history of pragmatism looks to a historian from the way it looks to a philosopher is shown by the eagerness of philosophers to overlook the forty years of mushy work Dewey did in this area in order to focus on his most rigorous, climactic work. See Thayer, *Meaning and Action*, 190–99, and Smith, *Purpose and Thought*, 96–112. This approach is understandable if one's aim is to recover

the completed structure of Dewey's philosophy; the approach makes less sense if one wants to understand the living tradition that Dewey had built before his *Logic* appeared.

23. The connection is emphasized by Morton White, *Social Thought in America: The Revolt Against Formalism* (New York: Columbia University Press, 1949); Eric F. Goldman, *Rendezvous with Destiny: A History of Modern American Reform* (New York: Vintage, 1952), 119–24; and most of the references to pragmatism that still appear in survey textbooks of American history.

24. William James, *The Principles of Psychology* (2 vols., New York: Holt, Rinehart, and Winston, 1890). See also the discussion of this work in John Wild, *The Radical Empiricism of William James* (Garden City, N.Y.: Doubleday, 1969), 1–262.

25. James, *Will to Believe*, 21, 92–93, 130.

26. Bertrand Russell, "Dewey's New Logic," in *The Philosophy of John Dewey*, ed. Paul Arthur Schilpp (Evanston, Ill.: Open Court, 1939), 143–56.

27. James, *Pragmatism*, 43–81.

28. Dewey, *Reconstruction in Philosophy*, 161–86; Dewey, *Quest for Certainty*, 254–86; James, *Pragmatism*, 75–76.

29. John B. Watson, *Behaviorism* (New York: People's Institute, 1925).

30. This was particularly true in the 1930s, when Dewey himself sometimes supported socialist candidates for public office.

31. Bertrand Russell, *Mysticism and Logic and Other Essays* (New York: Doubleday, 1917), 46–57.

32. Sinclair Lewis, *Arrowsmith* (New York: Signet, 1925).

33. Robert A. Millikan, *Science and the New Civilization* (New York: Charles Scribner's Sons, 1930).

34. See, for example, Henry S. Pritchett, "Science (1857–1907)," *Atlantic Monthly*, (November 1907): 613–25.

35. See, for example, the numerous publications during the 1920s of Edwin E. Slosson, including Edwin E. Slosson, *Chats on Science* (New York: The Century Company, 1924).

36. Oliver Wendell Holmes, Jr., *Collected Legal Papers* (New York: Little, Brown, 1920). Holmes was often claimed as a prophet of the pragmatist tradition, and it is a mark of the strength of this tradition that such claims went unchallenged for so long. Of the many warm accounts of Holmes as a "liberal" and as a "pragmatist," the most eloquent is Henry Steele Commager, *The American Mind: An Interpretation of American Thought and Character Since the 1880's* (New Haven, Conn.: Yale University Press, 1950), 385–90. For a reading of Holmes more representative of the scholarship of the last twenty years, see Yosal Rogat, "The Judge as Spectator," *University of Chicago Law Review* 31 (Winter 1964): 213–56. See also G. Edward White, "The Rise and Fall of Justice Holmes," *University of Chicago Law Review.* (Fall 1971), 51–77.

37. The recognition that Peirce, James, and Dewey shared something important philosophically was first promoted by James himself, and it was acknowledged almost as readily by Dewey as it was resisted by Peirce. This much is often said in histories of pragmatism; what deserves more attention is the process by which the idea of single "American Pragmatism" was kept alive after James's death, especially during the 1920s and 1930s. Dewey and Dewey's followers played a very large role in this process and helped to persuade most Americans who took an interest in the matter that Dewey's work was the logical culmination of the pragmatism of Peirce and of James. So it is that one can responsibly analyze "pragmatism" as a presence in American intellectual life without taking up the texts of C. I. Lewis or of the later Royce; elements in their work that a discerning historian *of philosophy* might call "pragmatic" simply were not assimilated into the tradition constructed by American intellectuals under the dominating influence of Dewey. For a document of Dewey's that is representative of the process, see "The Development of American Pragmatism," in John Dewey, *Philosophy and Civilization* (New York: G. P. Putnam's Sons, 1931), 13–35.

38. Lucid, brief analyses of C. I. Lewis and George Herbert Mead in the context of the work of Peirce, James, and Dewey can be found in Thayer, *Meaning and Action*. Although Mead has recently enjoyed a considerable vogue in several of the human sciences, he was not widely known beyond

philosophy prior to his death in 1931, except in the circles of "Chicago social science." For Mead in that setting, see Egbert Parnell Rucker, *Chicago Pragmatists* (Minneapolis: University of Minnesota Press, 1959). Lewis was very much a philosopher's philosopher from the onset of his career in the 1910s through his death in 1964; his role as an examplar of professionalism in philosophy is discussed ably in Kuklick, *The Rise of American Philosophy: Cambridge, Massachusetts, 1860–1930* (New Haven, Conn.: Yale University Press, 1977). For a cogent and illuminating account of Lewis's philosophic work, see ibid., 533–62. Cf. Flower and Murphey, *History of Philosophy in America*, Holt, vol. 2, 891–958.

39. Joseph Ratner, "Introduction to John Dewey's Philosophy," in *Intelligence in the Modern World: John Dewey's Philosophy*, ed. Joseph Ratner (New York: Random House, 1939), 5, 57, 61, 115, 187, 227, 241.

40. Horace M. Kallen began writing articles about James and about pragmatism in 1910, contributed in 1917 to Dewey's pivotal anthology, *Creative Intelligence*, edited in 1925 the Modern Library edition of James's writings, and was involved in numerous symposia, *Festschriften*, and commemorative volumes honoring James and Dewey in later years. See Dewey et al., *Creative Intelligence*, 409–67; *The Philosophy of William James: Drawn from His Work*, ed. Horace M. Kallen (New York: Holt, 1925), 1–55; Horace M. Kallen, "John Dewey and the Spirit of Pragmatism," in *John Dewey: Philosopher of Science and Freedom*, ed. Sidney Hook (New York: Holt, 1950), 3–46. *Festschriften* for Kallen himself were meeting grounds for keepers of the pragmatist flame. See, for example, Sidney Ratner, ed., *Vision and Action: Essays in Honor of Horace M. Kallen on His 70th Birthday* (New Brunswick, N.J.: Rutgers University Press, 1953). Sidney Hook's operations began with Sidney Hook, *The Metaphysics of Pragmatism* (Chicago: Open Court, 1927). His other writings included *John Dewey: An Intellectual Portrait* (New York: John Day and Co., 1939). Hook also had a tour of duty similar to Kallen's on the symposia-*Festschrift* circuit of the 1940s and 1950s. For a good example of Hook's writings as they consolidate and interpret the pragmatist tradition, see "The Centrality of Method," in *The American Pragmatists: Selected Writings*, ed. Milton R. Konvitz and Gail Kennedy (Cleveland, 1960), 360–79. The essay begins with an epigram from Kallen. Kallen, who was widely known also for his exposition of "cultural pluralism," died in 1974; Hook was one of the pragmatist tradition's most forceful, capable, and visible defenders until his death in 1989.

41. Horace M. Kallen, "Pragmatism," *Encyclopedia of the Social Sciences*, ed. Edwin R. A. Seligman and Alvin Johnson (15 vols., New York: Macmillan, 1930–1935), vol. 12, 307–11.

42. Charles Forcey, *The Crossroads of Liberalism: Croly, Weyl, Lippmann and the Progressive Era, 1900–1925* (New York: Oxford University Press, 1961).

43. Walter Lippmann, *Drift and Mastery: An Attempt to Diagnose the Current Unrest* (New York: Macmillan, 1914). For an effort to determine this text's historical significance, see David A. Hollinger, "Science and Anarchy: Walter Lippmann's *Drift and Mastery*," *American Quarterly* 29 (Winter 1977), 463–75.

44. Frederick Barry, *The Scientific Habit of Thought: An Informal Discussion of the Source and Character of Dependable Knowledge* (New York, 1927); James Harvey Robinson, *The Mind in the Making: The Relation of Intelligence to Social Reform* (New York, 1921); Paul H. Douglas, "The Absolute, the Experimental Method, and Horace Kallen," in Ratner, ed., *Vision and Action*, 39–55; Lyman Bryson, *The New Prometheus* (New York: Macmillan, 1941); Lyman Bryson, *Science and Freedom* (New York, 1947).

45. For William Heard Kilpatrick's career at Teachers College, see Lawrence A. Cremin, *The Transformation of the School: Progressivism in American Education, 1876–1957* (New York: Macmillan, 1961), 215–24. Another work, although presented as in part a history, is richly revealing as a statement of the "progressive" educational philosophy inspired by Dewey. See John L. Childs, *American Pragmatism and Education: An Interpretation and Criticism* (New York: Macmillan, 1956).

46. Papini's aphorisms about pragmatism, published in Italian, became known to Americans primarily through James's own rendering of them. See William James, "G. Papini and the Prag-

matist Movement in Italy,'' *Journal of Philosophy, Psychology, and Scientific Methods* 3 (June 21, 1906): 337–41.

47. Of the many accounts of the rise of this idea, the most discussed is Robert H. Wiebe, *The Search for Order, 1877–1920* (New York: Hill and Wang, 1967), 133–63. See also William E. Nelson, ''Officeholding and Powerwielding: An Analysis of the Relationship Between Structure and Style in American Administrative History,'' *Law and Society Review* 10 (Winter 1976): 188–233.

48. R. G. Tugwell, *The Brains Trust* (New York: Macmillan, 1968), 93–105. The New Deal is perhaps the most noticed of many instances in the history of pragmatic rhetoric in which the use of that rhetoric seems to have concealed from its users the unarticulated assumptions that guided their own experimentation. See especially Thurman W. Arnold, *The Symbols of Government* (New Haven, Conn.: Yale University Press, 1935), and Thurman W. Arnold, *The Folklore of Capitalism* (New Haven, Conn.: Yale University Press, 1937). See also the critique of Arnold by Sidney Hook, ''The Folklore of Capitalism: The Politician's Handbook—A Review,'' *University of Chicago Law Review* 5 (April 1938): 341–49.

49. Richard Rorty, ''Dewey's Metaphysics,'' in *New Studies in the Philosophy of John Dewey*, ed. Steven M. Cahn (Hanover, N.H.: University Press of New England, 1977), 45–74. Cf. the different interest in Dewey manifest in the work of Willard van Orman Quine, *Ontological Relativity and Other Essays* (New York: Columbia University Press, 1969), 26–29.

50. Louis Hartz, *The Liberal Tradition in America: An Interpretation of American Political Thought Since the Revolution* (New York: Harcourt, 1955); Daniel J. Boorstin, *The Genius of American Politics* (Chicago: University of Chicago Press, 1953). Of the many works purporting to find ''pragmatic continuities throughout American history, these two still repay the effort to come to grips with them critically.

51. Michael Brint and William Weaver, eds., *Pragmatism in Law and Society* (Boulder, Co.: Westview Press, 1991).

52. Richard Poirier, *Poetry and Pragmatism* (Cambridge, Mass.: Harvard University Press, 1992).

53. James T. Kloppenberg, ''Objectivity and Historicism: A Century of American Historical Writing,'' *American Historical Review* 94 (1989): 1011–30.

54. Philip Selznick, *The Moral Commonwealth: Social Theory and the Promise of Community* (Berkeley: University of California Press, 1992).

55. Cornel West, *The American Evasion of Philosophy: A Genealogy of Pragmatism* (Madison: University of Wisconsin Press, 1989).

56. See West, *Evasion*, 7: ''My own conception of prophetic pragmatism . . . serves as the culmination of the American pragmatist tradition.'' This book is most successful as a vindication of the calling of philosophically informed cultural criticism, bolstered by a series of sympathetic case studies in the performance of this calling. The book's title can easily mislead readers into expecting more of a history of an intellectual movement than West actually provides. It is interesting that West does not include Oliver Wendell Holmes, Jr., C. I. Lewis, George Herbert Mead, Alain Locke, or Horace Kallen.

57. The democratic center of Dewey's project has been emphasized, once again, in Robert B. Westbrook, *John Dewey and American Democracy* (Ithaca, N.Y.: Cornell University Press, 1991).

58. The pragmatic tradition's *via media* between narrower Enlightenment models for knowledge and radically anti-Enlightenment ideas has been emphasized in James T. Kloppenberg, *Uncertain Victory: Social Democracy and Progressivism in European and American Thought, 1870–1920* (New York: Oxford University Press, 1986).

2

William James and Richard Rorty: Context and Conversation

George Cotkin

Richard Rorty's appropriation of John Dewey as a precursor is well known. Rorty has announced that he is "a Deweyan philosopher who also thinks of himself as a reformist, bourgeois, Dewey-style liberal."[1] For Rorty, Dewey's philosophy seeks to overcome hackneyed dualisms of subject and object, mind and matter, experience and nature. Moreover, Rorty admires Dewey's refusal to remain mired in *fach* philosophy and the traditional puzzles of epistemology. Of course, Rorty's Dewey is a creation. Many find Rorty's vision of Dewey as an arch antifoundationalist and a rejecter of professional philosophy to be a gross misrepresentation.[2] Rorty acknowledges that his espousal of Dewey has not always demonstrated sufficient familiarity with the philosopher's corpus. But Rorty continues to find himself more comfortable with Dewey than with any other American philosopher: "Maybe I haven't read the right things in Dewey, but I can't see what he'd have against me."[3]

The snug fit between Dewey's philosophy and Rorty's antifoundationalist crusade is not at issue here. Rorty can choose whomever he wishes for his philosophical grandfather. But it is surprising that Rorty should find in Dewey, more than in William James, an appropriate ancestor.[4] After all, much of Rorty's recent work—after he employed Dewey, Heidegger, Quine, and Davidson in *Philosophy and the Mirror of Nature* (1979) to upset correspondence theories of truth and to undermine notions of foundationalism—would seem to have a most appropriate and obvious precursor in James. Both James and Rorty are powerful advocates of pluralism, wanting to present a world that is constantly in the process of making itself—a world that contains a multitude of stories in James's language or an endless number of vocabularies in Rorty's terms. Both

James and Rorty may be seen as romantics, seeking to enthuse the realm of the personal with excitement, responsibility, and creativity. In the public sphere, both adhere confidently to liberal assumptions. James and Rorty are each highly sensitive to the dangers of the imperial self, and hence proclaim the importance of respect for the "other." Moreover, James, certainly more than Dewey, possessed a firm sense of the tragic, a belief in limitations that would seem closer to Rorty's own recognition of the constraints upon revolutionary expectations and utopian hopes. Finally, quite as much as Dewey, James along with Rorty wanted to move away from a purely philosophical discourse to enter into the world of the public intellectual, albeit to an audience largely confined to the educated and middle classes.

Despite their powerful affinities, an important distinction exists between James and Rorty that will be a focus of this essay. James and Rorty hold strikingly different conceptions of cultural politics; they disagree about the necessity and value of a firm distinction between the private and public spheres of experience, and on the value of philosophy for public debates. For James, the private and public are intertwined, incapable of meaningful separation. His philosophical vision is designed to impel the individual into the public world on the same terms in which the individual creates his or her private sensibilities. In contrast, Rorty draws a Maginot Line between the public and private realms. For Rorty, selfhood, as a creative and continuous process, is where the action is to be found. The public practice of politics is complacently consigned to the assumptions of tepid and traditional liberalism. Thus, Rorty maintains that "within our increasingly ironist culture, philosophy has become more important for the pursuit of private perfection rather than for any social task."[5]

Each perspective may be understood and explicated through a historical contextualization. James's perceptions of the interplay between the private and the public were a function of the specific historical forces that defined his era and of his own particular understanding and overcoming of these concerns. Rorty's emphasis upon the split between the public and private may be seen as a continuation of the "end of ideology" notion of the 1950s and the sober view of the dangers of romantic and subjectivist judgments being written into a political agenda.

A conversation between James and Rorty may help to correct problems inherent within each of their approaches. If James's conflation of the personal with the political too often dangerously skirts the border line of the vitalistic or imperialistic mentality, then Rorty's sharp division between the two realms too often renders the public sphere tepid and uninviting. Importantly, James and Rorty share a fear of what James once called "desiccation" in the private sphere. But James also wanted to have the public realm as a sphere where the life "*in extremis*" of the private individual had an opportunity to play itself out. This ideal sends shivers up Rorty's privatistic spine.[6]

The desiccation that James confronted was at once expressed in metaphysical, intellectual, and cultural terms. It threatened the private sanctity of the individual will and it also eroded the fiber of public life. It must be noted that this fear of desiccation in the second half of the nineteenth century was not a generalized phenomenon. It raged especially virulently among the upper and middle classes and among those who followed a life of the mind. The etiology of desiccation, otherwise commonly referred to as neurasthenia, was mixed, but its effects could be numbing, provoking the sufferer to adopt a "nightmare" or "bass note" view of life. Surcease from the neurasthenic malady appeared possible only in the darkened chambers of the bedroom, where the harsh light of modernity and metaphysical doubt might be shut out.

From the early 1860s until well into the 1870s, William James had faced the specter of depression and debility as both a private and public reality. His depression was, in part, the result of a conflict of wills between him and his father over vocational direction—William wanting to pursue art, his father preferring him to study science. But the personal aspects of this conflict are only part of the story. James, in common with many from his generational cohort, experienced malaise as a personal and philosophical response to a historically specific set of circumstances. The value, and sometimes the possibility of free will came under attack, and the question of whether life was worth living in such a world suddenly became central for many intellectuals.[7]

This malaise, or notion of life as *tedium vitae*, could be laid at the doorstep of modern scientific certitude and confidence. By the mid-nineteenth century, the demands of Calvinistic religion had spent their force for James and many of his friends. The religious imperative to act with faith, to believe that one's actions were morally justified, seemed to be compromised by what James later characterized as the scientific stance of doubt. Contemplation and doubt, rather than action and belief, by the 1870s had become the required and respectable frame of mind. But James later wrote in "Is Life Worth Living?": "Too much questioning and too little active responsibility lead . . . to the edge of the slope, at the bottom of which lie pessimism and the nightmare or suicidal view of life."[8]

Metaphysical concerns combined with this scientistic melody to play for James a tune of inaction, doubt, and debility. As a young man, James had trembled at the apparently distinct ideals that the universe was fully determined or absolutely undetermined. In many ways, these perceptions were the flip sides of the same coin that translated into the currency of depression. The new God of science, in James's worst nightmares, presented a world that was mechanical and utterly determined. Everything that transpired was part of a long, inexorable chain of events that banished moral responsibility and free will from the world. James ruefully reported in 1869 that "we are Nature through and through, that we are wholly conditioned, that not a wiggle of our will happens save as the result of physical laws."[9]

At the same time, James feared that the universe was totally indeterminate. Drift and uncertainty hobbled James when he confronted a universe that was nothing more than "mere cosmic weather," in the sobering characterization of his early philosophical mentor, Chauncey Wright.[10] In James's own language, the universe was sometimes simply "restless" as well as an "abyss of horrors." Behind the illusion of law and logic, he worried, was nothing except for chance occurrences. Although he would later use this ideal in his mature philosophy as a rationale for the individual to write his or her own message upon the shifting sands of the metaphysical beach, the young and insecure James in the 1860s and 1870s found this vision frightening. It plunged him into the twilight existence of the neurasthenic, or it threatened him with the fear of becoming an epileptic cowering in the corner of loneliness and depression.

Philosophical problems corresponded with cultural concerns. Of course, the early Jamesian views of the universe did not have to translate into depression and debility. After all, determinism—no less than indeterminism—could be, and often was, capable of being turned into a prescription for hope and progress. All phenomena might be part of an either divine or natural plan for future well-being. Individual will and freedom were given sanction by this view, so long as the exercise of free will was in the direction of the preconceived order. But for many in James's cultural and class cohort, the metaphysical nightmares that hounded them were joined by the rather odd conviction that the modern world was an unexciting venue for action. Phenomenal description and metaphysical speculation commonly became confused as explanations for the neurasthenia or *tedium vitae* then common.

At first glance, the thought that the second half of the nineteenth century was a tedious or desiccated period seems absurd, nothing more than mere affectation. Without exaggeration, historian Howard Mumford Jones called the era an "Age of Energy." But James and others felt strangely distant from the movement that swirled around them. Diagnosticians of the neurasthenia that afflicted the elite classes in this period often explained it as caused by the rise of modern city living, which created high levels of anxiety and confusion. The cacophony of sounds grated against the refined and sensitive nervous systems of the elite classes, causing them to succumb to the neurasthenic malady.

Thus, the context for James's initial thinking about the private and public, no less than the philosophical realm, may be situated around the problems of desiccation and *tedium vitae*. These concerns, James believed, were metaphysical and cultural in nature. Resolution of the problems associated with neurasthenia became central to James's psychology and philosophy, professional as well as popular. Solution began with the individual reconstituting himself or herself, in Rortyean terms, by rewriting the texts of their lives in a new vocabulary. But, in the process of this creation, the individual also had to reconceptualize the metaphysical and public realms, coming to see them as the arenas in which the private self must be allowed to realize its ideals. Private virtues and reconceptualizations, for James, must become transformed into public virtues. James did this by developing a therapy for the reconstitution of the self that would, in turn, become a discourse of heroism in the public sphere.

By the 1870s, William James had begun to awaken from these cultural and philosophical nightmares. The chapters on "Will" and especially on "Habit" in *The Principles of Psychology* (1890) may be read as his confrontation and solution to the horror of the abyss and the *tedium vitae* of modernity. In essence, James's program wanted to reclaim the private self away from the debilitation and desiccation of doubt through a regimen of habit and training of the will. In his emphasis upon habit, James's prescription was Victorian rather than Rortyean postmodern in suggesting the possibilities of refashioning the self.

James was not always confident, however, about the success of redescription. He recognized that the individual was confronted with a variety of stimuli, some of which pushed him or her back into a state of debility. Most importantly, the creation of an identity was caught up in history—the habits and modes of behavior that the neurasthenic expressed were accumulations, and therefore not easily jettisoned. In his more pessimistic moments, James admitted that "in most of us, by the age of thirty, the character has set like plaster, and will never soften again."[11]

But for many, the plaster needed to be recast. To reconstitute the self required, in James's therapeutic formula, first the decision to proceed. Here James borrowed in theory, if not in practice, from Renouvier's theorem that the first act of free will must be to act as if one were free. Unfortunately, the decision to act was not sufficient in and of itself, especially given the legacy of accumulated habits of inaction. Thus James's notion of habit formation stressed small gains leading up to the development of a new selfhood. In the language of Victorian moralists, James told his readers to educate their nervous system to become "our ally instead of our enemy." Next, the individual must "Never suffer an exception to occur till the new habit is securely rooted in your own life." Other suggestions centered around seizing the first opportunity to make a change and learning to focus attention and effort in the desired direction. In the end, the reconstitution of the self, away from dessication to "energetic volition" depended upon "a little gratuitous exercise every day."[12]

James connected the reconstitution of the self with a reconceptualization of the public sphere. James was often ambivalent, even after his youthful bout with depression, about the possibilities of heroic interaction in the bourgeois world of bureaucracy, rationality, and comfort. How, James asked, could the individual practice "energetic volition" in the bourgeois "tea-table elysium" world?[13] James demanded "a universe for which our emotions and active propensities shall be a match." Life must be experienced "in its wild intensity" when we were caught up in the "Rembrandtesque moral chiaroscuro" of strife and hardihood.[14]

James wanted to transform individual personality from a narrative of tedium and desiccation into a story of heroism and excitement. This could only be achieved by conflating the private and public realms. The private individual must, by careful cultivation of useful habits, gain the ability to enter into the world, to escape from deadening doubt or mere sentimentalism. The world, in turn, must be open to that individual but, even more, it had to offer sufficient inducements for the exercise of heroism.

The moral economy of the public world, for James's discourse of heroism to function, had to be based on a scarcity model. Wealth and immediate gratification weakened the possibility of new heroic narratives. Asceticism and hardihood became essential for the heroic exercise of the will. The newly formed personality, James seemed to maintain in *Principles of Psychology*, could not be confined to the private realm; there it would wither and die. In fact, the larger the challenges from the public world, the greater the possibilities that were offered to the individual:

The huge world that girdles us about puts all sorts of questions to us, and tests us in all sorts of ways. . . . The world thus finds in the heroic man its worthy match and mate; and the effort which he is able to put forth to hold himself erect and keep his heart unshaken is the direct measure of his worth and function in the game of human life. He can *stand* this Universe. He can meet it and keep up his faith in the presence of those same features which lay his weaker brethren low. He can still find a zest in it . . . by pure inward willingness to take the world with those deterrent objects there. And hereby he becomes one of the masters and the lords of life. (1182, v.2)

The universe that James described in his mature philosophy was open yet resistant to the creative hand of individuals. In James's tragic view of life, evil was always present. Progress could be gained but it would not be absolute. The presence of evil demanded heroic exertions on the part of the individual. In *The Varieties of Religious Experience* (1902), the saints that James studied and respected had all undergone personal transformations that impelled them outward into the world, to fight evil, to convert souls, to reform institutions. There was a happy fit between the private compulsion to reform and the public need for amelioration of evil. The saint no longer lived within himself or herself, but through new qualities of asceticism, spiritual enlargement, purification, and charity, these individuals read their personality onto the pages of history. James recognized that religious excitement could become "pathological," but he never ceased to welcome its passion as a palliative for the *tedium vitae*.

Sainthood might not be possible for all men, but James wanted all men to experience heroism. In his own discourse on heroism, he emphasized frequently that the universe presented us with all types of situations that called forth the often dormant heroic instincts. Thus, natural disasters such as earthquakes or shipwrecks were evaluated quite as much in terms of their power to compel the individual into public feats of heroism as they were discussed as disasters of vast magnitude.[15]

"The beauty of war . . . is that it is so congruous with ordinary human nature."[16] This lesson became essential to James's views on the relation between the private self and public possibilities. It caused him to actually welcome the initial bellicosity of the Spanish-American War, to even respect the jingoistic mob spirit for its ability to shake individuals out of their lethargy. Indeed, in his most famous argument against war, "The Moral Equivalent of War," James made a far stronger case for the allure and importance of war in developing the race and in exciting the passions of individuals than he did in presenting his arguments against it. Furthermore, James always felt distanced from his allies in the antiimperalism movement because they lacked the respect for war as a transformer of the personality. "War is the *strong* life; it is life *in extremis.*"[17]

James's discourse on heroism, with its emphasis upon the private self engaging the world energetically, was highly problematic. It threatened domination by having the individual's perceptions read outward onto the public realm—a problem that Rorty's bifurcated cultural politics seeks to avoid. Yet James recognized the problem and its implications in both philosophy and politics—and so did his critics. *Pragmatism* (1907) was viewed by its opponents as an application of James's heroic narrativization upon the philosophical text of truth. To Bertrand Russell, pragmatism relied upon "iron clads and Maxim guns" as the "ultimate arbiters of metaphysical truth."[18] In the public realm, the danger existed that the individual, awash in personal emotions, might fall victim to a radical subjectivism that reduced the world to "private theatricals" or impelled the individual to confuse philosophical conceptions with individual realities.

If some ways, Theodore Roosevelt represented James's greatest desires and worst nightmares. On the one hand, Roosevelt was the renarrativized individual propelled into the public world. His early bouts with physical weakness and depression had been tossed to the side, replaced by an energetic confrontation with the world. On the other hand, Roosevelt was an arch jingoist imperialist. The problem, from James's perspective, was not always with Roosevelt's energetic effusions as such, but with his philosophical and personal blindness to the rights and realities of people different from himself. To James, Roosevelt was an Hegelian politician, someone who applied abstract conceptions to concrete situations. Hegelian absolutism and Rooseveltian imperialism, then, both practiced their own forms of blindness to the plurality and individuality of possibilities. Each easily transformed itself into a "big, hollow, resounding, corrupting, sophisticating torrent of mere brutal momentum and irrationality."[19] James's ship of cultural politics was threatened by the possibility of individual narratives, turned into abstractions, working to obliterate the validity of different visions.

James's solution to the problem of dominance that might be connected with the newly energized, renarrativized self, was twofold. In his public and professional philosophy, he continued to rail against all forms of abstractionism and absolutism. Such monistic visions, James reiterated often, misread the plurality of the world, reducing too tightly the belly-band of the universe. He also developed a doctrine of openness, a public expression of his philosophical doctrine of pluralism, that emphasized a recognition of the intractability of the "other." In perhaps his most compelling statement on the issue, "On a Certain Blindness in Human Beings," James offered a parable designed to allow the individual to reconstitute itself without seeking to dominate another person. James recalled encountering in the North Carolina mountains a scene of magisterial beauty and purity, but his rapture was compromised when he happened upon the ramshackle shack of a squatter, who had despoiled the natural sublimity of the environment. At first, James is disdainful, but as he ruminates on the matter, he finds that this squatter, too, has a vision, one that perceives the shack and ragged fence as accomplishments, as a writing of the creative will upon nature. Now, James understands the inner value of each man's vision. Thus, for James, the necessity was not to create a foundation for truth that might apply for everyone, but to allow a variety of truths to coexist within the world of philosophical and every-day discourse.[20]

Of course, James was not always successful in this endeavor, nor did he necessarily want to be. He refused, as he made clear in "The Moral Philosopher and the Moral Life" (1891?), to prescribe, through any "closet-philosopher's rule" some type of abstract formula for moral desires. He felt more comfortable in recognizing the "pinch" between desire and reality, and in hoping that the universe had enough room to reconcile competing visions. Unfortunately, the power of James's parable becomes dulled, as the developmental vision of the squatter comes into conflict with the conservationist desires of the environmentalist. The solution, James would no doubt say, did not lay in developing an abstracted truth about the situation. Any solution must begin in the recognition of the validity and purposefulness of the competing visions. Thus, in part, the intended appeal of pragmatism as a method was in its ability to empower possibilities and to mediate between disputes. But, of course, that did not resolve the problem.

Richard Rorty confronts a world that is quite different from James's. Rorty inhabits a universe that has seen all too often the dangers of the heroic person-ality *in extremis*. Rorty is, unlike James, not enthused with passion for radical transformations of the public sphere. He lives as the humbled philosopher, fol-lowing Adorno, in believing that the Holocaust, Stalinism, and the cloud of Hiroshima have rendered impossible old ways of thinking about Jamesian ideals of public exuberance. Yet Rorty continues to believe that poetry is possible, so long as its song is confined to the ears of the private imagination.

The agenda of Rorty's important recent work, *Contingency, Irony, and Soli-darity* (1989) is a logical extension of his earlier attacks against foundationalism in philosophy.[21] In his new work, Rorty attempts to develop the implications of an ethics of selfhood and community that can flourish without foundationalist claims. Nor does he flinch from his vision of an "aestheticized culture" in a world that is unfinished and unresolved, a world where there is no essential human nature and no truths out there waiting to be discovered. In good prag-matist fashion, Rorty's universe is contingent and so is his notion of the indi-vidual and of ethics. Drawing on the postmodern emphasis on language, Rorty presents people as a function of their languages, and their languages are contin-gent. Thus the key to creativity lies in the individual redescribing himself or herself by developing a new vocabulary. Through redescriptions and metaphorical forays, a brave new world may be forged. "It is changing the way we talk, and thereby changing what we want to do and what we think we are" (20).

Rorty is aware of the Nietzschean connotations of this program, and with Orwell, he was worried that in a world without fixed truths, without firm foundations, and with constantly changing vocabularies and equations (the $2 + 2 = 5$), domination threatens. But Rorty does not believe that a position in favor of abstract truths, buttressed by presumably foundationalist arguments, does anything to lessen the possibility of domination. Freedom grows out of the ability to recreate oneself and one's culture by the development of new vocabularies, and the toleration of this enterprise. This process is controlled, in Rorty's system, by the traditions that a society has developed.[22] And, equally importantly, Rorty presents one commandment as the nonfoundational foundation for his version of liberalism: "Liberal ironists are people who include among these ungroundable desires their own hope that suffering will be diminished, that the humiliation of human beings by other human beings may cease" (xv).

Rorty's cultural politics are designed to allow a maximum amount of creativity in the private sphere and a minimal amount of cruelty in the public sphere. In the private realm, the romantic impulse is allowed full sway, creating new vocabularies, taking ironic stances, and playfully redescribing everything that comes into its path. The model for the private realm of creativity is the poet, the maker of metaphors, of "new words, the shaper of new languages . . . the vanguard of the species" (20). In the public sphere, the pragmatist conception rules the roost, designed to increase human solidarity, to diminish pain and cruelty, and to celebrate the assumptions of a liberal polity. Rorty wants "an intricately-textured collage of private narcissism and public pragmatism."[23]

Although Rorty might believe, in the language of *Plessy v. Ferguson*, in the possibility of a doctrine of separate but equal for the public and private spheres, in practice Rorty's reconstitution of the public and private is not based on equality. Rorty waxes eloquent about the possibilities of the poetic within the private realm, but seems to approach the public sphere with a weary sigh. The public role of the philosopher is sharply constrained: "we should not assume it is our task, as professors of philosophy, to be the avant-garde of political movements."[24] In discussing the public, although Rorty admits to being less than comfortable with the status quo, nonetheless, he repeatedly celebrates the virtues of "bourgeois democracy."[25]

In addition, Rorty's agenda for increasing human solidarity and lessening the cruelty of the domination of an aestheticized public realm upon the individual resides mainly in a call for strong poets to redescribe the world, to begin evoking a better world in the realm of imagination and metaphor. Somehow, the works of great novelists will convert the public to liberal democratic ideals and human solidarity. But this ideal seems pallid and beside the point, even according to Rorty's own prescriptions. After all, Rorty rejects abstracted notions of human solidarity, noting that during the Nazi era, individuals did not save Jews from concentration camps because of an abstract dedication to the human race. Instead, they saved individual Jews because they identified with them as neighbors, fellow soccer players, or close friends. Thus, Rorty's hopes for a renarrativized public realm seem beside the point. Moreover, exhaustion and lack of imagination characterize his discussions and descriptions of the public realm: "We liberals have no plausible large-scale scenario for changing that world so as to realize the 'technical possibility of human equality' " (181).

How did Rorty achieve this strange amalgam of private creativity and public desiccation? To understand the origins and logic of his thoughts on political culture, it is necessary to examine the background and context for Rorty's formulations. The context of Rorty's philosophical and personal development is not as clear as James's. There is some evidence that Rorty went through a private crisis similar to James's, one defined by vocational anxieties. As Rorty narrates his own personal development, he originally wanted to be a poet. But his father, James, who had published a book of his own poetry, quashed such plans with critical comments.[26]

By age seventeen, Rorty had decided next to follow a career in philosophy. He met with immediate success if not contentment, receiving his Ph.D. from Yale. After a short time teaching at Wellesley, he was hired at Princeton. At Princeton, Rorty came face to face with the power of analytic philosophy. He worked in that field—and certainly learned to employ many of its methods and to learn its language—but he felt "sheer terror" at the thought of continuing to work within its assumptions and methods. To a lesser degree than James, Rorty went through a period of depression—"one year of clinical depression"—when he found himself incapable of writing anything.[27]

The personal depression that was tied into his professional imperatives dissipated when Rorty decided to abandon analytical philosophy and to hitch his star to the American pragmatists and to the continental philosophers (he had always been drawn to Heidegger). Such a shift did not work wonders for Rorty's relations with his Princeton colleagues, who, he states, "started telling graduate students, 'It's a waste of time to do your dissertation under Rorty' [who was viewed by them] as 'some sort of crank.' " But Rorty persevered with new resolve, and he found his creative possibilities freed: "The philosophic prose began pouring out of the typewriter. Suddenly it was a pure pleasure, and it's been that way ever since." In sum, Rorty had effected a private transformation by rewriting the text of his professional life. Such a reconstitution of the self, out of the depths of despair, would become a *sine qua non* for Rorty's emphasis on the valuable possibilities of the reconstitution of the self through the creation of new, original narratives—so long as they are confined more to the private rather than to the public realm.[28]

Private and professional problems alone do not account as the context for Rorty's emphasis on the firm dividing line between the private and the public spheres. It is also an outgrowth of a particular political and cultural milieu. At first glance, Rorty's background would suggest an inheritance of political and public activism—the social gospel minister Walter Rauschenbusch was his maternal grandfather, and his father, James Rorty, was a well-known New York intellectual and, for a time, a member of the American Workers Party. By the 1950s, James Rorty had come to refer to himself as a "Taft Republican" and a committed anticommunist.[29] Thus, one presumes, the mood of the Rorty household, like that in the mansions of the minds of many New York intellectuals, was one of suspicion for utopian plans of public transformations, along with a belief that ideological Romanticism leads directly into political domination. Therein lay, perhaps, the origins of Rorty's strongly held belief that "It is only when a Romantic intellectual begins to want his private self to serve as a model for other human beings that his politics tends to become antiliberal."[30]

Rorty's politics are sufficiently complex to defy reduction to a newer version of the politics of the New York intellectuals. But there are clear and important affinities. Although he disagrees with the scientism and antagonism to continental philosophy in the work of Sidney Hook, he finds in Hook a fellow traveler and valued teacher. For Rorty, Hook had the good sense to resist, like James Rorty, the siren songs of the communists in the 1930s and later. Hook's importance as a public philosopher resided in his debunking of the philosophical pretensions of his professional brethren and in his allegiance to the tradition of American democracy.[31]

In the same vein, Rorty's current position as a bourgeois liberal, philosophical antinomian, and cultural avant gardist, has some affinities with the ideas of another New York intellectual, Daniel Bell.[32] Analysts of Bell commonly emphasize his rejection of his Marxist past and, in the 1950s, his coming to terms with the triumph of liberalism in his formulation of an "end of ideology." But the end of ideology was not meant as a complete celebration of American values. To be sure, Bell did believe that the ideologies of communism and fascism were defunct, and his evaluation of liberalism may be seen as suggesting that liberalism was not an ideology. But, as Howard Brick has recently emphasized, Bell's book *The End of Ideology* was importantly subtitled "The Exhaustion of Political Ideas in the Fifties."[33]

Thus, Bell and Rorty become joined by their belief that traditional ideologies have spent themselves, have revealed their shallowness and demonstrated their political viciousness and totalitarian tempers. But in the face of such failures, Bell and Rorty have little to offer other than an espousal of social democratic ideals. If Bell at least continued to maintain faith in liberal planning in the public realm, Rorty seems to have given up the public realm as the interesting area of contestation in favor of the exciting possibilities of the private realm, where no ideology can ever hold the individual captive, since new vocabularies and ways of thinking are the lifeblood of human existence.

The connection with the New York intellectuals could be expanded to include Rorty's commitment to an ironic stance. Faced with the decline of their utopian fantasies, Reinhold Niebuhr, Sidney Hook, and Richard Hofstadter all found themselves increasingly drawn to an ironic view of life, as well as to a tragic sensibility. Niebuhr's *The Irony of American History* and Hofstadter's *The*

American Political Tradition may be read as crucial documents in the development of an ironic sensibility that Rorty has inherited and expanded, albeit in
the new language of postmodernism. And, Rorty's recent emphasis on the limitations of political reconstruction, the dangerous hubris inherent in revolutionary
movements to transform human nature, has a striking resemblance to Hook's
essay "The Tragic Sense of Life." Indeed, Rortyean pragmatism may be seen
as attempting to develop a pragmatism of ironic and debunking scope, marked
by a sense of limitations and tragedy that begins perhaps with Jonathan Edwards,
continues with Emerson (especially in the essay "Fate"), and culminates with
William James. Where John Dewey fits into this chastened perception remains
unclear.[34]

   Intellectual pedigree alone does not establish meaning. Rorty's emphasis on
the division between the private realm of creativity and his niggardly emphasis
on the public sphere may also be accounted for by his own understanding of
some of the crucial political events of the modern age. The experiments of Stalin
and other totalitarian movements to transform human nature, to recreate a new
public body, have proven to be abysmal failures, testaments to domination not
liberation. They have failed, in Rorty's view, because they have been based on
a false notion of possibility—they have assumed such an entity as human nature.
And, secondly, they have rejected the ideal that the polity must seek to limit
cruelty. Images of the totalitarian dictatorships of the 1930s continue to haunt
the pages of Rorty's philosophical speculation. And with good reason. "Hitler-
like and Mao-like fantasies" are the stuff that repression is based on, especially
when such transformative visions of the private self are read out onto the public
realm. Rorty's respect for Orwell as an analyst of the totalitarian sensibility are
revealing in this context. Orwell understands, in Rorty's reading of him, that
cruelty is not simply a political method, it is an end in and of itself, one that is
closely connected to the utopian hopes of totalitarian regimes. The strength of
Orwell's writing was to describe the devastating similarities of totalitarianism
whether marching under the banner of Hitler or Stalin. In sum, "the job of
sensitizing us to these excuses, of redescribing the Soviet Union, was Orwell's
great practical contribution" (171).

   The dangerous experiments in totalitarian engineering are not, in Rorty's view,
distant memories. Totalitarian dreams continue to lurk behind even the best-
intentioned ideals of transformation. Although he finds much that is valuable in
the work of Michel Foucault, Rorty becomes nervous with what he sees as Foucault's romantic need to project his "desire for private autonomy out onto politics." Intellectuals must drop "the assumption that" there must be "some
interesting connection between what matters most to an individual and his purported moral obligations to this fellow human beings." No such obligations exist
in Rorty's most recent formulations on the political responsibilities of the intellectual. The only obligation that seems powerfully compelling, beyond vague pronouncements about diminishing cruelty, is the desire for "self-overcoming and
self-invention" in the private realm.[35]

If Orwell "wrote exactly the right books at exactly the right time," then one suspects that doing that is Rorty's desire as well. The books and articles that passionately stream from Rorty's vigorous pen are designed to support individual creativity in the private realm and to minimize cruelty and to achieve a nonfoundational human solidarity in the public realm. Rorty's writings express a sense of exhaustion in the wake of failed utopian experiments in politics and failed foundationalist enterprises in philosophy. On the one hand, there are valuable lessons to be learned through Rorty's valid fears of the domination inherent in utopian schemes based on abstracted conceptions of truth and human nature. On the other hand, Rorty's ideal of human freedom and political possibility becomes powerfully stagnant and abstract, if not beside the point.

Criticisms of Rorty's cultural politics, with the division between public and private as central, are numerous and compelling. The work of recent feminist theory may be said to rest, in part, upon demonstrating that the line between the public and private is nonexistent or at least blurred. Moreover, vocabularies are gender based and quite capable of leading to the domination and abuse of women within the hallowed sphere of the private realm. In addition, Rorty's model of the strong poet and conversationalist appears to presume that all groups in society have the same access to the conversation, that those groups that have been excluded from the public sphere will be allowed to enter into the discourse. But even though Rorty is open and pluralistic about the inclusion of these groups into the conversation, his own work is singularly silent on how to achieve that end. Thus, not surprisingly, exhaustion and irrelevancy are the words that best describe the realities of Rorty's public realm.[36]

In a significant lecture, "Feminism and Pragmatism," presented as the Tanner Lecture on Human Values at the University of Michigan in December, 1990, Rorty has seemed to nudge himself away from an exclusive emphasis on the private realm as the space where the individual engages in the liberating act of redescription. Rorty now speaks more of individuals working together to form linguistic communities, where narratives of prophecy and reconceptualization become the norm. In keeping with his antifoundationalist convictions, Rorty recommends that such renarrativizations should be without recourse to realism or universalism; instead they must be based simply on the ability to imagine a different set of future possibilities, based on hopes and desires of the individuals joined into the linguistic community. Applying this formulation to the work of female liberation, Rorty suggests that "groups build their moral strength by achieving increasing semantic authority over their members, thereby increasing the ability of those members to find their moral identities in their membership of such groups."[37] This new language need not remain ghettoized to a single group. In the best of all Rortyean worlds, "The new language spoken by the separatist group may gradually get woven into the language taught in the schools" (248). And thus does social change ensue through the creation of new, nonfoundationalist narratives.

What jars in Rorty's nod to individual reconstruction as a group activity is his continued refusal, as just noted, to contextualize the possibilities for renarrativization and his inability to countenance the value of assumptions about human rights as either foundational or simply highly efficacious. Although the construction of narratives is now viewed as a community enterprise connected to a struggle for freedom, Rorty pays little attention to the preconditions for speaking and for being heard; there is really no analysis of the local mechanisms that exert power, that define, in Foucaultian terms, the direction that actions such as linguistic redefinition may take.[38] After all, Rorty may glibly announce (claiming authority from Dewey) that "if you find yourself a slave, do not accept your masters' descriptions of the real; do not work within the boundaries of their moral universe; instead try to invent a reality of your own by selecting aspects of the world which lend themselves to the support of *your* judgment of the worthwhile life" (241).

Unfortunately, this is easier said than done. The heroic nature of slave resistance, as historian Eugene Genovese has brilliantly demonstrated, was a function of the slaves' ability to work *within* the linguistic *and* ideological structure of their masters' assumptions; in this manner, they were able to expand the physical, if not always the logical, space for freedom. But such a revisioning was always constrained and limited by the circumstances of bondage, the control of literacy, and the circulation of power. Verbal reconstructions of the slave personality and concomitant increase of freedom did occur, but only within the boundaries of an ideological consensus. The edges of this consensus were, to be sure, contested terrain, but they were not ultimately malleable to the utopian imaginings of the slaves, either as individuals or as a collective community. To work effectively at redescription meant for the slaves to employ the language of Christian religion, and to use tribal beliefs, Enlightenment notions of human rights, as well as the ideology of paternalism, to forge their own world.[39]

This brings up the second and final point: Rorty's quick dismissal of human rights when too closely connected to foundationalist notions of humanity, to some ahistorical notion of humanity. When William James employed an ideal of human rights—as in his denunciations of American imperialism's effects upon the rights of Filipinos—he protested within a historical tradition of universal rights, derived from the American and French revolutions, and natural rights theory. This tradition was viewed by James as having a reality constructed and made material by its survival within the context of historical development. The issue was not simply, as Rorty would have it, the dangers of an anchored historical truth claim, but rather the survival and pragmatic usefulness of thinking about humanity in terms of inalienable rights. In this sense, religion, in James's view, was pragmatically useful precisely because it helped the individual to engage energetically in real struggles. Likewise, one suspects, the tradition of human rights with all of its associations with transcendent truth claims, was embraced by James as not only a useful and real tradition, but also as a future hope that must be nourished and respected. The failure of human rights was blamed less on its presumed grounding within foundationalist ideas than in its failure to be realized by the struggles of humans, in the failure of individuals and institutions to honor its assumptions. For James, human rights talk must be honored for its survival value in Darwinian terms, and in the recognition that its universalist agenda ought to be made more inclusive and powerful.

Thus the conversation between Rorty and James, who share so much in terms of their philosophical language and assumptions, begins with James demanding that Rorty commit himself to the public sphere, to struggle against the real powers with the aid of traditions. The individual and the social, the private and public, in James's view are the arena for reconstruction. Linguistic revision, while certainly acceptable to James, must not be allowed to become, as it is for Rorty, something that exists without the constraints of historical, social, class, race, and gender limitations. Even if James did not discuss these constraints fully, he would not reject their defining power. Rorty would do well to pay more attention to them as the preconditions for the linguistic possibilities that he so powerfully celebrates.

In addition, James would chide Rorty for seeming to rest comfortably as a modern example of the philosopher cum-cultural-critic who is playing the waiting game of the scientist. Remember in James's "Will to Believe" how he bites with venom into the cold arteries of scientists such as Huxley and Tyndall who reason that in the face of insufficient evidence, the scientist must withhold judgment. In certain situations, nonmomentous options, James called them, this is quite reasonable. But when this scientific waiting game was applied to questions of morality, reform, or even belief, then the results of waiting for additional evidence translated into an unacceptable, if unacknowledged, choice not to act. Instead, James wanted the individual to passionately engage life, to choose an option rather than to rest satisfied with the exhaustion of previous solutions or the paucity of present prescriptions.

Rorty posits that one of the lessons he has learned from Orwell is that "we could no longer use our old political ideas, and that we now had none which were of use for steering events toward liberal goals" (175). James would tell Rorty to make choices in the public sphere and to approach them with passion— for James, philosophy must be "passionate vision." He would say to Rorty that it is "Better [to] risk loss of truth than chance of error" when confronted by issues that are largely based on faith and belief.[40]

But Rorty would also have some sage advice for James. For all the allure of James's discourse on heroism, and despite his oft-preached admonitions against the domination of the "other" and in favor of pluralism, Rorty would recognize that James's position can easily lead to a celebration of action where the domination of the strong over the weak individual becomes common. If Rorty understands that in the totalitarian state cruelty is an end in and of itself, he also comprehends how the emphasis on a vitalistic notion of life *in extremis* may allow such an ideal to predominate, to shut out opposing ideals. The chastened liberalism of Rorty might be a decent palliative to lessen the vitalistic tendencies in James, tendencies that allowed James to initially support the Spanish-

American War and to take pleasure in the atavistic realities of some entity that James confidently described as human nature.

Perhaps, in closing, the upshot of this conversation and compromise between James and Rorty would be an image of the public and private realms as indistinct, both in need of passionate attempts to rewrite their vocabularies and to right the specific wrongs that serve to support cruelty and injustice. The wariness, based on the "intransigent fact" of the "bad news" of the events of the last forty years, that Rorty brings to the possibility of transforming the public realm would be joined by James's sober reflections, based on his own bout with depression, on the difficulties of transforming the language of our selves.

"The Utopian dreams of social justice in which many contemporary socialists and anarchists indulge are," wrote James in *The Varieties of Religious Experience*, "in spite of their impracticality and non-adaptation to present environmental conditions, analogous to the saint's belief in an existent kingdom of heaven. They help to break the edge of the general reign of hardness, and are slow leavens of a better order."[41] Pragmatism, in either its Jamesian or Rortyean variants, must seek to "break the edge of the general reign of hardness" of conduct and possibility in the private and public realms. And this can only be safely accomplished by an at once sober and passionate engagement with the worlds of the private and public selves.

NOTES

1. Richard Rorty, "Two Cheers for the Cultural Left," *South Atlantic Quarterly* 89 (Winter 1990): 228.

2. See the critical readings by Ralph W. Sleeper, "Rorty's Pragmatism: Afloat in Neurath's Boat, But Why Adrift?" *Transactions of the Charles S. Peirce Society* 21 (Winter 1985): 12, and John J. Stuhr, "Dewey's Reconstruction of Metaphysics" *Transactions of the Charles S. Peirce Society* 28 (Spring 1992): 161–76.

3. Danny Postel, "Richard Rorty, a Post-Philosophical Politics: An Interview by Danny Postel," *Philosophy & Social Criticism* 15 (1989): 202.

4. To be sure, Rorty often points to James as a fellow-traveler in the quest for philosophy as edification. But he clearly does not place the burden of the created tradition of antiphilosophy in America upon James's shoulders so much as upon Dewey's.

5. Richard Rorty, *Contingency, Irony, and Solidarity* (Cambridge: Cambridge University Press, 1989), 94.

6. James to L. T. Hobhouse, August 12, 1904, in *The Letters of William James*, ed. Henry James, Jr. (Boston: Atlantic Monthly Press, 1920), vol. 2, 208–9.

7. The vocational dispute between James and his father is discussed in Howard M. Feinstein, *Becoming William James* (Ithaca, N.Y.: Cornell University Press, 1984). For a general analysis of the philosophical and cultural problems of the *tedium vitae*, see George Cotkin, *William James, Public Philosopher* (Baltimore, Md.: Johns Hopkins University Press, 1990).

8. In William James, *The Will to Believe* (Cambridge, Mass.: Harvard University Press, 1979), 39–40.

9. James to Tom Ward, March [?] 1869, *Letters of William James*, vol. 1, 152–53.

10. James employs Wright's idea in *Pragmatism* (Cambridge, Mass.: Harvard University Press, 1975), 54 and *The Will to Believe*, 49.

11. James, *Principles of Psychology* (Cambridge, Mass.: Harvard University Press, 1981), vol.

1, 126. It is important to note that Jamesian psychology, in contrast to Rorty's idea of the self, was quite clear in believing that there was such a thing as human nature, based on the development and hardening of instincts that had proven useful to the species in the struggle for existence. This recognition of the hard-core stuff of the individual, led James to be less than sanguine about the possibility of a transformation of the self in a more pacifistic direction.

12. Ibid., 126, 127, 130.

13. William James, "The Dilemma of Determinism," in *The Will to Believe*, 130.

14. James, *The Will to Believe*, 71, 130, 290.

15. George Cotkin, "William James and the 'Weightless' Nature of Modern Existence," *San Jose Studies* 12 (Spring 1986): 7–19.

16. William James, *The Varieties of Religious Experience* (Cambridge, Mass.: Harvard University Press, 1985), 291.

17. William James, "The Moral Equivalent of War," in James, *Essays in Religion and Morality* (Cambridge, Mass.: Harvard University Press, 1982), 163. None of this is to deny that James was a powerful, indeed heroic, opponent of imperialism. It is simply to suggest that James was absolutely fascinated by the heroism associated with war.

18. Bertrand Russell, "Pragmatism," *Edinburgh Review* 209 (1909): 363–68.

19. William James, "The Philippine Triangle" (1899), "The Philippines Again," (1899), and "President Roosevelt's Oration," (1899), all in William James, *Essays, Comments, and Reviews* (Cambridge, Mass.: Harvard University Press, 1987), 152, 161, 162–66.

20. William James, "On a Certain Blindness in Human Beings," in *Talks to Teachers on Psychology* (Cambridge, Mass.: Harvard University Press, 1983), esp. 133–34. Rorty is aware of this narrative and uses it for similar purposes in *Contingency, Irony, and Solidarity*, 38.

21. Rorty, *Contingency, Irony, and Solidarity*. Subsequent references to this text will appear in parentheses in the text.

22. Rorty's emphasis on traditions, local and compelling, has a strong affinity to James's move in *Pragmatism* to present truth as a process while also announcing that truths are built on previous truths that are part of our traditional inheritance. For more on this, see Cotkin, *William James*, 164–69 and Hilary Putnam and Ruth Anna Putnam, "William James's Ideas," *Raritan* 8 (Winter 1989): 27–44.

23. Charles B. Guignon and David R. Hiley, "Biting the Bullet: Rorty on Private and Public Morality," in *Reading Rorty*, ed. Alan Malachowski (Cambridge, Mass.: Basil Blackwell, 1990), 343.

24. Quoted in Carlin Romano, "Naughty, Naughty: Richard Rorty Makes Philosophers Squirm," *Village Voice Literary Supplement*, June 1987, 15.

25. See Richard Rorty, "Postmodernist Bourgeois Liberalism," *Journal of Philosophy* 80 (October 1983): 583–89 and "The Priority of Democracy to Philosophy," in Malachowski, ed., *Reading Rorty*, 279–302.

26. Biographical information on James Rorty is in Alan Wald, *The New York Intellectuals: The Rise and Decline of the Anti-Stalinist Left from the 1930s to the 1980s* (Chapel Hill: University of North Carolina Press, 1987), 54–55. Biographical data on Rorty's crisis is from L. S. Klepp, "Every Man a Philosopher-King," *New York Times Magazine*, December 2, 1990, 117–18. Also see, most recently, Rorty's revealing explanation for his own public/private perceptions "Trotsky and the Wild Orchids," in *Wild Orchids and Trotsky*, ed. Mark Edmundson (New York: Penguin Books, 1993), 29–50.

27. Klepp, "Every Man," 118.

28. Ibid.

29. Wald, *Intellectuals*, 272.

30. Richard Rorty, "Foucault/Dewey/Nietzsche," *Raritan* 9 (Spring 1990): 2.

31. Richard Rorty, "Pragmatism Without Method," in *Sidney Hook: Philosopher of Democracy and Humanism*, ed. Paul Kurtz (Buffalo, N.Y.: Prometheus Books, 1983), 259–74.

32. See the suggestive comments on the connection with New York intellectuals in Christopher

Norris, "Philosophy as a Kind of Narrative: Rorty on Postmodern Liberal Culture," *Enclitic* 7 (Fall 1983): 157.

33. Howard Brick, *Daniel Bell and the Decline of Intellectual Radicalism: Social Theory and Political Reconciliation in the 1940s* (Madison: University of Wisconsin Press, 1986), 6.

34. On American intellectuals and the tragic sense of life, see Richard Wightman Fox, "Tragedy, Responsibility, and the American Intellectual, 1925–1950," in *Lewis Mumford: Public Intellectual*, ed. Thomas P. Hughes and Agatha C. Hughes (New York: Oxford University Press, 1990), 323–37. On Sidney Hook's view of the tragic dimensions of pragmatism, see his "Pragmatism and the Tragic Sense of Life," in *Contemporary American Philosophy: Second Series*, ed. J. E. Smith (London: George Allen and Unwin, 1970), 170–93. Rorty's discussion of Hook and the possibilities of philosophy as cultural criticism is in his "Professionalized Philosophy and Transcendentalist Culture," in Rorty, *Consequences of Pragmatism* (Minneapolis: University of Minnesota Press, 1982), esp. 68–70. Also see George Cotkin, "Middle-Ground Pragmatists: The Popularization of Philosophy in American Culture," *Journal of the History of Ideas*, forthcoming.

35. Rorty, "Foucault/Dewey/Nietzsche," 5–7. Rorty joins with Lyotard in opposition to meta-narratives while holding to a form of "cosmopolitanism" that favors, without foundations, persuasion over force. See Richard Rorty, "Cosmopolitanism Without Emancipation: A Response to Jean-Francois Lyotard," in Rorty, *Objectivity, Relativism, and Truth* (Cambridge: Cambridge University Press, 1991), 211–22.

36. Critiques of Rorty's public and private split, and of his cultural politics are: Nancy Fraser, "Solidarity or Singularity?: Richard Rorty Between Romanticism and Technocracy," in Malachowski, ed., *Reading Rorty*, 303–21; Dorothy Leland, "Rorty on the Moral Concern of Philosophy: A Critique From a Feminist Point of View," *Praxis International* 8 (October 1988): 273–83; Jonathan Ree, "Timely Meditations," *Radical Philosophy* 55 (Summer 1990): 31–39; Cornel West, *The American Evasion of Philosophy: A Genealogy of Pragmatism* (Madison: University of Wisconsin Press, 1989), 209–10. For Rorty's strongest division of the public and private realms in terms of leaving the problems of the public realm (such as world hunger) to the work of technological innovation rather than imagination, see his "Love and Money," *Common Knowledge* 1 (Spring 1991): 12–16.

37. Rorty, "Feminism and Pragmatism," *Michigan Quarterly Review* 30 (Spring 1991): 231–58. Hereafter, references to this work will be cited in the text.

38. For Foucault's emphasis, see "The Subject and Power," the Afterword to Hubert L. Dreyfus and Paul Rabinow, *Michel Foucault: Beyond the Structuralism and Hermeneutics* (Chicago: University of Chicago Press, 1983), esp. 220–21.

39. Eugene Genovese, *Roll, Jordan, Roll: The World the Slaves Made* (New York: Pantheon, 1974).

40. William James, "Will to Believe" in James, *The Will to Believe*, 30.

41. James, *Varieties*, 287.

3

Community Without Fusion:
Dewey, Mead, Tufts

James Campbell

My intention in this chapter is to examine one aspect of community that is of particular importance to us at the present time from the point of view of Social Pragmatism; my hope is that this chapter will contribute a bit to our attempts to understand and foster fulfilling community. The aspect of community that I will be considering is social fusion, the ability of the group to "swallow up" individuals and make them virtual automata in the collective actions of the group. As human experience continues to prove, religious, racial, political, and other groups are able to draw from their members such singleness of devotion that they willingly sacrifice and, on occasion, die for what they take to be the good of the group. While this kind of self-sacrifice may seem noble, and on occasion even heroic, my suspicion is that most of the time it is better understood as the result of a more-or-less blind loyalty to some skewed presentation of the common good. That living a life of such loyalty is emotionally fulfilling I will not dispute; that it demonstrates in addition any necessary connection to what is socially beneficial, I doubt.

I am using the work of the Social Pragmatists—such thinkers as John Dewey, George Herbert Mead, and James Hayden Tufts[1]—because they manifested in their life and work the dual emphases of community and individuality. On the one hand, they demonstrated an interest in the fostering of community as a key element in human well-being. For them, human fulfillment is made possible by, and takes place only within, vibrant and enduring community situations. On the other hand, they also demonstrated a clear recognition of the need to maintain some "distance" between the individual and the community itself. To be a moral agent, they emphasized, a person must be more than simply the agent of the group. Individuals must be both rooted in their group and capable of some critical evaluation of it for there to be satisfactory communal life.

If we consider various aspects of our long history as a human race, recognizing the importance of community is unavoidable. Humans are social creatures who both need and enjoy the companionship of their fellows, and who gather in groups in hopes of living well. Within this human trait, the question of group self-identity—the question of "who we are" as a group—looms large. Every grouping, from the smallest transient club or society to the United Nations or the various "universal" churches, has to define itself in ways that make clear to members and nonmembers alike who is, and who is not, properly a member. Included in any self-definition are answers to such problems as how the members are to conduct themselves with regard to the projects of the institution and in relation to one another, and how the members of the group are to conduct themselves with regard to the projects of other institutions and in relation to outsiders. For long-lived groups, this sense of "who we are" as a group usually contains within it an imaginatively embroidered sense of our past: where we came from, how we have met the challenges of former times, and so on. This sense of "who we are" also offers us some direction for the future: how people like us should act, where we should be headed, how we will overcome the problems that we encounter along the way. This sense of past and future further helps us to forge our group-identity at present and to act as "people like us" should act.

These abstract musings on the nature of community sketch out one of the key aspects of our social lives, one part of the complex web of human existence: we live in groups that help make us what we are. These relationships take on a special importance in times of crisis, especially in times of increased intercommunal tension of the sort that can lead on the political level to warfare. In these instances, the crisis results in a sharp separation between those who are part of our group—"us"—and those who are not—"them." In these cases, the phrase "external foe" becomes redundant. These cases also lead to an increased sense of unification with our fellows, a state of connectedness in which the key similarity of membership in the group can overpower any other consideration.

This powerful sense of oneness with our fellows in times of tension, still more powerful in times of hostilities, is an experience that is immensely pleasurable to individuals like us, individuals whose lives are normally segmented by the many problems of living. In this unification, we find a release from the everyday pressures of individual living and we can slide into the comfortable bliss of a homogenizing group life. Complex moral questions are simplified into matters of conformity; complicated orderings of priorities fall "naturally" into place; painful separations from others within the group are bridged. There is also the pleasure and excitement that arises from the anticipation of having our traditions and values proven to be better than those of the outside antagonist (also redundant).

There is, as we all know, great danger here. The complex questions that are simplified, the complicated systems of priorities that are ordered, and the formerly necessary separations that are bridged were originally recognized to be complex and complicated and necessary for reasons that should not be forgotten. But we accept, and even enjoy, the new situation. Tufts writes of the wartime power of the nation-state to order the lives of its citizens: "On the one hand no institution has commanded nobler devotion or inspired loftier art; on the other, none has lent itself so ruthlessly to the destruction of every human interest and value, or has practiced so consistently what in common life we call crime."[2] The widespread power of many other groupings to provide this feeling of oneness demonstrates that more than nation-states are able to extract this sort of heedlessness from us; but, as Tufts notes, states are without peer in doing so. Faced in such situations with a foreign enemy (also redundant), members of many groupings can overlook necessary moral distinctions, forget fundamental priorities, and join forces with admittedly unsavory characters who, whatever their faults, are at least "on our side." In the face of the emotional power of this social fusion, we can set aside the problems of the everyday life of society—the now seemingly petty domestic matters like job security and procedural justice—and concentrate on how to defend ourselves and our fellows from the sinister machinations of the alien devils (also redundant). Moreover, too often in the interest of furthering the social efficiency felt necessary for security, we abandon factors in our social life that have actually made us more efficient and secure. We are in particular willing to narrow our intellectual inquiries and accept limitations on public information. Included among these limitations must be even propagandizing by official governmental agencies and by unofficial agencies like the mass media who are fearful of appearing unpatriotic in perilous times. Such narrowing and limitations, further, make it more likely that our fusion will continue into the future.

These manifestations of social fusion arise in critical situations, yet they are related to more general aspects of human grouping. The way people can fuse with community in times of warfare is connected with the way they can unite behind a local sports team facing a deciding game or a beleaguered politician under pressure from "outsiders." The relationship between these critical situations and the more general ones opens up fundamental questions about the nature of the self and the community. From the individual point of view, an important issue to consider is the connection between our sense of self and our need for a group identity. From the social point of view, an important issue to consider is the possibility for a society to balance itself between a centrifugal collapse into isolating individualism and a fusion that absorbs individuals without remainder into the group's actions. I will consider first the general analysis of individuality and community found in the work of the Social Pragmatists, and then the application of their analysis to this situation of social fusion. The final section will introduce some additional themes that merit future consideration.

INDIVIDUALITY AND COMMUNITY

If we turn to the examination of the nature of human individuality and community found in Social Pragmatism, we see immediately its power to engage the problem that we have been examining. The core of the explanation of social fusion found there is its understanding of the nature of the self. Rather than seeing the self in terms of either separateness or permanence, the Social Pragmatist analysis emphasizes emergence within the social context. The self cannot be simply understood as having a pre-set trajectory which it should follow or from which it will go astray. Nor can the self be simply understood on some seed or plant analogy according to which it is to "blossom" in its predetermined way by making only incidental use of the resources present in society for nourishment—that is, without being essentially modified by its growing conditions. Nor can the self be simply understood as an individual who must resist the interference of others if his or her life-plan is not to be diverted from its presumed proper path. Rather, the emergent self is social through and through, growing within and because of communal life. The reason the problem of fusion is such an important problem for us is that we have a self that is truly social: developing in a situation of shared living.

Without denying the reality of inherent physical limitations on the developing social self, the Social Pragmatists concentrate on the socially grounded process and its possibilities. In particular, they discuss the origin of the self as something not present at the birth of the individual but developing—emerging—over the course of living communally with other individuals. Individuals grow to a sense of self-consciousness *through* the communities in which they live, not simply *in* them. We adopt the values of our group and area—be it in Ohio or in Tyrol— and we evaluate ourselves, initially at least, by whether and how we measure up to the group's general ideal of a good person. As Mead put it: "He becomes a self in so far as he can take the attitude of another and act toward himself as others act."[3] Dewey's formulation is similar: "An assembly is formed within our breast which discusses and appraises proposed and performed acts. The community without becomes a forum and tribunal within."[4] As growing, semi-developed selves we have enemies and friends, worthy goals and taboos, presented to us by our group. The way our group does things, Dewey continues, becomes the proper way: "What is strange or foreign . . . tends to be morally forbidden and intellectually suspect."[5] We thus all too often find our moral, political, and aesthetic values as easily—and with as little actual thinking—as we find our idioms of speech and familiar telephone numbers. This is because these socially derived values are not the restraints upon us that the individualistic analysis would suggest as much as they are reinforcers within our selves. These socially dervied values are, for good or ill, part of what we are.

This pragmatic understanding of the social nature of the self also makes an examination of the role of custom important. Part of the power of custom results from the importance of institutions to the successful life of the community. Given the virtually infinite number of possibilities for ordering the necessary ongoing activities of the group—for controlling sexual activity and systematizing the raising of children, for distributing work and disposing of the economic output of the group, and so on—the institutional system employed must be, and must be felt to be, powerful. Institutions order our shared lives. Should we like to pretend that such "anthropological" themes are irrelevant to our "modern" society, a simple glance at some of our various customs proves the contrary to be true. For example, we need only compare the very different procedures by which two different contemporary political entities control automobiles. In each instance, the governmental entities act very differently to inspect, license, tax, and insure automobiles in order to bring the necessary regularity to the realm of automobility in their society. Yet in each instance, these largely arbitrary procedures—at least this is how they are seen by outsiders—are seen to be natural and proper, and superior to the confusing and chaotic procedures in effect elsewhere.

If we take another example and consider this theme of the importance of custom from the point of view of the potential forms of diet that could be adopted by a society, two clearly distinguishable questions appear. One is the question of the historical accuracy or authenticity of the particular diet of the group. This question, however difficult it may actually be to answer in any particular case, is in theory simply a matter of consistency with the group's traditions. A second question is the nutritional adequacy of the diet in question: that is, we can wonder to what extent the historically authentic form of diet for a certain group is sufficient for a healthy life. We can question, for example, the nutritional adequacy of the traditional diet of the Syrian farmer or the New England fisherman. We can further consider the relationship between such traditional practices and contemporary realities: is the traditional diet, however adequate once, now adequate? In a similar fashion, we can surely wonder whether a particular set of controls that functioned more-or-less reasonably well as a system of automobile management at an earlier time remains adequate with regard to our contemporary ecologically based difficulties. (Following along this line of thought, it would also seem reasonable to contend that a system of constitutional guarantees found to be adequate at some past point might now—because of what it protects and fails to protect—be inadequate and in need of revision.)

This question of continued adequacy suggests the ongoing need to reconstruct our customary values, traditions, and institutions—to adapt them to changes in our social life. Unfortunately, many of our customs—especially those that are felt to be closest to our social "core," like sexual values and religious and political symbols—are not the sorts of topics that we are likely to think critically about. We have felt the need to "sacralize" them, perhaps as a means of quieting our own doubts about their validity, perhaps as a tool in shaping our children's behavior, perhaps as a justification for punishing those who fail to conform. In any case, we now find ourselves in the position of being unable to change our customs without abandoning part of what we believe we as a group are. We are a people, for example, who champion heterosexual monogamy as the proper form of coupling, oblivious to the contemporary realities on both counts; we are a people who find it necessary to defend the literal interpretation of religious texts and the idolization of political objects, even though both are more properly seen as symbolic.

Sacralization, in these and other cases, limits evaluation. Our normal stance, it seems, is to assume too quickly the concurrence of our customary practices and proper conduct. For Mead, custom too often becomes morality: "As a rule we assume that this general voice of the community is identical with the larger community of the past and the future; we assume that an organized custom represents what we call morality."[6] Operating under limitations like these, we can find ourselves blind to problems of significant import. A society seems to be able to understand situations as problematic only as they appear inappropriate according to its own customs. For example, for reasons having to do with the individualistic tenor of our inherited social self, we in America find ourselves blind to the problems of the poor and the sick, or at least unable to organize any adequate level of social action to deal with poverty and illness. In countries whose customs are more oriented toward socialism, poverty and illness are problems to be addressed socially, because they challenge values present in their image of an adequate society. At the same time, problems that we in America would find patent—for example, governmental involvement in what we see as matters of private business or family life—often go unrecognized and unaddressed in these lands. In each case, the members of the society in question cannot see what the members of the other see.

With this consideration of the role of society and custom in the shaping of the self, the pragmatic discussion of the social self is, however, only half-finished. Human individuals are not just members of groups. We are equally importantly able to transcend the group. In addition to the conventional and habitual aspect of the self that Mead calls the "me," he also discusses the "I": "The 'I' is the response of the individual to the attitude of the community as this appears in his own experience."[7] Each of us develops, at the time that he or she becomes a self with a conscious recognition of what it is to be a good person according to our group's ideal, the ability to distance ourselves from this ideal. This "I" is the reactive part of the self, the source of distancing or separation from the collective flow of the group. We need to recognize, of course, that this aspect of the self grows slowly, by means of the gradual realization of the degree to which our actions are ordered for us by society's customs, a realization that takes place largely through encounters with other possible modes of living. And we need to recognize as well the individual difficulty of balancing this knowledge of other modes of living against our own frequent sacralizations without succumbing to some form of crippling relativism.

For pragmatic social thought, evaluation of plans and goals is an ongoing necessity. This criticism of society, if it is to be effective, embodies both the

"I" and the "me." Effective social critics, in other words, are individuals firmly rooted in the life of their community who see there problems and possibilities of resolution and who try to bring this perspective before the public. In doing so, Mead notes, the critic does not simply attack his or her society. Rather, "the individual appeals, so to speak, from a narrow and restricted community to a larger one."[8] He means "larger" here in a moral sense: the actual group has by choice or accident adopted customary ways of acting that overlook important values, often values that it itself upholds in some weakened or distorted form, and the individual with a grasp of broader experience can recognize and point this out. As an example here we might consider the relationship between a social critic and a society like our own that has long tolerated serious restrictions on democracy while at the same time championing democracy as the only fit form of human association. If successful, the critic makes the community a different and enriched one by causing it to confront and overcome the contradictions between its values and its practices. An essential point in all of this social reconstruction is the process of discussion that makes the social growth happen. The effective social critic thus discusses and attempts to justify proferred courses of action through interaction with others and through this process of cooperative inquiry we discover the common good.

This role of social critic is, of course, played by all of us at one time or another. We are all able to "step back" and evaluate our social situation because we are all familiar with more than one. All of us have experienced the way in which even young children can criticize the decisions of their parents in the light of what they consider to be the more enlightened policies that operate in their friends' families. The complex "me" that should be present in anyone who lives in our multicultural world is a storehouse of historical and contemporary facts and relationships of importance to social evaulation. We can always learn more, of course, to enable us to better perform this task of social evaluation, and real education to enable us to understand and learn from others will have to be part of any educational program that proposes to follow the ideas of Social Pragmatism. We can thus take as one of the main goals of our organized educational institutions the attempts to strengthen our children's ability to understand themselves as both socially rooted and as more broadly ascendant, to make them increasingly cognizant of the need for reference groups against which to evaluate their lives and increasingly able to choose what reference groups they will use to do this. In this way we hope they will realize the difference between a choice between tradition and novelty on the one hand, and what is morally justifiable and what is not on the other. Certainly, I do not mean to suggest that this will be a simple process, but we need to foster a conscious awareness both of the power of custom in our social lives and of our need to demand more than consistency with our past ways of acting.

Seeing the individual self as being capable of social criticism, and recognizing our central role as critics, make the process of evaluation and enactment of primary importance. The attempt to construct a better world is the attempt to bring into reality social goods through the process of cooperative inquiry. In this process, the members of the group attempt to recognize and address the problems of society in ways that advance the common good. We need to listen to the other members of the group to get a sense of the traditional evaluations that have been felt to be compelling. We need also to listen to the various social critics who challenge aspects of our customary lives by attempting to prove that they are outdated. At the same time, this construction of a better world incorporates the growth of the individuals who live there. For the social self, however, this growth means not disengagement but greater involvement, not independence but responsibility. The ideal is to develop as a contributor to the efforts of the community to address the problems of social life. In Mead's formulation, "the attainment of that functional differentiation and social participation in the full degree is a sort of ideal which lies before the human community."[9]

In their own lives and work, the Social Pragmatists attempted to play this role of rooted social critics, advocating the advancement of the common good and the growth of individuals. Their roots came from their sense of the American past; their criticisms, from their sense of the failures of American life to make use of the possibilities contained in cooperative inquiry. Their essential faith was that these failings could be overcome. We could build communities that are both enduring and supportive of individuals; we could foster individual lives that are both rooted and growing.

SOCIAL FUSION

We can return from this Social Pragmatist analysis of the human situation to the problems that were laid out in the beginning of this chapter. We find ourselves, because of aspects of the social nature of the self, prone to be drawn into fusion with the group in which our hatred for outsiders makes us behave in ways that fall short of the requirements of moral agents. We expand our sense of "us" and lower the critical stance with which we regard our collective actions; we isolate and imprison and kill "them." The themes that we have considered indicate that we cannot expect a simple solution to problems as serious as these. Nor can we expect a permanent solution. In fact, it is necessary to recognize that the analysis of Social Pragmatism does not offer a direct solution to these problems at all. What it offers, however, is a wedge for understanding them, and thus suggestions for trying to bring about change toward the possibility of community without fusion.

This wedge consists in the analysis of the social self that we have considered. Human individuals live in part within the group and in part beyond it. Part of their self-identity is the group-identity within them. The "me" aspect of the self is that aspect that roots and connects the individuals as members of society who care about its furtherance; and, if the "me" is only thinly provided with a perspective on the outside, it cannot connect their self-identity with anything but their chance group. Especially in times of crisis, the "me" presents them with the importance of concern for the group in a heightened fashion, as well as with suggestions for the correct actions to advance its welfare. The part of the self-identity that is beyond this group, the "I" aspect of the self, is that aspect that enables the individual to step outside of this communal flow and evaluate and challenge the society's assumptions and plans. Although harder to maintain in times of crisis, the "I"—especially if it can draw upon the fuller "me" that results from participation in multiple groups—enables the selves to challenge facile and parochial assumptions and decisions. In this way, the Social Pragmatists' position offers us a way of understanding social fusion of the sort we find in crises as a potential element in any community organization. At the same time, the Social Pragmatists' position also enables us to see that such fusion need never be accepted as an unopposable element in our communal lives.

Let us first consider under this Pragmatic analysis an easy case, an instance where social fusion is possible but where the import of the situation is relatively modest. We can, for example, understand quite clearly the tension that is present in the lives of children who are members of some sports team when they are forced to decide between increasing their chances of victory by operating (slightly) outside of the rules—say by using an over-age player—or maintaining a commitment to something higher than just winning. While the collective pressure on the team might be toward victory at all costs, each child recognizes more-or-less clearly that a victory in sports is of value only within some regulating context and that a victory attained by cheating is tainted. The ease of their concluding that seeking victory in defiance of the rules would be wrong results in large measure from the unimportance of the community to the self. It is "just a team" or "just a game"; the situation, in this case at least, can be resolved quite quickly in favor of fair play. We realize, of course, that in any particular instance, the situation could still involve painful choices for the children involved and that, although it should be easier for the parents than for the children to accept an honest defeat, this might not happen either. And we can especially realize the problem of the isolated child or parent who rises in the face of a generally accepted willingness to circumvent the rules and says that "all is not right."

If we turn, however, to the really tough issues, to the fusion possible in the face of an external foe, the situation becomes much more complicated. For example, when the community is gripped by the reality of an impending external confrontation, or actually engaged in hostilities, the level of social fusion is far higher than in the prior case. War, Mead writes, can make "the good of the community the supreme good of the individual."[10] In such a case, for individuals who are skeptical about the merits of the belligerent policies of the community to declare that "all is not right" is personally risky. Similarly, suggestions that would otherwise be rationally entertained with regard to some situation in which we are not deeply engaged—for example, policy recommendations in the face of the ongoing collapse of what was Yugoslavia—are now greeted as deadly challenges to the survival of the group. When we are standing face-to-face with threatening foreigners (also redundant), we do not want to hear that our community might have chosen a less militant path of action, or that negotiations have not yet proven futile, or that an alternative analysis of the situation paints the actions of both sides in various shades of gray. We often accuse these critics at least of harming "the war effort" and endangering those who are (about to be) engaged in combat; we often suspect them of actual deliberate subversion or treason. Once we are fused together to fight, the raspy voice of such individuals is just one more problem standing in the way of victory.

My interest in these generalizations, of course, is in the social impact of the fusion brought about by these crusades against the outsiders, not in any moral evaluation of the individual crusades. Some such endeavors seem to be justifiable even if most of them are not. But my point is that they all—the justifiable and the unjustifiable— *feel* equally good to those who can fuse with the group in this crusade against the perceived evil. (This experienced thrill of unification, of course, is felt equally powerfully by those on the opposing side who have fused themselves together to resist what they take to be our foul designs.) There is, Mead maintains, "a peculiar sense of exaltation" when the "I" and the "me" can "fuse," and Dewey writes of the power of the feeling of "a mystical sense of fusion" that can arise from a "a sense of union with others."[11] There is the sense of doing important things, the sense of urgency that enables us to join ranks in spite of the petty problems of the everyday and to the exclusion of merely domestic concerns: "in the common attack upon the common enemy," Mead writes, "the individual differences are obliterated." Oftentimes, the level of fusion between the "I" and the "me," between the self and the whole group, is so complete that, as he continues, "One loses himself in the whole group in some sense, and may attain the attitude in which he undergoes suffering and death for the common cause."[12] In these cases, when group success in the crusade becomes more important to an individual than continued personal existence, social fusion is complete.

These theoretical considerations suggest some practical applications. Without attempting to minimize the fundamental difficulties with attempts to address this problem, it is possible to suggest that instances of social fusion are not insurmountable. The keys to our attempts to overcome fusion are two. The first is to recognize that at present all violence against the alien foe (also redundant) must be presented as defensive in nature, as having been forced upon us by their outrages. For example, the nation-state now realizes, Tufts writes, that "It must make its wars appear wars of self-defense."[13] The sad chronicle of the intervening years shows, of course, that they have managed to do this quite successfully. In the three-quarters of a century since he wrote, there has been no shortage of state, or other such, hostilities, and the present international situation should not incline us toward blind optimism for the future. Still, Tufts's point is an important one.

If hostilities will receive the popular support of a group only insofar as they are perceived as being required for self-defense against a foreign aggressor (also redundant), then the wedge provided us by Social Pragmatist thought might be inserted here. If it ever becomes truly clear to us that we can fight the others only when fused together by their crimes, and to them that they can fight us only when fused together by ours, the skepticism of the members of both groups about these presumed crimes will grow. By means of the careful cultivation of an enriched "me" among the members of the society, and by means of the widespread distribution of accurate information, the ability of governmental leaders to convert inherited situations into bleeding injustices and the ambiguous activities of other groups into unequivocal provocations will be weakened. Even recognizing the broad meaning that "self-defense" is capable of achieving, and the difficulties involved in really learning to understand members of other groups, and the repeated failures of the mass media to seek out and distribute accurate information, this suggestion that we bristle every time we see the word "defense" or any of its many synonyms is not vacuous. It is simply very hard to put into action in our world, where so much of our common life is based on emotion.

The second key in our attempts to overcome fusion is to recognize the degree to which it results from the emotions. We *feel* ourselves different from the others; more importantly, we *feel* ourselves superior to them. They think and act in ways that are different from—and thus not as good as—ours. There is also an intellectual element to fusion: we search for a rationalization for our hostile response in terms of their past deeds, present preparations, or future intentions, a rationalization that is usually not hard to construct in our scarred and suspicious world. But primarily social fusion is a matter of emotions—what Mead calls the "fears and hatreds and cupidities and individual greeds and jealousies"[14]—that are utilized to fuse society into a group willing to fight. Even when we move to the more respectable end of the emotional spectrum, we find that patriotism is still an emotion, however rationally justifiable in terms of the objective state and situation it may on occasion be.

Mead is very clear on the potential for a resolution. What we need to do, he writes, is "to reach a sense of being a nation by means of rational self-consciousness." The term that he uses here is "international-mindedness,"[15] and he means for both parts to be taken seriously. "International" refers to an expansion of our sense of self beyond membership in the nation-state; "mind-edness," to an emphasis on the mental origins of this new self-image. In this way, we should try to expand our "me" by various educational means beyond our chance rootings in space and time to include an appreciation for the customs and values of others. Also included is the deliberate attempt on the part of citizens in the various nation-states to reorient themselves with their minds and with science toward serious contemporary social problems—of which there is surely no shortage—to supplant the traditionally important points of contention. Environmental pollution, AIDS, and overpopulation can certainly be recognized to be problems at least as severe as our inherited border disputes and religious controversies, and their prolongation and broadening will continue to harm the common interest. Moreover, cooperative efforts to address these contemporary social problems will help us to begin to dissolve the inherited ones by demonstrating that the members of these other groups are not as foreign as we previously thought, and are just as interested as we are in solving these problems. As Mead writes, "The measure of civilization is found in the intelligence and will of the community in making these common interests the means and the reason for converting diversities into social organization."[16]

International-mindedness would thus involve us in attempts to create a new sense of the common good—one that is truly common, not one predicated upon enhancing goods for "us" without benefits for, or even at the cost of, "them." Should pollution or AIDS or overpopulation be eased, all would surely benefit. It should be possible in this way to begin to transcend our traditional conflicts in an intellectual fashion and to recognize our real common enemies, and to build a broader community of those who see themselves as endangered. The very diversity of this new rational community when contrasted with the traditional group would guarantee a broader selection of possible responses, and discussion should help to make the actual choices better. International-mindedness would actually be better for treating real problems.

The intellectual recognition of this new class of common enemies, even if no longer easily personifiable as an external foe, should still allow for some level of emotional engagement. It will admittedly not yield the intense pleasure found in social fusion, but the pain and suffering that these common enemies cause are just as acute and long-lasting as the pain and suffering we attributed to any external foe, and our efforts to oppose them are even more clearly self-defensive. Moreover, even if the potential victims who are to be saved are not members of what was originally "our" group, the relief we feel at their deliverance should come to be experienced as just as real. Benefits to those with whom we are learning to cooperate in the search for the common good can be learned to be benefits to us.

How successful we might be developing international-mindedness we do not yet know. We have not yet tested what Tufts calls our ability "to discover and point out how far intelligent methods of cooperation may supersede conflict as an international process."[17] We are without any real experience; we are just starting out. Europe, our key testing ground at present for the creation of international-mindedness, is the scene of new and wondrous possibilities that are trying to grow out of the ashes of centuries of nationalistic hatred and conquest. Elsewhere in the world, especially where conflicting sides feel able to fortify their hostile claims with theological corroboration, the potentials are currently more limited. Here at home, we find our efforts to turn to the new problems of ecology and human well-being hampered by inherited internal discords as severe as any found in the international sphere and by an appallingly weak sense of the world beyond our borders that could appear as a source of examples of diversity and multiculturalism. But, if we attempt to use the wedge provided by the social sense of the self that we have considered, and concentrate on developing a realistic sense of defense of the group through international-mindedness, community without fusion will become less of a dream.

CONCLUSION: SOME REMAINING QUESTIONS

In this chapter I have attempted to explore, through a development of themes found in the works of the Social Pragmatists, one aspect of the topic of community: the extent to which a group is able to fuse its members into social automata. My aim has been to try to understand the origin of this problem and to uncover how it might be addressed. I believe that there is a fundamental soundness to the approach of the Social Pragmatists, and that the wedge provided by their social understanding of the self is a crucial one that merits further development in our attempts to understand and improve community. At the same time, I realize full well the sketchiness of my efforts here, the crudeness of distinctions that need to be made with the greatest of precision, the meagerness of elaborations that need to be developed in the greatest of detail. I recognize as well that several issues central to the topic of community without fusion have not been addressed at all. In the space that follows, I would just like to mention a few of these considerations.

The first of these considerations is the question of the possible legitimacy of social fusion justified by the hostile actions of outsiders, a question that I have repeatedly sidestepped in the above analysis. Is it not necessary to recognize and take into account that sometimes the hostile outsider (also redundant) really is hostile, and that sometimes measures that are presented as self-defense really are self-defense, and that sometimes an action of presumed heroic self-sacrifice for the common good really is heroic? In such cases, it would seem that the members of an endangered group are justified in efforts to secure the group's future well-being, efforts that from some points of view might include tolerating or fostering what I have been negatively describing as social fusion.

My response would be to agree that such efforts might sometimes be justified, although my emphasis in this response would be on the *sometimes*. My reticence here is grounded in the complexity of the process of justification itself, a topic I save for another time, and in the same psychological reality that grounded my avoidance of the question of justification throughout my analysis. I am referring here to the fact that, because cases of fusion all *feel* equally good to those who are caught up in them, those who are fused seldom move beyond the feeling of intense pleasure and devotion to attempt any careful analysis of the justifiability of their cause. Moreover, should those who are fused be challenged to analyze their situation, they tend to be terrible judges of it, frequently more concerned with eliminating the challengers than with justifying their own actions. Consequently, I believe that it is a mistake to attempt to evaluate particular instances of fusion to decide on their justification, especially since this evaluating would have to be carried out under the pressure of the fusion-generating situation itself. It seems to me that it is far better to attempt to avoid fusion entirely. If we could develop the more rational approach of international-mindedness and prevent the slip into social fusion, those cases in which our defensive self-sacrifice in the face of a certifiable enemy were justifiable would be recognized with our brains, not with what Mead calls "our diaphragms and the visceral responses."[18] It would be somewhat more difficult, no doubt, to organize an effective defense under these restrictions on fusion; when necessary, however, it could be done.

A second consideration that has not been directly examined above is the nature of the common good. The efforts suggested by the Social Pragmatists to address our common problems all assume the ability to advance a common good that has remained below the level of recognition. I have suggested above that, at least in the cases of environmental pollution, AIDS, and overpopulation, we have clear instances of common problems whose easing would advance the common good. Moving beyond such obvious global examples, however, to more particular problems will be difficult. This is a result of the fact that, as we begin to move away from problems that endanger all groups, we will have to consider differences among groups. Moreover, even if we concentrate just on the global problems, we recognize that we need to pay special attention to differences in the distribution of costs and benefits in our attempts to address these problems. For example, efforts to advance the common good by slowing population growth will of necessity place more burdens on the members of some groups than on others and assist the members of some groups to a greater extent than they will others. No problem short of total human extermination, and no good short of a presumed universal salvation, would allow for complete distributive equality.

The repetition of such phrases as "the problem" and "the common good" should always remind us that, as C. Wright Mills writes, *we* is "the most tricky word in the vocabulary of politics." Particularly when our focus is on the collective welfare of the community, we tend to slide over important distinctions and fail to recognize potential conflicts. "What is a 'problem' to one 'group' is not at all problematic to another," Mills continues; "it may well be a satisfactory 'solution'."[19] It is thus necessary for all who emphasize community to emphasize as well the need to foster a critical distance from it. As important as it is for the social critic to point to specific problems and to offer potential solutions, it is equally important that the critic ever remind us of the potential distinction between *what we see as a problem* and *what is a problem*. To maintain that there is such a distinction, and ultimately a common good, and to maintain that this common good is to be attained through cooperative inquiry, is not to move too far toward an understanding of the complex topic of the common good. Far more needs to be done.[20]

A third consideration that has not appeared above is some examination of the very broad topic of the nature of community. In particular, I have not considered whether without fusion we would still have a community. My answer, as my title suggests, is affirmative—although admittedly it would not be exactly the same kind of community as before. A community of the sort that the Social Pragmatists discussed, a community that attempted to keep the "I" and the "me" in balance while being less emotional in its procedures, would not have to be the cold and scientistic group that it might be expected to be. It would, however, need to strive to be more rational, more respectful of the possible contributions of the cooperative activities of mind and science, than communities with which we are familiar. It would also have to be a community that emphasized education as a means of awakening and keeping awake the spirit of critical citizenship among the members of the populace.

These and other properties of a fulfilling community life still need to be explored; but let me close with a reconsideration of the duality theme discussed above. Community requires a sense of self-identity that offers a past and a future, a sense of "us" and "them," of constitutive choices and collective debt; but, equally importantly, a community needs an inquiring and challenging spirit that attempts to preclude individual absorption into the group. Up to the present, we have lived with little deliberate concern for this balance, often losing it to social fusion in times of crisis. Now we will need to be more concerned. In the pluralistic world of the future—should we manage to achieve this world—the new communities will not be ones without a social core. They will, however, have to be communities without a core based in fusion. We have yet to demonstrate that the healthy varieties of self-respect and cohesiveness that can be developed by helping to feed hungry people or by establishing hospitals in areas of great need can provide this necessary social core and can function in ways that are just as psychologically satisfactory as the varieties of self-respect and cohesiveness that result from attempting to dominate others. It is becoming increasingly clear, however, that the other benefits of the former approach far outweigh those of the latter, and this must at some point begin to incline us toward attempting to advance international-mindedness.

NOTES

1. I have attempted to develop further the interrelated thought of these figures in *The Community Reconstructs: The Meaning of Pragmatic Social Thought* (Urbana: University of Illinois Press, 1992).

2. James Hayden Tufts, *Selected Writings of James Hayden Tufts*, ed. James Campbell (Carbondale: Southern Illinois University Press, 1992), 186.

3. George Herbert Mead, *Mind, Self, and Society from the Standpoint of a Social Behaviorist*, ed. Charles W. Morris (Chicago: University of Chicago Press, 1934), 171, 155, 194.

4. John Dewey, *The Middle Works, 1899–1924*, 15 volumes, ed. Jo Ann Boydston, (Carbondale: Southern Illinois University Press, 1976–1983), 14:216.

5. Dewey, *Middle Works*, 9:21.

6. Mead, *Mind, Self, and Society*, 168.

7. Ibid., 196.

8. Ibid., 217.

9. Ibid., 326.

10. George Herbert Mead, *Selected Writings*, ed. Andrew J. Reck (Chicago: University of Chicago Press, 1981), 355.

11. Mead, *Mind, Self, and Society*, 273; John Dewey, *The Later Works, 1925–1953*, 17 vols., ed. Jo Ann Boydston, (Carbondale: Southern Illinois University Press, 1981–1990), 13:89.

12. Mead, *Selected Writings*, 215–16, 235.

13. Tufts, *Selected Writings*, 233, 187. See William James: "Only when forced upon one, only when the enemy's injustice leaves us no alternative, is a war now thought permissible" ("The Moral Equivalent of War," *The Writings of William James*, ed. John J. McDermott, [Chicago: University of Chicago Press, 1977], 661). For a further consideration of James's discussion of the moral equivalent of war, see Campbell, *The Community Reconstructs*, 19–21.

14. George Herbert Mead, "National-Mindedness and International-Mindedness," *International Journal of Ethics* 39, no. 4 (July 1929): 386.

15. Mead, *Selected Writings*, 363, 355.

16. Ibid., 366.

17. Tufts, *Selected Writings*, 236.

18. Mead, *Selected Writings*, 364.

19. C. Wright Mills, ed., *The Marxists* (New York: Dell, 1962), 19; C. Wright Mills, *Sociology and Pragmatism* (New York: Oxford University Press, 1966), 412.

20. I have attempted to carry this theme a bit further forward in my paper, "Democracy as Cooperative Inquiry," in *Philosophy and the Reconstruction of Culture: Pragmatic Essays after Dewey*, ed. John J. Stuhr (Albany: SUNY Press, 1993), 17–35.

4

Pragmatism, Technology, and Scientism: Are the Methods of the Scientific-Technical Disciplines Relevant to Social Problems?

Larry A. Hickman

As a part of a more general retreat from the optimism that accompanied the successes of Enlightenment science and the technological revolutions of the last several centuries, serious doubts have been registered in some quarters regarding the applicability of the methods of the scientific-technical disciplines to the solution of social problems.

These doubts have taken several forms. They have ranged from arguments that the scientific-technical disciplines in fact exhibit no coherent method, all the way to claims that such methods are coherent within their own sphere but inapplicable to social problems. Claims of the latter type have at times amounted to charges that attempts to apply the methods of the scientific-technical disciplines to social problems amount to "scientism," or the apotheosis of science. At other times such claims have amounted to assaults on what some have called "the cult of expertise" in industrial democracies.

An important source of insight into these matters can be found in the work of John Dewey. Dewey sought to develop a rigorous characterization of the methods of the scientific-technical disciplines and to demonstrate their relation to the methods of other productive disciplines including the arts, the practice of law, and the writing of history. He also sought to relate these highly productive methods of inquiry to other methods that he regarded as less productive, such as magic and religion. In all this, one of his foremost goals was to demonstrate some of the ways in which the methods that have proven inquirentially valuable, such as those utilized in the scientific-technical fields, could be applied toward the resolution of pressing social ills.

An important element of Dewey's reconstruction of this material was his argument that the debates that take place as a part of experimental inquiry within the scientific-technical disciplines should be distinguished from two further classes of debates. They differ from those that take place between the partisans and the critics of scientific-technical disciplines, and they also differ from those that take place completely outside of scientific-technical communities, that is, without the benefit of experimental techniques.

Differences of opinion between two paleontologists, for example, regarding whether evolution is characterized better by gradualist or by punctuationalist accounts, are radically different from debates between scientists (such as paleontologists) and nonscientists (such as creationists). This is so because in the former case both sides of the debate are committed in principle to experimental methods, whereas the participants in the second type of debate do not share that commitment. Debates between two nonexperimentalist camps, as for example those between the proponents of two radically different religious or political ideologies, are different still.

One of Dewey's central contentions was that disagreements within the context of scientific-technological inquiry admit of techniques of analytical evidence-gathering and experimental testing that are notably absent in some other more popular and more commonly utilized forms of inquiry. The successes of the scientific-technical disciplines have, he argued, been based upon methods of ''discriminating and arranging data that evoke and test correlated ideas.'' Those ideas are in turn ''employed as *hypotheses*, and are . . . of a form to prescribe . . . determinations of facts'' (LW12:485).[1]

Present in this remark is the germ of Dewey's characterization of the ways in which means and ends interact, not just as a part of inquiry within the scientific-technical disciplines, but within any inquiry that is systematically productive. Data are employed as the means of eliciting and extracting new ideas in a particular instance of inquiry. Ideas, in their role as hypotheses, serve as the means for further isolation and selection of the facts of the particular case under review. Neither ends nor means are privileged, and conclusions reached are always susceptible to further inquiry in the event that new doubts should arise, as does in fact frequently occur.

But it is important to note Dewey's contention that scientific-technical fields do not provide the unique location of successful inquiry. Dewey claimed the same special place for debates between and among individuals who undertake critical and productive work in the arts. It was Dewey's view that although the arts and the sciences address different questions and perform different types of services, they nevertheless share a common method of inquiry, which he often called the ''method of intelligence.'' Put another way, even though the arts and sciences utilize different tools and operate with different types of materials, they nevertheless exhibit common logical or inquirential strategies insofar as they bring problematic situations within their respective fields to a fruitful conclusion. The point here is that both types of activity—the arts as well as the sciences—

are capable of producing novel ways of adjusting unsettled or problematic situations.

The arts, Dewey suggested, "express" meanings, whereas the sciences "state" them. Nevertheless, both types of enterprise, when successful, are bound to criteria by means of which the elements and facts of their selected problem areas are subjected to critical appraisal, to honesty with respect to materials, to evaluations within a peer group or community of inquiry, and to relevance with respect to cultural-historical contexts.

In addition to tactical inquiry in the scientific-technical disciplines, the arts, law, historiography, and elsewhere, there is thus in Dewey's view also an over-arching strategic method of inquiry in operation. Further, this general method undergoes continual refinement as it transacts business with its more tactically oriented tributary disciplines. This is what Dewey called the general pattern of inquiry or the method of intelligence.

Dewey's characterization of this overarching method is itself an idea, a complex hypothesis about the general features of inquiries that have proven successful. As an idea about the general pattern of inquiry, it has been elicited from data that includes elements of the history of scientific technology, the histories of the arts, and even the history of proto- and non-scientific-technological methods of inquiry. As a hypothesis about the characteristics of successful inquiry, it serves as a guide to the further determination of the facts of that case. Moreover, refinement of the relevant facts leads to further improvement of the hypothesis, which in this particular case involves the methods according to which a general theory of successful inquiry may be characterized in an ever more precise manner.

One of the principal differences between successful and unsuccessful inquiry is that unsuccessful methods of fixing belief tend to terminate prematurely the give and take between the means and ends of a particular process of inquiry. Unsuccessful methods tend to avoid or dismiss experimentally based challenges to their received doctrines. Facts are selected because of their support for conclusions accepted in advance and often without qualification; new data are consequently denied or ignored and improved hypotheses are stillborn. In broad terms, this is the difference between scientific technique and ideology.

It is for this reason that even though less productive methods such as religion and magic have had some remarkable successes (defined in terms of their ability to produce satisfactory adjustment to changing conditions and to control situations that are perceived as undesirable), they have nevertheless historically proven less likely to produce such reliable results over the long haul.

Dewey was by no means the first to advance the general outlines of this theory of inquiry. He was in fact following up on the suggestions laid out in C. S. Peirce's 1877 essay "The Fixation of Belief" and in William James's "The Will to Believe," published in 1896. Peirce had argued that the alternatives to the scientific method, among which he included the methods of tenacity, authority, and intuitive plausibility (or what he termed *a priori* reasoning), were all less reliable than the method utilized by scientific technology. Peirce was quick to admit, however, that some nonscientific methods, such as authority, have proven to be more dependable than others, such as tenacity.

For his part, James had taken a different tack to a similar conclusion. He had argued that the primary virtue of the method of science resides in its technique, its method of experimental testing. Even though the "truth of truths" might come its way as hunch, revelation, flash of insight, or dream content, James argued, science "would decline to touch it. Such truth as that, she might [say], would be stolen in defiance of her duty to mankind."[2]

Like Peirce and James, then, Dewey had high praise for the methods of the scientific-technical disciplines, and he thought that their methods operate as a kind of exemplar for arriving at the truth[3] of a matter. As had his two predecessors, Dewey argued for the extension of this method into other areas of human inquiry, including the social sciences, that have thus far proved resistant to its application.

But Dewey went further to suggest that when generally successful methods of inquiry are enumerated and examined, tactical methods such as those utilized in the arts, in law, and in historiography (to take three of his examples) obviously stand as essential partners alongside those utilized by the scientific-technical disciplines. Each of these bodies of tactical method provides material for a more generally applicable pattern or strategy of inquiry, and each is in turn tested by the more general pattern. As I have indicated, Dewey called this general strategic pattern of inquiry "the method of intelligence," and he called its study "logic."

As James had, Dewey recognized well enough that even received methods of inquiry that do not take full advantage of the method of intelligence are often nevertheless the source of enormous energy, and that they frequently issue products that serve as stimuli that broaden and deepen discourse in the scientific-technical fields, in the arts, and elsewhere. This is particularly true when, as James put it, options are live, forced, and momentous, and when acceptable evidence for or against a particular viewpoint or course of action is scant or absent. This is arguably the main thesis of James's essay "The Will to Believe," and it is a theme that Dewey developed in dozens of books and essays.

But Dewey also argued that the products of such methods, because their claims are usually premised on luck, tradition, economic interests, or intuitions of various sorts, nevertheless inevitably require for their sustained success the enhanced focus and refinement that can only be brought about by the application of the method of intelligence. He was particularly critical of social theory and practice based on overly generalized goals or ends that are themselves assumed to be exempt from analytical inquiry.[4]

DEWEY'S TREATMENT OF INQUIRY

This argument of Dewey's—that many social problems are remediable by the application of the type of inquiry that has proven successful in the scientific-technical disciplines, the arts, and law—has been both broadly and profoundly misunderstood. Before turning to the arguments of some of Dewey's critics, however, and before attempting to answer the question posed in the title of this essay, namely whether or not it is possible or desirable to apply the methods of the scientific-technical disciplines to social problems, it will be helpful to examine a bit more closely Dewey's general treatment of inquiry, especially as it functions in the scientific-technical disciplines.

First, a central feature of Dewey's theory of inquiry is his rejection of realism, whether of the metaphysical or the scientific variety. One variety of scientific realism, for example, advanced in a recent essay on the philosophy of technology, holds that science reveals the "lawful fine structure of reality," and that reality is just the "final structures" of the world.[5]

Dewey's alternative to scientific realism was instrumentalism, or the view that science works in a piecemeal fashion with interlocking sets of problems, fashioning and improving upon tools as required. Proffered solutions are not so much reflective of a preexisting reality as they are tools for the resolution and reconstruction of the difficulties encountered in previously reconstructed solutions that have subsequently proved untenable. What counts as the facts for a particular sequence of inquiry is determined in the course of that very sequence of inquiry. In other words, in the course of inquiry some data recede into the background at the same time that others become more prominent. In Dewey's view, there are no absolute or free-floating facts; facts are always facts-of-the-case.

In a related move, Dewey reserved the term "object" to refer, as he put it, to "subject-matter so far as it has been produced and ordered in settled form by means of inquiry; proleptically, objects are the *objectives* of inquiry" (LW12: 122). Nevertheless, it is not necessary for each inquirer to begin *ab ovo*; there exists prior to any particular sequence of inquiry a rich storehouse of objects, that is, a base line constituted by things that "have been previously determined as outcomes of inquiries" (LW12:122).

Second, as I have already suggested, the activities of the scientific-technical disciplines utilize a family of tactical methods that operate in a relation of transaction or feedback with a more general pattern of strategic inquiry. In the broad sense of the term, Dewey characterized "inquiry" as "*the controlled or directed transformation of an indeterminate situation into one that is so determinate in its constituent distinctions and relations as to convert the elements of the original situation into a unified whole*" (emphasis in original) (LW12:108). This statement characterizes successful inquiry wherever it occurs, whether in scientific-technical disciplines, in the arts, in the practice of law, in the writing of history, or in inquiry into social problems. If the scientific-technical disciplines have exhibited more success in the utilization of this method than have other disciplines, then that success is not due to any special or privileged place occupied by them. It is due instead to the fact that their material has tended to be less complex and more manageable than that of other disciplines.

In other words, although the methods developed and utilized successfully in the scientific-technical disciplines have contributed greatly to the refinement of the pattern of inquiry, their methods are only contained in it as a part, and are not exhaustive of it. The continuing refinement of the methods utilized by the general pattern of inquiry, the method of intelligence, is also affected by advances in the methods of the other areas of inquiry just enumerated.

The pattern exhibited by the general method of intelligence, now taken to be inclusive of the scientific-technological and other disciplines, is itself a logical tool, an abstraction that has been constructed on the basis of past outcomes that have proven successful. But this pattern is, however, generated as a byproduct of inquiry, not as a direct result of it. Just as in agricultural practice, the aim of a particular sequence of inquiry is the resolution and reconstruction of a particular problem. And just as in the case of agriculture, when tools appropriate to a problem are invented or improved they are the byproducts, not the direct goal, of the relevant practice.

Third, the methods of inquiry utilized in scientific-technical disciplines undergo constant change. They may evolve, as they have since the seventeenth century, or they may devolve, as they did during the period that was marked by the breakup of the Roman Empire and the onset of the early Middle Ages. Methods utilized by the scientific-technical disciplines may even evolve at the same time that the methods utilized in social inquiry devolve. There is ample evidence to conclude that this situation occurred during the early stages of the first Industrial Revolution, that is, the revolution that introduced industrial machinery to Great Britain.

Scientific-technical methods are in constant need of corrective feedback that can only be secured by involvement with actual cases of successful scientific-technical practice and at the same time by transaction with the general method of inquiry. The general method of inquiry, like the methods of those disciplines tributary to it, is a general characterization made at a specific time. It is itself a tool that is open to continuing improvement, just as are the tools of carpentry. It is in this sense that the method of intelligence is said to be "self-corrective." (It should be obvious that the present account of this process is itself fallible, that is, open to continuing revision. The publication of this chapter is just a snapshot of an ongoing inquiry.)

Fourth, there are vast areas of experience within which the method of intelligence does little or no work, but from which it may receive interesting and important materials for its use. The contents of dreams, the insights of religious mystics, folktales and folk remedies, and even the most vile crimes committed by one human being against another:[6] all these and myriad other elements of human experience may serve as materially important within situations calling for inquiry.

Fifth, emphasis within inquiry is not on the origin of material to be tested, but rather on the analysis and ordering of that material, on the selection from it of elements that are appropriate to the problem at hand, and on the checks and tests utilized within a community of inquiry in order to maintain standards of evidence, relative disinterestedness, and honesty.

THE CHARGE OF INSTRUMENTALISM

As I have indicated, Dewey's position with respect to these matters has been profoundly misunderstood. His critics have tended to grasp neither the import of his general theory of inquiry, nor his view concerning the ways in which methods that have proven successful within the scientific-technical and other disciplines may be applied to social problems.

Among Dewey's harshest critics have been some of the members of the Frankfurt School, such as Max Horkheimer, and some of their recent partisans such as W. A. Paringer. Horkheimer accused Dewey of reliance on what he called "instrumental reason," which he identified as an outdated Enlightenment positivism or scientism coupled with an uncritical faith in the institutions and goals of industrial technology.[7] Since these arguments have begun to resurface in the work of some of the contemporary critics of Dewey's philosophy of education, I shall address them at some length.

Horkheimer accused Dewey and the other pragmatists of preoccupation with means at the expense of ends;[8] of emphasizing practice to the detriment of theory;[9] and of attempting to abolish philosophical thought altogether in favor of an apology for crass commercial and industrial experimentalism.[10] "Pragmatism," wrote Horkheimer, "in trying to turn experimental physics into a prototype of all science and to model all spheres of intellectual life after the techniques of the laboratory, is the counterpart of modern industrialism, for which the factory is the prototype of human existence, and which models all branches of culture after production on the conveyor belt, or after the rationalized front office."[11]

Horkheimer was, in short, charging Dewey with espousing what Langdon Winner has called "straight-line" instrumentalism. As Winner crisply characterizes it, straight-line instrumentalism "begins with a preconceived end in mind. Then one decides upon an appropriate instrument or organization of instruments to achieve that end, usually weighing the advantages of two or more alternative instruments. Next comes the actual *use* of the instrument in the way established for its successful exercise. Finally, one achieves certain results which are judged according to the original end."[12]

When judged in terms of the general remarks on Dewey's theory of inquiry that I have sketched in the previous section, Horkheimer's criticism appears to be badly misdirected. My aim in the next few paragraphs is not to demean Horkheimer, however, but to utilize his criticism as a tool for constructing an enhanced understanding of Dewey's position.

First, straight-line instrumentalism depends on some sort of scientific or metaphysical realism to provide its inflexible goals. But such realism is more apparent in Horkheimer's own view than in that of Dewey. Horkheimer contended that "objective truth" should be "pursued for its own sake" as a "concept of an order or hierarchy, of static or dynamic structure, that would do full justice to things and nature.''[13] Dewey viewed matters quite differently. He held that such generalizations as "absolute truth" and "essential structures"[14] usually serve only to short-circuit inquiry, and that the legitimate role for metaphysics lies in its provisional generalizations about the generic features of existence.

Second, Dewey did not seek to measure all experience by scientific-technical analysis, as Horkheimer claimed. He did not even think that scientific-technical inquiry should serve as the pattern for all forms of inquiry. It was rather his view that much of human experience, especially within the domain of simple aesthetic delight, has no need of inquiry because it is not problematic. Further, even where inquiry is called for, the methods of the scientific-technical disciplines constitute only one important source of insight among others (including but not limited to the methods of the various arts and legal practice) into ways of understanding and improving on a pattern of inquiry that is more general than that employed in the scientific-technical disciplines. His theory of inquiry is thus considerably broader than his theory about the methods of scientific technology.

Third, Dewey did not disregard "any speculative capacity of reason as distinct from existing science,"[15] as Horkheimer claimed. But speculation was for Dewey not the same as contemplation, which he regarded as static and passive. Speculation functioned for Dewey as an important means of the determination of further facts of a case and of the setting out of refined hypotheses. Speculation, unlike contemplation, was in Dewey's view both experimental and productive.

Finally, Horkheimer's charge that Dewey's method of inquiry was irremediably subjective is also misdirected. He took particular offense at Dewey's suggestion that intelligence effects a "projection of the desirable in the present," and an invention of "the instrumentalities of its realization."[16] Horkheimer claimed to see only two possible interpretations of this remark: either that it accepts in an uncritical way the desires of people just as they are, or that it accepts some notion of objective desirability, which he argued was foreign to Dewey's subjectivist approach. In the former event, philosophy would be reduced to popularity polls; in the second the pragmatists would have abandoned the subjectivity that he thought they had championed elsewhere and would have taken the first step on the road of critical thought, a road on which Horkheimer regarded himself as an experienced traveler. But it is clear that Horkheimer did not think of himself and Dewey as traveling the same road.

Dewey's account of inquiry was in fact not subjectivistic. He argued that successful inquiry always takes place within a community because it is only within such venues that adequate checks and tests can be performed. This argument lies at the heart of the extended discussion of the difference between what is (subjectively) "desired" and what is (objectively) "desirable" that Dewey developed in the tenth chapter of *The Quest for Certainty*, a work that appeared almost two decades before Horkheimer published his remarks.

THE CHARGE OF SCIENTISM

The charge made by some of Dewey's critics that he was a proponent of a naive Enlightenment scientism calls for further special attention. I take scientism to have at least three important components: the view that the methods of the natural sciences are paradigmatic for all other areas of experience, the view that the conclusions of the natural sciences are universally applicable to all other areas of experience, and the view that the natural sciences are objective or "value free."

There is widespread agreement among philosophers of science that one of the most radical critics of scientism has been Paul Feyerabend. In assessing the extent to which Dewey's views are scientific, a brief comparison of his views to those of Feyerabend may prove helpful.

At the very heart of Feyerabend's position seem to be the following claims. First, the methods of scientific technology are not static, but evolve through time. The methods utilized by the scientific-technical disciplines today are, for example, quite different from those used in the seventeenth century. Second, the processes of scientific discovery are not generalizable, but rather, in his famous phrase, "anything goes." There has been considerable confusion regarding this claim. Probably the best way to read Feyerabend on this point is not that anything goes in the testing phase of inquiry, but that anything in fact goes in the phase of inquiry that involves the formation of hypotheses, that is, the getting of ideas for further development. Third, science is not universal but perspectival, that is, culture-bound. Different assumptions and worldviews promote different solutions to similar problems. Medical science, for example, has developed in the Orient differently than it has in the Occident. Fourth, science operates in its own domain and does not have hegemony over other types of experience. To expect that the methods of the scientific-technical disciplines should be applicable to the visual arts or to law would be to claim too much for those methods. Fifth, in true democracies, science should be "de-established" just as religion has been. This has been and continues to be a controversial point. Recent debates concerning the relation of "big" science to "small" science illustrate what this claim might mean in practical social terms. The struggle over funding for the Texas Supercollider constitutes an excellent case study for this point.

Dewey's positions on these matters are the general subject of this chapter, so I will not reiterate them here. Nevertheless, two points should be made. First, except for Feyerabend's final point, each of these views (which many of Feyerabend's readers have generally regarded as radical) was present also in Dewey's treatment of science in his 1938 *Logic: The Theory of Inquiry*. Second, if Feyerabend's final point, that science should be "de-established," means that members of scientific institutions should be just one of many voices that play a role in the determination of public policy in a democratic society, then Dewey was clearly in agreement on that point as well.

A full comparison of Dewey's philosophy of science to that of Feyerabend is well beyond the scope of this chapter. I nevertheless present this brief outline of an argument in support of my claim that Dewey's view of scientific technology was hardly an example of scientism. It was not a "mainstream" view during his lifetime, nor is it now.

NIEBUHR'S CRITICISM OF DEWEY

Looking back on Dewey's work from the perspective of the 1990s, it is not difficult to find points at which he stumbled, and even blundered, as he sought to apply his instrumentalist brand of pragmatism to the concrete problems of his own times and places. Nevertheless, I believe that his central insights remain applicable to the social difficulties of our own time.

To demand, for example, as Dewey did, that the claims and methods of religious communities and their leaders should be open to the same experimental tests that are applied to all others who seek to influence public opinion and policy is as appropriate now as it was in 1934, the year that Dewey published *A Common Faith*. To hold fast to this point is not to attempt to establish a hegemony of science over religion, as some religionists have claimed, and it is not to deny the important role of religious insight and motivation as materials for intelligent inquiry. It is rather a challenge to the proponents of various religions to abandon their own pretense to privilege, to join in public debates on equal terms with those whose primary activities take place in other areas of inquiry, and to accept the general criteria of experimental testing that characterize the successful application of the general pattern of inquiry to meaningful public discourse.

These matters were the focus of Dewey's attention in *A Common Faith*. One of his central concerns in that work was to frame a reply to Reinhold Niebuhr, whose own book *Moral Man and Immoral Society* had appeared just two years earlier. Niebuhr had accused Dewey of mislocating the source of social ills in "the failure of the social sciences to keep pace with the physical sciences which have created our technological civilization."[17]

In this matter he thought that Dewey had gotten the cart before the horse: social justice would be improved, if it all, not through the application of scientific-technical methods in education, but through a type of social conflict whose primary motivation would be the "absolutizing moral principle" he termed Christian love, and whose primary tools would be "the right dogmas, symbols and emotionally potent oversimplifications."

"They [industrial workers] may," Niebuhr claimed, "be very scientific in projecting their social goal and in choosing the most effective instruments for its attainment, but a motive force will be required to nerve them for their task which is not easily derived from the cool objectivity of science."[18]

Niebuhr's position on the political spectrum was certainly far removed from that of the Christian fundamentalists of his and our own time who have seen Dewey's pedagogy as a major threat to their own agenda. Nevertheless, the arguments Niebuhr used to support his position are remarkably similar to those advanced by the fundamentalists. In each case there is an appeal to the method of straight-line instrumentalism. In each case there is an inflexible social agenda, an inflexible principle, and a conviction that desired goals can only be achieved by means of utilizing irrational and oversimplified dogmas.

In his reply to Niebuhr, Dewey recognized the important place of ideals and emotions as motives for change, especially within the kind of problem-solving that leads to the control of matters that are not as we wish them to be. But he also denied that there is any "religious" experience *simpliciter*, and argued instead that those "elements and outlooks that may be called religious" (LW9:8) should be emancipated from their servitude to the ideologies of sectarian religious institutions, including, by implication, the one espoused by Niebuhr. He sought to reconstruct the noun "religion" as "religious," an adjectival term that would refer to the qualities of energy and enthusiasm that infuse and motivate all those experiences that produce enhanced adjustment within life's situations.

Dewey thus argued that undesirable social situations could be improved by education in the methods of experimental inquiry, that is, by improving citizen competence in the methods utilized by the general pattern of intelligence. He further argued that such methods were among the primary tools of democracy. But whereas he admitted that religious ideals and emotions may prove an aid in the struggle to achieve worthwhile ends, and he added that they frequently serve as important stimuli to the application of the methods of intelligence, he also argued that such ideals and emotions are themselves in continuing need of refinement by just those types of experimental methods that have proven successful in the scientific-technical disciplines and elsewhere.

Niebuhr and Dewey were thus advancing very different notions of democracy. For his part, Niebuhr claimed that the Christian religion had at its disposal a uniquely powerful tool, one that was much more effective than those utilized by the scientific-technical disciplines. Whereas the instruments and conclusions of the latter were tentative, he argued, Christian love constitutes an "absolutizing moral principle" that is capable of "imparting transcendent worth to the life of others."[19] He held that democracy would result, if at all, when social conflict was coupled with Christian love and applied to solve immediate social ills.

Implicit in Niebuhr's argument was the claim that the Christian religion offered the greatest hope for the resolution of human problems because it was the most evolved of the world's religions. Dewey countered by suggesting that if religious thought had evolved (and he thought it had), then there was certainly no reason for its progress to stop with Christianity as it was understood and practiced in the 1930s. Its next stage might be a common faith, that is, one that would transcend sectarian differences and allow for common efforts to solve common problems.

A primary tool of advancing and refining such a common faith, Dewey argued, would be the method of intelligence. Just as the methods of scientific technologies transcend national borders and sectarian religious divisions, and just as the methods and products of the arts constitute an international "language," so could the experimental methods of the general pattern of inquiry be applied across boundaries previously thought impermeable, and this with an aim to the solution of social ills.

Dewey's approach was thus the inverse of Niebuhr's. He argued that the methods of democracy and scientific technology, motivated by a common faith in the desirability of an improved future and expressed in terms of experimental action undertaken to determine what courses of action are worthy of being desired, constituted the best hope for humankind. History has shown that no "absolutizing moral principle" is available within any particular religion, since each has claimed its own as absolute and since religious institutions have frequently resorted to open conflict with one another regarding whose principle is "more absolute."

Fortunately, however, no "absolutizing moral principle" is required for intelligent inquiry. On this question Dewey aligned himself against Niebuhr and on the side of Aristotle, who had argued that in matters of morals and social justice, intelligence works not from, but toward, first principles.

Dewey's notion of the motivating factors in the use of intelligent inquiry was thus much more sophisticated than that of Niebuhr, and it reflects his commitment to continuing reconstruction of the methods of the scientific-technical disciplines and the arts in their ongoing transactions with the general pattern of intelligence.

For his part, Niebuhr seemed to prefer a utilitarian version of the arts that would render them subservient to political aims. To use a now famous phrase of Walter Benjamin, Niebuhr seemed to want to "aestheticize politics." Dewey's reply was that wherever the arts are utilized as little more than ancillary to the political, then inquiry in the arts is stifled and their larger contribution to desirable social ends is cut short. But where the arts flourish, that is, where artistic materials are expressed in ways that are intelligent, then several felicitous consequences ensue. First, experience is enriched because its aesthetic dimension is augmented and refined. Second, advances in inquiry within the arts feed into and enrich our understanding of the general pattern of intelligence. Third, improvements in the general pattern of intelligence serve to inform and ameliorate methods in the sciences, in law, and elsewhere, with corresponding social gains. The same argument, of course, may be employed against the capture of the scientific-technical disciplines, law, or historiography, by political expediency.

Dewey's program for the enhancement of the role of the arts in social and political inquiry, and the corresponding enrichment of social life that would result from the refinement of the arts, revealed a much deeper grasp of the possibilities of the arts than was evident in Niebuhr's work. In fact, Dewey's position was in certain ways similar to that of Benjamin, who claimed that it would be much more productive to politicize art than to aestheticize politics, as the Nazis had done. By this I take Benjamin to have meant that aesthetics must play a role in a total program of social and political amelioration, and not be limited to a kind of veneer designed to mask and make palatable preconceived and therefore unreconstructed and unreconstructable social ends. Put another way, both Dewey and Benjamin were saying that "the right dogmas, symbols and emotionally potent oversimplifications" that Niebuhr thought essential to political progress in fact tend to restrict social and political amelioration because they promote the "cult" values of art over their critical and expressive possibilities.

PARINGER'S CRITICISM OF DEWEY

Important elements of Horkheimer's and Niebuhr's criticisms of Dewey's instrumentalism have resurfaced in recent assaults on his philosophy of education. W. A. Paringer's *John Dewey and the Paradox of Liberal Reform* provides an excellent example. Drawing from arguments advanced earlier by members of the Frankfurt School, as well as from the work of other radical philosophers of education, Paringer has argued that Dewey was guilty of a naive optimism that ignored the realities of the American power structure, a structure that he thinks legitimates itself through the use of brute power and oppression rather than through democratic institutions. Like Niebuhr before him, Paringer contends that "democracy begins only after reasonably egalitarian conditions and structures have been prioritized."[20] "In identifying 'scientific' with 'democratic,' " writes Paringer, "Dewey made a similar mistake to the one Plato had made. . . . Both presumed an epistemological basis (idealism) for their social theory."[21]

Paringer calls upon a passage from Marcuse to buttress his point: "Today, domination perpetuates and extends itself not only through technology but *as* technology . . . and provides the great rationalization of the unfreedom of man and demonstrates the 'technical' impossibility of being autonomous, of determining one's own life."[22]

In other words, Marcuse and Paringer have held that it is the very methods of the scientific-technical disciplines as they are practiced that have entrenched the patterns of inequality and oppression that are apparent in American society. Far from being a part of the answer to social problems, however, as Dewey thought they were, the methods of the scientific-technical disciplines are in Paringer's view a part of the problem.

What has Paringer to offer as an alternative to the methods of scientific technology? He tells us that his approach "begins with a critical stance towards one's reality and engages in the contradictions which the option-makers have hidden. *While not abandoning the empirical means of science* critical theory takes aim at hidden coercions, at the concrete contradictions consequent to any world picture, at an entirely different sort of emancipation" (emphasis added).[23]

I believe that there is a serious flaw in this line of argumentation, and that it betrays a misunderstanding of Dewey's program. Dewey's general pattern of inquiry, which stands in a relation of transaction to the methods of scientific technology, is capable of absorbing the agenda of the critical theorists insofar as they desire to engage in a critique of underlying ideologies and assumptions. Every account that Dewey provided of his general method of inquiry includes as one of its components just such a moment of analysis in which an inquirer or a community of inquiry delves as deeply into previously held assumptions as is possible within that situated process of inquiry. It was Dewey's contention that this pattern works in the arts no less than in the scientific-technical disciplines.

What Dewey's general method of intelligence is *not* able to do, however, is to accept the notions of absolute truth and absolutizing moral positions that seem to be essential ingredients within the program advanced by Paringer.

CONCLUSION

It is now time to draw together the arguments within this essay and to propose a succinct answer to the question posed in the title. My suggestion has been that the methods of the scientific-technical disciplines, together with the methods of other disciplines that have proven successful, such as the arts, law, and historiography, nourish and are refined by an overarching pattern of intelligence. This pattern of intelligence functions as a kind of "liaison officer" for applying methods developed by the several disciplines to problems that are characterized as social. Dewey argued strenuously that the methods of the scientific-technological disciplines, though they in no sense exercise hegemony or even deserve to do so, have in fact set the pace for other areas of human inquiry because their subject material is less complex than that of the social sciences, because of their refinement over time of the methods of hypothesis-construction and testing, and because of their ability to develop and relate abstract meanings in ways that may be referred back to and that alter matters that are concretely existential.

Dewey at times called his general method "instrumentalism," and at other times he used the term "technology." Since the terms "technical" and "technological" are utilized as well to refer to methods that are ancillary to the general method of inquiry, his equivocal use of these terms has been a source of some confusion. Why would Dewey insist on calling his general method of inquiry "technology"?

I believe that the answer to this question lies in Dewey's contention that every successful inquiry involves the invention, use, and development of tools and other artifacts to solve human difficulties. This process may involve the concrete, tangible tools and artifacts normally associated with hardware technology, but it may also involve the noetic or conceptual tools and artifacts that do their work at more abstract levels of operation. Dewey's definition of inquiry is thus more or less his definition of technology in one of its broadest senses.

From Dewey's instrumentalist point of view, then, it makes little sense to condemn technology as the source of human ills, as Paringer, Horkheimer, and Marcuse have done. If the resources of a society have become concentrated in the hands of too few individuals, and if social ills result, then it is not technology *ueberhaupt* that is at fault, and it is certainly not the method of intelligence that has failed. The fault rather lies with a failure to employ technology to solve human problems. Just as Dewey continually argued that wherever democratic institutions fail to work properly there is a need for more, not less, democracy, he also argued that wherever technological institutions fail to enhance desirable human goals there needs to be more, not less, technology (taking the term in the broad sense in which he utilized it).

There are therefore good grounds for applying the methods that have proven successful in the scientific-technical disciplines to social problems. The scientific-technical disciplines, like the arts, law, and historiography, are themselves socially situated and cannot be divorced from social concerns. Conversely, no social problems exist outside the context of the physical conditions that the scientific-technical disciplines have been developed to address. It is for these and other reasons enumerated above that Dewey thought that "social phenomena cannot be understood except as there is prior understanding of physical conditions and the laws of their interactions. Social phenomena cannot be attacked, *qua* social, directly. Inquiry into them, with respect both to data that are significant and to their relations or proper ordering, is conditioned upon extensive prior knowledge of physical phenomena and their laws. This fact accounts in part for the retarded and immature state of social subjects. . . . Without physical knowledge there are no means of analytic resolution of complex and grossly macroscopic social phenomena into simpler forms" (LW12:486).

NOTES

1. References to John Dewey's work are to *The Collected Works of John Dewey*, edited by Jo Ann Boydston and published by Southern Illinois University Press in three series: as *The Early Works* (EW), *The Middle Works* (MW), and *The Later Works* (LW). Citations utilize these designations followed by volume and page number.

2. William James, *The Will to Believe and Other Essays in Popular Philosophy* (New York: Holt, 1897; Cambridge, Mass.: Harvard University Press, 1979), 27.

3. "Truth" was a term that Dewey took great care to reconstruct. He argued that because of the absolutist sense traditionally carried by that term, the more fallibilist term "warranted assertibility" served his purposes better.

4. See, for example, Dewey's remarks in LW12:489, *ff.*

5. Albert Borgmann, *Technology and the Character of Contemporary Life* (Chicago: University of Chicago Press, 1984), 28.

6. One example would be the experimentation on hyperthermia undertaken by Nazi researchers on concentration camp inmates. Another example would be the notorious syphilis studies done on Southern blacks in the 1930s and 1940s in this country, studies that became the basis for much important knowledge about that disease.

7. Max Horkheimer, *Eclipse of Reason* (1947; reprint, New York: Seabury Press, 1974), 45, n. 29.

8. Ibid., 46.

9. Ibid., 48.

10. Ibid., 49.

11. Ibid., 50.

12. Langdon Winner, *Autonomous Technology* (Cambridge, Mass.: MIT Press, 1977), 28.

13. Horkheimer, *Eclipse*, 45–46.

14. Ibid., 55.

15. Ibid.

16. Dewey, MW10:48, quoted in Horkheimer, *Eclipse*, 53.

17. Reinhold Niebuhr, *Moral Man and Immoral Society* (New York: Charles Scribner's Sons, 1932), viii.

18. Ibid., xv.

19. Ibid., 71.

20. William Andrew Paringer, *John Dewey and the Paradox of Liberal Reform* (Albany: SUNY Press, 1990), 42.

21. Ibid., 55.

22. Herbert Marcuse, *One-Dimensional Man* (Boston: Beacon Press, 1964), 158. Quoted in Paringer, *Paradox*, 55.

23. Paringer, *Paradox*, 57–58.

5

The Perils of Personality: Lewis Mumford and Politics After Liberalism

Casey Nelson Blake

MUMFORD AS USABLE PAST

Amid the lively discussions of liberal, communitarian, and radical politics currently taking place among historians and political theorists, Lewis Mumford's name remains strangely absent. The revival of interest in his work among ecologists, urbanists, feminist theorists of housing, and cultural historians has not yet touched those engaged in rethinking and renovating American political culture, even as their debates rehearse many of the themes of Mumford's career. Whether in the form of Richard Rorty's resurgent pragmatism, the communitarianism of Robert Bellah, Alasdair MacIntyre, William Sullivan, and Sheldon Wolin, or the neo-Marxism of Richard Bernstein and American followers of Jurgen Habermas, recent efforts at constructing a new, postliberal opposition return to issues that preoccupied Mumford at the earliest stages of his career, and that form a backdrop to his entire life's work. Chief among the questions that Mumford addressed in the 1920s and 1930s, which now concern his successors, are those that plumb the cultural crisis of democratic politics: the severing of the bonds of fellowship and community in advanced industrial society; the warning sense of a "public good" and of a vernacular idiom capable of expressing such an ideal in a secular culture; and the antagonism between the instrumental language of statecraft and technique, on the one hand, and the symbolic language of aesthetic experience and moral judgment, on the other. Despite Mumford's renown as an architectural critic and a sociologist of cities and technology, these are the critical issues that undergird virtually every one of his works. As he wrote Van Wyck Brooks, in the midst of working on the lectures that became *The Golden Day*, "I find, consolingly, that my standards in architecture and literature are one, so that the good life that hovers in the background has, at all events, a unity of interior and exterior."[1]

The mood of skepticism about received liberal dogma and of wary hopefulness about possible alternatives that pervades Mumford's early work links those writings to current efforts at a postliberal politics. Like many of his successors, he was shaken by the outcome of a bloody, apparently pointless war overseen by liberals. The result was an uneasiness about the state, and about progressive claims for "scientific" state-sponsored reform, that has since become the dominant mood among chastened liberals and radicals in the 1980s. In reaction, Mumford undertook a project that still remains the central focus of much current political debate. Forsaking the "scientific" claims of progressive thought, which likened the actions of reformers to the technical achievements of the engineer or applied scientist, Mumford sought to ground a democratic politics in the give-and-take of a public conversation, and in the associational ties of a common culture. Such an alternative would not repudiate scientific method, or even many of the fruits of technical innovation, so much as it would return political understanding to its roots in the broader cultural dialogue of which science was only a part. Mumford's "cultural turn" in the 1920s and 1930s, then, anticipates by half a century the current intellectual ferment about the politics of language, culture, and symbolic meaning. It also anticipates the return to a republican idiom of "community" and the "common good" advocated by Robert Bellah and other proponents of a renewal of American politics and culture.

Like Mumford in the 1920s, contemporary advocates of a revitalized public culture condemn what Alasdair MacIntyre calls "the bifurcation of the contemporary world" into two separate spheres, equally indifferent to the claims of public discussion: "a realm of the organizational in which ends are taken to be given and set and are not available for rational scrutiny and a realm of the personal in which judgement and debate are central factors, but in which no rational social resolution of issues is available."[2] Between the dictates of administrative rationality and the "emotivism" of the socially unencumbered self, there exists no middle range of cultural practices to ground public and private behavior in what Mumford called "the good life." When Bellah and his associates demand an understanding of community, in which "the individual self finds its fulfillment in relationship with others in a society organized around public dialogue," they echo Mumford's belief that the crisis of "personality" in industrial society requires a comprehensive rethinking of American culture and politics.[3] In their search for a politics after liberalism, Bellah, MacIntyre, and other critics of "the bifurcation of the contemporary world" return to a project of personal and public renewal that preoccupied Mumford more than a half-century ago.

This chapter aims at making Mumford's early explorations of "the good life" available to the contemporary discussions surrounding the reconstruction of a public culture, and does so in the spirit of Mumford's own understanding of what it means to shape a "usable past." Far from bending the past to fit current ideological imperatives, the "usable past" that Mumford sought in his writings was intended to give a historical dimension to a common culture. History, in his view, was "usable" insofar as it allowed citizens to reflect on the past conditions that shaped their experience, and to grasp the potential for change that lay within themselves and their society. "Establishing its own special relations with its past," Mumford wrote in 1925, "each generation creates anew what lies behind it, as well as what looms in front; and instead of being victimized by those forces which are uppermost at the moment, it gains the ability to select the qualities which it values, and by exercising them it rectifies its own infirmities and weaknesses."[4] Mumford's work may be "usable," then, not as a crutch for one or another position in the current controversy about American politics, but as a way of deepening the historical resonance of that discussion and of taking note of opportunities missed and of mistakes made in its previous formulations. Above all, I will argue that his work provides a lesson in the ambiguities of "community," a word that reappears throughout Mumford's writings and that has quickly emerged as the cornerstone of all current efforts to transcend the deadlock of American liberalism.

Mumford's work has so much to offer contemporary debates about the recovery of a democratic culture because it directly addresses the need to reconceive of individualism as an ideal of selfhood achieved through participation in a common artistic and civic project. At the center of all of Mumford's concerns is his interest in renewing "personality" through a revitalized democratic community life. The personal, in Mumford's work, is never *merely* personal: it always involves questions of politics and culture that transcend the limitations of private life. But this admirable goal of personal and public renewal has taken very different forms at different stages of Mumford's career, as he has alternated between blueprints for utopian, neotechnic organization and more modest hopes for moral leadership by small groups that have rejected the premises of a modern technological society. In either case, Mumford has been at best tentative, and at worst neglectful, in his treatment of the conflicts—within a polity, or between the individual and the community, or even within the self—involved in overcoming our current cultural predicament. To be faithful to Mumford's project, then, requires going beyond the terms of Mumford's own work; it requires that contemporary communitarianism assess the perils, as well as the promise, of a politics of personality.

INSURGENT PERSONALITY

In the closing pages of *Technics and Civilization* (1934), Mumford argued that the reaction against "the denial of the organic and the living" in a machine civilization could take one of two forms. The first would involve "the use of mechanical means to return to the primitive," a resurgence of destructive impulses that, left unchecked by any collective moral discipline, would harness the power of new technologies in a final assault on civilized life. Against this prospect of libidinal and mechanical apocalypse, Mumford posed his own vision of personality, community, and a renewed vitalism. The alternative to the cult of power, he explained, "involves the rebuilding of the individual personality and the collective group, and the re-orientation of all forms of thought and social activity toward life."[5]

Of the three constituents of Mumford's vision of cultural renewal, it was the "rebuilding of the individual personality" that had absorbed most of his attention until the publication of *Technics and Civilization.* Throughout the 1920s, Mumford returned again and again to the crisis of personal identity in a corporate industrial society—a theme he inherited from the circle of cultural critics associated with the journal, *The Seven Arts*, in 1916–1917. Like Brooks, Randolph Bourne, Waldo Frank, and Harold Stearns, Mumford believed that a culture of self-expression and personality was replacing the Victorian culture of self-reliance and character. In this regard, he and his forerunners at *The Seven Arts* were part of a much broader cultural upheaval that centered on the emergence of "personality," which has become a central topic in recent cultural histories of the early twentieth century. The late Warren Susman, Jackson Lears, and other historians have traced the widespread interest in "personality" as a successor to the Emersonian ideal of "character" to the emergence of a therapeutic culture of mass consumption. While nineteenth-century Americans from the middle class extolled self-discipline and training in moral virtues through literary and religious education, advocates of personality equated success with the cultivation of personal charm and the ability to win friends and influence people.[6] In this view, the recurring fascination with personality, personal growth, and self-fulfillment in the writings of Mumford and his predecessors suggests that theirs is another example of cultural radicalism gone wrong. Once again, the attempt to delineate a counterculture—in this case, what Susman called a "culture of personality"—only fuels the dominant culture's capacity to promote new forms of privatistic, and ultimately conformist, experience as a means of liberation.

Despite the value of this argument as an interpretation of the rhetoric of personality in advertising, popular psychology, and other manifestations of mass culture, it fails to do justice to the search for personality that engaged, first, the *Seven Arts* group and, later, Lewis Mumford.[7] For these critics, the reconstruction of the self required neither therapeutic self-absorption nor the rootless individualism celebrated in the popular notion of self-reliance. Instead, the creation of a full personality involved a reciprocal process of cultural and self-renewal. Mumford and the earlier *Seven Arts* writers sharply distinguished their conception of personality from the therapeutic gospel of affability and charm by insisting that personal growth was only possible within a project of enlarging the domains of civic life and culture, which in turn required the active participation of the individual in his or her community. Personality was the realization of the self in tension—or in dialogue—with its environment, not psychic adjustment to dominant institutions. As Bourne wrote in 1916, "All our idealisms must be those of future social goals in which all can participate, the good life of personality lived in the environment of the Beloved Community."[8]

The radical personalism that Mumford inherited from the *Seven Arts* group dovetailed with the view of organic equilibrium he had learned from his mentor, Patrick Geddes. Geddes's vitalistic biology led Mumford to a view of nature as a dynamic interpenetration of dead and living matter, and of human development as a dialectic of subjective consciousness and objective conditions. As he explained in *Technics*, Geddes held that "every form of life . . . is marked not merely by adjustment to the environment, but by insurgence against the environment." It followed, then, that an organism was "both the victim of fate and the master of destiny: it lives no less by domination than by acceptance." In human life, "this insurgence reaches its apex," because aesthetic experience and historical knowledge allow men and women to glimpse the limitations of their given surroundings and, on occasion, transcend them.[9] Mumford received the same message from both Geddes and the *Seven Arts*. The highest achievements of "personality" were possible only through sustained efforts at shaping the public world and, in so doing, making both that world and oneself more human, more fully "personal."

The need to create the conditions for insurgent personality compelled Mumford to articulate a political position in the 1920s that still resists easy characterization. Despite the publicity surrounding his curt dismissal of "the pragmatic acquiescence" in *The Golden Day* (1926)—and his subsequent debate with John Dewey in *The New Republic*—Mumford was not as far from Dewey's pragmatism as he and others (including Dewey) may have believed. In his arguments for cultural renewal, Mumford was not merely recycling the Romantic critique of utilitarianism, whatever his indebtedness to the English Romantics, from William Blake to William Morris. Nor was Dewey a latter-day positivist, oblivious to the cultural concerns that motivated Mumford. What both men missed in their heated exchanges during the 1920s was their convergence on the importance of symbolic language and communications in providing a cultural foundation for a participatory politics.[10] Mumford's position, like that of Bourne, Brooks, Frank, and Stearns before him, is best seen as a highly subjectivist variant of pragmatism that drew on Romanticism as a corrective to perceived weaknesses in Dewey's thought.

Mumford owed more to Dewey than he usually acknowledged. Like Dewey, he argued that cultural life needed to be grounded in "experience"—the point of convergence between human consciousness and the environment, and the fertile ground of real personal growth. Dewey's philosophy of mind in conscious interaction with society directly paralleled Mumford's own conception of personality developing through experience. Moreover, Mumford shared Dewey's interest in renewing the democratic ideal of a free public sphere based on a shared culture of critical inquiry, which is what both men meant when they spoke of the promise of science or scientific method in recreating a democratic community life. Finally, Mumford found in pragmatism and in the Romantic critique of capitalism a common veneration of the craftsman as the apogee of realized selfhood. According to Dewey and Morris, craftsmanship transcended the industrial division of theory and practice by giving individuals the fruits of historical experience; it allowed the self to be crafted in interaction with the physical and cultural worlds. The culture of craftsmanship provided a symbolic language and a practice in which personality could engage its environment, without succumbing to its premises.

Mumford did differ with Dewey, and with mainstream pragmatism, in his hostility to the state as an agency of scientific reform and in his insistence that a new politics first required a prolonged attention to aesthetic and moral values. In his earliest essays for *The Dial* after World War I, Mumford targeted the state as a threat to culture and values. "Civil life means association," he wrote in 1919, "with the family, the trade union, the grange, the chamber of commerce, the professional institute, the church, the theater, and the forum intermediating between the life of the individual and his life as the member of a political (military) state."[11] Such mediating institutions provided the context for a culture of personality, and as Mumford's thinking developed in the 1920s, he tried to distinguish his "culturalist" conception of community from the progressive ideal of state-sponsored social unity. The politics of "culturism" was "rooted in the integrity of the local community," he argued, "in its common *shul*" and other local organs of civic life, not in the nation-state.[12] By 1930, Mumford had become even more resolute in this regard. "As an expression of the will to power, the state is an enemy of culture," he declared.[13] The centralized state had emerged victorious during World War I because bureaucratic means of organization, pioneered in the factory and the corporation, had already loosened the cultural bonds that held together local communities.

Mumford's hostility to the state as an agency to reform was always a submerged element in his debates with Dewey and other progressives over the role of culture in a democratic politics. Fearful that Dewey's work displayed a tendency to overlook the subjective dimensions of experience, Mumford sought to ground a new politics of democratic community in a shared set of aesthetic practices and symbols and in a common understanding of moral values. In Mumford's view, aesthetic experience and values stood at the crossroads of public life and private conduct, creating a cultural "second nature" that would sustain the critical capacities of individuals in search of personality and a revitalized community life. They were the resources needed in the "insurgence" of the human organism against its conditions, and in the rebuilding of regional cultures as alternatives to the nation-state. Like the *Seven Arts* critics, Mumford challenged the pragmatists to broaden their conception of experience to acknowledged the significance of art and values in fostering shared bonds of community and a consciously informed social practice.

By the mid-1920s, then, Mumford had already arrived at the point of departure for his mature work and at an intellectual position best considered as an aestheticist pragmatism. Convinced of the need to foster personality through a collective project of cultural renewal, Mumford sought alternatives to the bureaucratic structures of authority and association in modern industry and the wartime state. The language of symbolic interaction provided exactly such an alternative, he believed; it deepened the potential for personal experience as it enriched a democratic community life. Much of Mumford's earliest writing on these themes seemed hardly political, but questions of community and cultural democracy were never far from his mind as he began his career as a critic of American architecture, literature, and culture. In the late 1920s and early 1930s, Mumford turned to a more explicitly political formulation of his views on culture, personality, and community, a shift in emphasis that became fully apparent with the publication of *Technics and Civilization* in 1934. With this turn to politics and sociology, Mumford revealed both the potential and the limitations of his "culturism" as a critique of modern culture.

AGAINST AHAB: MUMFORD'S CULTURAL ETHIC

"I have never been a Liberal," Mumford wrote in a 1930 statement of "What I Believe" for *The Forum*, but he added that "if I cannot call myself a revolutionist now, it is not because the current programs for change seem to me to go too far: the reason is rather because they are superficial and do not go far enough."[14] Geddes's organicism had left Mumford ill-disposed toward either classical liberalism or Marxism, with their emphasis on political conflict, competition, and struggles over rights. Instead, Mumford elaborated on the neorepublican and anarchist radicalism of Henry George, Ebeneezer Howard, Peter Kropotkin, and Thorstein Veblen, which confirmed his hostility to the nation-state and reinforced Geddes's biological view of community as a healthy organism. Mumford's communitarian politics shared with the radicalism of these turn-of-the-century thinkers a defense of a balanced, organic community of producers against the invasive forces of speculation, monopoly, and war. In this regard, Mumford's politics were more populist than socialist. Following George's lead, Mumford tended to attack finance capitalism as a parasitic force that dissolved mutualistic social bonds and promoted feverish commercial expansion at the expense of any sense of the common good.

The merits of this populist political tradition, in Mumford's eyes, lay in its emphasis on cultural issues and on the importance of local community as a counter to state power—questions ignored by most progressives and socialists. But the very advantages of a populist defense of producers' commonwealth were also the causes for its most serious limitations as a radical politics of personality and community. These limitations were rarely acknowledged or confronted openly in Mumford's work, even as he tried to adapt this radical tradition to the challenge of interpreting and criticizing an advanced industrial culture. Yet they posed challenges to his own critical project that clearly influenced his thinking in this period. If local communities had in fact been "invaded" and colonized by metropolitan cultures, and their institutions replaced by those of the wartime state and the national market, then the task of self-renewal and cultural reconstruction had to confront questions of power and conflict. Mumford's ideal of a communitarian culture had to come to terms with those institutional arrangements that prevented self-fulfillment and deformed public dialogue. This, in turn, required a project that fortified the critical self—the oppositional self—as an adversary of its surroundings, even as it sought reconciliation with others in a new community. Moreover, it required formulating a culture of opposition that fostered the "organic" values of "wholeness" and "equilibrium" that dominated Mumford's Geddesian political vocabulary, without embracing the undemocratic, "mechanical" unity that had been constructed on the ruins of a civic culture. The challenges facing Mumford as he sought to reconstruct a radical communitarian politics, then, were twofold: the ideal of the cultural self had to be salvaged from the adjustment of the acculturated self to its surroundings; and the promise of community had to be predicated on a realistic appraisal of the threats to its attainment posed by modern social relations.

In his writings from 1929 and 1930, Mumford confronted these challenges by addressing the ethical issues at stake in a communitarian politics of personality. Mumford's biography of Herman Melville, his statement of belief in *The Forum*, and a contemporary polemic against the conservative New Humanism of Irving Babbitt and Paul Elmer More articulated the need for moral reconstruction as the first step toward the renewal of community life. If, as Alan Trachtenberg has argued, Mumford's early politics rested on "a social aesthetics—a grounding of social criticism upon an aesthetic premise"—then so too did his ethics.[15] Mumford looked to the language of symbolic form to provide a successor to prophetic religion as a resource for the critical "personality" and as a common ground for a democratic politics.

Mumford's *Herman Melville* (1929) may be unreliable as biography, but its significance lies in its effort to view Melville's struggle with a hostile culture, and with his own despair, as a usable past for a twentieth-century culture of personality. In Melville's Captain Ahab, Mumford recognized both the Promethean drive of a technological society and the destructive impulses at work in every person's "insurgence" against his or her given state. The very gifts that saved human beings from animal existence beckoned with the promise of limitlessness: of freedom from all inherited restraints and traditions, and of personal reconciliation with an ideal world. The result, the cult of "meaningless force," of the great white whale, drove Ahab to his death and propelled industrial societies to an unending quest for limitless power.[16] It was Melville's accomplishment in his later work—*Clarel* and *Billy Budd*—to find in culture a means of maintaining a tension between his own aspirations to transcendence and acceptance of his limitations. The doubled nature of human life as both creature and creator of its environment made culture the proving-ground for human aspirations and the realm where men and women were compelled to recognize their own mortality. In Mumford's cultural ethics, the creation of forms and symbols provided a stern but not despairing lesson in moral realism. The legacy of culture was, indeed, restraining and, to the Promethean mind, a hindrance to the realization of the human will. Yet only such restraints made possible the transcendence of human limits on terms other than Ahab's: they transmuted the will-to-power into forms, values, and the other durable artifacts of a common culture. "Man's defence lies within himself," Mumford wrote, "not within the narrow, isolated ego, which may be overwhelmed, but in that self which we share with our fellows and which assures us that, whatever happens to our carcasses and hides, good men will remain, so to carry on the work, to foster and protect the things we have recognized as excellent."[17]

By choosing Melville as his source for a personal ethics, as opposed to Emerson or Whitman (the culture heroes of choice for his friends Brooks and Frank), Mumford made clear the importance of a recognition of human limits, of "the tragic sense of life," for his own vision of community. Melville's life and work brought Mumford face to face with the problems of evil, tragedy, and the inescapable sense of loss that plagued Melville as he confronted an indifferent world. Mumford's encounter with Melville left him convinced of the moral shabbiness of American liberalism, and of the need to find a secular equivalent to the insights into human nature once provided by religion. As he argued in 1930, in "What I Believe" and "Towards an Organic Humanism," those committed to renewing democratic community required an ethical middle ground between acquiescence and the pursuit of personal boundlessness that fueled the technological will-to-power. "If a religion be that which gives one a sense of the things that are worth dying for, this community with all life, this sense of a central purpose in oneself, inextricably bound up with the nature of things, even those accidents and brutal mischances that are so hard to assimilate—this faith may be called a religion."[18]

That religion, for Mumford, was a religion of culture, but culture conceived as an inherently dynamic, self-critical, and self-limiting form of human endeavor. Mumford's religion acknowledged that there would always be friction between individuals and their community; far from seeking to erase such conflict, radicals should seek to exploit it as a spur to cultural creativity. "The real problem of life," he wrote, "both for men and societies, is to keep the organism and the environment, the inner world and the outer, the personality and its creative sources, in the state of tension wherein growth and renewal may continually take place."[19] By maintaining personality in a state of tension with its environment, culture could provide individuals with the moral resolve to resist accommodation and the ability to enjoy the fruits of limited victory.

Mumford's moral insights into the connection between the Promethean promise of technology and the cultural crisis of the boundless self became the major theme of his work after World War II. They played a smaller role, however, in *Technics and Civilization*, the first volume of his "Renewal of Life" series. There, as in his other major work of the 1930s, *The Culture of Cities*, Mumford located the origins of modern technology in the collapse of the symbolic universe of medieval Christianity, but he failed to follow up on this observation in his neotechnic program of alternatives. Writing of the seventeenth century, he explained how technology filled a spiritual absence left by the disintegration of Catholic metaphysics. In an "empty, denuded world," bereft of familiar cultural landmarks, "the invention of machines became a duty. By renouncing a large part of his humanity, a man could achieve godhood: he dawned on this second chaos and created the machine in his image: the image of power, but power ripped loose from his flesh and isolated from his humanity."[20] This indictment of the scientific contempt for a value-laden, cultural world, might have led Mumford to develop his cultural ethics into a very different alternative to paleotechnic technology from that which emerged in the final chapters of *Technics*. Instead, the promising argument for moral renewal as a foundation for a new culture that had inspired the Melville biography and his 1930 essays now took a back seat to an ambiguous attempt to create personality and community within the context of a technological culture of organicism. "This development of value within the machine complex itself," as Mumford called his portrait of a neotechnic culture, relinquished the tension between personality and its environment that was critical to his cultural religion.[21] By attempting to give a modern, scientific basis to communitarian politics, Mumford had come to substitute technological *Gemeinschaft* for his original vision of a democratic community.

THE CAMERA EYE: NEOTECHNICS AND
THE OBJECTIVE PERSONALITY

Mumford's decision to seek organic values "within the machine complex itself" reflected not only his indebtedness to Geddes's idea of neotechnic synthesis, but his own attempt to overcome the elegiac tone of some of his early work—particularly *The Golden Day*—which had drawn fire from Mumford's friend Waldo Frank, as well as from John Dewey. In a review of *The Golden Day*, Frank complained of the "wistful and vague" nature of the book's conclusion. Mumford was in "in love with the gesture, the dream, the childhood faery of our past: yet he rejects the *body*—our present interim of the Machine and of the romanticisms of the Machine—whereby alone this promise from our past may be organized into a living future." Anticipating his own argument for cultural synthesis in *The Rediscovery of America* (1929), Frank held that "future spiritual action must rise organically from the facts of our hideous present," including the facts of modern industrialism.[22] For Frank, the example of Alfred Stieglitz's life and photography showed that it was possible for an artistic prophet to promote cultural wholeness by mastering industrial technology. In correspondence, Mumford assured Frank that he agreed that an organic culture must accept the benefits of "the Machine" in order to transcend its sterilities. This, he explained to Frank, had been the basis of his critical endorsement of architectural Modernism, in which he sought to move beyond the architects of the International Style by reintegrating humanistic values with the efficiency and crisp aesthetics of industrialism.[23] A similar perspective on industrial culture had informed much of his theory of the "fourth migration" for the Regional Planning Association of America during the 1920s, in which electricity, the automobile, and the radio would permit a return to nature by way of modern technology.[24] But it was only in the early 1930s that Mumford elaborated on the cultural implications of such a project by insisting that mechanization and a technical worldview were irreversible gains and the resources for a postindustrial organic synthesis.

By accepting the technical disavowal of religious and aesthetic experience as the first step to a new cultural synthesis, Mumford essentially jettisoned the morally grounded communitarianism of his work from the late 1920s. "In Our Stars: The World Fifty Years from Now," a 1932 sequel to "What I Believe" for *The Forum*, registered the shift in emphasis in Mumford's thinking. Though he mentioned the presence of "humane and well-balanced personalities" populating his 1982 utopia, the overwhelming focus of Mumford's essay was on new techniques and new technologies—buildings built as "bubbles of glass"; "the utilization of the merchant marine for education"; solar energy; scientific agriculture; and "selective mating"—all designed to overhaul the "slums of thought" that needed to be razed along with ghetto neighborhoods. Mumford acknowledged that citizens of this world would have to cultivate "a whole new series of initiatives in the culture of the personality itself," including the "counter-balancing forces" of "communal and personal discipline," in order to prevent their mechanized utopia from becoming "a well-drilled beehive," but even this qualification revealed how much ground had been lost since his *Forum* piece two years earlier.[25] In Mumford's previous formulations of a communitarian politics, it was exactly such "initiatives in the culture of the personality" that took center stage in his analysis, and that dictated both the need to overcome a technocratic civilization and the construction of a more humane alternative. Now, if such initiatives played any significant part in Mumford's work in the mid-1930s, it was as an ambiguous humanistic backdrop to more pressing technical concerns—or worse, as a set of "counter-balancing forces" that checked the excesses of an organicist technology. By 1937, Mumford was fully in step with the progressive consensus on the need to extend "the socialized disciplines of the factory, the laboratory, the accounting office, and the administrative bureau" to the organization of "the community as a whole."[26] Writing in a foreword to a symposium on social planning, Mumford's only real dissent from the technocratic implications of such an approach lay in his insistence that philosophers, teachers, and sociologists join economists and engineers in forming "new human values," and that their plans reflect some wider democratic ferment in culture and values.[27] What had begun as revolution in art and "values" had come of age in the 1930s as a program to supplement social planning by technicians with cultural planning by humanistic professionals.

Technics and Civilization, published in 1934, caught Mumford in midcourse between his moral communitarianism and his enthusiasm for a postindustrial cultural synthesis.[28] Penetrating insights into the mechanization of thought in the paleotechnic age coexist in that text with neotechnic proposals that seem only to reproduce such developments on a broader scale. Prescient warnings against the dangers of technological determinism prepare the way for organicist solutions founded on the assumption that "the machine is a communist" that fosters collectivist modes of thought.[29] Morrisite indictments of the capitalist division of labor set the stage for praising the managerial innovations of Frederick Winslow Taylor and Elton Mayo. Despite Mumford's belief that the cult of mechanical power derived from the breaking of cultural restraints on humans' self-destructive impulses, the conclusion of *Technics* celebrates technology for wiping the slate clean of unnecessary cultural clutter and promoting a functionalist aesthetic of "precision, calculation, flawlessness, simplicity, economy."[30] For all the side-glances to the need to cultivate personality, it was the "objective" personality type that Mumford identified as the place where true personal development must begin. "A modulation of emphasis, a matter-of-factness, a reasonableness, a quiet assurance of a neutral realm in which the most obdurate differences can be understood, if not composed, is a mark of the emerging personality."[31] And as befit an objective personality, there now existed an "objective" human environment, which Mumford defended as a site of future cultural renewal. "The concept of a neutral world," Mumford explained, "untouched by man's efforts, indifferent to his activities, obdurate to his wish and supplication, is one of the great triumphs of man's imagination, and in itself represents a fresh human value."[32] In a Hegelian twist, the great white whale of untamed, unacculturated power that haunted Melville returned in *Technics* as the bearer of cultural renewal, community, and personality.

Mumford's confusion about the relationship between cultural renewal and modern, neotechnic, developments in science and industry reflects more than an optimism that later gave way, in the two-volume *Myth of the Machine*, to cultural pessimism. Nor does such confusion reveal only Mumford's indebtedness to Geddes's chronology of civilization, Frank Lloyd Wright's efforts to reconcile the Ruskin-Morris tradition with a machine aesthetic, and Thorstein Veblen's dichotomy between an atavistic capitalism and "an instinct of workmanship," however much these predecessors contributed to Mumford's thinking. The tensions and contradictions running through *Technics* are indicative, instead, of much deeper problems in the very concepts of personality and community that underlie Mumford's work in this period.

Such problems are evident, above all, in those moments in *Technics* in which Mumford directly addresses the intersection of technology and personality in the neotechnic era. The psychological portraits of such archetypal figures as the hunter and the miner in the early chapters of the book advanced Mumford's claim about the interdependence of technical, cultural, and psychic change, and he was eager to note similar processes at work in his own time. For Mumford, the displacement of the mirror by the camera as the central medium of self-presentation marked a turning-point in human consciousness that accorded with his own theory of an emerging culture of organicism. The invention of the mirror had literally reflected—and, through reflection, reinforced—the emergence of an introspective psychology, Mumford held; the intertwining of bourgeois individualism and its polished image was nowhere more evident than in the work of the seventeenth-century Dutch portrait painters. The psychology of self-reflection depended on a technology of reflection that allowed a Rembrandt or a Hals to peer into his own image in search of something stable in a world in which outer certainties were dissolving. The result was less reassuring than Mumford believed in *Technics*: fascination with the isolated self revealed the self's reliance on the very mirrors used to keep it in focus, and hence prompted Baroque artists to document its fragmentation.

In the twentieth century, however, it was the camera that was busy laying waste to the bourgeois psychology of self-reflection and introspection. Like his contemporaries Bertolt Brecht and Walter Benjamin, Mumford believed that the medium of photography was the harbinger of a new social psychology, in which individuals viewed themselves from all three dimensions—as in Cubist painting—and perceived the self as a creature of its environment. "The change is from an introspective to a behaviorist psychology, from the fulsome sorrows of Werther to the impassive public mask of an Ernest Hemingway," Mumford wrote. The "constant sense of a public world" that intervenes in Hemingway's fiction and causes its protagonist to imagine "himself as a public character, *being watched*," testified to the camera's success at opening up the self to public inspection. "The change is significant: not self-examination but self-exposure: not tortured confession but easy open candor: not the proud soul wrapped in his cloak, pacing the lonely beach at midnight, but the matter-of-fact soul, naked, exposed to the sun on the beach at noonday, one of a crowd of naked people."[33] Such an interpenetration of personality and its community was even more evident in the motion picture, which not only promoted a Bergsonian consciousness of time as a constant process of overlapping relations, but also forced upon the audience a relativistic understanding of its own relation to artistic subject matter. "Without any conscious notion of its destination, the motion picture presents us with a world of interpenetrating, counter-influencing organisms: and it enables us to think about that world in a greater degree of concreteness."[34]

Such passages, with their intuitions of the profound psychological implications of technical innovations, are reminders of Mumford's genius as an interpreter of cultural change, but they also raise serious questions about his understanding of personality as an interactive form of selfhood and of community as an organic social group. In his positive view of the photographic self, Mumford approached the very position he had sought to avoid in his explorations of personality in the 1920s. Hemingway's self-conscious characters are, in Mumford's description, self-less: they open themselves up to the camera so as to divest themselves of interiority and privacy. They exemplify an objective personality type insofar as they are open to all points of view, and are given neither to internal conflicts nor to opposition to their culture. Far from fostering an insurgent, transformative personality, Mumford's psychology of the camera reconstitutes the self as a creature of its environment, lost in the crowd of sunbathers on a summer holiday. With Brecht and Benjamin, Mumford was oblivious to the authoritarian and conformist potential of a culture of photographic publicity, in which the camera functions as an instrument of self-surveillance and as a check against self-absorption. Nor did Mumford consider the possibility that the relativism promoted by the experience of viewing films might produce, not the "whole," relational self set firmly in its surroundings, but the fragmented psychology of dissonant, incommensurate images that now pervades postmodernist art. In this regard, the organic community Mumford proposed was one in which there remained little room for insurgence and few possibilities for the critical function of personality. As in so many other aspects of his argument in *Technics*, Mumford embraced a technological solution to the crisis of bourgeois individualism, which—as much of his own work suggested—required a deeper resolution at the level of culture, ethics, and politics.

BEYOND MUMFORD: CULTURAL RENEWAL AS POLITICS

In a penetrating review of *Technics* for the journal *Christendom*, Reinhold Niebuhr pointed to two major faults in Mumford's analysis and program for renewal. Niebuhr held that Mumford's distinction between "the coal and iron period of civilization and the more recent 'electricity-and-alloy' complex" was adequate in terms of technology, but added that "Mr. Mumford is writing more than a history of technics."[35] Despite the revival of organic forms in industrial design, Niebuhr found little reason to believe that the class divisions and dehumanizing effects of paleotechnic civilization were in any way lessened in an electrochemical age. More significant, though, was the book's weakness on religion. "Science did indeed 'widen the domain of the symbol,' " as Mumford argued, "but unfortunately it frequently destroyed the permanent myth with the primitive myth and substituted some naive credulity for a majestic faith." Niebuhr recognized a kindred spirit at work in Mumford's praise for medieval culture and "the organic aspects of life," but he found baffling his dismissal of myth and other forms of prescientific knowledge.[36] Without a greater sensitivity to religious culture, *Technics* verged on becoming but one more example of the "naive" religion of progress.

Niebuhr's critique reflected his own understanding of political and moral realism. The first element of Niebuhr's criticism, which drew on his recognition of the inescapability of political conflict, found echoes during the 1930s and 1940s in the reactions to Mumford's work by such secular leftists as V. F. Calverton, Mike Gold, Meyer Schapiro, Sidney Hook, and James T. Farrell, all of whom savaged Mumford's "evolutionary" radicalism and his inattention to questions of class and social tensions.[37] These critics may have retreated to easy Marxist cliches in their attacks, but they did recognize the aversion to any serious analysis of power relations and conflict in Mumford's communitarianism. In *Technics*, Mumford's holistic approach to culture blinded him to the institutional impediments to the creation of a democratic community life. "Paleotechnic ideals still largely dominate the industry and the politics of the Western World," Mumford acknowledged, but the "class struggles" and "national struggles" that he cited as evidence of such backwardness suggested that such conflicts were irrelevant to the construction of a new culture.[38] Mumford's hostility to statist politics translated in *Technics* to an avoidance of any politics—of any conflict over power, that is—that went beyond humanistic education and propagation of new neotechnic advances. The danger of Mumford's "culturist" radicalism, then, lay in its confusion of cultural form with political function. The evidence of holistic symbols in modern culture, and the new interest among managers and technicians in social science, did not necessarily promise more democratic social relations. In fact, the very opposite trend may have been at work during the second industrial revolution: namely, the transference of programs of technical control of production to the producers themselves.[39] Without the transformation in values upheld in Mumford's early work, and a corresponding break with industrial power relations, the adoption of a holistic approach to culture would be more likely to foster an authoritarian system of bureaucratic controls than it would a democratic politics of community.

Even as Mumford later soured on the promise of "neotechnic" industry, he still held firm to a communitarian politics that obscured conflicts over power in modern society. In the 1940s and 1950s, Mumford's work took up the example of the withdrawal of early Christians from Roman civilization as a model for twentieth-century communitarians in a decadent industrial culture.[40] That theme of cultural withdrawal remained a dominant motif in subsequent writings. In 1970, *The Pentagon of Power* endorsed a politics of retreat that sought "not to capture the citadel of power, but to withdraw from it and quietly paralyze it." Only such initiatives, Mumford believed, would "restore power and confident authority to its proper source: the human personality and the small face-to-face community."[41] Whether as neotechnic organicism or as decentralist radicalism, Mumford's communitarianism could never envision a politics of sustained conflict or engagement with the dominant institutions of modern politics. Community could take shape on the margins of power, or come into full bloom under the electric lamps of neotechnic technology, but not in a prolonged contest for power.

Not until the 1940s did Mumford grasp the full implications for his own work of Niebuhr's moral realism, with its insistence on an Augustinian psychology of humans' divided nature. Yet Niebuhr was correct to note a similar sensibility in parts of *Technics*, although these were only echoes of the ethical explorations of personality in Mumford's previous writings. There were certainly points of convergence between Mumford's secular religion of culture, as outlined in *Herman Melville* and his essays from 1930, and Niebuhr's realist appraisal of the inherent conflict between human aspirations and limitations. But Mumford's positive view of culture as a means of confronting that conflict, and of making it a way to enhance lived experience, left him less attentive than Niebuhr to the religious dimensions of a critical ethics. With his faith in symbolic language, Mumford was in the end closer to such cultural prophets as Erich Fromm or Carl Jung than he was to thinkers like Niebuhr or Freud, despite his deepening appreciation in the 1940s of their insights into the fissures within the human psyche.[42] To Niebuhr, faith was a way of allowing individuals to speak truth to culture; it preserved the independent, critical self from the blandishments of a therapeutic ethos. Mumford had argued that his ideal of a common culture was capable of generating its own tensions, and that the realization of personality required the insurgence of the self against culture, even as it forged the self through aesthetic experience. But in *Technics*, Mumford let those tensions slacken: neotechnic community absorbed the self, then remade it in its own image. Instead of deepening the critical stance of his cultural religion, Mumford lashed out at "the rubbish of earlier cultures," including "superstitious forms of religion" that kept the masses "in a state of emotional tutelage to the very forces that were exploiting them."[43]

The tragedy of this dismissal of traditional religious ethics was that Mumford's previous works laid the foundation for a far more compelling alternative to technocratic culture than that outlined in *Technics*. It was not until *The Pentagon of Power* that the full implications of his early treatment of ethics for a critique of technology became apparent. There, Mumford looked to culture as a force for restraining the dual reign of "the automation and the id," whose interdependence he had first glimpsed through Melville's eyes.[44] Mumford's later work suggests that community must grow out of a moral consensus that recognizes the conflicts within the self, and that adopts an ethic of containment as an alternative to the technological culture of boundlessness.

"In taking an organic model," Mumford wrote in 1970, "one must renounce the paranoid claims and foolish hopes of the Power Complex, and accept finiteness, limitation, incompleteness, uncertainty, and eventual death as necessary attributes of life—and more than this, as the condition for achieving wholeness, autonomy, and creativity."[45] But the muddled notions of wholeness and community in Mumford's *Technics* point to the need for an even more resolute acceptance of finitude than Mumford advocated, one that acknowledges the limitations of personality and community themselves. As responses to the crisis of bourgeois individualism, theories of the "relational" self and of "communities of memory" still beckon with the promise of rootedness, nurturance, and a mutualistic sense of connection with and responsibility toward others.[46] But, as *Technics* demonstrates, the invocation of such values should not be confused with their realization, which may, in fact, require an initial determination to foster strong individuals and a realistic acceptance of conflict. Whatever the virtues of communitarianism as a democratic alternative to liberalism and Marxism, it cannot reject out of hand the emphasis of those traditions on a contested public sphere and their suspicion of claims to organic social unity.[47]

In contrast to contemporary advocates of communitarian democracy, Mumford looked in the 1920s and 1930s to the realm of culture—and particularly to the dynamics of symbolic language—as the source of political renewal. Mumford's efforts to restore the rich fabric of aesthetic experience and moral judgment rent by the culture of industrialism make his work of vital importance to contemporary debates about American public culture. According to Mumford, a public culture must be *cultural*, and not narrowly political: it must engage personalities in the creation of cultural form, as well as in the open-air debates of local democracy. A language of public dialogue, in Mumford's view, would have to invigorate art, music, architecture, and craftsmanship, in addition to the terms of political discourse. Here, then, Mumford's communitarianism still has a great deal to teach his successors about the cultural dimensions of civic renewal.

So too does Mumford's own struggle with the slippery implications of community for a new ethics and a new politics. If Mumford's different approaches to the problem of community in the 1920s, 1930s, and after offer anything to contemporary communitarians, it lies in their earnest attempts at reconciling an organicist social ideal with concrete cultural practice. *Technics and Civilization* offers one road to such a reconciliation, *Herman Melville* and *The Pentagon of Power* another. Admiration for Mumford's insights into the predicament of personality in modern culture should not blind us to the shortcomings of many of his own gestures toward a communitarian alternative, in particular his aversion to the political responsibilities of a "culturist" radicalism. The recognition that the crisis of American politics is symptomatic of a profound cultural crisis ought not to foster illusions that culture alone will produce new communities. Likewise, the understanding that the fully consummated self is the cultural self, rooted in communal practices, does not necessarily entail the elimination of boundaries between the self and community. Paradoxically, a recognition of the limits of community may best serve the cause of community; a renewed appreciation of the antagonism between "personality and its creative sources" may hold out the greatest promise of a socially grounded self. Such a view requires a resolve to live with conflicts usually blunted by the mutualistic ethos of community—to maintain that cultural "state of tension," as Mumford put it, "wherein growth and renewal may continually take place."[48]

NOTES

1. Lewis Mumford to Van Wyck Brooks, July 22, 1925, in Van Wyck Brooks, *The Van Wyck Brooks Lewis Mumford Letters: The Record of a Literary Friendship, 1921–1963*, ed. Robert E. Spiller (New York: E. P. Dutton, 1970), 30.

2. Alasdair MacIntyre, *After Virtue: A Study in Moral Theory*, 2nd ed. (South Bend, Ind.: University of Notre Dame Press, 1984), 34.

3. Robert Bellah, et al., *Habits of the Heart: Individualism and Commitment in American Life* (Berkeley: University of California Press, 1985), 218.

4. Lewis Mumford, "The Emergence of a Past," *New Republic* 45 (November 25, 1925): 19.

5. Lewis Mumford, *Technics and Civilization* (New York: Harcourt, Brace, & World, 1962), 433.

6. See Warren Susman, " 'Personality' and the Making of Twentieth-Century Culture,'' in *Culture as History: The Transformation of American Society in the Twentieth Century*, ed. Warren Susman (New York: Pantheon, 1984), 271–85; and T. Jackson Lears, "From Salvation to Self-Realization: Advertising and the Therapeutic Roots of the Consumer Culture, 1880–1930,'' in *The Culture of Consumption: Critical Essays in American History 1880–1980*, ed. Richard Wightman Fox and T. Jackson Lears (New York: Pantheon, 1983), 1–38.

7. For a fuller discussion of this issue, see Casey Nelson Blake, *Beloved Community: The Cultural Criticism of Randolph Bourne, Van Wyck Brooks, Waldo Frank, and Lewis Mumford* (Chapel Hill: University of North Carolina Press, 1990), and "The Young Intellectuals and the Culture of Personality,'' *American Literary History* 1, no. 3 (Fall 1989): 510–34.

8. Randolph Bourne, "Trans-National America,'' in *The Radical Will: Randolph Bourne Selected Writings, 1911–1918*, ed. Olaf Hansen (New York: Urizen, 1977), 264.

9. Mumford, *Technics*, 319.

10. See, for example, Dewey's argument in *The Public and its Problems* (1927) that "communication can alone create a great community,'' an idea fully compatible with Mumford's position in the 1920s. "Our Babel is not one of tongues but of the signs and symbols without which shared experience is impossible.'' John Dewey, *The Public and its Problems* (Chicago: Swallow Press, 1954), 142. See also Robert Westbrook, "Lewis Mumford, John Dewey, and the 'Pragmatic Acquiescence,' '' in *Lewis Mumford, Public Intellectual*, ed. Thomas P. Hughes and Agatha C. Hughes (New York: Oxford University Press, 1990), 301–22, which notes the convergence of Mumford's and Dewey's thinking in the 1920s and 1930s.

11. Lewis Mumford, "Patriotism and its Consequences,'' *Dial* 66 (April 19, 1919): 406.

12. Lewis Mumford, "A Search for the True Community,'' in *The Menorah Treasury: Harvest of Half a Century*, ed. Leo W. Schwartz (Philadelphia: The Jewish Publication Society of America, 1964), 863.

13. Lewis Mumford, "What I Believe,'' *Forum* 84 (November 1930): 264.

14. Ibid, 263.

15. Alan Trachtenberg, "Mumford in the Twenties: The Historian as Artist,'' *Salmagundi* 49 (Summer 1980): 34.

16. Lewis Mumford, *Herman Melville* (New York: The Literary Life, 1929), 185.

17. Ibid., 186–87.

18. Mumford, "What I Believe,'' 268.

19. Lewis Mumford, "Toward an Organic Humanism,'' in *The Critique of Humanism: A Symposium*, ed. C. Hartley Grattan (New York: Brewer and Warren, 1930), 358–59.

20. Lewis Mumford, *Technics*, 51.

21. Ibid., 55.

22. Waldo Frank, "Dusk and Dawn,'' in Frank, *In the American Jungle, 1925–1936* (New York: Farrar and Rinehart, 1937), 177.

23. See Lewis Mumford to Waldo Frank, March 13, 1927, Waldo Frank Papers, Department of Special Collections, Van Pelt Library, University of Pennsylvania. See also Mumford's letter to Alfred Stieglitz, July 20, 1933, Alfred Stieglitz Papers, Beinecke Library, Yale University, in which Mumford makes a similar case for reconstructing an organic culture within the confines of modern technology and explicitly cites Stieglitz, among others, as one of the pioneers of such a culture.

24. See Carl Susman, ed., *Planning the Fourth Migration: The Neglected Vision of the Regional Planning Association of America* (Cambridge, Mass.: MIT Press, 1976).

25. Lewis Mumford, "In Our Stars: The World Fifty Years from Now,'' *Forum* 88 (December 1932): 341, 342.

26. Lewis Mumford, Foreword to *Planned Society Yesterday, Today, Tomorrow: A Symposium by Thirty-Five Economists, Sociologists, and Statesmen*, ed. Findlay MacKenzie (New York: Prentice-Hall, 1937), v.

27. Ibid., ix.

28. I have addressed the shortcomings of *Technics* in Blake, *Beloved Community*, 283–86, and "Lewis Mumford: Values Over Technique," *Democracy* 3 (Spring 1983): 125–37.

29. Mumford, *Technics*, 354.

30. Ibid., 351.

31. Ibid., 362.

32. Ibid., 361.

33. Ibid., 243–44.

34. Ibid., 343.

35. Reinhold Niebuhr, "Our Machine Made Culture," *Christendom* 1 (Autumn 1935): 187.

36. Ibid., 189.

37. See Mumford's exchange with V. Calverton, "A Challenge to American Intellectuals," *Modern Quarterly* 5 (Winter 1930–31): 407–21; Mike Gold to Lewis Mumford, n.d. [1934], Lewis Mumford Papers, Department of Special Collections, Van Pelt Library, University of Pennsylvania; Meyer Schapiro, "Looking Forward to Looking Backward," *Partisan Review* 5 (July 1938): 12–24; Sidney Hook, "Metaphysics, War, and Intellectuals," *Menorah Journal* 28 (August 1940): 327–37; and James T. Farrell, "The Faith of Lewis Mumford," in James T. Farrell, *The League of Frightened Philistines and Other Papers* (New York: Vanguard Press, 1945), 106–31.

38. Mumford, *Technics*, 213.

39. See David F. Noble, *America by Design: Science, Technology, and the Rise of Corporate Capitalism* (New York: Alfred A. Knopf, 1979).

40. For one example for this argument, see Lewis Mumford, *The Conduct of Life* (New York: Harcourt, Brace, 1951), 244–92. Note that MacIntyre also calls on the example of the early Christians in the closing lines of *After Virtue*, 263: "What matters at this stage is the construction of local forms of community within which civility and the intellectual and moral life can be sustained through the new dark ages which are already upon us. . . . We are waiting not for a Godot, but for another—doubtless very different—St. Benedict."

41. Lewis Mumford, *The Myth of the Machine, Vol. 2: The Pentagon of Power* (New York: Harcourt, Brace, Jovanovich, 1970), 408.

42. See Richard Wightman Fox, "Tragedy, Responsibility, and the American Intellectual, 1925–1950," in *Lewis Mumford: Public Intellectual*, ed. Thomas P. Hughes and Agatha C. Hughes, (New York: Oxford University Press, 1990), for further discussion of the differences between Mumford and Niebuhr.

43. Mumford, *Technics*, 408–9.

44. Mumford, *Pentagon*, 350.

45. Ibid., 394–95.

46. For examples of contemporary appeals to replace individualism with a "relational self," see Bellah et al., *Habits of the Heart*; MacIntyre, *After Virtue*; Carol Gilligan, *In a Different Voice: Psychological Theory and Women's Development* (Cambridge, Mass.: Harvard University Press, 1982); and Thomas C. Heller et al., *Reconstructing Individualism: Autonomy, Individuality, and the Self in Western Thought* (Stanford: Stanford University Press, 1986).

47. In this regard, see Jane J. Mansbridge, *Beyond Adversary Democracy*, rev. ed. (Chicago: University of Chicago Press, 1983), and Jeffrey Stout, "Liberal Society and the Language of Morals," *Soundings* 69 (Spring-Summer 1986): 32–59, both of which question whether communitarian democracy adequately resolves the deadlock of an "adversarial" politics.

48. Mumford, "Toward an Organic Humanism," 359.

Part II

Pragmatism, Positivism, and the Linguistic Turn

Introduction

David Depew

American philosophy was changing rapidly in the 1940s. Imprecisely referred to as the rise of "analytic philosophy," these changes were provoked by the migration of many first-rate minds from Germany and Central Europe following the rise of Nazism. Among other interesting and learned folk, this intellectual diaspora brought to America a number of prominent members and fellow travellers of the Vienna Circle of "logical positivists," notably Herbert Feigl, Hans Reichenbach, Rudolf Carnap, Gustav Bergmann, and Carl Hempel. Their influence was destined to be enormous.

In this first instance, these philosophers urged the discipline to liberate itself from the overly psychologistic cast that had characterized it throughout the nineteenth century. This could be achieved by taking what Bergmann called "the linguistic turn." On the surface, what Bergmann was commending was an innocent piece of methodological advice, according to which philosophers might hope to solve their traditional problems if they agreed to formulate these problems as problems about language.[1] But the linguistic turn was something more than a heuristic recommendation. Its most abiding achievement was its analysis of meaning in terms of "truth-conditions." Following the pioneering work of Gottlob Frege, Bertrand Russell, and Ludwig Wittgenstein, meaning was conceived as a property of whole sentences, rather than of individual words. The meaning of a sentence was then declared equivalent to the set of conditions under which it would be correct to assert, or more generally to utter, it. The truth-conditional account of meaning was best set out by the Polish logician Alfred Tarski, who eventually settled in Berkeley. The sentence "Snow is white," for example, is true. But it is true if and only if snow is in fact white. For these are its truth-conditions. The *meaning* of a sentence, moreover, is equivalent to its truth-conditions. All this may sound utterly trivial. But in spite of the simplicity of these claims, the truth-conditional analysis of meaning carries substantive philosophical freight. For one thing, truth, rather than being obscure and distant, turns out to be something lying at our feet all the time. It is simply what happens to sentences when their truth-conditions are fulfilled, as Rorty puts it. Second, the truth-conditional analysis of meaning implies that if you cannot state truth-conditions for a proposition, then that proposition makes no sense at all.

The logical positivists distinguished themselves among other advocates of the linguistic turn by using the second of these claims as a weapon to declare that, with the exception of the empirically verifiable or falsifiable claims of science, nearly everything people say is, strictly speaking, meaningless. They claimed, for example, that ethical statements are merely emotive expressions rather than meaningful propositions. They also claimed that philosophy itself, where it does not restrict itself to rationally reconstructing and justifying scientific method, and to demarcating the rationality of science from everything else, is nothing but a set of pseudo-propositions. Indeed, some of the more consistent positivists thought that even this second-order activity itself was, strictly speaking, nonsense—important nonsense perhaps, but nonsense nonetheless.

European positivists felt strongly about this because for some time they had been battling a wave of intellectual irrationalism whose diffusion through European culture had, in their view, predictably resulted in the political, social, and ethical disaster that was now at hand, from which many of them were fleeing for their lives. Intellectually, the disaster had started when modern logic, mathematics, and physics—fields to which most of the new positivists had contributed or had studied—had undermined Kant's conviction that the categories under which we have any experience at all are uniquely consistent with Aristotelian syllogistic logic, Euclidian geometry, and Newtonian physics. These convictions had formed the basis of the European educational system for some time. Their collapse allowed a generation of philosophical irrationalists, from Friedrich Nietzsche and Henri Bergson to Martin Heidegger, to rise to a prominence they presumably would not otherwise have enjoyed and, directly or indirectly, to give aid and comfort to increasingly bad regimes. Heidegger, for example, attempted to preserve the fundamental Kantian claim that experience has *a priori* structuring principles by locating these principles at primitive, intuitive, prescientific levels of symbolic and emotional processing. The result of this neo-Romantic turn was to dismiss the controls of logic and scientific method as manifestations of a technological will to power, to concentrate ideological influence in the hands of antirationalists, and to reinforce the destructive forms of social and political irrationalism with which Heidegger not only sympathized but actively connived.

Appalled by this flirtation with the demonic, the Vienna Circle defended the guiding role of scientific method in society, especially in societies making the difficult, and extremely dicey, transition to modernity. (That is why they considered themselves to follow in the positivist tradition inaugurated by August Comte). They did this by attacking as meaningless the Kantian idea that there are any substantive *a priori* truths at all. For the logical positivists, meaningful statements fall into only two classes: the in-principle verifiable claims of empirical science, and the analytically true or false, but empty, calculi of logic and mathematics, which are used to track and concatenate sensory information. There is no room for synthetic *a priori* propositions. That meant that there is no room for metaphysics. For ever since Kant metaphysics had been understood on the Continent as the study of synthetic, or substantive, *a priori* propositions: propositions about the structural preconditions for having coherent experiences and for attaining knowledge. For the logical positivists, metaphysics, so construed, was nothing but a set of "pseudo-propositions" about "pseudo-problems," a conviction that Heidegger's muddy indulgences in deep speculation about Being *qua* Being did nothing to disconfirm. What goes by the name metaphysics either casts a glow of significance onto what is merely emotive, or, like Kant's Newtonianism, elevates some contingent result of scientific inquiry to an unrevisable status that cannot fail to retard the growth of science and to give scandal when it proves ephemeral. By this reworking of Hume's two-pronged "fork" between "relations of ideas" and "matters of fact," the new positivists attempted to launch a second Enlightenment, whose relation to the new physics would recover the lost relationship between the first Enlightenment and Newton.

Having neutralized metaphysics in this way, logical positivists—or logical empiricists as many of them preferred to call themselves—developed a philosophy of science with a number of distinctive components: (1) philosophy of science is what remains of philosophy after its earlier pretenses had been cut down by the verification principle ("scientific philosophy"); (2) the scientific method is the only method of acquiring knowledge ("scientism"); (3) scientific theories are instruments for predicting and controlling phenomena, rather than pictures of some underlying metaphysical reality ("phenomenalism"; "antirealism"); (4) scientific theories may originate by any number of psychological processes, but what matters is that theories are (in principle) empirically confirmable by experimental testing of the predictive statements that they deductively entail ("primacy of the mode of justification over the mode of discovery"; demarcation of science by verification"; "antipsychologism"); (5) scientific theories are composed of deductively arranged propositions that follow *more geometrico* from a set of axioms ("hypothetico-deductivism"); (6) scientific explanations are deductive applications of well-confirmed laws to cases, with the result that prediction and explanation are distinguished only by the temporal position of the investigator ("covering law model of explanation"); (7) progress in science depends on and is pushed forward by the effort to reduce the empirical generalizations and laws of less general sciences to those of more fundamental sciences, notably physics ("reductionism," "unity of science program"); (8) questions of value, being neither confirmable nor falsifiable, can and should be separated from questions of fact (''fact-value dichotomy''); and (9) ethical claims are strictly speaking meaningless emotional responses (''emotivism'').[2]

Since the early 1930s, reports about the Vienna Circle had been appearing with some regularity in American philosophy journals. (These are reviewed by Daniel J. Wilson in the essay that follows this introduction.) A. J. Ayer's influential positivist tract, *Language, Truth, and Logic*, appeared in 1936. In 1937 Charles Morris published a book of essays entitled *Logical Positivism, Pragmatism, and Scientific Empiricism*. Bright, science-minded graduate students were soon gravitating to places where the new philosophy was being taught. But the Vienna Circle influenced American philosophers most deeply perhaps in the person of Rudolf Carnap, whose ambition to analyze scientific theories into sense-data reports by way of elaborate logical transformations had been sketched in *The Logical Structure [Aufbau] of the World* (1928). In 1934, Carnap emigrated to the United States through the good offices of W.V.O. Quine, a young American logician from Harvard who had studied with him in Europe, and of Charles Morris, who found a place for him at the University of Chicago. There Carnap remained until 1952, when he spent two years at Princeton's Institute for Advanced Study before assuming the deceased Reichenbach's position at UCLA.

When they arrived in America, Carnap and his fellow émigrés were appalled to find how deeply mired in crude psychologism American philosophers still were. Deweyan pragmatists even gloried in it, believing that a fully naturalistic philosophy must be grounded in an evolutionary account of the mind, and accordingly in logic treated as a set of adaptive traits aimed at inductively and abductively facilitating an intelligent animal's way around in the world. Even realists, who defended the *a priori* status of logic against their pragmatist enemies, had failed to take the linguistic turn, and hence had failed to shift the weight fully from induction to deduction. As a result, they had failed to distinguish questions of justification sharply enough from psychological and sociological questions about discovery. Accordingly, Carnap was relieved when he found at Chicago, which was by then sinking into the neomedievalizing atmosphere that had been imposed by Robert Maynard Hutchins, Richard McKeon, and Mortimer Adler, at least one person who was eager to break out of these quagmires. That was Charles Morris.

Morris had maintained a pragmatist presence at Chicago after Mead and Tufts had ceased to be active, and after the connection between the university and the city's progressive community had become little but a distant memory, by refocusing pragmatism around Peirce's theory of signs (''semiotic''), his reworking of logic for a processive and probabilistic world. As editor of the *Journal for Symbolic Logic*, Morris was eager to infuse his tradition with the intensified stress on formal logic that the positivists had brought with them to America. He explored with Carnap conditions for convergence between their research communities, and helped devise ways to make the new movement better known. From Morris, meanwhile, Carnap claimed to have gained some understanding of Dewey's and Mead's pragmatism and at least some sympathy for its hapless ambition to be a "scientific philosophy." (As Hickman's report about the Frankfurt School's conception of it shows, pragmatism was badly understood in Europe as an expression of America's vulgar commercial mentality.) Carnap also became comfortable working in terms of the semi-Peircean distinctions Morris drew between syntactics, semantics, and pragmatics.

The informal rapprochement among pragmatists and positivists soon bore fruit. Since the 1920s, American philosophy had been stuck in an unstable stalemate between pragmatists and realists, with realists increasingly in the ascendancy. For even if they had not yet taken the linguistic turn, the realists' defense of the formal or *a priori* nature of logic had enabled them to defend philosophy's control over conceptual, as distinct from empirical, problems, and so to portray themselves as protectors of the discipline's professional status in a rapidly professionalizing academic environment. Mired in their musty, turn-of-the-century *ethos*, pragmatists seemed to "critical realists" like Sellars and Lovejoy oldfashioned and unprofessional, and, in their self-bestowed role as "public philosophers," little better than advice columnists.

Morris's courtship of Carnap was based on a perception that the tables could be turned if pragmatists were willing to abandon their psychologistic view of logic. They could do so by reinterpreting the pragmatic criterion of meaning in terms of the language-oriented verificationist theory of meaning. Pragmatism's positive attitude about the beneficial effects of science on society could then be reinterpreted along the lines proposed by positivist philosophers of science. In one stroke, this would make American realists, rather than pragmatists, look dated. The initiative succeeded so well that American realism virtually disappeared from the scene until, beginning with the work of Wilfrid Sellars, it, too, began belatedly to take a linguistic turn.[3] If positivism had not come to pragmatism's rescue, we are willing to say, it might have been pragmatists, rather than realists, who were relegated to a seldom read and seldom discussed past. As it turned out, memories of the heroic deeds of the classical pragmatists were kept warm and their textual remains venerated in part because the positivists, while exoriating the crudities of the classical pragmatists, saved their reputations as forerunners of their own scientific philosophy. (For more on this subject, see Wilson's essay in this volume.)

It soon appeared, in fact, that pragmatists could be at least as much help to positivists as positivists could be to pragmatists. Even its most ardent advocates had long recognized that the strict positivist position contained insoluble difficulties. For one thing, the logical status of the verification principle itself was unclear. It was neither a definitional nor a purely empirical claim. In addition, Carnap's strenuous efforts to show how sense data can be combined by logic to support up-to-date physics had succeeded in showing instead that the same data can be equally well explained and predicted by many different logical schemes and frameworks of theoretical entities. In response to these difficulties, Carnap took what he described as a pragmatic turn (*sensu* Morris). He acknowledged that choices between one "language" or ontological framework and another are "pragmatic": Such choices are to be judged by what is most consonant with and useful for the economical pursuit of up-to-date predictive science. But, Carnap claimed, this "ontological relativity" does not lead to the metaphysical relativism against which logical positivism had arisen in the first place.[4] For there is no matter of fact on which we might base a general or antecedent preference for one interpretive framework or another. It was the truth-conditional analysis of meaning that made this point persuasive. "Five is a prime number" is true *if* one chooses to use a framework of numbers. But the bare statement "Numbers (or substances, or universals) exist," is neither true nor false. For "external questions" about ontologies do not have truth-conditions that differ from those that apply to the "internal questions" that they make possible. This analysis reaffirmed positivism's view of philosophy as a set of pseudo-problems without denying their indispensibility as "frameworks of entities," and without regressing to Kant's belief that *a priori* questions can be approached frontally and answered noncontextually.

Soon Quine was arguing that Carnap's ontological relativity entailed an even greater degree of pragmatism than Carnap suspected. For one thing, since each language has its own way of identifying and individuating objects, "linguistic relativity implies referential opacity": Two languages will cut the sensational field up differently, even where they appear to pick out nominally the same thing, say a "rabbit" in English. Accordingly, we cannot justify the choice of one ontological framework, or scientific theory, over another by deciding which better accounts for and aggregates isolated or theory-neutral pieces of data. As the French physicist Pierre Duhem had already argued, unit-for-unit comparison must be abandoned for more holistic and heuristic considerations. As Quine put it, "Our statements about the external world face the tribunal of sense experience not individually but only as a corporate body."[5] Quine's view favored Jamesian coherence over Russell's ideal of logical construction and his correspondence theory of truth. For it meant that the project of reducing molecular to atomic propositions, each of which names a single sensory datum, cannot conceivably form the philosophical basis for theory choice in science.

More trenchantly still, Quine argued that if pragmatic criteria for theory choice are all we have, the revered distinction between analytic and synthetic statements, and hence between conceptual frameworks and empirical truths, must be abandoned. In making comparisons between rival ontologies we can choose to hold this or that statement more or less closely to our breast, and can "redistribute" truth values accordingly. No statement, however, including the allegedly analytic definitions and synonymies that are built into our preferred languages ("All bachelors are unmarried men"), will be immune to rejection or revision. Hence the very notion of a distinction between necessary (analytic) truths and revisable, empirical (synthetic) statements collapses:

In repudiating such a boundary I espouse a more thorough pragmatism [than Carnap]. Each man is given a scientific heritage plus a continuing barrage of sensory stimulation; and the considerations which guide him in warping his scientific heritage to fit his continuing sensory promptings are, where rational, pragmatic.

This famous sentence, written in mid-century at the end of Quine's most famous paper, "Two Dogmas of Empiricism" (1951), radicalized the kind of pragmatism that Quine's Harvard teacher, C. I. Lewis, had inherited from James. At the same time, it implied answers to the positivists' conundra about the logical status of the verification principle and the disciplinary status of philosophical inquiry that seemed to Quine to echo Dewey more than James. By turning issues about theory choice into questions whose answers are to be guided by what the best physicists currently say about what objects really exist, what psychologists experimentally tell us about behavior, and how well field linguists and anthropologists manage to devise translation manuals between the languages of different cultures, Quine claimed to be returning to Dewey's "naturalized epistemology." "When with Dewey we turn . . . toward a naturalistic view of language and a behavioral view of meaning," Quine wrote in "Ontological Relativity" (1968), "we recognize . . . that 'meaning is primarily a property of behavior.' " In this way Quine was able to restore Dewey's naturalism about philosophical questions without wallowing in his psychologistic, and overly inductivist, interpretation of logic and semantics.

American pragmatism breathed new life into itself in this way. It is no less true, however, that in the process pragmatism was positivized and scientized. It was now clear that philosophy's only job was to keep ontology lean and mean enough to legitimate a thoroughly scientific worldview, and to help shift power to those who participate in or at least honor that worldview. ("Philosophy of science," Quine is reported to have quipped, "is philosophy enough.") Viewed in this light, the classical pragmatists now appeared as tender-minded prophets of hard-headed saviors whose shoes they were hardly worthy of tying. Where, for example, Dewey had tried to naturalize the intention-laden and meaning-full world that humans share in their daily life by socializing and biologizing much that later came to be called folk-psychology, Quine's naturalism extended no further than "extensionalist" ontologies that allow the inferential apparatus of propositional logic to map onto a physical world that impinges on agents in such a way that bits of behavior are elicited and shaped in response to it. Inspired by ideas like these, and urged on by his colleague Quine, B. F. Skinner sought to assimilate human to animal behavior by explaining it on the model of natural selection, according to which blind acts are shaped by rewards and punishments meted out entirely by the exigencies of the external environment. Thus, in contrast to Clark Hull, a Columbia University behavioral psychologist who had once commended his colleague Dewey's *Logic: The Theory of Inquiry* as a good account of how social agents and those who investigate their behavior guide their activity by thought, the next generation of behaviorists assumed that the requirements of logical empiricist science could be met only by eliminating terms referring to the suspiciously mentalistic symbolic processes that, in Dewey's view, still seemed to intervene between stimulus and response. In this fashion, the positivization of the social sciences fostered redescriptions of psychological and social facts in terms that allowed social scientists to present their diagnoses and policy prescriptions as "value free" and the lived world they hoped to reengineer as a gigantic laboratory lying at their disposal. In this atmosphere, even Dewey's closest disciples, such as Ernest Nagel, adjusted the instrumentalist view of science to make it commend hypothetical-deductive explanations and the positivist project of unifying all the sciences by way of theoretical reduction. (Nagel's influential 1961 textbook, *The Structure of Science*, is a monument to pragmatized positivism of this sort.)[6]

Now in the evening of his long life, these developments made Dewey nervous. Pressed by Reichenbach to give his blessing to the new movement by contributing to the positivists' showcase yearbook, *The Encyclopedia of Unified Science*, Dewey's 1948 contribution consisted of a stinging, even insulting, attack on the positivists' emotive account of value:

When sociological theory withdraws from consideration of the basic interests, concerns, and actively moving aims of a human culture on the ground that "values" are involved, and that inquiry as "scientific" has nothing to do with values, the inevitable consequence is that inquiry in the human area is confined to what is superficial and comparatively trivial, no matter what its parade of technical skill.[7]

Dewey's wariness was stimulated by knowing that he had been down this road before. Having long since repented of his support for World War I, Dewey was vividly aware that even if the technocratic impulse that Mumford had called "the pragmatic acquiescence" did not apply to him, it did describe well enough what many social scientists who had formerly been allied with the progressive pragmatists believed. World War I had given professional social scientists a base from which to exercise increasing influence on public policy and the managerial practices of corporations. The National Research Council, which had come into being during the war, inspired the creation of a Social Science Research Council after it, through which huge amounts of money began to flow to professional psychologists, economists, political scientists, and sociologists, and to their universities, much of it from the Rockefeller Foundation. Among the social scientists most eager to participate in this effort were many who had been dissillusioned by the failures of their youthful populism, or whose hostility to the narrowness of their religious upbringings had resulted in a crusading scientism. They were eager to professionalize and scientize disciplines hitherto associated with the insufficiently quantified, and vaguely feminized, sphere of "social work" that Dewey and Jane Addams had inspired. The political conservatism of the 1920s, moreover, provoked many liberal intellectuals, including former pragmatists, to work from the top down rather than from the bottom up. Many political scientists, for example, embraced Walter Lippmann's conclusion—a product of his own disillusioned retreat from participatory pragmatism—that democratic consent must be manufactured from above because the masses are incapable of intelligent political judgment.[8]

By the 1920s, social scientists sharing some or all of these attitudes had found their way to philosophies of science, which ratified them. In particular they had found their way to prelinguistic positivists such as the eugenicist Karl Pearson and to disillusioned prophets of value-free social science like Max Weber. What Dewey feared was that the new breed of positivists who had arrived in the United States in the 1930s would stimulate and magnify these tendencies, and that the aftermath of World War II would recapitulate what had happened after World War I. Nor was he wrong. Both before and after World War II, logical positivism amplified, even if it did not create, the scientistic *ethos* within which a managerial "culture of expertise" acquired prestige at the expense of the more participatory forms of liberalism favored by Dewey. In the public sphere, it was now acknowledged that attempts to socialize or overly regulate production would be less effective than the creation of a society of mass consumption. If a "managerial revolution" was required to rationalize corporations in order to achieve that end, behaviorist psychologists were there to recast their theories in terms of the responses of organisms, including workers and managers, to stimuli unmediated by such unmeasurable, and seemingly metaphysical, concepts as mind. More generally, Dewey's old idea of a scientifically informed control of experience became reconceived as rule by a body of skilled experts, who, in a dangerous, complex, and tragic world, administer the schedule of rewards and punishments (carrots and sticks) that keep international affairs stable and at home maintain a consumption-oriented economy for a population whose role is largely restricted to happily consuming the "utilities" that the new class is supposed to be able to maximize by its managerial and technical skill. A new form of liberalism soon took shape on this basis. The emphasis was to be taken away from Dewey's idea of universal participation in democratic life and placed instead on protecting and enhancing the scope of personal choice in the private sphere that a well-managed consumption economy made possible. Positivism's clean distinction between fact and value played a role in this shift by making it easier to portray the ethical and aesthetic dimensions as sufficiently noncognitive, emotive, subjective, and expressive to ensure that no good reasons could conceivably be given why moralistic communities or invasive governments should constrain the private preferences of individuals. (By the 1960s the notion of human sexuality itself was "socially constructed" along these lines.)

The home of this new liberalism was the postwar American university, where the positivist dichotomy between fact and values was embodied in the disciplinary structure of a reconstructed and vastly expanded system of higher education that had been stimulated and paid for by the G.I. Bill. The social sciences were encouraged to assimilate themselves to the quantitative methods of the natural sciences, which were assumed already to be in accord with the canons of positivist philosophy of science. Most social scientists responded by obligingly exhibiting what came to be called "physics envy." Whatever disciplines could not meet this challenge were meanwhile unceremoniously dumped into a new bin denoted by an old world, "the humanities," a category that, as Bruce Kuklick elsewhere demonstrates, assembled a heterogeneous collection of fields whose objects and methods were deemed too subjective to meet verificationist criteria, but whose mission (to cultivate the sensibilities of students by curing them of the dogmatic attitudes toward values they had brought from their homes, churches, and provincial or ethnic communities) seemed too important to drop. The study of literature was the most important tool in this enterprise.[9]

What is in question here is not the need for experts. It is instead a certain conception of expertise: an objectivistic, external, nonparticipatory, technical conception of the relationship in which experts are assumed to stand to their society. Fostering that conception of expertise is how positivism helped create a new "meritocratic" governing and managing class or stratum, whose most powerful tools are informational technology and quantitative social science. It was by means of positivized pragmatism that the original Deweyan effort to sharpen the practical reason of a democratic culture by developing habits of controlled inquiry in the population as a whole—which is what Dewey meant by scientific method—was converted into a cult of often predictive theorizing within closed communities of experts, which would subsequently be "applied" to social problems. This is a mentality you will recognize in the naive verificationism and falsificationism of what passes for "scientific method" in many disciplines today, and that has been widely disseminated by the American school system. You will also recognize it in its preference for explanations couched in terms of the beneficial effects of competition between self-interested units (whether they be atoms, genes, individuals, firms, or interest groups) in securing maximally efficient outcomes for all, and in its too-facile appeal to the fact-value distinction to protect technical languages, and those who wield them, from the critical gaze of common sense and to minimize the cognitive content of much of our most important experience.

The plausible contention that this constellation of beliefs constitutes an ideology helps show that nothing could more ideological than proclamations of an "end of ideology" and its replacement by "value-free" "scientific management." Viewed in this light, it matters less than commonly believed that professional philosophers have retreated from the public role to which they aspired in the America of the progressives. One does not have to believe in Comte's "law of three stages" to see that "public philosophers" were important in America in a fleeting moment between the fall of public theologians and the rise of public social scientists. In his contribution to this volume, Kuklick rue-fully and wittilly traces the passing of that moment. Still, the disappearance of philosophers from the public scene does not mean the evaporation of the social power and influence of philosophy. Philosophy is most saliently linked to power by the fact that in their professional work philosophers create, commend, and criticize the conceptual frameworks and epistemic criteria within which what counts as objective knowledge in a society, and therefore secures access to the power that knowledge grants, are constructed and justified. Philosophers, that is to say, shape and warp the cognitive space in which knowledge and power appear by clarifying, amplifying, and justifying epistemological, ontological, and praxical norms. In this matter, professionalized philosophers have never really withdrawn from society. On the contrary, from increasingly powerful academies they continue to exercise enormous, if subtle and only retrospectively visible, influence on society. Logical empiricism and positivized pragmatism, for ex-ample, have demonstrably had, and continue to have, enormous effects on Amer-ica's culture, and even its policies. Well after the philosophical underpinnings for these ideas had ceased to interest professional philosophers, they had been all too successfully been exported to other disciplines and from there to the society as a whole.

The chapters in this section can be read against the background sketched in this introduction. Daniel J. Wilson gives a detailed account of how the linguistic turn and logical positivism were received by American philosophers, especially pragmatists. Wilson stresses the fact that in turning pragmatism's vague, hand-waving hymns to an experimentalist culture into detailed, hard-nosed analyses, logical positivists helped the pragmatists recover their influence. At the same time, the positivists' superior grasp of scientific method and of contemporary physics showed up the pragmatists as amateurs, speeding their eclipse. Bruce Kuklick traces the process by which public philosophers gave way to distinctly non-publicly involved professional philosophy. He argues that surrendering the role of public intellectual to pop scientists, pop psychologists, and pop social scientists may have delivered pragmatists from making fools of themselves in public in an age when knowledge was no longer an amateur affair. At the same time, he does not believe that this retreat did philosophy itself much good. For Kuklick does not believe that philosophy is the sort of thing that can very successfully ape the disciplines over which it formerly presided. Isaac Nevo goes on to tell how Quine, in blurring the line between conceptual and empirical claims, harked back to the holism of James, and so helped Harvard's distinctive pragmatic tradition make the linguistic turn. We may add that by naturalizing epistemology Quine certainly exposes philosophy to the expertise of other dis-ciplines. At the same time, however, Quine's positivistic inheritance protects these professional disciplines, and philosophy itself, from the scrutiny of com-mon social life and its discursive practices. Quine's positivized pragmatism ex-presses itself, for example, in a Skinneresque account of evolution in which the behavioral responses of organisms are elicited and shaped by the environment.

While Quine can justly say that he thereby inherits Dewey's naturalism, Quine's atomism about stimulus response units, his stress on individual rewards and punishments, and his tendency to transfer causality to a primarily physical rather than a social environment restores much of what Dewey was denying when he criticized the "reflex arc conception in psychology," and subverts the guiding role that Dewey assigned to the intentional and intelligent acts of cooperative individuals. This shift is part of what Randall Auxier calls "the decline of evolutionary naturalism in later pragmatism." For his part, Auxier believes that Dewey's view cannot be maintained except by treating evolutionary theory as naturalistic metaphysics. Perhaps Dewey's reasons for writing *Experience and Nature*, Auxier implicitly suggests, were not so misguided after all. There is in Auxier's essay a hint that Dewey's evolutionary naturalism could not have survived the linguistic turn intact. In the course of tracing the emergence of Rorty's philosophizing out of the thick and tangled background we have been reviewing, on the other hand, Rickard Donovan suggests that, to arrive at a more consistently evolutionary (and hence historicist) perspective than either Dewey or Quine achieved, what pragmatism needs is more rather than less of the linguistic turn, and that in Rorty's work it gets what it needs.

NOTES

1. The linguistic turn should not be identified with the logical atomists' and logical positivists' versions of it. The "Ordinary Language Philosophy" or "linguistic analysis" of the later Wittgenstein and J. L. Austin, which became dominant among professional philosophers in America by the 1960s, differs in nearly every way from logical positivism, but is no less a manifestation of the linguistic turn. Indeed, in their preference for the semantics and syntactics of natural, rather than formal, languages, ordinary language philosophers arguably took an even sharper linguistic turn. Significantly enough, the best guide to the issues that divide these two versions of the linguistic turn is Richard Rorty's anthology, *The Linguistic Turn* (Chicago: University of Chicago Press, 1967).

2. For a summary of these views, see A. J. Ayer, *Language, Truth, and Logic* (London: Metheun, 1935); and C. Hempel, *Philosophy of Science* (Englewood Cliffs, N.J.: Prentice-Hall, 1966).

3. Wilfrid Sellars was the son of Roy Wood Sellars. He explicitly took himself to be defending critical realism, which he called his "paternal inheritance," by making the linguistic turn instead of following his father's lead in rejecting it. Sellars did this by questioning how closely wedded linguistic analysis is to the empiricist tradition. For an account of what Rorty takes from Sellars while resisting his realism, see Richard Rorty, *Philosophy and the Mirror of Nature* (Princeton, N.J.: Princeton University Press, 1979).

4. See Rudolf Carnap, "Empiricism, Semantics, and Ontology," *Revue Internationale de Philosophie* 9 (1950): 20–40, reprinted in A. Rorty, ed., *Pragmatism* (New York: Doubleday, 1966), 396–411.

5. Willard van Orman Quine, "Two Dogmas of Empiricism," in Quine, *From a Logical Point of View* (Cambridge, Mass.: Harvard University Press, 1951). For Quine's epistemological naturalism, see his *Ontological Relativity and Other Essays* (New York: Columbia University Press, 1969).

6. Nagel's "hard-headed liberal" attitudes had been shaped by their first teacher, Morris R. Cohen of City University, more than Dewey. So had Sidney Hook's. On Cohen, see David A. Hollinger, *Morris Cohen and the Scientific Ideal* (Cambridge, Mass.: MIT Press, 1975). On behav-

iorism, positivism, and pragmatism, see L. Smith, *Behaviorism and Logical Positivism* (Stanford: Stanford University Press, 1986).

7. John Dewey, "Theory of Valuation," *International Encyclopedia of Unified Sciences*, Vol. 2 (Chicago: University of Chicago Press, 1939), 62–63.

8. On this topic see Dorothy Ross, *The Origins of American Social Science* (Baltimore, Md.: Johns Hopkins University Press, 1991).

9. Bruce Kuklick, "The Professionalization of the Humanities," in *Applying the Humanities*, ed. A. Caplan *et al.* (New York: Plenum Press, 1985), 41–54.

6

Fertile Ground: Pragmatism, Science, and Logical Positivism

Daniel J. Wilson

Some three decades after their emigration to the United States, two of the original members of the Vienna Circle recalled their initial impression of American philosophy and their warm welcome from their American colleagues. Herbert Feigl, the first to emigrate permanently in 1930, admitted that, before arriving, most members of the "Vienna Circle were largely ignorant of American philosophy." They had some knowledge of James and Dewey, but Peirce was largely unknown. What little he did know had convinced Feigl that the *zeitgeist* in America was "thoroughly congenial to our Viennese position." On arriving, Feigl and the others received "generous and friendly treatment," despite the "spirit of 'conquest' " with which they arrived, certain that they "had found a 'philosophy to end all philosophies.' " Rudolf Carnap, for example, who accepted a position at the University of Chicago in 1936, was "gratified to see that in the United States there was a considerable interest, especially among the younger philosophers, in the scientific method of philosophy, based on modern logic." He found here "a philosophical atmosphere which, in striking contrast to that in Germany, was very congenial."[1]

The congenial climate that both Feigl and Carnap discovered suggests that, in spite of their separate development, American pragmatism and Viennese logical positivism shared certain ideas and approaches which made possible the favorable reception of the European import in the 1930s and after. Where pragmatism had been one of the major schools of philosophy in the United States during the first three decades of the century, logical positivism and related empirical and analytic philosophies would dominate many of the philosophical debates in the next three decades. The ways in which the pragmatists had emphasized science and scientific method, empiricism, meaning, verifiability, and cooperation meant that not only would individual logical positivists find a congenial haven from the terrors of Nazi Europe, but that their effort to construct a rigorous, scientifically and logically based philosophy could be conceived as carrying the pragmatic program to new levels of rigor and scientific exactitude and certainty. The pragmatists had created the conditions in which logical positivism and other analytic philosophies could flourish and ultimately displace them as the dominant voice in mid-century philosophical debates.[2]

Beginning in the late nineteenth century, the pragmatists Charles Sanders Peirce, John Dewey, and to a lesser extent, William James, had participated in the movement to make American philosophy more rigorous and scientific. American philosophers of all persuasions had felt increasing pressure from the sciences in the professionalizing and specializing universities of the period. This pressure to emulate the methods, values, and successes of the natural and physical sciences induced what I have elsewhere called ''the crisis of confidence'' in American philosophy.[3] Many philosophers believed that unless they could remake philosophy along the lines of a science, it would be difficult to maintain a secure position in universities enamored of science and scientism. The pragmatists, to varying degrees, sought to develop a method imbued with the values and procedures of science so that philosophy could take its rightful place alongside the other sciences in the academy. Philosophers who were not pragmatists, such as Arthur O. Lovejoy and Morris Cohen, also incorporated a scientific orientation and method into their philosophies, so that, by 1930, when logical positivism began to be known in the United States, there was widespread agreement, if not universal assent, that a properly conceived philosophy adopted the methods and values of science, if it did not itself become simply another science.[4]

By sketching the efforts of American philosophers and especially the pragmatists to construct a more rigorous and scientific philosophy in the decades before 1930, those features of American philosophy that the logical positivists found congenial will become apparent. In addition, by examining the initial encounters between American philosophers and those of the Vienna Circle, it will be possible to reconstruct some of the ways in which these complementary traditions converged. They converged not only because of a complementarity of ideas, but because a number of younger American philosophers familiar with pragmatism and logical positivism, including Ernest Nagel, Sidney Hook, Albert Blumberg, and Charles W. Morris, made the connection. These younger men, trained in the American context, were interested in European philosophy, traveled and studied in Germany and Austria, met and worked with the logical positivists and other analytic philosophers, and ultimately encouraged the Europeans to emigrate to the United States. This personal connection facilitated the sharing of philosophical viewpoints and the assimilation of logical positivism in the American context. The ideas of the Vienna Circle would have become known at some point, but the particular circumstances of the 1930s, when some of the younger philosophers were seeking even more rigor and certainty than pragmatism had yet offered, and when the political circumstances in Europe necessitated the emigration of leading empiricist and analytic philosophers, meant that logical positivism and analytic philosophy could be regarded as building on pragmatism as the next step toward the ideal of philosophy as a science.

The question of the relationship between philosophy and science was one of the most important facing the pragmatists at the end of the nineteenth century. Earlier formulations of the relationship had conceived of science providing descriptive and explanatory information about the natural world, which philosophers then interpreted through a theological, moral, and philosophical lens. The publication of *The Origin of Species* in 1859 and the significant developments in the natural and physical sciences in the last four decades of the century had called into question the traditional relationship between science and philosophy. Science no longer needed a philosophical or theological imprimatur; scientists could now offer explanations of physical phenomena entirely within a scientific context. These scientific achievements were accompanied by a pervasive scientism. The values and methods of science were increasingly seen as the keys to progress and their application to fields beyond the natural and physical sciences eagerly awaited. In this intellectual and cultural climate, philosophers began to reexamine and reformulate the relationship of philosophy and science.[5]

James, Peirce, and Dewey all addressed the relationship of philosophy and science in the late nineteenth and early twentieth century. James was always constitutionally unable to declare finally for a single conception of philosophy. Sensitive to the achievements of science, he did not want to limit philosophy to only that which could be known by the scientific method. While he resisted reducing philosophy to science, he was equally opposed to subsuming all facts under some grand theory or absolute. Science was most valuable for its method which provided "a mere fragment of truth broken out from the whole mass of it for the sake of practical effectiveness exclusively. *Divide et impera.*" The methods of science were noted for their practical effectiveness, not their comprehensiveness. To assert more than this was, for James, to become one of the "votaries" before the "idol" of science. Without denigrating the very real achievements of scientific method, James believed that they were still limited. As he put it, "our science is a drop, our ignorance a sea." Furthermore, he thought that science "must be constantly reminded that her purposes are not the only purposes, and that the order of uniform causation which she had use for, and is therefore right in postulating, may be enveloped in a wider order, on which she had no claims at all." James repeatedly sought to steer a course between the excesses of religious belief and faith on the one hand, and the excesses of science worship on the other. Either position was mistaken, for "there is really no scientific or other method by which men can steer safely between the opposite dangers of believing too little or of believing too much. To face such dangers is apparently our duty, and to hit the right channel between them is the measure of our wisdom as men."[6] Thus, though James saw scientific method as essential to certain kinds of philosophical inquiry, and though he helped set psychology in America on a course to becoming more scientific, he always pulled back from extreme empiricist, materialist, and scientistic positions. Lived experience was more multifarious than could be contained within the formulations of any scientist.

In his training and early work as a scientist, Charles Sanders Peirce was more like the logical positivists than either James or Dewey.[7] Thus, when Peirce considered the relationship of science and philosophy, he did so as a practicing scientist well versed in the scientific method and the cooperative nature of scientific enterprise. Peirce regarded science and philosophy as compatible, indeed as complementary modes of inquiry. As he noted in an early journal entry: "Just as Science cannot advance without Philosophy—because (to use Kant's expressions) Induction pure is Blind—so Philosophy cannot exist without science—because Deduction pure is Void. Science and Philosophy must advance together." Even metaphysics was not unalterably opposed to science, though he conceded that current metaphysics was scientifically underdeveloped. "Every great branch of science," he wrote, "has once been in the state in which metaphysics is now, that is when its fundamental conceptions were vague and consequently its doctrines utterly unsettled: and there is no reason whatever to despair of metaphysics eventually becoming a real science like the rest." Peirce, unlike the logical positivists, sought to reform metaphysics, not to abandon it as meaningless. In addition, the motivation to scientific inquiry was important to Peirce. Scientific motivation was "a craving to know how things really were and an interest in finding out whether or not general propositions actually held good—which has over-balanced all prejudice, all vanity, and all passion." An inquirer possessed of this scientific spirit would spend his day in "laboratories and in the field . . . *observing*—that is perceiving by the aid of analysis,—and testing suggestions of theories." Since this method of observation was not limited to "natural objects," there was no *a priori* reason to prevent philosophy and metaphysics from becoming a science.[8]

From his earliest writings on science and philosophy, the idea of community was central to Peirce's conception of a science and to the pursuit of truth within a science. His notions of community were no doubt shaped by his working experience as a scientist in the Coast Survey. "Scientific progress," he wrote, "is to a large extent public and belongs to the community of scientific men of the same department, its conclusions are unanimous, its interpretations of nature are no private interpretations, and so much must always be published to the world as will suffice to enable the world to adopt the individual investigator's conclusions." The goal of science was truth: "The followers of science are fully persuaded that the processes of investigation, if only pushed far enough, will give one certain solution to every question to which they can be applied." These same results are possible for philosophy, if only the philosophers would emulate the scientists in motivation and method. The ultimate philosophy is not within the reach of any individual philosopher, but it is worth seeking for "the *community* of philosophers."[9]

Peirce returned repeatedly to the question of whether philosophy was then or could yet become a science. There was no denying that contemporary philosophy, particularly metaphysics, was in a "deplorable backward condition." In Peirce's view this condition resulted from the lack of scientific training among philosophers. Men not "nurtured in dissecting rooms and other laboratories" lacked "the true scientific *Eros.*" In addition to a scientific background, philosophers needed to be more firmly grounded in logic. His own philosophy, "and all philosophy worth attention, reposes entirely upon the theory of logic." Peirce often chided James and other philosophers for their neglect of logic: "People who cannot reason exactly (which alone *is* reasoning), simply cannot understand my philosophy,—neither the process, methods, nor results." Philosophers, however, must do more than simply deplore the neglect of logic or the present state of philosophy. They should commit themselves to bringing philosophy to "a condition like that of the natural sciences, where investigators, instead of contemning each of the work of most of the others as misdirected from beginning to end, cooperate, stand upon one another's shoulders, and multiply incontestible results." If these conditions were met in philosophy, then philosophers would soon join their scientific brethren in the collective pursuit of truth.[10]

Though not all of Peirce's statements on science and on philosophy as a science had been published before the 1930s, the general outline of his position was well known in the United States. Enough had been published or delivered as public lectures, in addition to the extensive philosophical correspondence Peirce conducted, for his views to be broadly disseminated among his philosophical colleagues. One example of the spread of Peirce's conceptions lies in Josiah Royce's Harvard seminar. Royce, who received high marks from Peirce for his understanding of logic, conducted a seminar that brought together philosophers and practicing scientists to examine such topics as "The Logical Analysis of Fundamental Concepts and their General Relations to Philosophical Problems" (1904–1906) and "A Comparative Study of Various Types of Scientific Method" (1910–1912, 1913–1916).[11]

Less well grounded in science than either James or Peirce, John Dewey's conception of science and philosophy evolved more during his long career than had that of either of the other pragmatists. Like them, he felt the attraction of science in the late nineteenth century, but his initial view of the relationship of science and philosophy was heavily colored by his early idealism and Hegelianism. He began by trying to merge philosophy and science in a Hegelian synthesis and only gradually came to appreciate the distinction between the two as he acquired a firmer understanding of scientific method. With the development of his instrumentalism, Dewey began to argue that the methods and results of scientific inquiry could be put to use solving human problems and toward achieving human goals.

Dewey readily acknowledged in the early 1880s the power of scientific method to permit "exact measurement" and to increase the "power of analysis.'' These methods had permitted scientists to achieve a number of significant interpretative and practical successes in the late nineteenth century and had contributed to the pervasive scientism of the period. As Dewey noted, ''Every important development in science contributes to the popular consciousness, and indeed to philosophy, some new conception which serves for a time as a most valuable category of classification and explanation.'' This development was not necessarily cause for celebration, since too much modern science was marked by an empty realism and materialism. No inquiry or ''accumulation of facts'' had much meaning unless tied to higher values: ''That science or philosophy is worthless which does not ultimately bring every fact into guiding relation with the living activity of man, and the end of all his striving—approach to God.''[12]

By the early 1890s, Dewey was moving away from an idealistic conception of science toward a greater emphasis on method and on logic. Although less insistent than Peirce on the primacy of logic, Dewey now argued that logic was a characteristic of scientific thought and necessary to the pursuit of truth. ''Logical theory,'' he thought, ''must be the endeavor to account for, to justify, or at least reckon with this scientific spirit.'' He still resisted dividing the world into the logical and nonlogical, or scientific and unscientific. Rather, he saw a continuum of methods for dealing with the world in which the logical and the scientific were more successful in achieving truth, in part because the logical and scientific investigators were more self-conscious about their methods. Ultimately, all knowledge, ''whether in the form of ordinary observation or of scientific thinking is logical, . . . the only difference is in the degree of development of the logical functions present in both.''[13] Dewey also opposed reducing philosophy to science or logic, but by the 1890s had accepted the logical and scientific methods as more certain routes to truth.

At the end of the century, Dewey began to develop an instrumentalism based on scientific method that could reconcile the divergent emphases of science and philosophy. Both ''report the actual condition of life or experience. Their business is to reveal experience in its truth, its reality. They state what *is*.'' Philosophy devoted itself to ''the more generic (the wider) features of life'' and science to ''the more detailed and specific.'' Instrumentalism stressed the application of scientific methods to the solution of human problems. As Dewey argued, ''*Reality is not to be read in terms of knowledge as such, but in terms of action.*'' Action reconciled ''the old, the general, and the permanent with the changing, the individual, and the new.'' Given the recent refinement of scientific and logical method, the dominant ''interest becomes the *use* of knowledge; the conditions under which and ways in which it may be most organically and effectively employed to direct conduct.''[14] This instrumentalism marked a significant move beyond his early views. Dewey now had a better understanding of science and scientific method and his conception was closer to that of practicing scientists. Philosophy remained a broader field than science, still dedicated to finding meaning in life, but science had clearly become the method of inquiry and reconciliation came in the instrumental actions to improve the human condition. It is this broader Deweyan instrumentalism that has provided the inspiration for some of the neopragmatic opposition to positivistic philosophies.

In the early twentieth century, Dewey put increased emphasis on scientific method and on the notion that science was "a body of systematized knowledge." For Dewey, the activity, the method, had clear primacy over the results. Science was not "a peculiar development of thinking for highly specialized ends; it *is* thinking so far as thought has become conscious of its proper ends and of the equipment indispensable for success in their pursuit." Science was "*regulated activity, i.e.*; conduct, behavior, practice" whose primary object was "to give intellectual control—that is, ability to interpret phenomena—and secondarily, practical control—that is, ability to secure desirable and avoid undesirable future experiences."[15]

Scientists were most interested in intellectual control, while philosophers emphasized practical control. The scientific method applied to philosophy would result in a philosophy that would be "instrumental rather than final, and instrumental not to establishing and warranting any particular set of truths, but instrumental in furnishing points of view and working ideas which may clarify and illuminate the actual and concrete course of life."[16] By these means philosophers would be able to eliminate perennial but unsolvable problems and focus attention on those problems that could be resolved rationally. This was not unlike the task that the logical positivists would later set themselves.

In his major works of the 1910s and 1920s, Dewey conceived of the role of the philosopher more broadly than the logical positivists later would. The philosopher was to mediate between the properly narrow, clarifying, and illuminating conceptions of the scientist and the broader human and social concerns that needed resolution. The modern scientist tries to "describe a constant order *of* change," to emphasize "something constant in *function* and operation." The philosopher who employs "experimental intelligence, conceived after the pattern of science," develops "guides of reconstructive action" to shape the resolution of those broader human concerns.[17] Without philosophy, the scientific clarification remained meaningless; without a scientific, "experimental intelligence," philosophy remained impotent.

Dewey returned to these themes again in *Experience and Nature* (1925) and *The Quest for Certainty* (1929). Scientific method remained the key to philosophic and social progress. The scientific method of knowing was a process through which certain results were attained by hypothesis, test, and validation. Knowledge, in all fields, not only science, "is an affair of *making* sure, not of grasping antecedently given sureties." These methods of knowing were appropriate to philosophy, but philosophers must not make the mistake of simply assimilating scientific results. They must, instead, adopt the scientific methods for their own inquiries. By adopting the empirical method, philosophers would secure "for philosophic reflection something of that cooperative tendency toward consensus which marks inquiry in the natural sciences." The philosopher could also serve as "a liaison officer between the conclusions of science and the modes of social and personal action through which attainable possibilities are projected and striven for." Finally, philosophy could play the role of the critic. Its "critical mind would be directed against the domination exercised by prejudice, narrow interest, routine custom and the authority which issues from institutions."[18] R. W. Sleeper has recently emphasized the ways in which Dewey's reconstruction of philosophy, embodied in his work of the 1920s and 1930s, directly challenged key tenets of logical positivism. While Dewey's contributions to pragmatism contributed to a climate favorable to a scientific, empirical, and analytic philosophy, his own contemporary work was significantly at odds with the logistic empiricism coming out of Europe.[19] Philosophy, in Dewey's view, should and could adopt the methods of science without becoming just another specialized inquiry. Philosophers needed to ensure that the clarifications and illuminations of the special sciences were brought to bear on solving the major social needs of humans.

James, Peirce, and Dewey were not the only philosophers in the early twentieth century who desired to make philosophy more scientific in at least some respects. Within the ranks of the American Philosophical Association (APA) in the first two decades of this century this goal was widely considered and discussed. Several times the theme of the annual meeting focused on questions of achieving greater agreement among philosophers. There "was pretty general agreement that agreement itself was at least desirable," but no consensus on how to achieve it. Ralph Barton Perry, Arthur O. Lovejoy, and others foresaw the possibility of greater agreement if philosophers would only give up their "traditional lonely individualism, and make an effort to cooperate with each other, and especially try to understand each other and to be understood."[20]

Lovejoy, in particular, was a strong advocate of making philosophy more scientific in at least some of its manifestations. His 1916 presidential address to the APA was a call to make philosophy more successful in resolving philosophical problems. If philosophers wanted to be more scientific, and Lovejoy thought they should, then it was "sheer dishonesty" of them "not to play *that* game according to the rules, to be content with a lower degree of rigor in scientific method, any smaller measure of established and agreed-upon results, any greater infusion of the idiosyncrasies of our private personalities." Philosophy, he argued, "will never acquire anything like the gait of a science until it becomes, to a much higher degree than is yet customary, methodologically self-conscious; until it becomes more systematic in its procedure, devotes relatively more attention to its technique, and, for a time, relatively less to the formulation of substantive conclusions." There was some danger of philosophy becoming nothing more than "dried, abstract, depersonalized arguments and counterarguments, destitute of all charm of style," but that might be necessary if philosophers were to hold to their "customary pretension to be dealing with objective, verifiable and clearly communicable truths." In replying to critics of his proposals, Lovejoy argued that "if philosophy is to be regarded as in any sense a science, it must share the *generic* attributes of all the sciences; it must have *some* definite method of inquiry, some systematic procedure in the observation of data and the verification of hypotheses.'' Not all philosophy need adopt the methods and values of science, but, for Lovejoy's argument, it made ''little difference *what* part of philosophy is conceded to be akin to science in its purpose and ideal to aim at depersonalized and universally verifiable truth. If only there be *some* such part, then to that part, and to all of it, and to it alone,'' his argument applied.[21]

Morris Cohen was another nonpragmatist to argue for making philosophy more scientific. Cohen, like James, acknowledged that ''philosophy is primarily a vision and all great philosophers have something in common with poets and prophets,'' but he also believed that philosophy, like science, must be ''vitally concerned with reasoned or logically demonstrable truth.'' Any serious philosopher should apply to his vision a critical judgment, ''rigorously logical rules of evidence,'' and ''arduous scientific technique'' so as to achieve ''order and consistency.'' Cohen, however, warned against too great a reliance on ''a new set of priests called scientists.'' The scientific method, nonetheless, was useful in curing ''speculative excesses.'' Scientists proceeded by logically testing assumptions, ''mathematically deducing their various consequences,'' and then testing them against ''such experimental facts as can be generally established.'' This method was simply a ''systematic effort to eliminate the poison of error from our common knowledge.'' Cohen, however, thought that philosophy needed to go beyond inquiry into particular problems to address the need for a ''comprehensive vision.''[22] Cohen, then, like James and even Dewey, thought that philosophy was more than a narrow and often barren technical specialization. Rigorous logical analysis was needed to securely ground philosophy, but the philosopher then needed to go on to develop his vision, his grander synthesis.

Not all American philosophers in the early twentieth century agreed that philosophy could or should become a science, as the debates in the philosophical journals and at the meetings of the APA demonstrated.[23] However, there was growing consensus by the 1920s that philosophy, if it was to remain a vital part of the academic community and to participate in its discourse, would need to acquire at least some of the characteristics of a science, if not exactly become a science itself. The views presented above suggest that philosophers should transform their discipline by placing greater emphasis on logical analysis, on empirically verifiable evidence, on scientific methods, and on cooperative endeavors. These programmatic statements going back to the late nineteenth century had not, however, succeeded in significantly transforming the practice of philosophy in America by 1930. They had, nonetheless, created an expectation, especially among younger philosophers, that this was how philosophy ought to be conducted. Thus, when word of the program, methods, and goals of the logical positivists began to reach the United States after 1930, some philosophers were prepared to see in this philosophical movement the next step. Whereas the American philosophers had repeatedly called for making philosophy more scientific, the logical positivists seemed to have succeeded. It is no wonder, then, that the logical positivists and their ideas found a congenial climate in the United States.

In the early 1930s, reports on the ideas and activities of the logical positivists began to appear in American philosophical journals, such as *Philosophical Review* and the *Journal of Philosophy*. Many of these essays did more than simply outline the Europeans' philosophical positions; they also made explicit connections between the European developments and pragmatism. Although the Europeans acknowledged that the pragmatists had worked along similar lines, they confessed to relative ignorance of American philosophy. It was primarily the Americans, trained in the pragmatic context, who tried to suggest the fortuitous convergence of heretofore separate philosophical traditions.

One of the first reports, Sidney Hook's 1930 essay, "A Personal Impression of Contemporary German Philosophy," drew attention to recent European developments. Hook's impression was not altogether favorable, as he thought that too much German philosophy was still mired in idealism and historical study. Only a few philosophers seemed cognizant of and willing to incorporate recent developments in science. During his year abroad, Hook was keenly aware of the "insularity of German philosophy." Of the American philosophers, only William James was known, and he was "more often 'refuted' than read." Among the men affiliated with the analytic and empiricist approach, Hook was most taken with Hans Reichenbach. Reichenbach and his colleagues won Hook's approval, in part, because they had, as Peirce long ago advised, come to their philosophical studies after a firm grounding in a specific scientific discipline. This gave analytic philosophers "a sense of concreteness and relevance lacking in the thin effusions" of the more historically minded thinkers. Hook suggested that the most interesting parts of Reichenbach's philosophy for American readers would be his work on probability and on a naturalistic interpretation of the *a priori*.[24] Though Hook did not specifically deal with the Vienna Circle, his emphasis on the high quality of work from the scientifically trained German philosophers downplayed the more traditional areas of German philosophy.

A year after Hook's report appeared, "Logical Positivism: A New Movement in European Philosophy" was published in the *Journal of Philosophy*. Jointly authored by Albert Blumberg, a philosopher at Johns Hopkins who had studied in Vienna, and Herbert Feigl, a member of the Vienna Circle then at Harvard, the essay attempted to summarize the most important doctrines of the Vienna philosophers and their allies. In it, Blumberg and Feigl also coined the term "logical positivism." They emphasized "recent advances in pure logic which have made this new type of philosophizing possible." These advances were primarily derived from the work of Wittgenstein, Frege, Russell, and Whitehead. The key idea was that "logic can not be contradicted by empirical facts precisely because it says nothing about them. Logic is *a priori* because it is analytic." Beyond this, the logical positivists emphasized the distinction between "knowledge by description" and "knowledge by acquaintance." Most radical of the positions was the thesis developed by Carnap "that knowledge consists of propositions concerning the formal characters of experience." The logical positivists' theory of propositions led into their theory of meaning. That is, "to know the meaning of a proposition is to know what must be the case if the proposition is true." The meaning of a complex proposition was to be determined by breaking it into its "component atomic propositions" and then following the above procedure. Blumberg and Feigl noted that the importance of such a theory would be "familiar in view of the contributions and discussions of pragmatism." They then discussed the relations between science and logical positivism and the implications for our understanding of science. Finally, they examined the significance of this new movement regarding the "nature and aim of philosophy." They argued that the "essence of philosophy" had as "its ultimate goal the purification of language, the elimination of meaningless assertions." In support of this view, they cited Wittgenstein's position that "the object of philosopy is the logical clarification of thought. Philosophy is not a theory but an activity." The chief activity of philosophy was to clarify the propositions of science and to analyze the traditional subject matter of philosophy, particularly metaphysics. For the new positivists, metaphysical propositions were "strictly speaking, meaningless, since a proposition has meaning only when we know under what conditions it is true or false." In this respect, logical positivists went beyond what they viewed as the "pragmatic rejection of metaphysics as superfluous."[25]

In subsequent years, several additional accounts of logical positivism appeared in American journals. For example, Ernest Nagel, in his *Journal of Philosophy* report on the Eighth International Congress of Philosophy (1934) in Prague, devoted considerable attention to the philosophers of the Vienna Circle who were at the congress. The logical positivists and allied philosophers dominated the sessions of logic. Nagel found them to be "the most interesting and vital philosophers present." He noted the presentation of the American, Charles W. Morris, who developed a "more inclusive form of pragmatism," and declared it "refreshing to find an American pragmatist accepting the results of modern logic." Nagel also cited Hans Reichenbach's theory of probability, and observed that "he has developed it independently and in great technical detail," but that in its essentials it was "familiar to all students of Peirce." He speculated that the surprise with which Reichenbach's views were heard testified either to "the inaccessibility of Peirce to European students, or to the provincialism of their reading habits."[26]

Several accounts of logical positivism and analytic philosophy appeared in the *Journal of Philosophy* in 1936. The American accounts, by John Sommerville of the City College of New York and Ernest Nagel of Columbia, explicitly addressed the similarities between logical positivism and American pragmatism. Sommerville was particularly concerned about the "social ideas" of the Vienna Circle. He noted that the logical positivists now preferred to be called "logical empiricists," and that this only made more evident the movement's "significant connections, some premediated and some unconscious, with the pragmatic thought of James and Dewey." Like James and Dewey, these new empiricists had given up the pursuit of absolute certainty in favor of unity through growth. The new positivists' emphasis on dealing with "the concrete material of the sciences" constituted "another bond of union with American pragmatism and instrumentalism," as did the belief in the essential predictive power of science. Sommerville believed that the unity of science that lay at the heart of the logical empirical school could only benefit American sociology and philosophy.[27]

Ernest Nagel's much longer "Impressions and Appraisals of Analytic Philosophy in Europe" attempted to summarize and criticize the current positions of the Europeans while giving passing notice to the ways in which this new philosophy was tied, often indirectly, to pragmatic concerns. Despite the differences from Cambridge to Vienna, Prague, and Warsaw, Nagel discerned four common themes among the analytic philosophers: a preoccupation with analysis and the clarification of meaning and implication; "concern with formulating the *method* of philosophic analysis"; little interest in the history of philosophy; and adherence to "a common-sense naturalism." Nagel acknowledged that American ideas had little influence on the European analytic philosophers in part because "American writings are not easily accessible, and in part because American thinkers are not sufficiently analytic for European purposes." Even if the Americans were little known in Europe, the similarity of their thought meant that "much in the following account will be familiar to American readers." Nagel went on to summarize and comment on the recent work of G. E. Moore and Wittgenstein at Cambridge, the Vienna Circle, particularly Carnap, and the Polish logicians. He especially noted the "missionary zeal" with which the Vienna Circle had "propagated its doctrines to all parts of the world," and the way in which its members had unwittingly followed "Peirce's advice that expert knowledge of some empirical subject-matter ought to be part of a philosopher's equipment."[28]

Although Hans Reichenbach was not a member of the Vienna Circle, the analytic philosophy with which he was associated was closely allied in intent and method with the logical positivists. His 1936 essay, "Logistic Empiricism in Germany and the Present State of Its Problems," was a review of the historical antecedents of contemporary empirical philosophy and an assessment of its current status from his point of view. He noted that modern empiricism was "initiated" by nineteenth-century developments in the natural and physical sciences and given a philosophical formulation by Mach in Europe and by Peirce, James, and Dewey in the United States. Logistic empiricism was not a new invention, but an "explicit formulation" of the ideas previously developed by Mach and the pragmatists. "The sole significant advance which it contributes is to be found in the conscious working out of a method, until now accepted in an instinctive way, and in the substitution of organized collaboration on the basis of a common method for unrelated individual effort." However, this statement demonstrates the lack of an intimate understanding of pragmatism, as Peirce and, to some extent, Dewey had already taken that step. In the course of his summary of recent developments, he credited Peirce and the pragmatists with recognizing the connection between predictive propositions and problems of probability and induction. He suggested, however, that the Americans had not gone further than to see "the general direction along which the solution of a problem lies," while the Berlin and Viennese groups had gone on to develop "a definitive theory."[29] Reichenbach, then, was willing to credit the pragmatists as forerunners who had seen the right path to truth, meaning, and certainty, but who had not fully developed the implications of their insight. His comments, as noted above, do not, however, reveal a close familiarity with the writings of the pragmatists.

These three essays from 1936 suggest similarities of viewpoint and emphasis among the pragmatists, logical positivists, and other analytic philosophers of the 1920s and 1930s. They do not, however, contain a sustained analysis of the links between the American and European philosophies. The two most comprehensive early analyses of the ties between pragmatism and contemporary European empirical and analytic philosophies came in the work of C. I. Lewis and Charles W. Morris. Lewis, along with Dewey, was one of the leading exponents of a pragmatic philosophy, while Morris, a younger philosopher at the University of Chicago, attempted to unite pragmatism, logical positivism, and traditional empiricism in a new synthesis he called "scientific empiricism." While acknowledging the largely separate traditions of logical positivism and pragmatism, both Lewis and Morris explored the similarity of temper, outlook, and standpoint.

Although Lewis examined the similarities and differences between pragmatism and logical positivism at some length in his 1933 presidential address to the American Philosophical Association, his most penetrating comparison of pragmatism and logical positivism was in an essay written for publication in *Revue Internationale de Philosophie* in 1940. Because of the German invasion of Belgium, it was not published until 1970 in his *Collected Papers*; nonetheless, it is an important statement of the difference between pragmatism and logical positivism even while it acknowledges certain similarities. Despite the difficulty of global assessments, Lewis hoped to develop a "comparison between views which approximate to one another at points which are important but diverge at others which are not less significant." He limited his examination to our four topics: "empiricism, the scope of science, the significance of metaphysics, and the status of evaluative and moral judgments."[30]

In addressing the topic of empiricism, Lewis noted that "both movements present themselves as forms of empiricism," especially regarding the centrality of "a conception of empirical meaning." Both movements would also declare meaningless any statement that could not be empirically verified in some sense. Pragmatists, however, put more emphasis on "active intent" than the logical positivists. The two groups also differed on the "fundamental fashion in which meaning is to be determined." The logical positivists found meaning in the logical, formal relations between sentences, while the pragmatists held to a broader conception of what constituted conceivable and acceptable modes of empirical verification. The result, according to Lewis, was a "very deep" difference.[31]

Regarding the scope of science, Lewis observed that "pragmatism and logical positivism represent generalization of attitudes which might be regarded as derived from natural science and as looking to science as the exemplar of knowledge in general." Pragmatists, however, never accepted the "physicalistic pan-scientism" of the Vienna School. Further, "science" connoted different things to the pragmatists and the logical positivists. For pragmatism, science connoted "the *method* of science and its experimental and instrumental point of view," whereas the positivists emphasized "the *content* of science as exact formulation in physical terms." The pragmatists did not want to restrict narrowly the definition of science, nor to regard such a narrow definition as encompassing all of science. Rather, the pragmatists were more inclined to give the term "science" a wider "meaning in which it signifies merely what is verifiable and thus coincides with 'empirical knowledge' in general." According to Lewis, some pragmatists, like James, would go even further and "deny exclusive significance, or perhaps even preeminence, to the scientific formulation of truth."[32]

On the question of whether "metaphysical statements are meaningful," Lewis noted that even "without discussion" it was clear that "pragmatists and logical positivists would not be in agreement." He noted that "Peirce identified himself with a metaphysical position," that James had criticized absolute idealism as false, not meaningless, and that he had also argued for "realism and pluralism" as well as for the "significance and possible truth of various more speculative metaphysical assertions," and that Dewey, who ordinarily avoided metaphysical questions, is "definitely a realist, and could not plausibly be interpreted as denying significance to all metaphysical issues." The pragmatists, according to Lewis, wanted to hold to the possibility that at least some metaphysical statements were meaningful and thus significant.[33]

For Lewis, the strongest contrast between the two movements came, "with respect to problems of evaluation and of ethics." Pragmatism was activist and instrumentalist and "could be characterized as the doctrine that all problems are at bottom problems of conduct, that all judgments are implicitly judgments of value, and that, as there can be ultimately no valid distinction of theoretical from practical, so there can be no final separation of questions of truth of any kind from questions of justifiable ends of action." The logical positivists, according to Lewis, believed that value statements were either "merely expressive" or *a priori* normative statements and, in either case, not subject to empirical verification. Lewis, however, rejected these alternatives in favor of "the essentially empiricist conception that value-judgments are verifiable in the same general manner as are judgments of other qualities." His position, of course, was tied to the pragmatic view that empirical verification embraced more than a narrow scientific procedure.[34]

From his perspective firmly within the pragmatic tradition, Lewis emphasized the differences between the two movements while acknowledging shared concerns. Whereas the logical positivists wanted to reduce each of the topics discussed to those positions that could be empirically verified or formally analyzed in a rather narrow sense, the pragmatists sought a wider conception, more activist and instrumental in intent and practice, and more closely grounded in ordinary human needs and experience. Pragmatism may have helped create a favorable climate in the United States in which logical positivism could flourish, but Lewis refused to surrender the broader conception of a scientific, empirical philosophy developed by Peirce, James, Dewey, and himself.

Charles W. Morris, on the other hand, believed that pragmatism and logical positivism represented converging strains of a scientific philosophy. In a series of essays published together as *Logical Positivism, Pragmatism, and Scientific Empiricism* in 1937, Morris hailed the emergence of "a new type of mind" among younger scholars: "That of the logician-scientist who is content neither with the verbiage of most philosophical speculation nor with the mere repetition of non-analysed and non-systematized scientific concepts and propositions." This development gave hope to the "old ideal of a unified science" in which philosophy and science became one. His own formulation of the unification of philosophy and science, which he called scientific empiricism, attempted to unite the logical and analytical rigor of the positivists with the broader range of the pragmatists. Finally, echoing both Peirce and the logical positivists, Morris suggested that any such "empirical synthesis must, like science itself, be a cooperative enterprise."[35]

Morris addressed the possibility of the convergence of pragmatism and logical positivism most clearly in "The Concept of Meaning in Pragmatism and Logical Positivism," published in his short book, and in "Peirce, Mead, and Pragmatism" published in *Philosophical Review* in 1938. In the essay on meaning he characterized pragmatism as an empirical philosophy with an "emphasis on biological and social categories" and logical positivism as a movement characterized "by its utilization of logical (or syntactical or grammatical) analysis." Pragmatism, he thought, needed "systematization and a more adequate treatment of the formal sciences." This it could acquire from its "European cousin." Logical positivism needed more "socially and biologically oriented analyses" of concepts. In addition, a dose of pragmatism would aid the logical positivists "in doing justice to the full range of interests which have generally characterized the activity of philosophers by saving it from the scholastic spinning of webs" of a too-narrow focus on logical analysis. He thought it possible that, "in spite of apparent divergences and real differences of emphasis," pragmatism and logical positivism could converge on a theory of meaning "wide enough to include the results of socially cooperative science, and to do justice to the logical, biological, and empirical aspects of the symbolic process, and yet narrow enough to exclude from claims to knowledge those expressions which are meaningless."[36]

In the essay on Peirce and Mead, Morris noted the difficulty of finding unifying threads within the pragmatic movement, but he believed "that there is a sustained unity to the pragmatic movement. Pragmatism reveals itself in all its phases as a series of constantly deepening analyses of a single set of theses.'' He focused on the theory of signs developed by Peirce and Mead, and acknowledged their significant differences, while emphasizing broad areas of agreement on the importance of semiotics in problems of meaning and knowledge. Toward the end of the essay, Morris looked to the future development of pragmatism. Recent pragmatists had, he thought, been devoted to ''more careful analysis and wider attention to fields subject to such analysis.'' At the same time, logical empiricism had emerged in the ''philosophical garden.'' Despite their differences, Morris thought that it was ''possible to regard the two traditions as complementary and convergent components within a wider and more inclusive movement'' which he called ''scientific empiricism.'' By incorporating more and more of Peirce's logical orientation, contemporary pragmatists were increasingly ''moving into the circle of interests which characterize the logical empiricists.'' Similarly, by stressing the ''instrumental significance of formal structures'' and by recognizing the partial verification of propositions, the logical positivists were ''moving with remarkable rapidity in the direction of typical pragmatic emphases.'' Morris concluded that ''in the light of such convergences—and many more might be mentioned on both sides—it does not seem unreasonable to think of pragmatism and logical empiricism as different emphases within a common movement.''[37]

Morris also considered the relationship between philosophy and science as approached by pragmatism and logical positivism. Morris rejected ''any conception of philosophy which regards philosophy as proceeding by methods other than those of science or as obtaining an order of certainty different from that obtained by science.'' What work, then, was there left for the philosopher that the scientist could not do better? Morris developed four possibilities for a scientific philosophy. The first and narrowest possibility was ''to identify philosophy with formal logic, so conceived however that this in turn becomes identical with the logic of science.'' This was the route laid out by Carnap. Philosophy could clearly fulfill this role; the important question was whether it could also do more. The second possibility envisioned philosophy as clarifying meaning. This entailed applying ''the method of logical analysis to all concepts and to all dimensions of meaning.'' This conception had long been characteristic of pragmatism and had more recently found adherents among the members of the Vienna Circle. The third possibility conceived of philosophy as ''empirical axiology,'' and was particularly indebted to the work of Dewey. Developing this notion of philosophy required the formulation of ''a general theory of science as an institution and science as a habit of mind'' and the elaboration of the implications of adopting scientific methods and values for the ''widest spheres of human life.'' The final possibility, according to Morris, was ''philosophy as empirical cosmology.'' Under this heading, the task of philosophy was to ''erect a conceptual scheme of such generality that it is confirmed by all data. It differs from science in the narrower sense only in generality, and not in method nor in the security of the results.'' Such a philosophy would be continuous with the specialized and narrower sciences, and would build on the certain results of science. The main difference, for Morris, between science and philosophy was the range of vision: "Philosophy is the most general science and the widest vision,—and the one because it is the other."[38]

Morris's efforts to bring about a reconciliation of pragmatism and logical positivism drew more heavily on the pragmatic tradition than on logical positivism. His stress on the importance of signs derived from Peirce and Mead; his Deweyan concern for the wider human implications of a scientific philosophy, and his resistance to reducing philosophy to a logical, semantical, or grammatical analysis of propositions, put him clearly within the pragmatic conception of a scientific philosophy. Logical positivism was a promising complement to pragmatism because it promised to sharpen philosophical analysis, to define more clearly the empirical conditions for the verification of meaning and knowledge, and to wed philosophy even more closely to the scientific method. But like James, Dewey, and Lewis, Morris refused to reduce philosophy or pragmatism to logical analysis and empirical verification of propositions. Convergence, as he envisioned it, meant drawing from both philosophical traditions, not reducing one to the other.

Thus the two distinct philosophical traditions of pragmatism and logical positivism experienced an uneasy convergence in the 1930s. The convergence was fostered primarily by Americans knowledgeable in the pragmatic tradition who saw in logical positivism the possibility of strengthening the tendencies toward analysis, empirical verification, and scientific method already present in pragmatism. The Americans tended to see the incorporation of logical positivism and its allied philosophies as a way to move philosophy forward, to eliminate the vestiges of sloppy, uncritical, and unscientific metaphysical thought. The logical positivists, however, tended to see pragmatism, when they considered it at all, as one of the empiricist and realistic predecessors to their more rigorous scientific, empirical, and analytic method. In their view, logical positivism delivered what pragmatism had only promised.

The congenial climate that Herbert Feigl and Rudolf Carnap found in coming to the United States in the 1930s was largely the product of pragmatism and the drive to make philosophy more scientific that had developed in America beginning in the late nineteenth century. The urge to make philosophy into a science grew out of certain developments within philosophic thought, particularly a revival of empiricism and realism, but also out of an academic and cultural climate in which the values and methods of science were held in high regard. By the 1930s it was evident, despite the progress toward a scientific philosophy, that American philosophy was insufficiently critical, analytic, and scientific in its methodology. For those philosophers familiar with European developments, logical positivism initially promised what the pragmatists had been unable and unwilling to achieve—a philosophy firmly and solely rooted in a scientific, empirical method. Closer study, at least by men like Lewis and Morris, revealed an initial reluctance to abandon the broader conception of philosophy embodied in pragmatism in spite of the undeniable appeal of logical positivism. Only later would pragmatism be pushed to the side as American philosophers concentrated on logic, analysis of language, philosophy of science, and epistemology.

Pragmatism had created the conditions of its own demise. It had raised expectations concerning empiricism, logical and critical analysis, and verification that it appeared unable to meet. First logical positivism, and then linguistic analysis and ordinary language philosophy, promised to fulfill these expectations. Even though analytic philosophy broke with the narrow verifiability criterion of meaning, it continued the positivist emphasis on analysis and the positivist rejection of a philosophical role in social reconstruction. By midcentury, as John Rajchman has observed, "mainstream American philosophy had become a specialized occupation with precise formal problems, one that eschewed public debate, disclaimed the requirements of literary or historical erudition, dismissed phenomenological and existential thought, and found little scientific and nothing philosophical in either psychoanalysis or Marxism. Philosophy had become a recondite recluse."[39] The triumph of analytic philosophy over pragmatism was not, however, long-lasting. Since the mid-1970s, at least, the analytic strain in American philosophy has come under attack from a variety of philosophers, including Richard Rorty, Richard Bernstein, and Hilary Putnam, who might be categorized as neopragmatic in their outlook. In emphasizing different aspects of the pragmatic tradition, these more recent philosophers have found various ways of overcoming analytic philosophy.[40] Pragmatism, then, not only created the conditions in which logical positivism and analytic philosophy could flourish in the United States, it also contained the seeds of the postanalytic philosophies that have attempted to move beyond the intraphilosophical analytic debates to restore a broader range of philosophical concerns characteristic of the work of Peirce, James, and Dewey.

NOTES

1. Herbert Feigl, "The Wiener Kreis in America," in *The Intellectual Migration: Europe and America, 1930–1960*, ed. Donald Fleming and Bernard Bailyn (Cambridge, Mass.: Harvard University Press, Belknap Press, 1969), 644–45, 630; Rudolf Carnap, "The Development of My Thinking," in *The Philosophy of Rudolf Carnap*, ed. Paul Arthur Schilpp, The Library of Living Philosophers, vol. 11 (LaSalle, Ill.: Open Court, 1963), 34, 40. Carnap recalled that his knowledge of pragmatism came mainly after he emigrated and was filtered through the work of Charles W. Morris and Ernest Nagel. Rudolf Carnap, "Replies and Systematic Expositions," in Schilpp, ed., *The Philosophy of Rudolf Carnap*, 860–61.

2. A somewhat similar argument is advanced by G. Schrader, "The Influence of Continental Philosophy on the Contemporary American Scene: A Summons to Autonomy," in *Aspects of Contemporary American Philosophy*, ed. Franklin H. Donnell, Jr. (Wurzburg: Physica-Verlag, 1965), 43–44; and by Morton White, *Toward Reunion in Philosophy* (Cambridge, Mass.: Harvard Univeristy Press, 1956), vii.

3. Daniel J. Wilson, *Science, Community, and the Transformation of American Philosophy, 1860–1930* (Chicago: University of Chicago Press, 1990), chapter 7, "Science and the Crisis of Confidence in American Philosophy."

4. Ibid., 180–82.

5. Ibid., 2–7, 56–57.

6. William James, "A Plea for Psychology as a 'Natural Science,'" in *Essays in Psychology: The Works of William James* (Cambridge, Mass.: Harvard University Press, 1983), 71; William James, "Is Life Worth Living?" in *The Will to Believe and Other Essays in Popular Philosophy: The Works of William James* (Cambridge, Mass.: Harvard University Press, 1979), 49–50; William James, *The Principles of Psychology: The Works of William James* (Cambridge, Mass.: Harvard University Press, 1981), 2:1179; and William James, "Preface," in *The Will to Believe*, 7.

7. On Peirce's early education and career with the U.S. Coast and Geodetic Survey, see Murray G. Murphey, *The Development of Peirce's Philosophy* (Cambridge, Mass.: Harvard University Press, 1961), 18–19, 97–105; Max H. Fisch, "Peirce as Scientist, Mathematician, Historian, Logician, and Philosopher," in *Proceedings of the C. S. Peirce Bicentennial International Congress*, ed. Kenneth L. Ketner et al., Texas Tech University Graduate Studies, no. 23 (Lubbock: Texas Tech Press, 1981), 13–19; and Joseph Brent, *Charles Sanders Peirce: A Life* (Bloomington: Indiana University Press, 1993).

8. Charles S. Peirce, "Private Thoughts, Principally on the Conduct of Life," in *Writings of Charles S. Peirce: A Chronological Edition*, vol. 1, *1857–1866*, ed. Max H. Fisch (Bloomington: Indiana University Press, 1982), p. 9; Charles S. Peirce, "[Critique of Positivism]," in *Writings of Charles S. Peirce: A Chronological Edition*, vol. 2, *1857–1871*, ed. Edward C. Moore (Bloomington: Indiana University Press, 1984), 127; Charles S. Peirce, "Lecture I: Early Nominalism and Realism," in *Writings of Peirce*, 2:315.

9. Charles S. Peirce, "Whewell," in *Writings of Peirce*, 2:339; Charles S. Peirce, "How to Make Our Ideas Clear," in *Writings of Charles S. Peirce, A Chronological Edition*, vol. 3, *1872–1878*, ed. Christian J. W. Kloesel (Bloomington: Indiana University Press, 1986), 273; Charles S. Peirce, "Some Consequences of Four Incapacities," in *Writings of Peirce*, 2:212.

10. Charles Sanders Peirce, "The Backward State of Metaphysics," in *The Collected Papers of Charles Sanders Peirce*, ed. Charles Hartshorne and Paul Weiss (Cambridge, Mass.: Harvard University Press, 1931–1935), 6:2; Charles Sanders Peirce, "Vitally Important Topics," in *Collected Papers*, 1:620; Charles Sanders Peirce to William James, December 26, 1897, in Ralph Barton Perry, *The Thought and Character of William James*, (Boston: Little, Brown, 1935), 2:419; Charles Sanders Peirce, "What Pragmatism Is," in *Collected Papers*, 5:413.

11. Wilson, *Science, Community* 136–37; see also Harry T. Costello, *Josiah Royce's Seminar, 1913–1914: As Recorded in the Notebooks of Harry T. Costello*, ed. Grover Smith (New Brunswick, N.J.: Rutgers University Press, 1936), 1–3.

12. John Dewey, "The New Psychology," in *The Early Works, 1882–1898*, edited by Jo Ann Boydston (Carbondale: Southern Illinois University Press, 1969), 1:53, 56; John Dewey, "The Obligation to Knowledge of God," in *The Early Works*, 1:62.

13. John Dewey, "The Present Position of Logical Theory," in *The Early Works*, 126; John Dewey, "The Logic of Verification," in *The Early Works*, 3:88–89; John Dewey, "Is Logic a Dualistic Science?" in *The Early Works*, 3:80.

14. John Dewey, "Introduction to Philosophy: Syllabus of Course 5, Philosophical Department," in *The Early Works*, 3:211, 229; John Dewey, "Significance of the Problem of Knowledge," in *The Early Works*, 5:21–22.

15. John Dewey, "Logical Conditions of a Scientific Treatment of Morality," in *The Middle Works, 1899–1924*, edited by Jo Ann Boydston (Carbondale: Southern Illinois University Press, 1977), 3:3, 39: John Dewey, "Science as Subject-Matter and as Method," in *The Middle Works*, 6:78; John Dewey, "The Evolutionary Method as Applied to Morality," in *The Middle Works* 2:19.

16. John Dewey, "Philosophy and American National Life," in *The Middle Works*, 3:77.

17. John Dewey, *Reconstruction in Philosophy*, in *The Middle Works*, 12:114, 134–35.

18. John Dewey, *Experience and Nature*, in *The Later Works, 1925–1953*, edited by Jo Ann Boydston (Carbondale: Southern Illinois University Press, 1981), 1:123, 134; John Dewey, *The Quest for Certainty*, in *The Later Works*, 248.

19. Ralph W. Sleeper, *The Necessity of Pragmatism: John Dewey's Conception of Philosophy* (New Haven, Conn.: Yale University Press, 1986), 134–35, 168–71.

20. James B. Pratt, "The Twelfth Annual Meeting of the American Philosophical Association," *Journal of Philosophy* 10 (1913): 91–92; see also, Wilson, *Science, Community*, 141–42.

21. Arthur O. Lovejoy, "On Some Conditions of Progress in Philosophical Inquiry," *Philosophical Review* 26 (1917): 132–33, 144, 148–50, 154–63; Arthur O. Lovejoy, "Progress in Philosophical Inquiry," *Philosophical Review* 26 (1917): 538, 543–44. See also, Ernest Albee, Charles Bakewell, et al., "Progress in Philosophical Inquiry and Mr. Lovejoy's Presidential Address," *Philosophical Review* 26 (1917): 315–31.

22. Morris R. Cohen, *Reason and Nature: An Essay on the Meaning of Scientific Method* (New York: Harcourt, Brace, 1934), ix, xi, 39–40, 79, 149. See also David A. Hollinger, *Morris R. Cohen and the Scientific Ideal* (Cambridge, Mass.: MIT Press, 1975).

23. Wilson, *Science, Community*, 148–49; 180–82.

24. Sidney Hook, "A Personal Impression of Contemporary German Philosophy," *Journal of Philosophy* 27 (1930): 144–47, 158–60.

25. Albert E. Blumberg and Herbert Feigl, "Logical Positivism: A New Movement in European Philosophy," *Journal of Philosophy* 28 (1931): 281–82, 285–87, 292–93; see also Feigl, "Wiener Kreis in America," 646.

26. Ernest Nagel, "The Eighth International Congress of Philosophy," *Journal of Philosophy* 31 (1934): 591–92; see also Edward Ginsburg, "On the Logical Positivism of the Viennese Circle," *Journal of Philosophy* 29 (1932): 121–29.

27. John Sommerville, "The Social Ideas of the Wiener Kreis's International Congress," *Journal of Philosophy* 33 (1936): 296–97, 300.

28. Ernest Nagel, "Impressions and Appraisals of Analytic Philosophy in Europe," *Journal of Philosophy* 33 (1936): 6–7, 9–10, 29–30.

29. Hans Reichenbach, "Logistic Empiricism in Germany and the Present State of Its Problems," *Journal of Philosophy* 33 (1936): 141–42, 152.

30. Clarence Irving Lewis, "Logical Positivism and Pragmatism," in *Collected Papers of Clarence Irving Lewis*, ed. John D. Goheen and John L. Mothershead, Jr. (Stanford: Stanford University Press, 1970), 92–93; see also Lewis's APA presidential address, "Experience and Meaning," in *Collected Papers*, 258–61, 270.

31. Lewis, "Logical Positivism and Pragmatism," 93–96.

32. Ibid., 99–100, 104.

33. Ibid., 104, 106–107.

34. Ibid., 107–9.

35. Charles W. Morris, *Logical Positivism, Pragmatism, and Scientific Empiricism* (Paris: Hermann et Cie., 1937), pp. 3–5; see also Charles W. Morris, "Some Aspects of Recent American Scientific Philosophy," *Erktenntnis* 5 (1935): 143, 148–49.

36. Charles W. Morris, "The Concept of Meaning in Pragmatism and Logical Positivism," in *Logical Positivism, Pragmatism, and Scientific Empiricism*, 22–23, 30.

37. Charles W. Morris, "Peirce, Mead, and Pragmatism," *Philosophical Review* 47 (1938): 110, 125–27.

38. Charles W. Morris, "Philosophy of Science and Science of Philosophy," in *Logical Positivism, Pragmatism, and Scientific Empiricism*, 7–11, 13–14, 18–20.

39. John Rajchman, "Philosophy in America," in *Post-Analytic Philosophy*, ed. John Rajchman and Cornel West (New York: Columbia University Press, 1985), ix.

40. For recent examples of the effort to overcome the positivistic and analytic strain in philosophy, see the essays in Richard Rorty, *Objectivity, Relativism, and Truth: Philosophical Papers, Volume 1* (Cambridge: Cambridge University Press, 1991), especially "Introduction," 12–17 and "Pragmatism Without Method," 75–77.

7

American Philosophy and Its Lost Public

Bruce Kuklick

In this chapter I characterize three periods of speculative thinking in America. The aim is dual. I consider how it came to be that contemporary philosophy— philosophy in my third period—differs so much from that in the other two, and I appraise the consequences to philosophy today of the loss of a sense of mission that, however differently conceived, sustained the earlier periods. To state this dual aim differently: the historical survey of the three periods will be grist for making some points about the *meaning* of philosophy in the United States and the rationale offered by professors for the utility of studying it.[1]

The first period extends from the middle of the seventeenth century, my starting point, to World War I and embraces those people commonly regarded as American thinkers from the early Puritans to the classic pragmatists. During this 250-year epoch a couple of broad themes stand out. Philosophers regarded human knowledge as one: knowledge of the world, knowledge of man, and knowledge of God were seen to fit together and support one another. Scientific knowledge was not identified with any narrow understanding of the work of the physical sciences, and, perhaps most important, few questioned the claim that religion was a cognitive enterprise that established truth. The thinkers of this period saw philosophizing as the means by which the ways of nature could be shown to be emblematic of the divine and, so, as the intellectual pursuit that best exposed the meaning of human experience. During this period thinkers also believed that their enterprise had consequences for mundane affairs: the philosopher was a public person.

For the Puritans this public role was essentially religious because theological concerns were at the heart of their society. The leadership was formally committed to a specific body of thought, and that thought was fundamental to a virtually theocratic culture. Technologia, the system of ideas that was the official philosophy of the college-educated New England elect, was surely derivative. It had its basis in medieval scholasticism, European Calvinism, and particularly the humanism of Petrus Ramus. Clergymen taught it to generations of students at Harvard and Yale and made it the intellectual core of their writing until the eighteenth century was well under way. While this system emphasized that existence must be understood in religious terms, it combined what we would today call science, philosophy, and theology. For the New Englanders the acquisition of knowledge was a duty because all of nature and all of history were divine works. Every field of study revealed something of the Lord's ways. The Puritan savant took all the world for his subject and taught how all areas of inquiry were interconnected and how all nature displayed God's activity in creating and governing the universe.

When the Puritans fully absorbed Newton and Locke—during the first third of the eighteenth century—their scientific and philosophical views shifted. Their religious ideas came to depend less centrally on scripture. But the seventeenth-century system had enjoined them to find a coherent intellectual order in the chaos of experience, a rational explanation of phenomena. Newton gave the New England intellectual elite *proof* of the order and plan in nature. In short, the new science was a blessing, a splendid confirmation of their doctrines, and a useful tool. The laws of physics could be regarded as descriptions of the mode of divine action, the will of God in action. Here was a demonstration of the rationality of the cosmos beyond anything the ministers had dreamed. The later Puritan divines could not conceive that the Newtonian world was self-subsistent; it was rather the most wonderful illustration of spiritual truth.

By this time colonial society had become more diverse, and the changing cultural milieu resulted in a decisive fight between defenders of the older and stricter Calvinism and those content with a religion less at odds with the demands of a wealthier and more sanguine society. But this battle between the likes of Jonathan Edwards, on the one hand, and Charles Chauncey and even Benjamin Franklin, on the other, should not blind us to the fact that there was agreement on the union of science, philosophy, and religion and on the revelation of the deity in nature. In fact, although Edwards was on the more traditional side of the controversy, he most thoroughly and successfully integrated the latest scientific and philosophical notions into a religious worldview. What seems to have separated Edwards from his contemporaries—aside from his genius—was that whereas Edwards was a theocrat, his peers were willing to expand the authority of nontheological thinkers in a society where various creeds flourished and religious institutions had to share power. There were divergent ideas of the role of the philosopher. Edwards thought of the American ministry as the leaders of a clerisy. His opponents believed that the theocracy was lost but that religious leaders could serve the community through concrete reforms, organizing it around universal moral principles, active good works, and practical piety. For example, Cotton Mather urged establishing reform societies to suppress disorder and immorality and to supply the sanctions necessary to maintain discipline in a more heterodox society. Franklin also sponsored voluntary associations to do good works, convinced that in a culture of multiple religious groups the leadership could only coalesce around practical measures.[2]

Accordingly, during the eighteenth century the philosophers' public function shifted from the religious to the social. As the colonies became the United States, the intellectual elite—commonly called the *philosophes*—assumed a distinctly political role. The providential deism of the Founding Fathers in their eyes surely amalgamated scientific and religious doctrines, even if the latter were not Christian, and their peculiar form of Scottish Enlightenment rationalism guided and justified their leadership from the Revolution to the Age of Jackson. The Declaration of Independence and the Constitution welded the secular and the sacred, and their authors, the quintessential public men of the period, saw philosophy as the synoptic integrator of their manifold concerns.

The characteristic Scottish philosophy that dominated American academic speculation in the nineteenth century returned to a broadly social public function from the preeminent political one. Philosophers spoke out on economic and education issues, for example, as well as on political reform and religious disputation. American promoters of the Scots also forsook non-Christian deism for more conventional forms of worship. But in their various defenses of Protestant denominationalism, nineteenth-century philosophers also defended science. They saw no conflict between an empiricist view of the world and a moderate and intelligent religion. A major aspect of the philosophic enterprise was interpreting scientific advances and religious doctrines to reconcile competing positions.

The Transcendentalists also swam in this main stream. Ralph Waldo Emerson's most sustained work is, after all, titled *Nature*, but the critical point to be made about the nineteenth century does not concern them. Nineteenth-century Scottish academic philosophers and theologians have received a bad press: they were just as socially engaged as more well known critics such as Henry David Thoreau and Emerson.

The philosophers of the Golden Age also treated the bases of both science *and* religion, redefining them in light of the work of Charles Darwin. The pragmatism of William James was typical of the result, and revered the scientific endeavor but rejected the privileged character of knowledge of the physical world. James affirmed that we could not rigidly construe cognition. The natural sciences and religion were each justified on the same grounds: they enabled us to survive in an only semi-hospitable environment. The speculators of the Golden Age, it also need be noted, altered again the the philosophers' public role. Almost inevitably because of the Darwinian controversy—the attacks by foreign evolutionary positivists on religion—philosophers pulled in their horns. They spent their time leading the educated, upper-middle class to a new and vital spiritual commitment. Their commitment to other aspects of public affairs slackened.

The era of World War I ends the first period during which philosophy bound science and sentiment together and during which the philosopher was also a public man. The second period is a transitional one, of philosophy between the wars; the third period is American philosophy after World War II.

It is ironic that enormous changes in philosophizing so rapidly followed the speculation of the Golden Age, the greatest achievements of American philosophy. Within fifty years of the work of Charles Peirce and William James, philosophers rejected the integration of science and theology and dismissed the public role of the philosopher. The spectacular synthesis of religion and Darwin that the pragmatists brought off succeeded only momentarily, and by the fourth decade of the twentieth century philosophers were deserting religion *en masse*. Despite the pragmatists' brief victory, things actually became unstuck for them in the science versus religion debate. Although we feel James triumphed in the academy, by World War II the intellectual defense of religion was unpopular and philosophers had simultaneously retreated to the ivory tower.

How were these dramatic changes heralded by the students of the thinkers of the Golden Age, the transitional philosophers of the second period? This first generation of purely professional philosophers in the United States rose to eminence between 1910 and 1950. But thinkers such as C. I. Lewis, Arthur Lovejoy, Ralph Barton Perry, Roy Wood Sellars, and Morris Cohen have not successfully engaged our attention. From the vantage point of sixty years they look dreary and unprepossessing. The group has received little philosophical study or historical examination. James put it well while he was training many of these men when he complained of "the gray plaster temperament of our bald-headed young Ph.D.'s, boring each other at seminaries, writing those direful reports of the literature in the 'Philosophical Review.' "[3]

The interwar philosophers may have been judged too harshly. In many cases they became the sorts of specialists James disliked, and they certainly backed away from any serious and sustained attempt to show religion justifiable in a modern technological society. Their defense of religion, if it occurred at all, was wary and implicit. There were few philosophical generalists bold enough to harmonize knowledge of the world and of the divine. But the transitional thinkers were *not* the young logical positivists of the 1930s. Bereft of the belief that philosophy could yoke physics and religious solace as *fin de siècle* speculation had, the philosophers of the second period seized on Science with a capital S as the human endeavor that could coherently order the world and justify a faith to live by. Many of these people had come to philosophy because they were troubled by the repercussions of the Darwinian controversy. They found philosophy unable to shore up their old creeds, but it did have the virtue of giving them a new one.

The philosophers of the 1920s, 1930s, and 1940s were only vaguely aware of the investigations of the hard sciences and had no sophisticated sense of "the philosophy of science.'' Yet they heralded science as the panacea of secular society. Indeed, they came to use the adjective ''scientific'' as an incantatory device when they wished to praise an enterprise and exempt it from criticism. Moreover, although these thinkers usually distinguished the realms of nature and morals, they also believed, somehow, that science could establish and justify a scheme of values and the good society. In crudest form their potent if confused legacy is with us today in the ideology of the social sciences. On the one hand, many social scientists hold, their investigations are value-free and ethics can be explained by a simple emotivism. Is and Ought are sundered. On the other hand, the expertise of social scientists somehow legitimates their speaking out on important questions of public policy. Is somehow implies Ought.

This philosophic paean to science and to a scientific politics undergirds the mentality of the representative philosophers of the transitional period; it is shared by the doctrinally diverse thinkers that I have mentioned above as well as—need I add him—the later John Dewey, a holdover from the Golden Age. Many social scientists still pay tribute to a scientific method that will answer all human problems and to a mechanistic view of social relations to which the method can apply. The enduring legacy of the second period is this marriage of a romanticized notion of science and a technocratic vision of morality.

Dewey and his younger peers did not forsake the American tradition. They were suspicious of the spiritual or at least of its alliance with science, but they promulgated a talismanic version of science that fulfilled many religious needs. The transitional generation also carried on the public tradition of American philosophy, broadening the Golden Age's emphasis and commenting on education, economics, and politics. The claims the scientific ideal made for the study of society allowed the interwar philosophers to speak for the liberal intelligentsia in popular forms of debate.

So we reach the third period and my attempt to characterize postwar philosophy. Recent speculation has rejected the defining traits of its predecessors—the need to make both knowledge of God and the world legitimate *and* the public role of philosophy. Before I can show how these developments arose out of the concerns of the transitional generation, it is helpful to note the social context in which the developments emerged. The professionalization of scholarship in the United States occurred roughly between 1880 and 1920. It encompassed several things. Various disciplines, limited fields of knowledge distinguished by special techniques and accepted sets of doctrines, grew up in the university. Universities defined the integrity of a discipline by the number of positions it would finance in a department. The training and placing of teachers in a field took place through an intensified apprenticeship leading to the doctorate and appointment as a college professor. The paraphernalia associated with the social organization typical of the modern professoriate came into existence: the scholarly bureaucracy in the university, the codification of ranks culminating with tenure, academic journals, and professional associations. While this process occurred before World War II, it was first entrenched as a social fact for the bright young men who exhibited philosophy's aspirations after the defeat of the Nazis. For them the goal was specialized research published for technically competent audiences in technical journals with popularizations frequently relegated to hacks, has-beens, and incompetents.

In this context the teaching of the transitional philosophers of the second period was crucial for those of the third period. These later speculators learned from their mentors that science was the area to study, and they moved from a relatively unsubtle comprehension of it to sophisticated work in logic, epistemology, and the philosophy of science. Simultaneously, however, they found that the accepted conception of a "scientific" morality would not bear scrutiny. They cast aside the attempt to amalgamate various forms of human understanding that had defined speculation in America since the seventeenth century. Belief that science could serve as key to the meaning and significance of human existence was abandoned. Almost as an afterthought, philosophers relinquished their public role.

After World War II, that is, the role of the discipline of philosophy in the culture changed dramatically from what it had been. The enterprise is no longer the synoptic integrator of the life of the mind, nor does it have much of a public function. The reasons for this are both intellectual and social. The location of all speculative endeavor in the university and its surrounding institutions and the efflorescence of the academic as a social type have narrowed the vision of philosophers, and the growth of expertise and specialization has reinforced this constricted outlook. Indeed, the alteration in philosophy in many ways just mirrors what has happened in many parts of the scholarly world. Philosophy, however, is a sort of limiting case. It once had the supreme role as the queen of the sciences; now it has next to none. It once was the premier public academic calling; now it has no such calling.

Many academics do still speak out on public issues, but those who do are rarely philosophers—Robert Bellah, Allan Bloom, Garry Wills, Stephen Jay Gould, Edward Wilson.[4] Overall, the philosophers of my transitional, interwar generation communicated their interest in the public function of philosophy not to their professional philosophy students, but to assorted social scientists.

There are also quasi-public scholars whose "blockbuster" academic books have had wide multi-disciplinary effects. But these people, too, are rarely philosophers. Examples are Thomas Kuhn in *The Structure of Scientific Revolutions* (1962); Clifford Geertz in *The Interpretation of Cultures* (1973); Stanley Fish in *Is There a Text in This Class?* (1980); Paul Kennedy in *The Rise and Fall of the Great Powers* (1987); and Richard Rorty in *Philosophy and the Mirror of Nature* (1979) and *Contingency, Irony, and Solidarity* (1989)—more later about this exception who proves the rule.[5]

Let me turn in this analysis of the present period to the chapter's second aim. The historical excursion provides material for understanding the meaning of philosophy today in American culture. I will try to answer two questions: Is the present situation good or bad? and Is it good or bad for the practice of philosophy in America? And I will end by offering a diagnosis for whatever ills philosophy may have and a prescription to cure them.

The pluses of specialization and professionalization in the university can be quickly recounted. It is a blessing that a professor has to know something now before he or she can waffle on about it. It is hard to object to the fact that wealth and family no longer give people an automatic right to speak out on public affairs, or that religious commitment is no longer a prerequisite for having something to say. Indeed, the fact that philosophers are no longer usually leaders in a civic dialogue because they do not have the requisite knowledge may also be a positive thing: the quality of the public performance of the philosophers has been dubious for the past two hundred years. The *philosophes*, the Founding Fathers, did just fine. Since that time, as institutions became the locus of speculation, it is more difficult to make out a positive case. The *ante-bellum* Scottish moral philosophers were not merely predictably conservative, but, more important, banal and often trivial, platitudinous, and jejune. The Golden Age did not do much better—it was unrelievedly genteel. World War I gave the transitional generation of philosophers an early and unique opportunity to mobilize the universities for the war effort and to produce the worst sort of anti-German propaganda. The philosophers also helped to drum dissidents out of institutions of higher learning. That is, I am suspicious of the notion of a vital public discourse led by philosophers (or by academics in general). We might all benefit if scholars were restricted to the Ivory Tower. The world might be better off if philosophy were kept pure. So, to answer my first question, it may not be so bad that philosophy has lost its public.

That does not mean, however, to turn to my second question, that it is good for philosophy itself. Disciplines are not Platonic concepts written in the minds of administrators and demanding to be realized to their fullest financial potential. Disciplines are strategies for investigation that have a cultural source and that can consequently change; their existence today depends in part on the politics of the university. Without a defensible mission, philosophy might be in the position of systematic theology, say, at the end of the nineteenth century, a discipline that by and large has gone out of business.

In some measure philosophers have recognized this. Many have plausibly argued that they can no longer function as authoritative cultural critics on the ground that what is called the knowledge explosion prohibits anyone from mastering anything more than a fragment of what we know, that the generalizer can be no more than a dilettante. But while they cannot contribute materially to the various branches of knowledge, some philosophers contend that they can clarify problems about the form of knowledge; philosophers can clear up conceptual confusions that prevent practitioners in various areas of inquiry from working most effectively. These philosophers point to the development of the field of cognitive science, courses in medical ethics and the like, and various interdisciplinary projects involving philosophy—some in evolutionary biology are noteworthy—to suggest a new role for philosophy as ground-clearer, rubbish-remover, and under-laborer.

On the other side, many students in various disciplines claim not to read philosophy or to be unable to understand it if they do read it. Many departments have positions reserved for methodologists or theoreticians who do their own "philosophy" out of whole cloth and are regularly castigated by philosophers because they are ignorant of the discipline's nuances. The social sciences, as I have suggested, have been theoretically oriented in this way for some time. In a comparatively recent development, much speculation that used to be the purview of philosophers has been taken over by literary theorists in many language departments. French intellectual fads have received tenure in departments of English in the United States, which often challenge philosophy departments for authority. It is almost as if a functionalist view of human society were true. Cultural criticism about objects of ultimate concern is a need that always will be served in one way or another. If professional philosophers will not do it, someone else will—in the United States today the social scientist or the literary critic.

This challenge to the self-image of philosophy has been reinforced in the last twenty years by a battle within the field itself. The "analysts" are the heirs to the postwar logicians and epistemologists; they are ensconced at the most prestigious schools and, if it may be said without prejudice, are an intellectual elite unconcerned with the alteration in the civic function of philosophy. Their opponents, the "pluralists," are not as intellectually prepossessing. They nonetheless have a more generous sense of what philosophy is, and they find lamentable the decline in the public role of professional speculation. The struggle between the two groups has centered on the constricted speculative views of the reigning analytic group and, secondarily, on the feeble mark this sort of philosophy has made outside its own disciplinary strongholds. Trained in the Anglo-American (analytic) tradition, Richard Rorty left it for a position in the Humanities and is roundly disliked by his previous comrades. For a time he was a sort of hero to the other side, the pluralists. But, to emphasize the troubles in metaphysical circles, the pluralists, after having a better look, also dislike Rorty for stealing their thunder; for vulgarly pillaging nonanalytic traditions and the history of thought about which, the pluralists claim, he knows nothing; for urging that philosophy is "over" when the pluralists still believe it can be restored to its synoptic role and vanquish the literary critics. That is, Rorty, the one philosopher with an academic and intellectual public, is in bad repute with both factions of professional philosophy.

All of this is to say that there is no definite answer to my second question: Is the change in role good or bad for American philosophy? Some people see a vital discipline in ferment; others see confusion, lack of purpose, and self-aggrandizement. The literary critics may look with glee on the internecine strife in philosophy. English departments have always been the most imperialistic of the humanities. The split within the professional philosophical camp of the enemy may allow them to divide and conquer. The possible triumph of the literary critics fills me with dread, I must confess. They are not knowledgeable of speculative traditions and have no training in understanding them. In any event the philosophers, whatever the quality of their public work, spoke out of a tradition or traditions of learning, and I am conventional enough to respect those traditions— not only unknown to, but repudiated by, literary critics. For my money we are in serious trouble when aggressive ignorance is a central variable in determining "public philosophy" today.

On the other side, I am almost tempted to say that professional philosophers deserve it. The ministerial posturing of the pluralists is only matched by their intellectual frugality. As a social group the analysts have only the barest sense of what the world is like beyond the confines the *Journal of Philosophy*. One understands why intellectual debate on these matters has become so divisive yet unenlightening.

What is the basic trouble? And what could be done about it? There are directions philosophers might take to restore unity in their own ranks and, perhaps, recover the ball from the literary critics. Some philosophers, as previously mentioned, believe there is still a role for them to play as intellectual ground-cleaners. Nonetheless, the philosophers have often run into scholars whose ground is to be cleaned who object to or ignore speculative labor. There is much to be said for the intransigence of the disciplinary practitioners. Epistemology, the central discipline of analytic philosophy, is germane to little else beyond itself because of the unrelenting penchant of philosophers to engage in their favored form of analysis without regard for substantive disciplinary knowledge. That is, philosophers are effectively convinced that investigation at an *a priori* level is licit, that exploration of what scholars actually know about the world is beside the point of their enterprise.

Yet at least one central strand of philosophical analysis is not committed to a traditional view of epistemology. Latter day "pragmatic analysts" such as Nelson Goodman and W.V.O. Quine of Harvard have attacked the old distinction between fact and theory, data and conceptual scheme, *a priori* and *a posteriori*. For these thinkers strict conceptual investigation is not possible; substantive demands shape theories taken to be merely the product of the free play of imagination. Any supposed collection of mere evidence is informed by the implicit constraints of some theory.[6]

From this insight I infer the usefulness of a version of the old Kantian notion of the synthetic *a priori*. At the basis of knowledge in various fields of inquiry are presuppositions that cannot be thought away but that also depend on the empirical. Their existence compromises various kinds of empiricism but also makes dubious the idea of any inquiry into concepts alone. It would follow that investigation of such a synthetic *a priori* would require the standard skills acquired by philosophers but also knowledge of the research paradigms in various disciplines. Successful investigation of this synthetic *a priori* might be relevant in the practice of disciplines. Philosophers would again speak as a sort of super discipline, as the pluralists desire.

In practice, however, philosophers have ignored the insight of the pragmatic analysts. Two stunning examples come to mind. They are powerful because they emanate from thinkers who embrace ideas of the pragmatic analysts, from whom I have extrapolated the idea of a synthetic *a priori*. Consider Quine's *Word and Object* and John Rawls's *A Theory of Justice*.[7] Quine has argued more strongly than anyone that the distinction between scheme and empirical content, the analytic and the synthetic as he called it, is unjustifiable. Rawls in the sphere of practical philosophy has participated in the overall pragmatic orientation of Quine's Harvard. Nonetheless, their most important works undermine the healthier direction of their pragmatism.

One of Quine's critical projects in *Word and Object* is to describe how translation from an unknown to a known language might take place, the way a scientist might comprehend a hitherto unknown tongue. Quine's conclusions in this study have been subject to enormous scrutiny in an extended literature. For all I know they may be right. What is puzzling, however, is that Quine pays no attention at all to the actual translation projects that have been successfully completed. As he says, anthropologists have relied on a trail of bilinguals; scientists start from the assumption of linguistic commonality, however indirect, and work from it. Quine's approach, as he puts it, is radical. It has no empirical precedent. Without even doffing his hat to anthropologists, he constructs a thought experiment about how translation should occur. Quine also omits consideration of the extraordinary achievements involved in the recovery of ancient languages, for example cuneiform and hieroglyphic. These also proceeded indirectly through "bilinguals," documents like the Rosetta Stone. In such projects anthropologists and archaeologists have concluded that the languages they have come to understand share certain fundamental similarities with, say, English, French, and German. For Quine this conclusion is a mere cultural prejudice, but a conclusion drawn in ignorance of how scholars work.

A Theory of Justice proposes to uncover what social arrangements exist in any society that could be said to be just. Rawls bases his explorations on our intuitions of what must pass for justice. In addition he argues for his position by cogitating on what any rational creature must want were that creature to be placed in a situation ignorant of his or her personal qualities and place in society.

Again, for all I know, Rawls's notions may be correct. Argumentation that begins in some sort of universal state of nature has a long and honorable lineage in the history of philosophy. Yet it has certain shortcomings. Rawls proceeds without even a nod in the direction of cultural relativism, of the actual differing conceptions of justice anthropologists may have discovered in cultures other than our own. He does not attend to the more truncated history of Western attempts at securing justice. There have, for example, been three striking attempts in the last 200 years to construct societies that were just. The Founding Fathers, the French Revolutionaries, and the Bolsheviks did not, of course, work without a sense of their personal qualities or their place in society. That would have been impossible, and these makers of new orders might have thought it peculiar to put aside their knowledge even if they could. So from Rawls's viewpoint Jefferson, Mirabeau, and Lenin made the philosophical error of using their experience. From the perspective I have been outlining, the error is to *disregard* experience. It is appropriate when trying to understand justice to examine the history of human efforts to achieve it.

Recent philosophy's besetting sin has been its failure to deal with the implications of the central insight of the pragmatic analysts. If philosophers were to see that the empirical and the conceptual were genuinely joined, they would see the aridity of merely *a priori* cogitation. The proclamation of a new synthetic *a priori* that emphasized the importance of both the substance and form of knowledge as legitimate and necessary for philosophers to study might reinvigorate their discipline. Philosophers might enjoy a new notoriety. Their ancient claims to be the queen science might again be fulfilled without the loss of professional status.

NOTES

1. This chapter is a relative of three other attempts of mine to come to grips with overarching themes in the history of American philosophy: "The Changing Character of Philosophizing in America," *Philosophical Forum* 10 (1978): 4–13; "The Professionalization of the Humanities," in *Applying the Humanities*, ed. Arthur Caplan et al. (New York: Plenum Press, 1985), 41–54; and "The Emergence of the Humanities," *South Atlantic Quarterly* 89 (1990): 195–206. Detailed citations for the historical points made in this essay may be found in two other pieces of my writings: *The Rise of American Philosophy: Cambridge, Massachusetts, 1860–1930* (New Haven, Conn.: Yale University Press, 1977) and *Churchmen and Philosophers: From Jonathan Edwards to John Dewey* (New Haven, Conn.: Yale University Press, 1977).

2. My discussion of the seventeenth and eighteenth centuries is dependent on Murray G. Murphey's work in Murphey and Elizabeth Flower, *A History of Philosophy in America*, 2 vols. (New York: G. P. Putnam, 1977), 1:14–45.

3. William James, *The Letters of William James*, 2 vols., ed. Henry James, Jr. (Boston: Atlantic Monthly Press, 1920), 2:228–29.

4. Robert Bellah and others wrote *Habits of the Heart: Individualism and Commitment in American Life* (Berkeley: University of California Press, 1985); Allan Bloom, *The Closing of the American Mind: How Higher Education Has Failed Democracy and Impoverished the Souls of Today's Students* (New York: Simon and Schuster, 1987); Wills, among many books, *Nixon Agonistes* (New York: Simon and Schuster, 1969); Gould, among many books, *The Mismeasure of Man* (New York: Norton, 1981); and E. O. Wilson, *Sociobiology: The New Synthesis* (Cambridge, Mass.: Harvard University Press, 1975).

5. On these points I have been helped by David A. Hollinger's essay-review "Why Can't You Be More Like Dwight MacDonald?" *Reviews in American History* (1988): 657–62.

6. The crucial exposition of this view is Willard van Orman Quine's "Two Dogmas of Empiricism," reprinted in Quine, *From a Logical Point of View*. (Cambridge, Mass.: Harvard University Press, 1951), 20–46.

7. Willard van Orman Quine, *Word and Object* (Cambridge, Mass.: MIT Press, 1960); John Rawls, *A Theory of Justice* (Cambridge, Mass.: Harvard University Press, 1971).

8

James, Quine, and Analytic Pragmatism

Isaac Nevo

INTRODUCTION

Quine's thesis of holism is justly regarded as the cornerstone of his naturalized epistemology. It is, to use Quine's own image, the crucial milestone in the development of post-Humean empiricism.[1] Quine's holism constitutes a transition from the individual sentence to the organized system of sentences as the basic unit of empirical meaning. This system-centered approach allows him to dispense with theoretical reductions by dispensing not with the empiricist rejection of nonempirical facts, but with traditional assumptions concerning uniqueness and determinacy in matters of scientific theory. It allows the holist to affirm, rather than abandon, the empiricist commitment to science without having to secure this position on some *a priori*, neutral foundation.

One of my aims in this chapter is to question Quine's narrowly linguistic understanding of the holistic turn, by considering the place of holism in grounding and qualifying the pragmatism of William James, a pre-linguistic-turn philosopher. While not forming a milestone on Quine's road, James's radical empiricism is informed by a holism that can be described as the transition from the individual sensation to the organized system of sensations as the basic unit of objective experience. Such phenomenological holism falls short of sustaining Quine's naturalism and behaviorism, for it is committed to the existence of ideas as intermediate entities between the objective and the subjective. It does, however, anticipate both Quine's ''shift to pragmatism,'' namely, the rejection of uniqueness in (theoretical) inquiry, and the epistemological limits Quine imposes on such pragmatism. Both anticipations are important for the purposes of this chapter.

They serve to expose the empiricist core of James's pragmatism, that is, its embeddedness within a modern, epistemology-centered, philosophical project.

The anticipation of Quine's holism is evident, for example, in James's image of experience as a mosaic that lacks a bedding of cement to fix its individual stones into position. The holistic import of this image is clear. Without the bedding, no image can count as the unique image of the mosaic. Rather, there are indefinitely many different configurations of the same colorful stones that could all count as the mosaic's overall image. Experience is thus construed as an underdetermined system, and a functional account of its subject and its object follows. Another image used by James is of experience as a web, a system of interconnected sensations that cannot be specified independently of one another. Admittedly, this construal of experience as a web is vaguer than Quine's analogous notion of the web of belief.² The difference lies in the linguistic mediation of Quine's web, which is lacking in James's, but this difference is one between different versions of holism, rather than a difference between an idea-centered and a system-centered approach to empiricism. From this perspective, Quine's five-milestone narrative is a Whiggish history of post-Humean empiricism. The third milestone, in particular, is a milestone in the implementation of a pragmatist insight, rather than a measure of the pragmatists' irrelevance for contemporary developments in empiricism.

Jamesian holism anticipates both Quine's notion of a web in which practical and theoretical considerations intertwine, and the epistemological limits Quine sets on his shift to pragmatism. Quine ridicules sense data as a "fancifully fanciless medium of unvarnished news," but goes on to secure a category of observation sentences by way of a behavioral (and communal) criterion.³ These observation sentences serve as the fixed stock of empirical input variously arranged in theory and translation. James too, I shall argue, confines considerations of expedience to the systematic organization of experience, and does not apply them to its sensationalist input. Correspondence, for James, remains a requirement of truth with respect to a special subclass of ideas that constitute "copies" of their objects.⁴ Such limits place James's pragmatism firmly within the empiricist tradition, and render all radical, antiepistemological attempts to appropriate it, such as Rorty's in *Consequences of Pragmatism*, highly problematic. The appeal to expedience is an epistemological alternative to traditional empiricism, not an alternative to epistemology as such. James's pragmatism, like Quine's, maintains the distinction between the theoretical and the observational. It harbors no hostility to the very idea of empirical observation. Rorty's attempts to break down the distinction between theory and mythology by first abolishing the distinction between theory and observation is foreign to James's way of thinking.

Thus, I will engage here in two parallel lines of polemics: against Quine, who fails to recognize the holistic character of James's empiricism, and against Rorty, who does not acknowledge the empiricist character of James's pragmatism. In different ways, I argue, both overlook the way in which holistic reasoning at once grounds and qualifies James's pragmatic account of truth and knowledge. The historical development of post-Humean empiricism is more complex than Quine's tale of five consecutive accomplishments suggests, and the outcome of these developments in post-Humean empiricism are philosophically more viable than Rorty's ridicule would lead us to suppose. My hope is to recover the sense in which James's pragmatism is a chapter in post-Humean empiricism, a correction to its reductionist zeal which continues, not abandons, the empiricist defense of science in the polemics of modernity.

QUINE'S HISTORICAL NARRATIVE

As Quine describes it, the holistic transition from sentences to systems of sentences as the basic units of empirical significance seems to depend historically on two earlier transitions undertaken for the same purpose, namely the transition from ideas to words, and from words to sentences. Holism, in other words, is described as a step within a more inclusive linguistic turn. Yet, Quine also attributes a holistic awareness to Peirce, for example, whose talk of concepts, as Quine points out, shows no trace of such linguistic turns and transitions. "Peirce," Quine notes, "was unquestionably aware that scientific theory confronts its evidence thus holistically." However, this awareness "is hard to reconcile with [Peirce's] facile account of pragmatic meaning,"[5] which is stated in ideational, rather than linguistic terms. The difficulty, I wish to argue, may be due more to Quine's narrowly linguistic formulation of his holism than to an inconsistency in Peirce's views. A similar case can be made with respect to William James, whose theory of truth is, similarly, holistic without being linguistic. In fact, James's holism is even more pronounced than Peirce's, since James is not committed to Peirce's conception of truth as an ideal terminus at which scientific theories converge. The assumption of such an ideal conversion tacitly introduces constraints on (holistic) revision of theory, and unlike Peirce (and Duhem, as it turns out), James took such revision to be governed only by practical, and not by ideal, conditions.

In its most provocative version, Quine's thesis states that the unit of empirical significance is the whole of science, not the individual sentence.[6] This formulation is doubly provocative, first in its emphasis on empirical significance rather than just empirical confirmation, and secondly in its emphasis on the whole of science, rather than on smaller segments of it which are sufficient for implying observation sentences. The latter excess is corrected in many of Quine's subsequent formulations. The former emphasis is governed by an implicit argument that was later to become an argument for indeterminacy. If the unit of verification is the whole of science, so the argument goes, then if meaning consists in verification conditions, nothing but the whole of science can be empirically meaningful. Individual (theoretical) sentences, in particular, are not. This argument, implicit in Quine's "Two Dogmas of Empiricism," becomes explicit in later work of his, most clearly in "Epistemology Naturalized."[7] It underlies

Quine's thesis of the indeterminacy of translation, for it purports to show that the empirical meaning, hence also the translation, of nonobservation sentences is, indeed, indeterminate. The argument rests, however, on a more basic thesis of evidential, rather than semantic, holism, which forms the ground level of Quine's epistemological project. Aspects of this, evidential, holism are also what one detects in the writings of Peirce and James. Empirical significance was not the focus of their concerns.

Quine's holism is, thus, primarily a thesis about method and justification, rather than meaning. It states that the unit of confirmation or "infirmation" in science is not the individual (theoretical) sentence, but rather the larger system of sentences. Within that unit, empirical data could all be accommodated in various, mutually incompatible ways. Consequently, no theoretical sentence could claim its own stock of verifying or falsifying experiences, and none are immune to revision in light of recalcitrant data. It follows, as Quine points out, that both reductionism and the analytic/synthetic distinction have to be discarded despite their empiricist credentials, while empiricism itself, if it is to survive, has to become more pragmatic in such matters as theory choice and ontological commitment. Much of Quine's subsequent philosophy, the fourth and the fifth milestones, could be traced back to these moves.

At the heart of Quine's evidential holism lies a Duhemian conception of theoretical revisability. By the problem of induction, we know, confirming evidence does not suffice to determine the truth of any particular hypothesis. By Duhemian reasoning, "infirming," or recalcitrant, evidence does not suffice to determine the falsity of any particular hypothesis, either. For given any failed prediction, it is only the inclusive disjunction of all the sentences from which it has been derived that is determinately falsified, not any particular hypothesis in that disjunction. Hence, logically speaking, different revisions are possible in such cases in the assignment of truth values to particular hypotheses, each with its complementary requirements for further adjustments that would bring the whole system of such hypotheses back to consistency. Since the choice of any such revision remains underdetermined by all relevant empirical evidence, empirical disconfirmation is subject to considerations that are practical, not purely cognitive, in nature. Far from being a measure of the pragmatists' irrelevance to post-Humean empiricism, the Duhemian notion of revisability is itself a pragmatic notion. It serves to uncover the practical nature of such theoretical endeavors as theory construction and experimentation, and it defines the scope within which practical maxims range without being, in James's phrase, challenged by fact.

Thus for James, "the scope of pragmatism" involves "first, a method: and second a genetic theory of what is meant by truth."[8] The method in question is the pragmatist analogue of the principle of verifiability, namely, the pragmatic maxim: the (practical) content of a claim is the sum total of the practical consequences of holding it to be true. The other component of pragmatism, namely the "genetic theory of what is meant by truth," is basically a holistic theory of belief revision, or what James calls "the observable process . . . by which any individual settles into new opinions."[9] The two components of pragmatism are inferentially linked in the following way: insofar as theories and opinions satisfy the pragmatic method, they can go beyond mere "copying" of experience only by being instruments, not final answers. As instruments, theories play a role within experience. Theories mediate between new experiences and old beliefs, and their success in doing so is the measure of their truth: "a new opinion counts as 'true' just in proportion as it gratifies the individual's desire to assimilate the novel in his experience to his beliefs in stock."[10] However, there is no single way of doing just that; rather, it is for subjective reasons that the old stock of truths/beliefs grows in just the way that it does. In other words, other possibilities are not, and cannot, be ruled out. The holistic character of this "genetic theory" of truth is thus a consequence of taking theories to be instruments in the reweaving of experience. As James puts it: "In the matter of belief we are all extreme conservatives." Beginning with "a stock of old opinions," the individual seeks to save as much of it as possible once he encounters a contradiction to them. The process of belief modification is the individual's way of escaping the "inward trouble" generated in him by such contradictions. It is in relieving such tensions that considerations of expedience enter the determination of truth.[11]

James's notion of belief revision is closely analogous to Duhem's. For Duhem, disagreement in the result of an experiment with an earlier prediction teaches the physical scientist that some one of his hypotheses is wrong, but "experiment does not show him the one that must be changed."[12] A process of revision ensues in which fact and theory cannot be expressed in isolation. Consequently, physical theory may leave room for incompatible "chapters," which the physicist is free to construct for his own convenience. James broadens this notion. For him, belief revision is the relieving of stress induced not only by recalcitrant experiments but also by such sources as interpersonal disagreements or motivational changes. Like Duhem, James emphasizes the underdetermined character of such revisions. Unlike the positivists who followed him, however, James sought no grounding for the pragmatic method in some *a priori* theory of language and meaning. True to the spirit of that method, he turned to the consequences of adopting it in an attempt to render the method plausible and workable. This generates his "genetic theory" of belief/truth, namely, the conception of experiences as a web, a system, in relation to which theoretical belief may be understood in terms of its function.

Notice also how James's "web" metaphor is generated from his pragmatic-holistic understanding of the role of theoretical truth. James argues that if one "forgets" that even the most absolute standard of truth "grows up endogenously inside the web of experience," then one "May carelessly go on to say that what *distributively* holds of each experience, holds also *collectively* of all experience, and that experience as such, and in its totality, owes whatever truth it may be possessed-of to its correspondence with absolute realities outside of its own being'' (my italics).[13] The distinction between the distributive and the collective senses of "experience" is the main conceptual instrument in James's radical empiricism which provides for conjoined, not merely disjoined, experiences. It is also a measure of James's holism. In saying that correspondence is required of objective experience only when taken distributively, James is noticing experience as a collective whole, a web, which meets the requirements of objective correspondence only through its periphery, its disjoined elements, not in its overall organization.

Duhem himself, to be sure, was fully aware of the pragmatist consequences of his method. An argument from holism to pragmatism, the converse of James's, is rigorously laid out in his work. Realizing that holism implies the underdetermination of theory with respect to empirical data, Duhem saw that his method (namely, the holistic method) permits logically incompatible theories to be equally supported (by empirical data). It follows, he argued, that theories should be taken as instruments that are more or less useful, rather than as pictures that are true or false, for otherwise the method of holism would be contradictory. Thus, he says: "The principle of contradiction is able to judge truth and falsity decisively. It has no ability to decide what is useful and what is not. Therefore, to require physical theory to observe a rigorous logical unity in its development would be to exert an unjust and insupportable tyranny on the intellect of the physicist."[14] Even though Duhem did not fully endorse this argument, there can hardly be a more concise formulation of the pragmatist consequences of holism.

As noted above, James and Duhem argue the converse of one another's argument. James argues from pragmatism (namely, the pragmatic maxim) to holism (the P to H argument). On this argument, theories (or ideas) that satisfy the pragmatic maxim (i.e., nonmetaphysical theories) and whose meaning is their practical consequences, are still not reducible to (not "copies" of) the consequences in question. This irreducibility is compatible with the pragmatic maxim, on the assumption that such theories (or ideas) function in organizing experience into coherent schemes, and it is in terms of such functional features that theories (or ideas) are irreducible to mere experience. Theories, in other words, organize experience in ways that are not fully determined by the experiences that are organized. Hence, the conjunction of pragmatism and nonreductionism implies that theories (or ideas) are tools in organizing experience, not pictures that mirror it. From this, holism, or what James calls a "genetic" account of truth, directly follows: Theories and ideas face the verdict of experience as organized wholes, not item by item. It also follows that no theory can claim uniqueness, for obviously, there is more than one way of organizing experience, that is, more than one way that truth can be generated from experience.

Duhem, for his part, argues from holism to pragmatism (the H to P argument). His argument is the following: Empirical hypotheses (theories) do not face their confirming instances individually, but only as organized wholes governed by underdetermined revisions. It follows that empirically equivalent but logically nonequivalent theories are equally sanctioned by holism. By the law of non-contradiction, such theories cannot be sanctioned as true or false, only as more or less useful. Thus, holistically sanctioned theories can only be tools, not pictures or mirrors of reality. From this, the pragmatic maxim follows: Nonfunctional "theories," for example, theories about ultimate reality that play no distinguishable role in organizing experience, may be safely eschewed as meaningless constructs. Here too, the hidden assumption is that empirical theories need not be understood as pictures of experience, but rather as functional (and irreducible) aids in organizing it. Thus, pragmatism follows from the conjunction of holism and the "tool theory" of theories. Hence, holism and pragmatism mutually imply each other, each in conjunction with assumptions concerning the irreducible function of theories in making experience cohere under an organized scheme. Much room remains, notwithstanding, for varieties in construing the precise function of theories, or the system in which their role is to be played.

This connection is, of course, more than a mere analogy. Duhem and the pragmatists mutually influenced each other. James, for example, cites "energetics," the (holistic) conception of science advocated by Duhem, as a case of "scientific Humanism," which makes the notion of scientific truth more flexible, and with which he was in agreement.[15] In two places James mentions Duhem by name as one among many for whom "human arbitrariness has driven divine necessity from scientific logic,"[16] and who are beginning to think that concepts like " 'matter,' 'mass,' 'atom,' 'ether,' 'inertia,' 'force' are not so much duplicates of hidden realities in nature as mental instruments to handle nature."[17] For his part, Duhem was troubled by the pragmatist consequences of his own holism, for it seemed to him to undermine the rationality, or cognitive authority, of the physical theorist. While realizing that his analysis "has found great favor on the side of many pragmatists," and that "they have applied it to the most diverse fields: to history, to exegesis, to theology," Duhem still attempted to distance himself from that movement.[18] To secure the physicist's claim to knowledge, Duhem was willing to postulate an ideal "terminus of theoretical progress, as the limit which theory endlessly approaches without ever reaching it."[19] In light of this ideal, the instrumental plurality of theories that his holism uncovers will be reduced to a single, though inaccessible, theory in relation to which knowledge will be claimed. Duhem's position, in short, was not unlike that of Peirce, the acknowledged founder of pragmatism, who was also inclined to postulate an ideal end to which all inquiry strives, and to define truth in terms of such an ideal. The ideal-terminus position, however, is incompatible with both holism and pragmatism, for the assumption that all theories will eventually converge on one ideal theory tacitly introduces (realistic) constraints on theoretical revision. From a holistic point of view, there is no reason to suppose such convergence to take place, and no reason to introduce such constraints. The limit theory is merely an unsuccessful attempt by Duhem to escape his own pragmatism, the pragmatism introduced by the holism of his own methodology.

As early as "Two Dogmas of Empiricism" Quine described his results as a shift toward pragmatism (the H to P argument), though unlike Duhem, Quine had no difficulty in accepting the pragmatist consequences of the argument. In that work, Quine extended the insights of holism from the issue of empirical confirmation to that of empirical significance. Through this extension, holism served to undermine not merely the empiricist dogma of reductionism, but also that of the analytic/synthetic distinction, along with all other intensional notions and theories. Consequently, Quine could offer a functional account of meaning and analyticity as a corollary of the functional account of belief revision presupposed by the shift-to-pragmatism argument. The converse argument (the P to H argument) can also be detected in Quine's early writings. Quine's rejection of empiricist reductionism, together with his (empiricist) rejection of trans-empirical meaning, yields his thesis of holism. Theories go beyond experience not by possessing trans-empirical meanings, but rather by organizing experience in various, underdetermined ways. All these are, no doubt, important and exciting extensions of both pragmatism and holism. The notions of function and system are rendered clear and precise, and a naturalist-behaviorist reorientation of epistemology is made possible. Nevertheless, the novelty of these moves is the novelty of extending an existing pragmatist-holist tradition on to a new terrain, rather than the novelty of introducing a wholly new argument. Of course, Quine is aware of his predecessors in holism and in pragmatism, but he does not recognize the holism of his pragmatist predecessors. The two theses, however, were thought to be related by their respective authors from their very inception.

On later occasions, Quine salutes Dewey's naturalism, and credits Dewey with "a naturalistic view of language and a behavioral view of meaning."[20] Similarly, Quine refers to Peirce as supplying the verificationist premise of the argument to indeterminacy, noted above, from holism and the verification principle.[21] Peirce, rather than Carnap, is singled out for this honorary reference, though, of course, the principle of verification is better known as a positivist, rather than pragmatist, principle. Quine is willing to read the principle of verification into Peirce's "pragmatic principle," thereby admitting Peirce into a brotherhood of empiricism. However, neither Peirce nor any other pragmatist is acknowledged to have contributed much by way of supplying the holistic premise of the argument. As was shown above, Quine only mentions Peirce's holism in passing, while questioning the possibility of such a holism within Peirce's sensationalist empiricism.

Quine's attitude to the pragmatist is clarified in his article, "The Pragmatist's Place in Empiricism." In that paper, Quine brings pragmatism to the test of post-Humean empiricism, which he describes in terms of the five milestones. Quine admits difficulty in finding a distinctive and shared "tenet of pragmatism," but his most poignant charge is that the pragmatists fail the test of shifting to a Duhemian, system-centered approach. This failure is accounted for by the prior pragmatist failure in not shifting the focus of their empiricism from ideas to words and, finally, to sentences. Quine concludes his account with the following remarks:

The professing pragmatists do not relate significantly to what I took to be the five turning points in post-Humean empiricism. Tooke's shift from ideas to words, and Bentham's from words to sentences, were not detectable in Peirce's pragmatic maxim, but we found Peirce's further semantic discussions to be sentence-oriented in implicit ways. Peirce seemed at odds with Duhem's system-centered view, until we got to Peirce's theory of truth; but this we found unacceptable. Other pragmatists were sentence-oriented in an implicit way, but still at odds with the system-centered view, until we made hypothetico-deductive sense of Schiller's humanism. On the analytic-synthetic distinction, and on naturalism, the pragmatists blew hot and cold.[22]

Quine goes on to express disappointment with respect to the prospects of finding pragmatist tenets that are shared and distinctive: "I have found little in the way of shared and distinctive tenets. The two best guesses seemed to be behavioristic semantics, which I so heartily approve, and the doctrine of man as truth-maker, which I share in large measure."[23] The second of these tenets is too vague to qualify as a pragmatist contribution to empiricism; the first is hardly just a pragmatist tenet. Behaviorism, like verificationism, is shared by most empiricists; hence Quine's inclination to dispense with the term "pragmatism" altogether.

Quine's judgment is excessively harsh. James's genetic account of truth, as well as the distinction between the distributive and the collective aspects of experience, that is, the claim that correspondence is required of experience only in its distributive aspect, exemplify a holistic, system-centered approach, even though the system in question is not one Quine would have much commerce with. Furthermore, the pragmatist tenet of man as truth maker is not independent of such holistic insights, for it is, if we follow James's line, only in the collective sense of "experience" that its truth, or objectivity, is man-made. In thus delimiting the truth-making tenet of pragmatism, holism, so conceived, qualifies as the fundamental tenet of pragmatism, though not, perhaps, one that is shared by all pragmatists. It is unfortunate that Quine turns a blind eye to this pragmatist tenet, by construing holism in excessively technical and narrow terms.

PRAGMATISM AS POST-MODERNISM

While Quine dismisses the pragmatists, Rorty embraces them. Pragmatism, he claims, "names the chief glory of [the American] intellectual tradition,"[24] and he has little difficulty in spelling out its main tenets. In spirit, Rorty's pragmatists are settlers in a philosophical West; they break with the whole philosophical tradition, rather than advance criticism within it. Pragmatism, as Rorty conceives it, is no mere holistic correction to the atomism of early logical empiricism. For logical empiricism itself was merely "one variety of standard, academic, neo-Kantian, epistemologically centered philosophy," which one could criticize without yet taking leave of the whole tradition. However, "The great pragmatists should not be taken as suggesting an holistic variation of this variant, but rather as breaking with Kantian epistemological tradition altogether.''[25] Thus, Rorty's account of pragmatism weaves together the American theme of breaking with a European tradition, and the Romantic (and European) theme of breaking with "epistemologically centered philosophy," that is, with philosophy as a quasi-scientific critique of the rest of culture in terms of its truth, or accuracy of representation. This picture of pragmatism, however, is somewhat of a *tour de force*. If anything, the pragmatist's Americanism manifested itself in a modernist, epistemologically naturalist attitude, which focused on the task of removing foundationalist roadblocks from the way of inquiry, rather than replacing inquiry with some other form of cultural activity. James's pragmatism had little to do with the antiepistemological insurrection Rorty is advocating in philosophy.

The pragmatist's greatest break with philosophy, their most Western frontier, was, according to Rorty, their view that "objects of philosophical theorizing," such as truth, knowledge, morality, and so on, have no essence. The point is explained with reference to James's definition of truth as "what is good in the way of belief."[26] James's deflationary definition, Rorty believes, is not really meant to be a definition at all. Rather, it serves as a warning against all definitions of truth. It is merely meant to suggest that "there is nothing deeper to be said: truth is not the sort of thing which *has* an essence."[27] Hence, no definition of truth would be possible. All other distinguishing features of pragmatism are consequences of this basic stance.

Among such consequences, Rorty lists the following: Words such as "truth," "knowledge," and so forth belong to what Rorty calls "the vocabulary of practise," not theory. Thus, "it is in the vocabulary of practise rather than of theory, of action rather than contemplation, in which one can say something useful about truth."[28] To expect otherwise is to expect that some theory of truth (or knowledge) can capture the general truth (essence) about it. But no such essences are to be found. Another consequence of the pragmatist's antiessentialism is that there is no distinction between facts and values, between descriptive and normative language. Again, to expect such a distinction is to expect what cannot be had, namely, a realm of neutral facts as the province of pure, untainted theory. It is to expect a theory of truth, or objectivity, that determines what belongs to the factual and what is merely "normative." But no such theory of truth exists. Thirdly, antiessentialism applied to truth, or to other "objects of philosophical inquiry," implies that there are no constraints on inquiry, save conversational ones. In other words, there is no trans-discursive standard of objectivity that can be universally applied. All constraints on inquiry are discourse-relative.

At bottom, Rorty's consequences of pragmatism are posed as exclusive alternatives. Either inquiry is practical in nature, value laden and purely conversational, or else truth has an essence that is independent of all contexts and theories. In other words, either one accepts that there are no nonconversational constraints on inquiry, or one is guilty of "essentialism" with respect to truth, that is, guilty of imposing harsh necessities on unsuspecting contingencies. In Rorty's scheme, one is always faced with a radical choice: action or contemplation, practise or theory, contingency or essence. There is a "fundamental choice which confronts the reflective mind," which Rorty describes in terms of accepting or evading the "contingency of starting points." Those who accept the contingency in question also "accept our inheritance from, and our conversation with, our fellow humans as our only source of guidance."[29] On the other hand, those who attempt to evade the contingency are hoping for a super-natural, or super-human, guidance, which would guarantee the correctness of their outcome. In Rorty's image, they hope to become a "properly programmed machine."[30] There is, for Rorty, no middle ground. These antinomies, however, are both false and unfaithful to the spirit of pragmatism and to Jamesian pragmatism, in particular. There is a way between the horns, and that way is given by Jamesian holism, which is entirely misconstrued in Rorty's account.

To go between the horns of Rorty's dilemmas, one needs only to invoke James's distinction between the collective and the distributive senses of such systemic terms as "experience," "inquiry," or "theory." Objective, nonconversational constraints can be admitted to apply to these systems distributively, yet all the gains of pragmatism may still be obtained by denying the existence of such constraints with respect to these systems when collectively specified. This is, in essence, Quine's system-centered approach, which allows the marriage of pragmatist antifoundationalism with empiricist epistemology. James, too, is an advocate of that approach. His account of truth, or actually "the true," as "merely the expedient in the way of our thinking," is not, as Rorty claims, the suggestion that truth has no essence. Rather, it is the suggestion that because truth's "essence" (or definition) is correspondence, it can only apply to experience when taken distributively, not when "experience" is specified collectively as a system of interconnected ideas.[31] Only "disjoint" ideas can serve as copies of their object and meet the demands of correspondence, but experience is not merely the sum total of such disjoint copies. Hence also, it is only the system of true ideas that is subject to considerations of expedience; it is not the individual, or disjoint, idea. The pragmatist's appeal to expedience, his rejection of metaphysical dogma and foundational stricture, does not call for the stronger, Rortyan, claim that there is nothing of interest to be said about truth, save in the vocabulary of practice, or that no correspondential (nonconversational) demands can be set on inquiry without invoking essentialist metaphysics.

Rorty is not entirely oblivious to the holistic nature of James's argument. With James, Rorty accuses the foundational tradition of the fallacy of composition. The "picture" metaphor fails us, he argues, when we turn from individual sentences to vocabularies and theories. Unlike James, however, Rorty goes on to commit an equally fallacious inference of division with respect to the components of the system of inquiry. In other words, he concludes that because the system of inquiry, taken as a whole, is governed by considerations of expedience, its components, too, are similarly governed. In Rorty's language, his conclusion is that inquiry does not admit of nonconversational constraints at all, not even with respect to its constitutive elements, because inquiry does not admit of such constraints with respect to its organizational features. Without such distributive, as opposed to collective, determinacy, holistic pragmatism loses its air of empiricism and naturalism. In place of holism, we get a Nietzschean drama, a contest of elemental forces—the Apollonian versus the Dionysian. All this, however, is highly unfaithful to the spirit of pragmatism.

All three of the tenets Rorty attributes to pragmatism are infected with this fallacy of division. The claim that it is only in the language of practice, rather than theory, that something useful can be said about knowledge, clearly does not apply distributively, for we can bring empirical tests to bear on theory, holism notwithstanding. Notice that such empirical starting points of inquiry are no less contingent than other starting points are, since our embeddedness in a particular natural environment, which impinges on our "surfaces," is still a contingent fact, but there is nothing particularly "conversational" in such starting points despite their contingency. Needless to say, this is an epistemologically important fact, a fact that can be exploited in nonfoundational, naturalistic, epistemologies. A similar point can be made with respect to the fact/value distinction. While there is no room for such a distinction at higher reaches of theory, where values such as economy, charity, and conservatism intertwine with more cognitive considerations, clearly this does not hold distributively, for as Quine notes, value-laden sentences could not count as observational. Hence, some distinction between the natural and the normative survives the holistic critique of our cognitive systems.[32] As for nonconversational constraints, here, too, the distributive and the collective diverge. Clearly, the guidance of our fellow humans would count more the further we are from the merely observational. James's experiential holism is, in this respect, much closer to Quine's view than to Rorty's. Let us now turn to examine James's doctrine of radical empiricism, where his holism comes to a head.

CONSEQUENCES OF HOLISM—JAMES'S RADICAL EMPIRICISM

James's holism, we saw, consists in the distinction between the collective and the distributive senses of terms like "experience" or "inquiry," together with his "genetic theory of truth," which claims that correspondence is required of true experiences only when the latter term is distributively specified. In "Radical Empiricism" James goes on to consider the consequences for empiricism of these holistic moves. He is, in effect, articulating the possibility of an empiricism without the Humean dogma that "ideas" are uniquely and individually derived from sensations. In place of that dogma, James offers an account of experience as a web that requires sensations of various functional descriptions, "conjunctive" as well as "disjunctive," in relation to which no clear boundary can be drawn between ideas and sensations. This functional diversity is expressed by the radical empiricist principle that "the relations that connect experiences must themselves be experienced relations."[33] James derives this principle from holism and the empiricist sensationalism that still held him captive. If experience is a holistic web, and if experience also consists in the possession of sensations, then some sensations must present their "object" by means of their relation to other sensations. Thus, although all experience consists in the possession of sensations, not all sensations present their object "disjointly."

Pleading the privilege of a skeptic, Hume describes an inconsistency between two principles that he cannot renounce: "*that all our distinct perceptions are distinct existences and that the mind never perceives any real connexion among distinct existences.*"[34] Hume's point is that if perceptions are distinct existences and the mind does not perceive real connections between distinct existences, then any notion of personal identity, that is, of connections between different perceptions, must be as chimerical as that of the causal nexus. A similar conclusion would seem to follow generally with respect to relations among perceptions. Not surprisingly, the thesis of radical empiricism has been taken by some interpreters to conflict with the second of Hume's principles, namely, the principle that the mind does not perceive "real connections among distinct existences." John E. Smith, for example, takes radical empiricism to imply that some real connections, for example, the connection of "withness," are directly perceived.[35] However, this interpretation of radical empiricism seems to evade a Humean point that most empiricists would find too important to give up. The holistic interpretation offers a better account. It is not that the mind can perceive "real connection among distinct existences"; rather, it is the first of Hume's two principles that has to be rejected, namely that "all our distinct perceptions are distinct existences." With respect to "real connections among distinct existences," James might join Quine in claiming that "the Humean predicament is the human predicament." But as a radical empiricist, he would go on to deny that all sensations could be specified with the requisite "distinctness" that Hume employs in his principles. Some perceptions, the radical empiricist claims, can only be specified with reference to other perceptions, through which they are related to the objects that these other perceptions present. In this form, radical empiricism constitutes a challenge to Hume's atomistic psychology without evading his skepticism about "real connections among distinct existences."

Now it might be claimed on behalf of Hume's skepticism that James's "relations that connect experiences" are as inexperienceable as Hume's "real connections among distinct existences" are, and that radical empiricism is, therefore, incompatible with the spirit, if not the letter, of Hume's second principle as well. If reference to one perception has to enter the experiencing of another, then the latter experience should count as the experience of a "real connection" that is every bit as obscure to the mind as the real connections among distinct existences that Hume was discussing. James's position, however, is more subtle than this objection gives it credit for. To deny that perceptions are (all) distinct existences is also to deny that "the relations that connect experiences" are objectively determined. If perceptions are not, as Hume claims, distinct existences, then the relations that connect them are not relations between independent terms, but are, rather, partly dependent on the way these perceptions, indeed the whole system of such perceptions, are specified (or what they are experienced as). But there is no single way to specify perceptions and experiences, and no single way to organize them as a whole. Thus, the relations that connect experiences are neither unique, given the experiences, nor objectively determined. Such relations, therefore, are not Humean "real connections" in another guise. This point may be brought out by saying that such relations are *merely* experienced; they are not experiences of predetermined connections. Hence, James's case for experienced relations that connect experiences is a case for the indeterminacy of such relations, not a case for their objective or independent existence.

James presents the program of radical empiricism differently in different places. In some places the thesis is presented in terms of the existence of conjunctive relations in experience. In this form I have quoted it above, and have shown it to be a consequence of James's holism with respect to experience. In other places, the program is specified in terms of the full argument for the indeterminacy of such (conjunctive) relations. Indeed, an explicit argument for the indeterminacy of the stream of experience is built into the program of radical empiricism, as James presented it in his 1909 preface to *The Meaning of Truth*. In that argument, James derives an indeterminacy thesis from premises that involve a pragmatist version of the verification principle, and the holistic thesis of conjunctive relations quoted above, in much the same way that Quine derives the indeterminacy of translation from the principle of verification and the holistic conception of language. Consider, for example, the following statement:

Radical empiricism consists first of a postulate, next of a statement of fact, and finally of a generalized conclusion.

The postulate is that the only things that shall be debatable among philosophers shall be things definable in terms drawn from experience. [Things of an unexperienceable nature may exist *ad libitum*, but they form no part of the material for philosophic debate.]

The statement of fact is that the relations between things, conjunctive as well as disjunctive, are just as much matters of direct particular experience, neither more so nor less so than the things themselves.

The generalized conclusion is that therefore the parts of experience hold together from next to next by relations that are themselves part of experience. The directly apprehended universe needs, in short, no extraneous trans-empirical connective support, but possesses in its own right a concatenated or continuous structure.[36]

This argument deserves a close scrutiny. The postulate may be taken as an early version of the principle of verifiability. Notice the status of the postulate given here to that principle. It is thus neither an empirical nor an *a priori* truth. By accepting the principle of verification as merely a postulate, James can join forces with traditional empiricism without becoming entangled in paradoxes of self-reference. This is very much the spirit in which Quine, too, accepts the

principle. Quine has attacked the principle of verification as a theory of senten-
tial meaning in terms of which sentence-synonymy and analyticity can be defined. But Quine still retains the principle as an empiricist postulate, which plays
an important role in any derivation of the thesis of indeterminacy. The statement
of fact, with which the argument proceeds, was already shown above to be a
consequence of Jamesian holism. To repeat, the claim that conjunctive relations
are experienced is, we saw, a consequence of the claim that experience forms
a system that satisfies objective criteria only distributively, not collectively, together with the more traditional empiricist conception of experience as the possession of sensations, or mental representations. For, again, it follows that some
experienced sensations satisfy the demands of objectivity only through their
reference to other sensations. Here, too, the analogy with Quine's argument is
striking. If scientific theory faces the tribunal of experience only as a collective
body, then some sentences at least face it only through their relations with other
sentences.

Quine's derivation of indeterminacy from these two premises, namely, holism
and the principle of verification, is fairly simple. If some sentences meet the
tribunal of experience only through other sentences, then the empirical meanings
of these sentences depend on their relations with other sentences, relations that
are not themselves determined by experience, as we know from Duhem. To
suppose that such sentences do have determinate meanings is to go counter to
the principle of verification that serves as the second premise of the argument.
Hence the indeterminacy Quine finds in the meaning and translation of such
sentences. The generalized conclusion in James's argument for radical empiricism is similarly derived. Some experiences are ''conjunctive'' in character in
the sense that they present experienced objects only through their relation with
other experiences. Such relations, however, are subject to much revision and
substitution, and they are not determined by the experienced objects themselves.
Hence the relations that connect experiences ''from next to next'' are indeterminate, for to suppose them to be objectively determined is to run counter to
the principle that things of an unexperienceable nature are not debatable among
philosophers.

James's conception of experience as an indeterminate stream is, of course,
naive and indefensible. Its basic problem is that in order to effect a naturalization
of philosophical dualisms, for example, the concept/percept dualism, it constructs the terms of the dualisms in question as functions in a nonnatural system
of ideas and experiences. Obviously, Quine's fifth milestone, as well as the
ghostly sixth milestone of behaviorism, have not been reached by James. But
my purpose in this chapter was to discuss the third milestone, namely, the holism
of James's account of experience, in order to establish the place of pragmatism
in the history of post-Humean empiricism. Rorty denies the latter description of
pragmatism as an empiricist (hence epistemology centered) critique, while Quine
denies the former description of the pragmatist's empiricism as post-Humean,
in any but the chronological sense. The account given here of the extent of
James's holism suffices, I hope, to correct both.

NOTES

1. See W.V.O. Quine, "Five Milestones of Empiricism," *Theories and Things* (Cambridge, Mass.: Harvard University Press, 1981) and "The Pragmatists' Place in Empiricism," *Pragmatism: Its Sources and Prospects*, ed. R. J. Mulvaney and P. M. Zeltner (Columbia: University of South Carolina Press, 1981).

2. For James's use of the "web" metaphor, see William James, "Humanism and Truth," in James, *The Meaning of Truth* (London: Longmans, Green, 1909), 91.

3. See W.V.O. Quine, *Word and Object* (Cambridge, Mass.: MIT Press, 1960), 2.

4. For a discussion of ideas as "copies" of their objects, see W. James, "Pragmatism's Conception of Truth," *The Writings of William James*, ed. John J. McDermott (New York: Random House, 1967 [1907]). See also W. James, "Humanism and Truth," in James, *The Meaning of Truth*.

5. Quine, "The Pragmatist's Place," 31.

6. For this formulation, see Quine, "Two Dogmas of Empiricism," in Quine, *From a Logical Point of View* (New York: Harper & Row, 1961), 42.

7. W.V.O. Quine, "Epistemology Naturalized," in Quine, *Ontological Relativity and Other Essays* (New York: Columbia University Press, 1969), 80.

8. William James, "What Pragmatism Means," in *The Writings of William James*, ed. John J. McDermott (New York: Random House, 1967 [1907]), 384.

9. Ibid., 382.

10. Ibid., 384.

11. Ibid., 382.

12. Pierre Duhem, "Logical Examination of Physical Theory," *Synthese* 83 (Dordrecht, The Netherlands: Kluwer Academic Publishers, 1990 [1913]), 185.

13. William James, "Humanism and Truth," 91.

14. Duhem, "Logical Examination," 186.

15. See James, "Humanism and Truth," 58.

16. See James, "What Pragmatism Means," 381.

17. See William James, "Percept and Concept—The Abuse of Concepts," in James, *The Writings of William James*, 249n.

18. Duhem, "Logical Examination," 187.

19. Ibid., 187.

20. W.V.O. Quine, "Ontological Relativity," in Quine, *Ontological Relativity*, 26–29.

21. Quine, "Epistemology Naturalized."

22. Quine, *Ontological Relativity*, 37.

23. Ibid.

24. Richard Rorty, "Pragmatism, Relativism, and Irrationalism," in Rorty, *Consequences of Pragmatism* (Minneapolis: University of Minnesota Press, 1982), 160.

25. Ibid.

26. Ibid.

27. Ibid.

28. Ibid.

29. Ibid., 166.

30. Ibid.

31. Consider, for example, the following statement of truth, taken from James's introduction to *The Meaning of Truth*: "Truth . . . is a property of certain of our ideas. It means their agreement, as falsity means their disagreement, with reality. Pragmatists and intellectuals both accept this definition as a matter of course." James, *The Writings of William James*, 311. James goes on to consider how this condition may be applied to ideas that do not constitute mere copies of their objects.

32. For a discussion of this issue see W.V.O. Quine, "Reply to Morton White," in *The Philosophy of W. V. Quine*, ed. L. E. Hahn and P. A. Schilpp (LaSalle, Ill.: Open Court, 1986), 661–65.

33. William James, "A World of Pure Experience," in James, *The Writings of William James*, 195.

34. See David Hume's Appendix, *A Treatise of Human Nature*, ed. Selby-Bigge (Oxford: Oxford University Press, 1978 [1888]), 636.

35. See in particular, John E. Smith's chapter on radical empiricism in his *Themes in American Philosophy* (New York: Harper and Row, 1970): "It is evident that radical empiricism depends heavily on the reality of relations; without them experience remains a bare *that*, not 'taken' at all but left merely as an undifferentiated whole of feeling." This interpretation seems to conflict with the one given below, in which "conjunctive relations" are taken to be indeterminate, rather than "real."

36. See James, *The Writings of William James*, 314.

9

Vanishing Frontiers in American Philosophy: Two Dogmas of Idealism

Ralph W. Sleeper

My title alludes to two famous papers. The first is John Dewey's essay on "The Vanishing Subject in the Psychology of James," first published in the *Journal of Philosophy* in 1940. The second is Willard Quine's "Two Dogmas of Empiricism," a paper read a decade later at the Eastern Division meeting of the APA and subsequently published in the *Philosophical Review* of January 1951.

Two brief quotations, one from each, will show why I have borrowed from them not just the style of my title but the theme of what follows. From Dewey the text is this:

Philosophy will not be emancipated to perform its own task and function until psychology is purged, as a whole and in all its special topics, of the last remnants of dualism.[1]

And this from Quine:

Carnap, Lewis, and others take a pragmatic stand on the question of choosing between language forms, scientific frameworks; but their pragmatism leaves off at the imagined boundary between the analytic and the synthetic. In repudiating such a boundary I espouse a more thorough pragmatism.[2]

There is more than one way to link these texts. The path that I take is, perhaps, the less familiar one. It leads across the map of "Classical American Philosophy" in its own way, exploring imagined boundaries and vanishing frontiers.

One result of this exploration is the discovery that two dogmas of idealism still haunt the territory. One is the belief that an impassable abyss divides the external "noumenal" world from the internal "phenomenal" world of experience. The other is a belief that some form of transcendental argument—or logic—is a viable bridge between them.

Though both dogmas have early roots in empiricism, I call them dogmas of idealism in recognition of their Kantian origins, and the fact that it is from that tradition that they have come to influence our own American philosophy from Emerson to Peirce, Royce, and Lewis. And it is by his repeated attacks on that tradition—and its dogmas—that John Dewey commenced its repudiation.

One consequence of that repudiation is the rejection of the "metaphysics of experience," as Kant called it, and its reconstruction as the metaphysics of existence. This antifoundational move against traditional "first philosophy" helps to close the gap between speculative metaphysics and natural science. Another effect is the healing of the schism between the epistemology of facts and the knowledge of values. Both are features of a reconstructed pragmatism, one that reassigns the tasks of both metaphysics and logic.

Relieved of its foundational role as "first philosophy," metaphysics is reconstituted as the background theory of criticism. Relieved of its normative role in relation to science, logic is reinstated as the empirical theory of inquiry. Both of these moves bespeak a more thoroughgoing pragmatism—and a more radical empiricism.

Kant's exclusion of the noumenal world of things-in-themselves from the phenomenal world of experience was, as I have said, anticipated by the empiricists. Hume's skepticism about our ability to experience anything like a metaphysically fixed and universally valued law of casuality, when placed in relation to Berkeley's contrary reduction of the real to experience, are signposts on the road to Kant's restriction of experience to the phenomenal world. Another is Leibniz's devotion to truths of reason that hold in all possible worlds, the stimulus for Locke's account of truths belonging to the essences of things, truths that are eternal and that can be found out only by examining our own ideas.

But it is the consequences of these dogmas and not their origins that concern me here. First among them is the restriction of experience implicit in the exclusion of the thing-in-itself from empirical access. Denied entry to this much of the external world, reason is turned inward upon itself and to the attenuated experience of the phenomenal world. Within these constraints the search for categories upon which to found the structures of knowledge becomes a quest for the *a priori* conditions of experience. It is a search that, deflected from the possibility of discovering the categories of being or of existence, throws reason back upon its own resources. Metaphysics, thus restricted to the content of experience and the *a priori* forms of its reception, becomes, as it were, a branch of logic; its categories are conceived as the *a priori* forms of experience and are reached as the logical products of transcendental deduction.

Kant's confidence in this deduction arises, no doubt, from the Aristotelian notion of essence. For it was on that notion that the syllogistic logic of subject-predicate relations and deductive inference was founded. But while Aristotle's logic was clearly based on his metaphysics—his "first philosophy"—Kant's procedure was to base his metaphysics on his logic, the "perfected form of the syllogism," as Dewey sometimes called it. This startling reversal—in which Dewey discerned the foundation of all "ontological logics" and condemned from time to time as "the philosophers' fallacy"—is the dark side of what Kant himself called his "Copernican revolution" in metaphysics.

Enthusiasm for Kant's two dogmas among nineteenth-century Continental metaphysicians and logicians was unrestrained, and a flourishing market was soon created for a variety of ways of understanding their consequences, or for rejecting them altogether by means of one reductionism or another. Absolute idealism was one alternative, and materialism another; the dialectical logic of the one suggesting the ontological structure of the other.

By the end of the century, of course, the market was dominated by this Hegelian turn in metaphysics. But in logic, transcending even Hegel, logical idealism was already at apogee in the "logicism" of Frege. For it was, after all, Frege who announced the final hegemony of transcendental logic. It is not just that logic gives us the laws of mathematics, or even the laws of nature, as some had supposed, but it is that "logic gives us the laws of the laws of nature."[3]

In tracing the path of this triumph of logical transcendentalism to America I pass over the British idealists, noting their contrary move in psychologizing logic after the manner of Mill, a move that issued in Shadworth Hodgson's fabulous four-volume *Metaphysics of Experience* by the end of the century, and that had a profound impact on William James.[4] I likewise pass over Emerson's transcendental turn, by acknowledging what John McDermott has poignantly—and accurately—called his "Spires of Influence" upon classical American philosophy, and move directly to the period following.[5]

It is the period of the birth of pragmatism and of the burgeoning influence of Charles S. Peirce. Recalling his early mathematical background it is easy to see why Peirce's philosophical development followed a path that suggests parallels with Frege's, avoiding by the narrowest of margins a final confluence. By the close of the century American mathematicians were already well conditioned by the work of Dedekind and others to accept that form of transcendental logic that issues in "logicism." But it was not until the work of Peirce that its wider implications were much debated here.

This doctrine, finally made famous by Frege and Russell, held that all mathematical forms can be derived from the forms of logic. Moreover, its corollary—that all the sciences rest ultimately upon these same foundations—was already at issue in America. Peirce's own father, Benjamin, had made it so by mid-century, even though he also held that it is more likely that logic can be derived from mathematics than the other way around.[6]

Charles himself was on the brink of accepting a version of the doctrine as early as his 1865 Harvard lectures "On the Logic of Science." He was still on the edge in his 1869 paper "On the Grounds and Validity of the Laws of

Logic." But it was this paper, as Max Fisch points out, that Peirce would later see had already "adumbrated" his nomination of logic to the position of "Critic," forecasting the transition from a view of logic as nonnormative to the assignment of logic to a normative role.[7]

Even this move in the direction of logicism, however, did not suffice to take him over the edge. Nor was it enough to commit him to either of the dogmas to which I am attending. Although Peirce was clearly well down the road to doing so in mathematics, his conception of the relation of logic as "Critic" to mathematics, and hence to metaphysics, had not yet been worked out. Nor would it be until the development of the doctrine of "synechism" in the 1890s. In that doctrine, Fregean logicism is transcended—or perhaps it should be said that it is contained in a higher synthesis—for it "carries along with it," as Peirce himself says, "first, a logical realism of the most profound type; second, objective idealism; third, tychism, with its consequent thoroughgoing evolutionism."[8] It was a stunning combination, not least for its striking discovery of an ingenious way of resolving the conflict between Darwinian and Lamarckian evolutionism.

This remarkable synthesis, as again Max Fisch points out, had already been implicit in Peirce's reaction to Darwinism from the beginning. "At least from the summer of 1859 onward, one of Peirce's main metaphysical concerns was to establish that, contrary to what some metaphysicians were saying, we can reason mathematically and logically about infinity and therefore about continuity. On that assumption, synechism became a regulative principle first of logic and then of metaphysics.[9]

It is not that Peirce rejects Darwinism and adopts the Lamarckian persuasion in revulsion from the Darwinian hypothesis of the descent of man from simian origins, but that he needs Lamarckism to account for the ascent of "Platonic forms."[10] He needs both theories. While Darwinism accords well with "fallibilism" and its expression in "tychist" cosmology, it is Lamarckism that allows for a superior account of the evolution of what he sometimes calls "Platonic forms" or "generals," and sometimes refers to as "Scotistic reals." The doctrine of synechism is designed to provide a transcendental argument that will continuously link them in the tandem processes of "evolutionary love."

It is not my purpose here to examine in detail the structure of that argument, but a sense of how it goes can be gleaned from Peirce's essay, "What Pragmatism Is."[11] There Peirce elaborates the point that synechism is intended to connect the real—which he defines as "being as it is regardless of what you or I may think about it"—with what is "destined" to be believed as a consequence of the continuity of inquiry. He wants to show that what is antecedently and independently real—thus noumenally real?—is a causally efficacious external constraint on the direction and process of inquiry.[12]

Peirce, of course, would not want the evident processive dualism of his synechism to be laid to his tacit acceptance of the Kantian dogmas, or their ghostly remains. But why not? Why not explain the shift from pragmatism to "pragmaticism" that way, as well as by invoking Peirce's reluctance to follow either

James or Dewey down the more radical paths of empiricism that they were exploring?

Royce, of course, shows none of Peirce's hesitancy. Rejecting James's metaphysics altogether, but clinging to Peirce's conception of continuity, Royce embraces not one, but both of Kant's dogmas. In two recent and important articles, Robert Burch has pointed out some of the remarkable consequences of this turn by Royce.[13] Among them is not merely Royce's realization of the link between his own form of transcendental argumentation and Kant's, exemplified in *The World and the Individual* and the *Lectures on Modern Idealism*, but the revival of his own interest in mathematical and logical studies that led to his fascination with Russell's turn to Frege in 1903, and to Russell's period of "Platonism" in mathematics and science that followed.

Moreover, Royce's capitulation to transcendental logic, complete by 1882, was, in many respects, recapitulated by Lewis. For, despite his rejection of both Peirce's latent and Royce's overt idealism—and his loyalty to James—Lewis's "conceptual pragmatism" owes more to Royce and to Peirce than we are in the habit of conceding. Despite the intention of the "Pragmatic *A Priori*," moreover, there is little in *Mind and the World Order* to remind us of either James or Dewey. In the end, as Quine suggests, it was his commitment to a transcendental logic that stopped Lewis short of the full commitment to empirical naturalism that James and Dewey had made.

In his superb new study of James, Gerald Myers show that it is not easy to say just when it was that James gave up on the two dogmas of idealism if, indeed, he ever did. But surely Dewey got it right when he saw, both early and late, that what may have been a commitment to at least one persistent conseqence of this dualism was already at the "vanishing" point in the *Principles of Psychology*—even if James himself was not yet prepared to acknowledge the fact. But Dewey was observing the development of James's psychology from a vantage point denied to James himself.[14] He had already rejected Peirce's program in normative transcendental logic by the time that the *Principles* was published. Unlike James, Dewey loved logic. He enjoyed teaching it and did so for most of his life. It might not even be too much to say that, in the end, he did his best work in logic.

Dewey's interest in refuting the claims of Kantian transcendental logic began early and never ceased.[15] Even while he was still under the influence of George Sylvester Morris, whose own 1886 book on Kant's first *Critique* adopts the line of psychologism in logic that Dewey briefly followed, it is clear that Dewey was less interested in defending psychologism than in rebutting the arguments of the transcendentalists.[16] In a series of articles published in *Mind* in the 1880s Dewey repeatedly argued the thesis that, as he succinctly put it in 1886:

In truth we do not go from logic to nature at all. The movement is a reverse movement. . . . The logical movement considered by itself is always balancing in unstable equilibrium between dualism and pantheism. . . . Logic cannot reach, however much it may point to, an actual individual.[17]

In this thesis, drawn from Hegel and distinguishing between symbolic "pointing" and actual "reaching," Dewey anticipates the now familiar distinction between a variable and its value, and the ontological implications thereof.

Just a few months after this appeared in *Mind* under the title "Psychology as Scientific Method," Dewey again attacked the method of transcendentalist logic and its "metaphysics of experience" in direct response to Shadworth Hodgson's criticism. It is abundantly clear from the tenor and tone of Dewey's response that his own rejection of the two dogmas of idealism that Hodgson's "metaphysics of experience" embraced was now complete. All that remained for Dewey was the reconstruction of psychology, and its method, as the "logic of experience" in the 1903 *Studies*.

Because I have tried to trace the process of that reconstruction elsewhere,[18] let me devote what remains of this chapter to a few of its consequences. Among them are those already noted by reference to Quine's essay on the "Two Dogmas of Empiricism." From the outset, Dewey's conception of logic as an empirical science erased the boundary between the analytic and synthetic. The alleged boundary between fact and value soon followed.

But are these the consequences of the system that Peirce was trying to work out? Was it, indeed, pragmatism at all? The evidence suggests that Dewey's earliest efforts at logical reconstruction had little or nothing to do with pragmatism, at least as conceived by Peirce in the *Scientific Monthly* articles of 1886–1887, even after James made them famous by his 1898 California address. Dewey had been attacking Peirce's conception of logic—if indirectly—all along, and so it is not at all puzzling that he failed to embrace those maxims and the tag attached. Moreover, as his 1896 essay on "The Reflex Arc Concept in Psychology" shows, Dewey did not yet think of James's radical empiricism as sufficiently free of the Kantian dogmas, either. Dewey was already introducing the transactional approach to inquiry and the "logic of experience" that were to occupy him for the rest of his life.

The fact is, I think, that Dewey was astonished to learn of James's enthusiasm for the 1903 *Studies in Logical Theory*, which does not so much as mention pragmatism or radical empiricism. Peirce's response to the *Studies* was, of course, very different and clearly came as no surprise to Dewey. Shocked at the naive impudence of Dewey's empirical approach to logic, Peirce showed—in a letter of 1905—that he well understood the challenge to the doctrine of synechism implicit in the *Studies*, and warned Dewey against further incursions into the territory that he had marked out for himself in the researches that had absorbed him—as he puts it—"for the last eighteen years."[19] It is easy to see why Dewey could not have believed himself a pragmatist at all.

In the end, of course, Dewey's acceptance of the epithet—or soft impeachment—of "pragmatism" would depend on how its terms were to be construed. There were many factors contributing to the studied phrases in which Dewey finally stated that construal in 1938, and of his acceptance of the tag that Peirce had invented so long ago. They appear in the *Introduction to Logic: The Theory of Inquiry* this way:

The word "Pragmatism" does not, I think, occur in the text. Perhaps the word lends itself to misconception. At all events, so much misunderstanding and relatively futile controversy have gathered about the word that it seemed advisable to avoid its use. But in the proper interpretation of "pragmatic," namely the function of consequences as necessary tests of the validity of propositions, provided these consequences are operationally instituted and are such as to resolve the specific problem evoking the operations, the text that follows is thoroughly pragmatic.[20]

Perhaps what has been misleading us all along is what appears just a few lines below. For there Dewey says this:

I should state explicitly that, with the outstanding exception of Peirce, I have learned most from writers with whose positions I have in the end been compelled to disagree.

But surely, we should not have been misled at all. For what follows is a thoroughgoing and systematic reconstruction of Peirce's doctrine of continuity, that is, of synechism.

Its consequences are those that we must expect from the final rejection of idealism and its persistent dogmas: a pragmatism that embraces its own "pragmatic realism" with its piecemeal character, and all the limitations, uncertainties, and vagueness that go with it.[21]

Putnam, Goodman, and others take a pragmatic stand on the question of choosing between realism and idealism, but their realism sometimes leaves off at the imagined boundary between the "internal" and "external" worlds. Quine does not seem similarly afflicted, although his insistence on the special treatment of abstract entities suggests that he is closer to Peirce than he would willingly concede, that a trace remains of the transcendental mathematicism of Peirce in at least this one segment of his ontology. Goodman would excise such traces by accepting Quine's abstract entities as parts of a world "version," one among many such versions in his vision of "irrealism." His pluralism in "worldmaking" is successor to James's.[22]

Donald Davison takes a pragmatic stand in respect to both Kant's dogmas, at least in rejecting the dualism of scheme and content, of mental states and mental objects.[23] But the theory of "truth without reference" seems to imply that transcendental arguments may sometimes be necessary. And Putnam at times seems to say outright that they are necessary.[24] Davidson invokes something like a transcendental argument in his efforts aimed at rescuing propositional attitudes from cognitive limbo. We need them, he tells us if we are ever to make sense of the world of our experience.[25] And Putnam, invoking a similar line to justify the objectivity of value judgments in his Carus Lectures, remarks on its connection to Peirce's line and that which moves both Apel and Husserl to versions of transcendentalism.[26]

But the unabashed acceptance of the Kantian dogmas by Husserl and Apel is hardly the style that leads to the more thorough pragmatism envisaged by either Dewey or Quine. Perhaps Putnam's troubles stem from the Kantian turn that he takes in *Reason, Truth and History*, for that suggests to Margolis—and I think that Margolis is right about this—the necessity that Putnam faces of working out a transcendental argument to resolve the dualism of internal versus external realism.[27]

In reconstructing Peirce's synechism to get rid of its dualist ontology, Dewey espouses a more coherent theory of experience and of inquiry, as well as the more coherent version of realism that goes with it. (More coherent because it is piecemeal, and not perfectly "holistic.") The reconstructed theory of the continuity of inquiry supports a more thorough pragmatism, one that recognizes, as Stan Thayer puts it, that "Logic has an ontology and ontology a logic; thought and things are causally linked in a circuit of existential transactions."[28]

Putnam sometimes seems to appreciate this feature of Dewey's methods, perhaps when he is reminded of it by Nelson Goodman, or Ruth Anna Putnam.[29] Then again, he sometimes forgets, perhaps when distracted by the lure of modal logics or the attraction of Kantian moral images. But it is just because our practices are causally linked with our standards that our practices are right and wrong depending on how they square with our standards; "And our standards are right or wrong depending on how they square with our practices," as Putnam himself once put it.[30] It is just such transactional linkages that replace transcendental arguments in pragmatism once these frontiers of classical American philosophy have vanished, and the necessity of the dogmas of idealism is banished from its logic. To paraphrase the quotation from Dewey with which I began: Philosophy will not be emancipated to perform its own task and function until logic is purged, as a whole and in all its special topics, of the last remnants of dualism.

NOTES

1. John Dewey, *The Later Works, 1925–1953*, 17 vols., ed. Jo Ann Boydston. (Carbondale: Southern Illinois University Press, 1981), 14:167.

2. Willard van Orman Quine, "Two Dogmas of Empiricism," in Quine, *From a Logical Point of View* (Cambridge, Mass.: Harvard University Press, 1951), 46.

3. William Kneale and Martha Kneale, *The Development of Logic* (Oxford: Clarendon Press, 1984), 448.

4. Shadworth Hodgson, *The Metaphysics of Experience*, 4 vols. (London: Longmans Green, 1898).

5. John McDermott, "Spires of Influence: The Importance of Emerson for Classical American Philosophy," in *Streams of Experience* (Amherst: University of Massachusetts Press, 1986), 29.

6. Max H. Fisch, "Peirce as Scientist, Mathematician, Historian, Logician, and Philosopher," in *Foundations of Semiotics*, ed. Achim Esbach (Amsterdam and Philadelphia: John Benjamins, 1983), xvii.

7. Ibid., xxvii.

8. Justus Buchler, *Philosophical Writings of Peirce* (New York: Dover, 1955), 352.

9. Charles Sanders Peirce, *Collected Papers of Charles Sanders Peirce*, 8 vols., ed. Charles Hartshorne, Paul Weiss, and Arthur W. Burks (Cambridge, Mass.: Harvard University Press, 1931–1958), 6:17ff; Fisch, *Foundations*, xxvii.

10. Peirce, *Collected Papers*, 6:14.

11. Ibid., 5:416–34.

12. Peirce's "Platonic forms" and "Scotistic reals" are, as he defines them, general objects (or universals) that are linked up with his objective idealism through the process of "evolutionary love." It is this process, he says, "whereby the existent comes more and more to embody those generals which were just now said to be destined." And, though synechism replaces the Hegelian dialectical logic with the processive logic of "evolutionary love," it was Peirce himself who acknowledged that it is "closely allied to Hegelian absolute idealism" (Peirce, *Collected Papers*, 5:433–34). Responding to this alliance, Charles Hartshorne, whose own reconstruction of Peirce's categorical scheme repudiates it, reflects upon the doctrine of synechism in a piece the title of which signals its contents, "Charles Peirce's 'One Contribution to Philosophy' and His Most Serious Mistake." In Peirce's synechism Kant's two dogmas are, of course, on their way out. That is "destined." But they have not yet vanished. It seems that when, in 1937, Dewey reviewed the volumes of Peirce's work put together by Hartshorne and Weiss, he was disposed to neglect the fact that they had not vanished altogether (Dewey, *Later Works*, 11:479–84). But, by then, Dewey had already worked out his reconstruction of synechism in the *Logic* that he would publish the following year.

13. Robert Burch, "An Unpublished Logic Paper by Josiah Royce," *Transactions of the Charles S. Peirce Society* 23, no. 2 (1987); Burch, "A Transformation of Royce's View of Kant," *Transactions of the Charles S. Peirce Society* 23, no. 4 (1987).

14. William James, as Ketner points out, was initially in awe of Peirce's enthusiasm for the logicizing of scientific method, but it was doubtless Royce's version of the Kantian dogmas that eventually put him off. For, as Ketner himself quotes James, "I owe more to (Peirce's) writings than to anyone but Royce" (Kenneth Laine Ketner, "Introduction" [to selections of C. S. Peirce], in *Classical American Philosophy*, ed. John J. Stuhr [Oxford: Oxford University Press, 1987], 20). Peirce, famously, was well aware of this defection and abandoned "pragmatism" to its fate at James's hands, espousing "pragmaticism" instead. What may have put James off—aside from the fact that he detested formal logic altogether—was Royce's startling discovery in 1892 that the laws of physics are determined by the transcendental laws of formal logic as expressed in geometry. Perhaps James simply couldn't stomach this expression of the "Absolute"! (See Burch, 1987, 566). Like the logics of both Peirce and Royce, Lewis's logic belongs to the history of mainstream developments that stem from Frege and Russell. And his metaphysics remains loyal to the Kantian paradigm of the "metaphysics of experience." Like Peirce and Royce, he remained committed to the search for the necessary conditions of experience, and so to a "first philosophy" as the necessary foundation for science. Once again the Kantian dogmas haunt the territory and distinguish his pragmatism from what Dewey, James, and Mead were working on.

15. It is a moot point whether Dewey's defection from transcendental logic was precipitated by having attended Peirce's lectures at Johns Hopkins or not. Regrettably, Hopkins allowed Dewey "attendance credit" for them and we cannot infer from that much of anything at all—even that Dewey actually attended them. But what is clear is that Dewey's publications on logical matters began soon after his graduation from Hopkins, and continued unabated for the rest of his life. And those writings were uniformly critical of the transcendentalist path in logic that Peirce was following.

16. George S. Morris, *Kant's Critique of Pure Reason* (Chicago: S. C. Griggs, 1886).

17. John Dewey, *The Early Works 1882–1898*, 5 vols., ed. Jo Ann Boydston (Carbondale: Southern Illinois University, 1969), 1:164–66.

18. Ralph W. Sleeper, *The Necessity of Pragmatism: John Dewey's Conception of Philosophy* (New Haven, Conn.: Yale University Press, 1986).

19. Peirce, *Collected Papers*, 8:243.

20. Dewey, *Later Works*, 12:iii–iv.

21. Dewey's metaphysics does not provide for a completely closed system. Thayer suggests that pragmatism is more of a "metaphilosophy" than a system, but Quine suggests that we should "hold out for a holistic" perspective, despite the fact that it may not apply across the board (H. Standish Thayer, "Pragmatism: A Reinterpretation of the Origins and Consequences," in *Pragmatism: Its Sources and Prospects*, ed. R. J. Mulvaney and P. M. Zeltner [Columbia: University of South Carolina Press, 1981], 17; and Willard van Orman Quine, "The Pragmatist's Place in Empiricism," in Mulvaney and Zeltner, eds., *Pragmatism*, 1981). In my view, Quine resolves this question nicely when he suggests the following: "It is an uninteresting legalism, however, to think of our scientific system of the world as involved en bloc in every prediction. More modest chunks suffice, and so may be ascribed their independent empirical meaning, nearly enough, since some vagueness in meaning must be allowed for in any event." (Quine, "The Pragmatist's Place," 27)

22. Nelson Goodman, *Ways of Worldmaking* (Indianapolis: Hackett, 1978).

23. Donald Davidson, "On the Very Idea of a Conceptual Scheme," *Proceedings and Addresses of the American Philosophical Association* 47 (1973–74): 1–21.

24. Putnam actually gives a transcendental argument in his essay on "Why Reason Can't Be Naturalized" in *Realism and Reason*. It results in this reflection: "If reason is both transcendent and immanent, then philosophy, as culture-bound reflection and argument about eternal questions, is both in time and eternity. We don't have an Archimedean point; we always speak the language of a time and place; but the rightness and wrongness of what we say is not just for a time and a place." It seems clear to me that there is no need to argue for the "transcendence" of reason in order to reach the conclusion that "the rightness and wrongness of what we say is not just for a time and place." (Hilary Putnam, *Realism and Reason* [Cambridge: Cambridge University Press, 1983], 247.) But perhaps that is because I don't know what "eternal questions" are, or how they could possibly be answered. Since Putnam seems to be saying that our reflection and argument is in eternity as well as in time, perhaps all of our temporal questions are also eternal. But, if that is the case, there would be no need for anything like a transcendental argument for the transcendence of reason; its transcendence would simply be analytic.

25. Hilary Putnam, *The Many Faces of Realism* (LaSalle, Ill.: Open Court, 1987), 21.

26. Ibid., 20–21, 53–56.

27. Joseph Margolis, *Pragmatism Without Foundations* (Oxford: Basel Blackwell, 1986), 281–307.

28. Thayer, "Pragmatism," 332.

29. The reference to Goodman's work as a "reminder" is to Putnam's "Foreword to the Fourth Edition" in *Fact, Fiction, and Forecast* (Cambridge, Mass.: Harvard University Press, 1983), ix. The reference to Ruth Anna Putnam's work as a reminder is to Putnam, *The Many Faces of Realism* (LaSalle, Ill.: Open Court, 1987), 78–79.

30. Putnam, *Realism and Reason*, ix.

10

The Decline of Evolutionary Naturalism in Later Pragmatism

Randall Auxier

"The development theory implies a greater vital force in Nature, because it is more flexible and accommodating, and equivalent to a sort of constant new creation."

Thoreau[1]

MIDDLE PRAGMATISM AND EVOLUTIONARY NATURALISM

I should begin by explaining what is meant in the present chapter by "later pragmatism" and "evolutionary naturalism." I will first explain "later pragmatism" and then proceed to "evolutionary naturalism." It will be necessary to employ the latter term a number of times before defining it. Forbearance by the reader will be appreciated.

Middle Pragmatism

In point of fact, this chapter focuses largely on what might be called "middle pragmatism"[2] in order to illuminate why "later pragmatism" is less evolutionary and less naturalistic (in one sense) than middle pragmatism. Middle pragmatism, as I understand it, is epitomized by the work of Dewey and Mead. Later pragmatism may be taken to begin with C. I. Lewis and to run through Quine and "naturalized epistemology."[3] "Neo-pragmatism" arose in reaction to inherent weaknesses in the latter, method-oriented epistemological pragmatism.[4]

It is also worth taking a moment before proceeding to characterize what is meant by "neo-pragmatism," which may be too easily confused with "later pragmatism." Neo-pragmatism is, I believe, epitomized by the work of Richard Rorty. If genuine pragmatism had really survived the dual onslaught of trendy existentialist irrationalism and literal-minded positivism in any recognizable form, it is doubtful that neo-pragmatism would have taken shape as it did (if at all). Neo-pragmatism on the whole exhibits all the quirks and bizarre features one would expect from a hybrid beast that wanders around constantly in search of its progenitors, so that once finding the most likely culprits, it may, in the fashion of Frankenstein's monster, condemn them for having created anything at all. Certainly both the later and middle pragmatists would have given this beast up for adoption, or institutionalized it, rather than be forced to look at it every day.

Unlike later pragmatism, I do not believe that most versions of neo-pragmatism are even the legitimate offspring of pragmatism. It looks rather like a teenager who stands out at the family reunion with the relatives gossiping about his bright red hair—which couldn't have come from anyone in the family. What is neo-pragmatism's bright red hair? As the editors have correctly pointed out in the introduction to this volume, all forms of authentic pragmatism are nonfoundational (both epistemologically and metaphysically), and this is certainly what neo-pragmatists claim for themselves. This is not, however, a sufficient condition for a genuine pragmatism, in my view, but a necessary condition only. A pragmatist must also avoid reductionism of all kinds, and be committed to pluralism and fallibilism. Further, a pragmatist must also be committed to the primacy of *praxis*, understood as inquiry in some defensible sense. This final feature is, in my view, incompatible with the antirealist stance of most neo-pragmatists—those who would deny to natural science the full weight of an excellent (perhaps *the* most excellent) form of *praxis*. Neo-pragmatism's bright red hair is not its antirealism, however. Antirealism is more like the spiked, Mohawk haircut, but not the reason for its bright red color. Antirealism is a rebellion neo-pragmatism expresses against its parents, but who were they? Neither the full-bodied, naturalized realism of middle pragmatism nor the narrower epistemological realism of later pragmatism is reconcilable with the neo-pragmatist relativization of scientific method and scientific practice (i.e., inquiry). So this feature may not come from within the marriage of middle and later pragmatism. It may be time to go looking for the milkman—who is rumored to have bright red hair.[5] A successful search could end in an overdue divorce, and I will contend below that indeed later pragmatism was unfaithful, and neo-pragmatism was born.

The main peculiarity of neo-pragmatism is that it tends to allow methodological (as opposed to metaphysical or epistemological) reductionism to guide its thinking, whether this ends in the hegemony of rational discourse and the quest for the ideal speech community (e.g., Habermas, whom some would call a pragmatist), or simply in shrugging one's shoulders at all serious objections (Rorty).

In either case, the process is at least as unpragmatic as the product. Methodological reductionism is common to both; a recessive gene in later pragmatism that only became visible when combined with the milkman's more manifest genetic make-up.

What do I mean by methodological reductionism? Basically, I mean analysis, especially the *reductio ad absurdum*. Amazingly enough, this is the primary tool of both extremes in contemporary philosophy, and of neo-pragmatism as well. Both on the Continent and in the United States philosophers have in recent decades faced many ultra-rationalistic forms of reductionism on the right hand and extreme irrationalism or relativism on the left. Both of these are sufficiently convinced by the force of *reductio ad absurdum* methodology that they are willing to stake their philosophical reputations on results obtained by means of it. Rorty's *Philosophy and the Mirror of Nature*[6] would arguably have no methodology at all if it were not for the repeated application of the *reductio* to the content of the view of human nature presupposed in analytic philosophies of mind and language. By the same token, in seeing the basic cracks and fissures in the metaphysics of presence, often via the device of *reductio*, deconstruction resolves not to ever make the mistake of building anything of its own. Instead, it dances gaily about the Cartesian boneyard pointing out now and again how everything in Western philosophy reduces itself to absurdity as if by magic— or by method, there being nothing left to distinguish them. Neo-pragmatism shares this tendency. As the editors argue in the introduction to Part III, neo-pragmatism is the revenge of the interpretive disciplines on the scientism that dominated the middle third of the century. Whether that scientism is American and British philosophy of science or French structuralism is of little consequence.

This shows that both the neo-pragmatists and the deconstructionists believe tacitly in the power of the *reductio*. Analytic philosophy also, in all of its forms, makes the same methodological commitment, aside from being an extreme view in several other ways. As I will show in a moment, authentic pragmatism does not give the *reductio* this much power. Yet, with extreme commitments of analysis and deconstruction as the dominant alternatives, even the well-known excesses of neo-pragmatism have a surprising look of sane moderation, in spite of its methodological narrowness.[7]

To summarize, I will work with middle, later, and "neo" as the important divisions within pragmatism. These categories are too quickly formulated to have much more than a suggestive structure, which may not be ultimately defensible or desirable. They do, however, help one to trace the fate of Darwin's discovery/invention through its courses, and that is the aim here. Evolutionary theory fares differently among different kinds of pragmatists. Below I will argue that evolution is a fundamentally diachronic or processive worldview that seeks to explain and integrate natural knowledge, including scientific understanding itself, as an emergent phenomenon within a cultural phase of natural history. The concern Darwin and the early and middle pragmatists showed for this basically temporal mode of approaching nature and culture has effectively disappeared from both later pragmatism and neo-pragmatism.

In my view, this change also marks the death of a viable pragmatism. This is not to say that all philosophers have been completely wasting their time for the past forty years. Yet, most of the lessons learned during this time have been negative, lessons that had already been learned in other times by other thinkers from whom we could have profited had we exhibited the nerve to do so. I am not alone in saying this. When Hilary Putnam (a fairly recent addition to classic pragmatism's ranks) was asked (at a lecture he gave on William James at Emory University in December 1991) whether analytic philosophy had been a waste of time, he could give no more decisive reply than to say that we never waste our time when we seek the truth sincerely, but *finding* the truth is not a requirement.

These categories of early, middle, later, and neo-pragmatism also assist us in seeing how the absence of evolutionary naturalism contributed to the decline of public interest in (and social conscience/activism among) persons who called themselves pragmatists through the 1940s, 1950s, 1960s and 1970s—later pragmatism. There has been some slight renewed interest among the educated public directed toward neo-pragmatism (as well as a fairly healthy interdisciplinary interest within academia), but it is difficult at present to tell whether this is anything more than a fad. In any case, one could not claim for neo-pragmatism anything like the audience enjoyed by early and middle pragmatism. I will discuss this in a limited way below, and I also refer the reader to the chapter by Bruce Kuklick in Part II of this anthology.

Evolutionary Naturalism

The decline of evolutionary naturalism was too gradual to be noticed by anyone as it was occurring (with the possible exception of Dewey, see below), and so there are not really any villains—consciously sworn enemies of evolution, naturalism, and temporalistic philosophy—who might be pointed out. Indeed, I am certain that by far most philosophers, whether pragmatists or not, from Dewey's death right up to the present would count themselves among the subscribers to the theory of evolution, in one form or another. I do not believe, however, that very many of them are entitled to call themselves real "Darwinians," since this would commit them to a holistic, culturally based, organic philosophy of natural history which is committed to the employment of scientific method and statistical measure, but without being reductionistic. They would be obliged to acknowledge the operation of chance in natural selection and the entire messy field of sexual selection. They would be forced to admit that no finite set of logically connected "laws" governs the phenomenon of selection, and thus, they would cease being so mesmerized by mere words. They could not properly call themselves Darwinian materialists, nor mechanists, for this is not Darwinism. In my view, it fails to even be evolutionism in any important way. I will argue this point below.

I have said that the decline of evolutionary naturalism was gradual. It was indeed on the horizon even as Dewey and Mead reached their acmes in the late 1920s and early 1930s.[8] Only a great "effort of thought" (as James might say) by Dewey and Mead aimed at maintaining a creative tension between two contrary tendencies in evolutionary naturalism prevented a decline through the 1920s, 1930s and 1940s. I believe that, whether they realized it or not, Mead (to some extent) and Dewey (to a great extent) found themselves increasingly isolated, intellectually speaking, even through that period in which their influence was greatest. There is evidence that suggests Dewey was well aware of what was happening to evolutionary thinking all around him. In the foreword to what is still the definitive book on the reception of evolutionary theory in American intellectual circles in the 1860s, 1870s and 1880s, Philip P. Wiener's *Evolution and the Founders of Pragmatism*, Dewey says:

[Wiener's] treatment of the "Foundations of Pragmatism" in terms of a deep, moving cultural current takes us to a time when America was still a symbol of the dawn of a better day and was full of hope with courage. It will be a happy day for American philosophy if, after a period of loss of nerve, this stirring account of the initial period of a movement (not an ism) recalls the wandering thoughts of American teachers of philosophy to the creative movement to which they belong as Americans, whatever school they belong to professionally.[9]

This was not only aimed at the rising popularity of analytic philosophy (although it seems that Dewey could see the writing on the wall in that regard), but also at the next generation of "pragmatists." Some of Dewey's very own students (such as Sidney Hook and Ernest Nagel) had already turned decisively toward one side or the other of the creative tension I shall describe—seemingly without the least interest in or sympathy for the continued efforts of their mentors to maintain a bridge over an ever-widening gulf.[10]

What is the character of the creative tension in evolutionary naturalism? We must first keep in mind that evolutionary naturalism is progressive, experimental, scientific, and practical. With that much said, let us consider a passage from Mead related to this creative tension:

Continuous advance in science has been possible only when analysis of the object of knowledge has supplied not elements of meanings as the objects have been conceived but elements abstracted from those meanings. That is, scientific advance implies a willingness to remain on terms of tolerant acceptance of the reality of what cannot be stated in the accepted doctrine of the time, but that must be stated in the form of contradiction with these accepted doctrines.[11]

Scientific progress involves a tolerance of contradictions because scientific descriptions are always incomplete and fallible. Yet, for Mead, this does not militate against a practical, scientific realism, but is rather a result of it. Realism is what compels a scientist/philosopher to accept tolerantly the contradictions between his current theory and the world he or she wishes to describe. Here the methodological reduction is averted. A *reductio* is not necessarily a falsification of some state of affairs. Middle pragmatism will not accept the ascendancy of language analysis because a thorough-going realism forces us to admit that our descriptions of reality provide us with only an incomplete and fallible map of the territory we truly wish to explore.

Diving fully into language analysis is like studying a map, and perhaps also the tools of map makers, without showing adequate concern for the territory to be explored. Eventually, later pragmatists failed to strike out into the territory at all, being satisfied with the map(s) they inherited from physics and interested only in the tools of the cartographers. Such is the philosophy of science in the last forty years.

Mead and Dewey were, however, experimentalists as well as philosophers. In that sense, they were map makers as well as explorers of the territory. They were also fully capable of talking intelligently about the tools of cartographers, the value of cartography, the emergence of cartography, and a full range of philosophical and self-critical questions that the best cartographers would ask. This seems to be a lost art among pragmatists and philosophers in general, and it perhaps supplies a justification for forbidding the philosophy of science to be taught without a scientist present (a rule once aptly suggested for City University of New York by Charles M. Sherover). So we must not mistake the map for the territory, or imagine that map making is not important to those who wish to talk about maps already made and tools of cartographers.

This is of course true for evolutionary naturalism as a philosophy. But what are the two contrary tendencies within this philosophy? The tendencies need labels to facilitate discussion, and so I shall call them, following a suggestion Dewey made very late in his life, ''cultural naturalism'' on the one hand, and ''mechanistic naturalism'' on the other. ''Evolutionary naturalism'' may be understood as the continued effort to keep these two tendencies in balance, although there can be little question, in middle pragmatism, which of the two tendencies is clearly emphasized. Cultural naturalism, understood as the effort to situate all human inquiry and all human value within an existential and cultural matrix (which does not claim for itself a value-neutral status), is quite clearly the predominant tendency of middle pragmatism. As Mead says:

The scientific attitude contemplates our physical habitat as primarily the environment of man who is the first cousin once removed of the arboreal anthropoid ape, but it views it as being transformed first through unreflective intelligence and then by reflective intelligence into the environment of a human society, the latest species to appear on the earth.[12]

This is not, however, antirealism or relativism (moral, epistemological or metaphysical). Still speaking of the scientific method, Mead says:

The order of the universe that we live in *is* the moral order. It has become the moral order by becoming the self-conscious method of the members of a human society. We are not pilgrims and strangers. We are at home in our own world, but it is not ours by inheritance but by conquest. The world that comes to us from the past possesses and controls us. We possess and control the world that we discover and invent.[13]

Is this cultural naturalism or mechanistic naturalism? It is quite clearly both, which is to say that it is evolutionary naturalism. The key to having both is in not assuming that scientific method is reducible to some automatic application of previously used techniques for enumerating or measuring natural regularities, or that any technique or set of techniques must necessarily hook up with reality *an sich.* But for Mead and Dewey, the scientific method is far more than just that. In expressing his nonreductive, humanistic take on scientific method Mead says:

The analysis of the fact-structure of reality shows in the first place that the scientist undertakes to form such a hypothesis that all the data of observation will find their place in the objective world, and in the second place to bring them into such a structure that future experience will lead to anticipated results. He does not undertake to preserve facts in the form in which they existed in experience before the problem arose nor to construct a world independent of experience or that will not be subject itself to future reconstructions in experience.[14]

Mead follows this passage with a detailed example from the work of none other than Darwin as a paradigmatic case of what he means here.

Within the larger field of study, that is, the existential and cultural matrix of inquiry, it is entirely licit to search for "mechanisms" that can be observed and reliably described, tested, and controlled. These mechanisms, however, are themselves (at best) features of the existential matrix of inquiry/appreciation[15] whose very description is a provisional matter, subject to further experimentation. At worst, what have been identified as "natural mechanisms" driving natural and cultural evolution may turn out to be purely conventional and/or customary, and thus are "knowledge" relative only to a certain set of historical and environmental contingencies—hence, the "mechanism" is a feature of the cultural, but not the existential, matrix of inquiry.

Yet, this "worst" case makes the result no less important. Indeed, quite the contrary is true. It only points out to us that these "mechanisms" are less easily known, circumscribed, and controlled than are those that are evidently features of both the existential matrix of inquiry *and* the cultural matrix. The ongoing articulation of the relations between the cultural and existential matrices of inquiry is taken by middle pragmatism to be one of the primary functions of philosophy. Hence, Dewey and Mead both developed methodologies that moved freely between these two matrices, allowing them to mutually illuminate one another. These are more like poles than independent fields of inquiry.

In both cases natural science is thought of foremost as a fallible, human endeavor in the service of self-knowledge (in the broadest sense). A mechanistic framework could be adopted for the purpose of forming and testing a hypothesis, but it could never be made into a metaphysical first principle. Materialism seeks to make a metaphysics from an overly narrow interpretation of a culturally emergent method, and neither Mead nor Dewey even so much as flirted with this idea. Nevertheless, natural science is held to be, beyond any question, the best mode and method of inquiry the human race possesses, and both Mead and Dewey believed in using it to the fullest extent possible in solving genuine problems.

The creative tension between nature and culture exemplified in the methodologies of Dewey and Mead corresponds quite literally to what we now distinguish as the social or human sciences and the natural or hard sciences. Dewey and Mead were neither social scientists nor natural scientists strictly, since their kind of naturalism would not accept the split. It is not as if natural science were not a social undertaking, or human beings were not natural beings. Dewey and Mead did not need Thomas Kuhn to tell them this. It will be a familiar fact to the educated reader that the tendency has been, in the middle and later part of the present century, for this same tension and split between nature and culture to reduplicate itself over again within the various special sciences, both natural and social. Certainly great minds such as Freud and Levi-Strauss could hold the two in creative tension to some degree, but as time has passed, nature and culture (and the study of them) have gone increasingly toward separate extremes. It is not unusual to find anthropology departments where the physical and cultural anthropologists do not speak to one another, psychology departments where the behaviorists and psychoanalysts do not speak, political science departments that are famous for their disputes between statisticians/demographers and political theorists, history departments where the historians of ideas war constantly with those who would have history become a science,[16] and even genetics departments where the population geneticists have little or nothing in common with those working under mechanistic paradigms.[17]

Many things might be said about the forces that have conspired to create this unhealthy situation. For instance, it should be noted that the very structure of the university has lent itself to the sundering of nature and culture. Darwin gave us both natural selection (1859) and sexual selection (1871) as explanations of evolution. It is quite understandable that the former was taken up by those working under a mechanistic framework, while the latter was more easily studied by the social scientists of that day. What goes unnoticed is that this tendency to divide the evolutionary labor was the death knell of evolutionary naturalism itself. Evolutionary thinking, and Darwin's full-fledged theory and philosophy, could survive only as long as did the creative tension found in thinkers like Dewey and Mead, and in others (now long neglected) who shared their general approach, such as Bergson, Whitehead, Scheler, Cassirer, and later, Charles Hartshorne and Arnold Gehlen. In a very real sense, all of these figures could be described as evolutionary naturalists, and all are nonfoundationalists—although only Dewey and Mead are really pragmatists, while the rest may best be described as persons who have significant pragmatic tendencies and sympathies.

In their struggle to give full weight and consideration to both nature and culture, Mead and Dewey set a standard that proved to be too high for the generation of pragmatists that followed them, what I have called later pragmatism. It is quite clear that Quine accepts the distinction between the natural and human sciences, and that he is interested only in the "ontology" of the former. If it is at least preliminarily clear what I mean by evolutionary naturalism and later pragmatism, then, I will now proceed to the main arguments. In what follows, I will attempt to explain and defend, from one point of view, *how* (and to some extent *why*) evolutionary naturalism declined. I should also like to say a word or two about the effect this has had upon both philosophy and the public.

THE BACKGROUND OF EVOLUTIONARY NATURALISM

Darwin's account of the origin of species has not exactly been received with enthusiasm by the mass of Americans. Yet American philosophers of science were among the first, the most penetrating and thoroughgoing evolutionists to be found in the world. Along with Dewey and Mead, I should mention Peirce, James, John Fiske, and James Mark Baldwin, among many others.[18] Each of these philosophers of science (for that is what each of them were, if science is not taken to be something divorced from history and human culture) took as his point of departure the "evolutionary hypothesis." The evolutionary hypothesis, which we might now simply call a fact,[19] mandated some major changes in our views about the nature of human knowing. While these changes were fairly widely accepted and followed out in the years 1871–1950 by the leading figures in the philosophy of science, they have been all but lost in the past half century by pragmatists and nonpragmatists alike.

As Ernst Mayr has complained repeatedly in his *Toward a New Philosophy of Biology*, most current philosophers of science, whether consciously or not, operate on a positively pre-Darwinian model of human knowing guided "by an almost exclusive reliance on logic, mathematics, and the laws of physics."[20] By this, Mayr means deductive logic and mathematics, and the universal applicability of strictly definable mathematical laws of physics. In brief, the past fifty years have seen philosophers of science lean very markedly in the direction of relegating all biological phenomena that cannot be accounted for by such a reduction to the rubbish heap of unknowability or nonsense. This has not been a perfectly universal tendency among philosophers of science. It has been prevalent enough, however, to lead Mayr and many of his colleagues in biology to the conclusion that philosophers of science for the most part, in Rip Van Winkle fashion, simply slept through the Darwinian revolution.[21] They were perhaps too busy quaffing ale and watching ghosts play at nine-pins. As I have already made clear, I am in sympathy with this conclusion. I believe that a fairly clear idea of what was lost and gained by leaning toward physics can be discerned, and that a recovery of what has been lost can be effected with an adequate show of courage in the profession of philosophy, although I admit I will be surprised if that happens.

It is a fact that the role of bringing the moral implications of recent science to the educated public—a role traditionally played by philosophers—has been taken over of late by practicing scientists. One can list quite a number of these popularizers off hand: Stephen Hawking, Carl Sagan, Stephen J. Gould, Frithjof Capra, Richard Feynman, Edward O. Wilson, Roger Penrose, and Richard Dawkins all spring immediately to mind. Most of them have first compiled impressive credentials in their particular sciences, and then sought to interpret the lasting significance and meaning of their work for the world. In a sense, to return to my earlier analogy, they have taken upon themselves the questions of the meaning and value of mapping the territory of reality—these are questions now largely abandoned by philosophers (pragmatists included—Rorty's pretenses aside, since we are talking about the *actual* public, which has rarely or never heard Rorty's name).

But good popular science is very often bad philosophy. Each of the scientists mentioned (with the possible exception of Feynman) can be caught in philosophical errors so basic that beginning graduate students in philosophy could be expected to avoid them.[22] A glaring recent example that might be given is Carl Sagan's growing interest in the field of ethics. In a recent number of the widely read Sunday insert, *Parade Magazine*, Sagan expounds a peculiar theory of morality in which various ethical principles are metaphorically associated with various sorts of metals (gold, silver, bronze, iron, and a number of alloys), and then "tested" according to a very cursory and oversimplified account of game theory. The result is billed as a "scientific test" for moral principles.[23] Even an analytic ethicist would find Sagan's ethics appallingly simplistic.

Why is Carl Sagan doing moral philosophy? It must be admitted that these scientists have stepped in to fill a void once occupied by philosophers like James, Fiske and Dewey. As philosophy strove to be a science (or at least "scientific") in later years, it abandoned its very important duty to situate recent scientific advances in their proper historical and moral context for the educated public.[24]

The acceptance of the evolutionary hypothesis by early and middle pragmatism had three basic implications, which were found unacceptable by later pragmatism and by the dominant philosophers of science from the 1940s through the 1960s. These were (1) that our knowledge of nature is rendered entirely inductive and probabilistic by the evolutionary hypothesis (this is the "cash value" of fallibilism); (2) that the philosophy of science becomes epistemologically subordinate to the philosophy of history under the evolutionary hypothesis; and (3) that a metaphysics that construes values to be the ground of facts must replace the older arrangement in which facts were taken to be the ground of values (insofar as values were thought to *have* any ground). This is a different way of stating that for evolutionary naturalists, culture mediates our access to and interpretation of the existential matrix of inquiry, and that value is an inexpungable aspect of all things cultural. I will comment on each of these points in turn.

Probability, and Deduction as Reduction[25]

The classic experimental/scientific method of prediction and control has long been taken to be the basis of human knowledge of the natural world. It is not stretching matters to claim that through the seventeenth and eighteenth centuries, and into the nineteenth, the prevailing interpretation of that method was that it afforded deductive certainty about relations among natural phenomena. From the middle of the nineteenth century until today, however, the deductive model has come under considerable fire. The attack was first launched from biology, and has been joined by physics during the last forty to sixty years (the quantum revolution).

Evolutionary theorists argued that their theory yielded little in the way of positive predictions, and, as Mayr says "it is even doubtful how to define 'prediction' in biology."[26] It is at best a statistical calculation of the likelihood of the occurrence of a given event, and at worst an educated guess based upon past observation.[27] In either case it provides no universal "laws," and even the term "law" has fallen out of use in biology (as it may yet in physics). For all of these limitations, biology still claims to provide us with "knowledge" that is as verifiable as any other sort.

Physicists have largely followed suit of late, having discovered that "law" is an uncalled for anthropomorphism. This happened, however, only after a century of fairly staunch resistance.[28] As Mayr puts it:

Natural selection with its emphasis on the chance nature of variation was not palatable to the physicists. This is why Sir John Herschel referred to it as the law of "higgledy-piggledy." Modern physics has theoretically abandoned such determinism, and yet, physicists are still far more deterministic in their thinking than biologists.[29]

As late as Einstein's famous debate with Bohr, the role of chance in the universe was hotly contested among physicists. To this day it is still shocking to many to hear a quantum physicist such as Feynman pronounce that science is not in the business of giving unassailable mathematical descriptions of the natural universe, but merely of calculating the probability of certain interesting events—with varying degrees of error.[30]

It is not my aim here to recapitulate Dewey's penetrating analysis of the human quest for certainty with its corresponding criticisms,[31] but it should be recognized that physics has only "caught up" with biology recently (if indeed it really *has* caught up), by seeing that the science we have habitually taken to be the exemplar of knowledge itself is in fact something rather shaky, by our pre-Darwinian epistemological standards—which are the dominant ones currently in use in the philosophy of science. Continued efforts by philosophers to couch induction within a larger deductive framework have met with only mixed success in philosophical circles, and have been almost universally ignored by working scientists.[32] As Dewey and Mead knew perfectly well, it simply does not matter to many or most scientists whether mathematics is the language of God or not, or whether a sufficiently general metalogic can provide a complete (or relatively complete) framework for the various accepted methods of calculating probabilities. One does not need Gödel's proof to reach this conclusion. What I am claiming, in short, is that evolutionary thinking is responsible for the rejection of methodological reductionism in middle pragmatism. Probability as the standard of knowing is an inextricable part of evolutionary thinking, and the deductive mode of thinking becomes only a phase of inquiry. A *reductio* settles nothing in science or inquiry.

Whether one is a classical logician, an intuitionist, a modal logician, or a quantified modal logician, logic is still deductive in mainstream philosophy, and in later pragmatism insofar as it has adapted itself to mainstream philosophy. This is the marital infidelity of later pragmatism I promised earlier to expose, and it provides suitable grounds for a divorce—and for disinheriting neo-pragmatism in the process. C. I. Lewis and Quine are the important transitional figures, since the former worked for a reconciliation of pragmatic logic and deductive logic while the latter gave up on this project, opting instead to concentrate on the logical presuppositions and deductive consequences of particular ontologies. For both of these later pragmatists, along with other post-Deweyan logicians and philosophers of science, a finite number of rules are employed in order to gain a strictly formal understanding of what we mean when we make a claim or series of claims that involve subjects and predicates, and their relations. Aside from Dewey's now neglected logic, our most influential accounts of logic in this century are not probabilistic, although many philosophers still believe, in an amazing act of self-deceptive anachronism, that deduction provides the cognitive ground of all probabilistic thinking.

Whether or not they are right is, at this point, a moot question. Scientists have assumed that *whatever* answer we philosophers may arrive at, it will not be sufficiently important for them to forestall their present investigations until such time as we give them the go-ahead on the probability question. While we spend our time investigating mathematical induction and transfinite set theory, they find us most uninteresting conversation partners, and continue to make discoveries and write the most widely read books in popular philosophy.

This may not be a good thing, since the philosophical interpretation of science seems always to end in moralizing. I am uncertain about whether it is good for Carl Sagan's or Stephen Hawking's social and moral philosophy to be more widely read than books written by people who at least know a little about the history and development of morality and cultural history—beyond who happened in any generation to hold Isaac Newton's chair at Cambridge, evidently the seat of all human wisdom in Hawking's view. Hawking, in fact, ended his popular book *A Brief History of Time* with the following statement:

However, if we do discover a complete theory, it should in time be understandable in broad principle by everyone, not just a few scientists. Then we shall all, philosophers, scientists, and just ordinary people, be able to take part in the discussion of the question of why it is that we and the universe exist. If we find the answer to that, it would be the ultimate triumph of human reason—for then we would know the mind of God.[33]

This sounds catchy enough, but as philosophy it is indistinguishable from the soupiest drivel the Enlightenment could have hoped to produce. Yet, unquestionably, more people have read that paragraph than any written by a professional philosopher since Dewey died. Do you, the reader, suppose that they believe Hawking? Do they take these for the most profound ideas our culture has to offer?

A better question is "How did this happen?" Where was Quine? Was it not his responsibility to prevent this? He was busy in his Harvard study deducing (via many-a-*reductio*) consequences from the ontology presupposed by physics, naturalizing epistemology, and leaving all the questions of value to the specialists in ethics. Is that pragmatism? Quine claimed it was. For better or worse, and with or without the consent of philosophers of science and later pragmatism, probability—which does not recognize the finality or authority of the *reductio*— is rapidly becoming the prevailing standard of knowledge all around us.[34] The idea of raw probability as the standard of knowledge is unsettling to many epistemologists.

What would a probabilistic epistemology look like? Is it merely the acknowledgement of chance and variation as "real" phenomena that disturbs epistemologists? I believe that there is much more involved than simply acknowledging the reality of chance in the universe.[35] This leads to the second major point I wish to discuss.

The Historicity of Evolution

For many years the philosophy of science (to which later pragmatism attached itself—in part by the agency of Ernest Nagel) has enjoyed a relatively unchallenged authority in determining the status, definition, and resolution of epistemological claims. The philosophy of culture and philosophy of history, when they were admitted to be more than mere nonsense, were relegated to the region of imagination, speculation, supposition, or at best pseudo-scientific fuzziness. The evolutionary hypothesis, however, threatens this order. As Theodosius Dobzhansky succinctly puts it:

Darwin ushered in a new understanding of man and his place in the universe. After him, the fateful idea that all things change, that they evolve, has become one of the cornerstones on which the thinking of civilized man is based. The universe, inanimate as well as animate matter . . . all have had a history and all are in the process of change at present.[36]

A few pages later Dobzhansky adds: "Under the new dispensation not even atoms are eternal and unchanging; they, too, have histories, and their histories and those of near and distant universes are chapters of the same grand cosmic process."[37] Evolution *temporalizes everything*, and the proud philosophic tradition from Parmenides and Plato, through Descartes and right down to our day, which favors the predominance of the essences as identified by their *logoi* (that is, by *logic*) was at best a useful illusion, and at worst an error on the grandest possible scale. The arrogance about the extent and depth of human knowledge that is presupposed in essentialist philosophies defies imagination. It is time for us to get over our childish arrogance, or primitive superstition, about the power of language.[38] The evolutionary approach recognizes that we can never show beyond all questioning that there is an essence of a thing which endures. This renders our ways of speaking, our *logic*, a provisional matter.[39]

In its place is put a Heraclitean worldview. Yet, as Heraclitus was no despiser of logic, neither were Dewey and Mead. Logic, if it is to yield anything like knowledge, must make sense of change not by dictating the universal laws according to which change must occur, but by attempting to provisionally describe whatever seems intelligible in it. Knowledge, then, is not the knowledge of a thing's definition, nor of what can be said of it truly as invariant, but rather of where it came from and where it might be going, if indeed its past exhibits *any* intelligible patterns that can, with warrant, be generalized into its future. What can be truly predicated of any given thing then becomes a derivative matter. The prior question is "When in the natural history of this thing do you wish to make this predication?" That question makes all the difference to any further determination of the truth or falsity of the predication itself, and logic and knowledge are temporalized, rendering them merely probable.

When Dobzhansky, the biologist, goes searching for the origin of evolutionary theory itself, he finds that Giambattista Vico, the eighteenth-century Italian philosopher, seems to be the source of the idea. This is a peculiarity worth exploring. It is quite commonplace to point out that evolution was an idea that was really "in the air" by the beginning of the nineteenth century, and that Darwin simply gave it the formulation that permitted its further development (no mean achievement).[40] But Vico, Dobzhansky thinks, is the source of the idea.[41] Who is Vico? Cassirer identifies Vico as the originator of the philosophy of history. Through J. G. Herder, Vico influenced the entire hoard of early nineteenth-century German thinkers who held that history is a rational and intelligible process.[42] Indeed, Dobzhansky traces this thread from Vico through Nietzsche down to Spengler and Toynbee. While none of these thinkers is an evolutionist in any ordinary sense, they do have in common that they believed knowledge is a cultural phenomenon, and that science is a certain manifestation of one part of culture (and not so laudable a manifestation at that).[43] Yet, evolutionary naturalists like Mead and Dewey, along with others like Cassirer, are good examples of thinkers who also held to the epistemological priority of cultural and historical knowledge, but who regarded science as its most rigorous and highly refined form.[44] So it is not accurate to conclude that all philosophers of culture and history—among which the middle pragmatists are surely to be counted—dislike or mistrust natural science. Nevertheless, the general position treats science and its form of knowing as only one among many forms of knowing, and the overarching business of philosophy is to understand culture and history so that the forms of knowing that science attains may be situated within it. This is nothing more than to say that middle pragmatism stresses its cultural naturalism over its mechanistic naturalism, but maintains the creative tension.

Can the same be said of later pragmatism? Certainly C. I. Lewis was interested in these sorts of questions. But there is a fundamental departure from this in Lewis's approach to facts and values. Lewis says:

A fact is something which is the case. Its being the case is independent of anybody's mention of it and independent of anybody's apprehension of it. . . . Both objects and events have space-time boundaries. But facts have no date or locus: once a fact, always a fact; and what is anywhere a fact is always a fact. More precisely, the ascription of time or place to a fact is bad grammar, though times and places may be constituents of facts.[45]

It is quite clear that this is at odds with the statements of Mead quoted earlier, and with those of Dewey that are to come. Lewis's definition of fact is distinctly and explicitly ahistorical. His recessive gene for bright red hair is beginning to manifest itself. This is another way of saying that "facts" for Lewis are not evolutionary.

What does it mean to claim that evolution, as a first organizing principle of all knowledge (i.e., *not* just as a theory of biological development, but also of cosmic development), relegates the traditional philosophy of science to a position subordinate to the philosophy of culture and history? The point is familiar enough, even if I have approached it from an unusual direction. The position sounds like, and probably is, a kind of historicism. This is not, however, an embracing of Rorty's worldview.[46] If Rorty's specter now looms large before the reader, we should at least recognize that his position is attained not by embracing evolution so much as by throwing up his hands in disappointment at the inability of traditional philosophy of science to provide anything that looks like the knowledge it purports to have.[47] As I suggested earlier, this might not have happened if Rorty had not first accepted methodological reductionism. I do not think that holding to probability as the measure, time as the base phenomenon, and history as the ground of intelligibility need necessarily entail Rorty's brand of historicism. I do not think Dewey and Mead are in fact historicists of that sort. Historicism of Rorty's type tends to reduce the nature/

culture tension to culture, eliminating large parts of nature in the process. Rorty's early history with eliminative materialism should not be forgotten. Why? Why can the creative tension not be retained? Answer: Rorty's belief in the power of the *reductio*; methodological reductionism; his bright red hair, styled in an antirealist, spiked Mohawk.

Dewey's and Mead's fallibilism (which serves as a check on methodological reductionism) allowed them to retain the creative tension between cultural naturalism and mechanistic naturalism, while avoiding the reductionism of neopragmatic historicism. Evolutionary naturalism does not entail that all knowledge is culturally relative, but merely that any particular knowledge claim is to some degree contingent upon the tools (*viz.*, "concepts") with which we are obliged to interpret the natural history of the thing we claim to know. This does, however, imply that the philosophy of history—guided by the supposition that evolution (in the broadest cosmic sense) grants the human mind access to whatever is intelligible in the development of the universe—the philosophy of history is epistemologically prior to anything one can say in the philosophy of science. This is nothing more than thoroughgoing evolutionism, since evolutionism is a philosophy of natural and human history.

On this account, then, philosophers of science can no longer afford to remain ignorant of history, for in doing so, they implicitly deny evolution. Middle pragmatism was historically informed. In practical terms, this means, as Putnam remarks, that one can no longer spend one's graduate education in philosophy simply learning by reputation which books one does *not* have to read, as has been commonly practiced in the profession. Pragmatists who allow themselves to forget the mistakes of the past are doomed to repeat them. The milkman only looks attractive to a dissatisfied wife. Her dissatisfaction may, however, be the result of her unrealistic expectations from marriage rather than some inadequacy in her husband. Middle pragmatism was a good, honest, and hard-working husband. He has grounds for divorce from later pragmatism, and she has learned the hard way that the red-headed milkman was making promises he could never keep.[48]

It should now be clearer why evolution has been so egregiously ignored in the analytic philosophy of science (the milkman), and why it disappeared from neopragmatism. One might say that the latter lacked the proper genetic endowment (puns intended). The question of whether one can remain a respectable philosopher of science, refusing to give in to utter relativism or some extreme form of historicism, while still taking evolution to be a first principle (whatever *that* means) is not a question I can resolve here. Still, it does point in the direction of the third and final area I wish to discuss: the question of value.

Facts and Values

By 1938, Dewey saw quite clearly what happens when one temporalizes logical operations. Formulas like *modus ponens* move from being abstract certainties to being concrete strategies for resolving problematic situations, strategies that have proven reliable or "warrantedly assertible," as Dewey puts it, in past inquiry.[49] There is no such thing in middle pragmatism as the pragmatic *a priori*.[50] There is no *a priori* at all.

It must be said in fairness to Lewis (the father of the "pragmatic *a priori*") that he never claimed the pragmatic *a priori* is ahistorical. In fact, he says the reverse.[51] However, two things should be said on this point that demonstrate the extent to which Lewis is unfaithful to middle pragmatism. Lewis was not in line with the historicity presupposed in the evolutionary approach, and he was not in line with the position it takes on facts and values. Let me briefly explain each of these.

First, Lewis did not consistently maintain the context in which the historicity of the evolutionary approach had to be interpreted. In 1929 he was, with White-head, willing to speak of "the Great Fact in the presence of which all explicit thought is silenced," and this does seem consistent with the historicity presupposed in cosmic evolution, *viz.*, God's or the Universe's development, even if it is not recognizably pragmatic.[52] But Lewis came to be much less taken with "cosmic history" as he matured. Still, this cosmic philosophy of history from his early work is the feature of his philosophy that supplied him with the context for claiming that the pragmatic *a priori* was itself historical. Without a cosmic philosophy of history, he would have to resituate the ground for the pragmatic *a priori*, and he did so in a very atemporal (i.e., nonevolutionary) fashion.

Asher Moore (in somewhat different words) pointed out this tension in Lewis's account of the *a priori*.[53] In his response to Moore, Lewis explicitly admitted that if the analytic/synthetic distinction should ever fall, so would his entire philosophy, including the *a priori/a posteriori* distinction[54] (which is his key point of departure from evolutionary naturalism and its historicity in my view). Lewis pointed out also that the erosion of the analytic/synthetic distinction would leave us with no way to distinguish physics from mathematics from psychology, noting that "this process of attrition has now begun; though perhaps the consequences, for logic and for the theory of knowledge, have not yet been squarely faced."[55] This is evidently an allusion to Quine's work on the subject. Lewis was a remarkably self-honest thinker. He is admitting defeat.

What is amazing is that Lewis seemed unaware of the fact that Dewey had already begun to face the consequences of precisely this "erosion" and "attrition" in his first attempt at a "genetic" (meaning evolutionary and naturalized) logic in 1903. By 1938 Dewey was dealing squarely with these difficulties with much greater success than in 1903. How could Lewis be oblivious to this? It is difficult for me to imagine, and yet equally difficult to deny. Lewis would not be the first to fail to grasp what Dewey was trying to do with logic and why he was trying to do it.

At least in the sense that psychology, physics, and mathematics are all involved in the process of inquiry, Dewey believes they do indeed have something quite important in common (although that does not mean we cannot distinguish them). He asserts that inquiry always takes place within a highly complex existential and cultural matrix in which unanticipated or unrecognized contingencies are an ineliminable factor, and that logic or any other tool of inquiry is only "knowledge" in proportion to its capacity to solve such concrete problems.[56] Thus, we recognize that Dewey's method and his logic are "genetic," giving primacy to growth, development, change, contingency, and chance, and that the answers we achieve through inquiry must be situated within a cultural context in order to have any meaning. Logic is therefore fully historical. This points us toward the second important point of departure between Lewis and middle pragmatism.

One of the results of Dewey's stance is that the notion of a "fact" that is supposed to be perfectly value-neutral is rejected in favor of the position that all facts *are* facts only insofar as they reflect the values presupposed by inquiry itself.[57] Inquiry is not a value-neutral affair, but can only be understood as the activity of a being *with* values, some objectively set (like conditions for survival), some less tangible (like pleasure). That the universe admits of interpretations that are efficacious to the beings who interpret it is not a matter about which we can inquire without presupposing it. Foundational epistemological skepticism is what Peirce said it was, an elaborate self-deception. This assumption of the intelligibility of the universe is one we cannot get away from, for we cannot bring ourselves to genuinely doubt it, just as Peirce argued.[58]

What this means is that values have been guiding our articulations of the "facts" at every stage (or better yet, value simply *is* the guiding of fact).[59] It is true that Lewis has a naturalized account of value. But for him, value is an aspect of either possible or actual *mind-independent* facts. I ask the reader to look once again at the quote from Lewis on facts and values above. For Dewey, there is no such thing as a mind-independent fact, and Lewis is the one guilty of "bad grammar." For genuine pragmatism, "mind" is not some phenomenon that stands outside culture, inquiry, and so on, but rather it is a description of a very basic feature of experience that we come to notice when we criticize the process of inquiry itself. Something wants to know, something experiences; we may call it mind if we wish in order to single out some features of it. Still, *calling* it "mind" does not magically call into existence some isolated, preexistent Being which *is* "MIND." Although this is not Dewey's view, an evolutionary pragmatist might even admit that, perhaps, an independent entity exists. Who knows? The supposition (fruitless though it may be relative to inquiry) cannot be ruled out *a priori*. But we certainly have no access to that entity *as such*, and our characterizations of it can be no more than provisional and historically situated in any case. James already threw the best light on it that a genuine pragmatist can manage, and he was far too lenient toward this view to suit many pragmatists.

There is a huge difference between the view of Mind or God thus described and that of Lewis. I submit that Dewey's view is evolutionary and Lewis's is not in this respect. We have, in fact, now found the precise place where evolutionary naturalism declined, and the central point of departure between middle and later pragmatism.

For middle pragmatism, the idea that value is the basis of all fact is not merely a convenient assumption, but a metaphysical first principle (insofar as there are such things, they are better known under Dewey's epithet, "generic traits of existence"). This is because metaphysics is a descriptive, cultural, and historical activity, along with science, according to middle pragmatism. The cosmic theory of evolution is one articulation of this assumption, since "evolution" is itself hardly a value-neutral conception. This is to say that there is more to the notion of evolution, both biological and cosmic, than just ceaseless change.[60] By merely affirming the priority of change one does not thereby get an account of the *order* of the universe. One must also offer some *interpretation* of the order that can be discerned in change. Both are necessary components of any truly evolutionary philosophy. One is required to say that the sorts of changes that human beings *notice* in their surroundings are also the ones that appear to be intelligible to them, and that the general pattern of all change, insofar as human beings can make it intelligible to themselves, is what is meant by "evolution." Evolution is thus a highly general concept for organizing not just individual experience and observation, and not merely human history, but the growth of the entire universe insofar as it is intelligible to human beings.

As with the question of God, Mind, and such, the question of whether the universe is intelligible in itself, aside from our activity of symbolizing it for our finite minds (and contrary to Lewis's claims), is not a question that inquiry or philosophy can address *scientifically.* Philosophers must remain vigilant about this point. Of course we cannot help supposing that there is some analogy between our symbolizations of the universe and the universe as it is—we can speculate about this, but little else (and Dewey certainly does speculate about it).[61] Anything stronger rests on problematic metaphysical assumptions about what symbolization can really accomplish—and authentic pragmatism is not searching for the Omni-word. If that is what truly underlies the more recent forms of realism, and I say it does, then genuine pragmatism does not partake in that kind of realism. That search is not pragmatic in any way, and still less pragmatic are all the weird mutations of Plato that lie beneath the varieties of foundationalism and essentialism that constitute the arid philosophical landscape of the late twentieth century.

The recognition of fallibilism in method places human values at the ground of facts and anthropomorphizes the universe—by transforming the universe as we know it into the symbols through which the human mind comprehends all that is intelligible in the cosmos. "Evolution," then, is a tiny human map of the cosmos which, when one takes it out exploring, makes it possible to classify and organize nearly every possible phenomenon humans have run across. The problem is that this concept promises very little in terms of prediction about the future, and relinquishes the classical conception of knowledge in favor of probability. Knowledge is not of "what is"; it is of what may be.

Thus, if evolution is to be given its due, epistemology must take account of its cultural and historical surroundings, and admit the ascendancy of the metaphysics of history, including both natural *and* human history. Both are necessary conditions of value, while value is a necessary condition of all facts, and facts are the building blocks of knowledge.

This brings me to my conclusion. Much philosophical resistance comes from the fact that the evolutionary approach to the philosophy of science anthropomorphizes, or rather, *humanizes* science. This is something later pragmatism and professional philosophers of science have striven to avoid—an illicit avoidance that Kuhn called their hand on many years ago. The humanization of science, they believe, threatens to politicize knowledge, relativize epistemology, and open the door to wholesale metaphysical speculation upon anything and everything. I do not think this is a very realistic fear. One could hardly call Dewey and Mead irresponsible in their speculations, and they knew all of the dangers perfectly well. However, the humanization of the *philosophy* of science does render it contingent and fallible, and forces us to say that scientific knowing may or may not be good for us, but in either case it is *not* primary. Mainstream philosophy of science evidently wishes to maintain the comfortable facade that it is *not* in the business of simply *symbolizing* the universe so as to make its vastness intelligible to the finite understanding. Rather, philosophers have wished to claim that they have (or nearly have, or can get) the tools with which to say how the universe is, in itself, independent of the processes of human knowing. This is what Lewis did in his definition of fact, and what Dewey and Mead explicitly avoided doing in their interpretations of scientific method. Bald metaphysical and/or epistemological realism is a very strange thing to assert, and one rarely hears it anymore. But as a methodological presupposition it is still very prevalent in our time in the various strains of realism that are so popular. One need only find someone who thinks a *reductio* settles things to locate the phenomenon of which I speak. Such people are by far the bulk of philosophers today.

Early in this century, physics seemed to offer a model (which it has now greatly modified) whereby philosophy could ignore its humanity for a while longer—but only by learning to ignore Dewey and Mead. Consequently, what *had* been a singularly progressive reception in American intellectual circles to the idea of evolution died out with Dewey. The philosophy of science lost its nerve and turned its efforts back to the older essentialist forms of logic and methodology, and the hard-won progress in genetic logic has been subsequently forgotten. With it, evolutionary thinking and evolutionary naturalism died also.

It was inevitable that philosophers educated in such an antiquated way of thinking as essentialism should have also lost their ability to communicate with the educated public. Neither is it surprising that the scientists themselves should have stepped in to fill the void created by the new scholasticism of this recent strain of professional philosophy, which is only now loosening its death-grip on the American intellectual community. So the educated public thinks Hawking is a philosopher, and that science is perfectly objective and has a corner on truth. It looks to Carl Sagan for moral guidance. Philosophy lost its nerve and vision in the 1950s and either through cowardice or ignorance has failed to regain it. We cannot face the public for we have nothing of value to tell them (many having claimed that value is not the proper subject matter of knowledge). It is high time philosophy caught up to science, and again played its mediating role between the findings of hard science and their moral meaning in our world. This must begin with: (1) abandoning deductive/essentialist systems of reasoning for inductive/probabilistic ones; (2) acknowledging the priority of the philosophy of history and culture to the philosophy of science; and (3) embracing the metaphysical priority of value to the meaningfulness of any and every fact.

I advocate that we begin by returning the concept of evolution to and restoring the influence of Darwin on philosophy. Dewey's logic must be taken up and improved upon, advanced by means of incorporating developments in statistics, and humanized still further so that the relation between moral and statistical value cannot be ignored. Professional philosophy and especially pragmatism must become morally aware and politically responsive, socially critical and publicly accessible. The alternative is further wasted effort and still more wasted lives learning lessons that have already been learned and forgotten.[62]

NOTES

1. Henry David Thoreau, *Faith in a Seed and Other Natural History Writings*, ed. Bradley P. Dean (Washington, D.C.: Island Press, 1993), 102. Thoreau is speaking about Darwin specifically in this context.

2. I would prefer to call this period "mature pragmatism," and I believe this is indeed the proper way of understanding the period dominated by Dewey and Mead. I have chosen the ineloquent term "middle pragmatism" because "mature pragmatism" clearly betrays evaluative judgments that are best asserted openly rather than packed into the labels one chooses. Of course, I could also use the standard term, the "Chicago School," for this same group, but I prefer to keep its relation to the other periods more present to mind with the reader than the standard phrase allows.

3. For more detail on this transition in pragmatism please consult the chapters in this volume by Daniel J. Wilson and Isaac Nevo.

4. My interpretation of neopragmatism is largely inspired and guided by my deep agreement with David Depew and his recent work. While I am incorporating many of his insights into my interpretation, I do not cite him in every single case. It should be made clear, however, that the polemics are my own responsibility, and I shall leave Professor Depew to get himself in trouble, or to avoid it, in any way he sees fit.

5. I speak metaphorically here, not of R. Milkman, the editor of *Perspectives on Evolution* (Sunderland, Mass.: Sinauer Assoc., 1982).

6. Richard Rorty, *Philosophy and the Mirror of Nature* (Princeton, N.J.: Princeton University Press, 1979).

7. It seems that everyone has written an article refuting some aspect of Rorty's interpretation of pragmatism. I recommend James S. Gouinlock, "What Is the Legacy of Instrumentalism? Rorty's Interpretation of Dewey," *Journal of the History of Philosophy* 28, no. 2 (April 1990).

8. For more on this, please consult James Campbell's chapter in this volume.

9. John Dewey, "Foreword," in Philip P. Wiener, *Evolution and the Founders of Pragmatism* (Cambridge, Mass.: Harvard University Press, 1949), xiv (emphasis mine).

10. One of the clearest and best attempts at keeping the two tendencies balanced is George Herbert Mead's essay "Scientific Method and the Moral Sciences," in *Selected Writings*, ed. Andrew J. Reck (New York: Bobbs-Merrill, 1964), 248–66.

11. G. H. Mead, "Scientific Method and the Individual Thinker," in Mead, *Selected Writings*, 173.

12. Mead, "Scientific Method and Moral Sciences," 265.

13. Ibid., 266.

14. Mead, "Scientific Method and Individual Thinker," 193.

15. In this chapter, I will speak in the same breath of both "inquiry" and "appreciation of the consummatory aesthetic experiences for which humans strive" as if these two are on equal footing in middle pragmatism. The reason is that an interesting ongoing debate in the Dewey literature leaves in doubt the question of whether inquiry itself is the bottom line on human interest and value (as Larry Hickman persuasively argues), or consummatory aesthetic experience, rare though it is, is at the center of what drives the human animal (as Thomas Alexander has persuasively argued). See Larry Hickman, *John Dewey's Pragmatic Technology* (Bloomington: Indiana University Press, 1990); and Thomas Alexander, *John Dewey's Theory of Art, Experience, and Nature: The Horizons of Feeling* (Albany: SUNY Press, 1987). It may well be that this is a matter of emphasis more than a fundamental difference, but that question is beyond my present scope.

16. For a good popular discussion of the particular problem of history and the sciences, and the more general problem of the humanistic versus the scientific approaches to various disciplines, see Stanley L. Jaki, "History as Science and Science in History," *The Intercollegiate Review* 29, no. 1 (Fall 1993): 20–27.

17. Good discussions of this tendency with particular application to evolutionary theory can be found in Marjorie Grene, *Science, Ideology, and World View* (Berkeley: University of California Press, 1981), and also in a book by Richard Levins and Richard Lewontin, *The Dialectical Biologist* (Cambridge, Mass.: Harvard University Press, 1985).

18. The best book on this is Philip Wiener's *Evolution and the Founders of Pragmatism*, cited above. It contains chapters on Peirce, James, Fiske, Chauncey Wright, Nicholas St. John Green, and Oliver Wendell Holmes Jr., as well as discussion of numerous others.

19. Theodosius Dobzhansky, the noted evolutionary biologist and father of modern genetics, has nicely summarized the current state of the evolutionary "hypothesis" as follows:

> In Lamarck's and Darwin's times evolution was a hypothesis; in our day it is proven. Another proven hypothesis is that the earth executes a complete revolution on its axis once every twenty-four hours. When a hypothesis has been thoroughly verified, we may take it as a safe guide in our thinking and working activities. . . . The business of proving evolution has reached a stage when it is futile for biologists to work merely to discover more and more evidence for evolution. Those who believe that God created every biological species separately in the state we observe them but made them in a way calculated to lead us to the conclusion that they are products of an evolutionary development are obviously not open to argument. All that can be said is that their belief is an implicit blasphemy, for it imputes to God an appalling deviousness.

Theodosius Dobzhansky, *Mankind Evolving* (New Haven, Conn.: Yale University Press, 1962), 6. In the passage, Dobzhansky makes it clear that a confirmed hypothesis is merely a guide for future inquiry—a view that closely echoes Dewey's notion of warranted assertibility. Similarly, in calling evolution a "fact," I do not mean to give the impression that it is beyond all questioning or is perfectly value-neutral. Please consult the final section of this chapter for what is meant by "fact." Ernst Mayr, perhaps the foremost living evolutionary biologist, echoes Dobzhansky, saying that "the basic theory of evolution has been confirmed so completely that modern biologists consider evolution simply a fact." Ernst Mayr, *Towards a New Philosophy of Biology* (Cambridge, Mass.: Harvard University Press, 1988), 192. Dobzhansky himself repeats these claims with a bit more detail in his *The Biological Basis of Human Freedom* (New York: Columbia University Press, 1956), 6 *ff*.

20. Mayr, *New Philosophy*, v, see also 9–11, 188–89, 258. Mayr points out that "in short, theories of biology violated every canon of 'true science,' as philosophers had derived them from the methods and principles of classical physics. Even after the conceptual framework of physics changed quite fundamentally during the nineteenth and twentieth centuries, a mechanistic approach continued to dominate the philosophy of science. As a result, biology was referred to as a 'dirty science,' an activity . . . not much better than 'postage stamp collecting' " (p. 9). Later Mayr says that "with a few exceptions . . . philosophers have been essentialists and physicalists. In spite of sincere efforts by some of them, they have been quite unable to adopt population thinking, the concept of historical narratives, . . . the absence or at least irrelevance of laws (as defined by the physicists) in evolutionary biology, the invalidity of much of reductionism . . . and various other basic concepts of evolutionary biology. The anti-Darwinian arguments of certain philosophers (including some contemporary ones) are to such a degree beside the point that, to a competent evolutionist, it is almost embarrassing to read them" (pp. 188–89). It is difficult to be certain exactly who Mayr has in mind here, but he is particularly critical of Philip Kitcher in the book (see pp. 317, 338–39), and one would expect eliminative materialists, other physicalists, and most reductionists to fall under the shadow of suspicion. See also Mayr's "How Biology Differs from the Physical Sciences," in *Evolution at a Crossroads*, ed. David Depew and Bruce Weber (Cambridge, Mass.: MIT Press, 1985), 43–63.

21. I do not wish to make my claims any more broadly than the facts warrant. There are a number of philosophers who have emerged since the late 1960s who do in fact take evolution as the starting place for their philosophies of science, although none are really pragmatists, and all have reductive tendencies. The major books include: David Hull, *Philosophy of Biological Science* (Engelwood Cliffs, N.J.: Prentice-Hall, 1974), *The Metaphysics of Evolution* (Albany: SUNY Press, 1989), and *Science as a Process: An Evolutionary Account of the Social and Conceptual Development of Science* (Chicago: University of Chicago Press, 1988); Elliot Sober, *The Nature of Selection: Evolutionary Theory in Philosophical Focus* (Cambridge, Mass.: MIT Press, 1984); Michael Ruse, *The Philosophy of Biology* (London: Hutchinson, 1973). Landmark articles include: Mary B. Williams, "The Logical Status of the Theory of Natural Selection and Other Evolutionary Controversies," in *The Methodological Unity of Science*, ed. M. Bunge (Dordrecht: Reidel, 1973); R. N. Brandon, "Adaptation Explanations," in Depew and Weber, eds., *Evolution at a Crossroads*, cited above, and "Adaptation and Evolutionary Theory," *Studies in the History and Philosophy of Science* 9 (1978): 181–206; J. Beatty, "The Synthesis and the Synthetic Theory," in *Integrating Scientific Disciplines*, ed. W. Bechtel (The Hague: Martinus Nijhoff, 1986); William Wimsatt, "Teleology and the Logical Status of Function Statements," *Studies in the History and Philosophy of Science* 3 (1972): 1–80.

22. In most cases these are errors of begging an important epistemological or metaphysical question. For instance, Richard Dawkins does this in the book he takes to be the best philosophical statement of his view, *The Extended Phenotype* (Oxford: Oxford University Press, 1982). Here he first announces his intention to present not a scientific account of life evolving, but to "advocate" a total, philosophical viewpoint about how it is best interpreted:

> This is a work of unabashed advocacy. . . . What I am advocating is not a new theory, not a hypothesis which can be verified or falsified, not a model which can be judged by its predictions. . . . What I am advocating is a point of view, a way of looking at familiar facts and ideas, and a way of asking new questions about them. (p. 1)

Thus, it is "philosophy" (in one common way of looking at that word), and not science. Yet, only a few pages later he openly acknowledges that he takes the correctness of Darwinism for *granted* in his account:

> With the exception of a few genuine opponents of Darwinism, who are unlikely to be reading this, we are all in this together, all Darwinians who substantially agree

on how we interpret what is, after all, the only workable theory we have to explain the organized complexity of life. (p. 35)

Darwinism is ordinarily taken to be a theory of life rather than a total philosophy, but if Dawkins means to base his philosophy on an interpretation of it (and he does), then considerable work would still need to be done toward defending his view from those "genuine opponents." Yet, he refuses to address the idealistic, vitalistic, religious, and naturalistic accounts of the same phenomena, which are the only other competing total interpretations of the process. He also advocates materialism without defending the view. It may be fine for a working scientist to assume Darwinism or materialism for the purposes of his or her work, and to present data and results on the basis of that assumption. But it is not all right for someone who wishes to "advocate" a total philosophical interpretation of something to ignore the viable alternatives. This begs all of the hardest questions and leads Dawkins on an odyssey of anecdotes and hasty generalizations that are insufficient as science and question-begging as philosophy.

I do not mean to single out Dawkins for ridicule, but I use him as an example because he *announces* his intention to be overtly unscientific. Still, these sorts of features are to be found to greater or lesser degrees among even great twentieth-century philosopher-scientists, such as Einstein and Heisenberg.

23. Carl Sagan, "How Can Games Test Ethics? A New Way to Think about Rules to Live By," *Parade* (November 28, 1993): 12–14. I thank Torrey Curtis for bringing the article to my attention.

24. As Mayr says, "Darwin's emphasis on variations, populations, chance, and pluralism started a new era in the philosophy of nature, an insight that can no longer be ignored even though there are still some philosophers who only read each other's writings or the literature of the physical sciences" (Mayr, *New Philosophy*, 258).

25. For an excellent exchange on the question of whether Darwinian evolutionary theory is compatible with reductionism (especially methodological reductionism), see David J. Depew and Bruce Weber, "Introduction," and "Innovation and Tradition in Evolutionary Theory," Marjorie Grene, "Perception, Interpretation, and the Sciences," Ernst Mayr, "How Biology Differs from the Physical Sciences," and Francisco Ayala, "Reduction in Biology: A Recent Challenge," all found in Depew and Weber, eds., *Evolution at a Crossroads*, cited above. For more extended discussions of probability which are basically compatible with my analysis, see Theodore M. Porter, *The Rise of Statistical Thinking: 1820–1900* (Princeton, N.J.: Princeton University Press, 1986); Ian Hacking, *The Taming of Chance* (Cambridge: Cambridge University Press, 1990); L. Krüger, L. Daston, and M. Heidelberger, eds., *The Probabilistic Revolution*, 2 vols. (Cambridge, Mass.: MIT Press, 1987), and G. Gigerenzer, *How Probability Changed Science and Everyday Life* (Cambridge: Cambridge University Press, 1989).

26. Mayr, *New Philosophy*, 32.

27. Peirce has an interesting comment on the predictive capacity of evolutionary theory that warrants mentioning:

Mr. Darwin proposed to apply the statistical method to biology. . . . Darwin, while unable to say what the operation of variation and natural selection in any individual case will be, demonstrates that in the long run they will adapt animals to their circumstances. Whether or not existing animal forms are due to such action, or what position the theory ought to take, forms the subject of a discussion in which questions of fact and questions of logic are curiously interlaced.

"The Fixation of Belief," in *The Writings of C. S. Peirce*, vol. 3, ed. Christian J. W. Kloesel (Bloomington: Indiana University Press, 1986), 244. In a sense, the aim of the present study is to show how these issues have unfortunately become "unlaced" since Peirce's time, and then to lace them back up again, if possible.

28. See Ilya Prigogine and Isabelle Stengers, *Order Out of Chaos: Man's New Dialogue with Nature* (New York: Bantam Books, 1984), esp. 207–32.

29. Mayr, *New Philosophy*, 4.

30. See Richard Feynman, *QED: The Strange Theory of Light and Matter* (Princeton, N.J.: Princeton University Press, 1985) who, in the context of discussing the way in which quantum electrodynamics comes by its data says:

> Does this mean that physics, a science of great exactitude, has been reduced to calculating only the *probability* of an event, and not predicting exactly what will happen? Yes. That's a retreat, but that's the way it is: Nature permits us to calculate only probabilities. Yet science has not collapsed. (p. 19)

See also 77–78. This "retreat" into probability as the standard of prediction should not be confused with the "retreat" signaled by Heisenberg's uncertainty principle. For, as Feynman points out, one must be in some sense *expecting* certainty before an *un*certainty *principle* even makes sense. The uncertainty principle is completely irrelevant to the probabilistic procedures of present quantum physics, and a dinosaur of a concept from an old paradigm that just will not seem to die in popular and philosophic thinking (see 55–56).

31. See John Dewey, *The Quest for Certainty: A Study of the Relation of Knowledge and Action* (New York: Capricorn Books, 1960).

32. I do not wish to assume that "induction" is by any means a clear and univocal term. Different sciences and different philosophers understand its meaning and limits in rather different ways.

33. Stephen Hawking, *A Brief History of Time* (New York: Bantam, 1988), 175.

34. It is only fair to point out that the idea of treating probability as the source of our knowledge of nature is an idea at least as old as Aristotle. See the discussions of *epagoge* at 72b29, 105a10–19. Moving from the phenomena to our *talk* about them requires that we begin from "probable premises," as Aristotle states in Book I of the *Prior Analytics*. I thank Fred Marcus for bringing these passages to my attention. A number of later thinkers, including Vico (see discussion below), carried this view forward.

35. It may be worth noting at this juncture that Peirce made a valiant effort to incorporate the reality of chance into his fallibilist epistemology under the name "tychism." The strategy was to incorporate chance without giving up intelligibility (see *The Writings of Charles S. Peirce*, 3:308 ff.). Numerous Peirce advocates believe his efforts succeeded, but many of the controversies in Peirce scholarship also center around the adequacy of his epistemology and theory of truth/verification. Dewey may be said to have attempted the same thing regarding the reality of contingency and chance in his *Logic: The Theory of Inquiry* (New York: Henry Holt, 1938) and again in collaboration with Arthur F. Bentley in *Knowing and the Known* (Boston: Beacon Press, 1949).

36. Dobzhansky, *Mankind Evolving*, 1.

37. Ibid., 4.

38. Whitehead made an interesting analogy along these lines once:

> To know the truth partially is to distort the Universe. For example, the savage who can only count up to ten enormously exaggerates the importance of the small numbers, and so do we, whose imaginations fail when we come to millions.

Alfred North Whitehead, *Adventures of Ideas* (New York: Macmillan, 1933), p. 243. This should help to keep us mindful of our tendency to feel so self-assured in the extent of our knowledge.

39. It should be clear that when I use the term "evolution" in this way, I mean more than a biological theory of the descent of humankind via natural and sexual selection. Along with Dobzhansky, I employ its "cosmic" meaning, of which the biological theory is but a special instance. There is nothing unusual or original about employing the word in this way. Henri Bergson certainly used it this way in *Creative Evolution*, trans. Arthur Mitchell (New York: Henry Holt, 1913), and before him John Fiske also used it in this fashion in *Through Nature to God* (New York: Houghton, Mifflin, 1899). It could be argued that Herbert Spencer defined evolution "cosmically" still earlier, although his notion of the cosmos was somewhat more materialistic and reductive than Fiske's and Bergson's. Many thinkers since (including Whitehead) have subsequently used the term "evolution" in this way.

40. For a fuller account of how existing evolutionary ideas were brought together by Darwin, see Gertrude Himmelfarb, *Darwin and the Darwinian Revolution* (New York: W. W. Norton, 1962), 168–94. Himmelfarb notes similar connections with Anaximander and Empedocles as I have given below (in note 41).

41. Ibid., 2 *ff*. Dobzhansky does not think that the Greeks had the idea, and also argues that while the Christians had the idea of a historical development, it is not sufficiently close to evolution to claim that Christianity is the source of the idea. However, Anaximander had ideas so close to those of evolution that it is unfair to say the Greeks did not have the idea, as evidenced by the ancient reports in the following fragments:

> Anaximander said that the first living creatures were born in moisture. . . . Further he says that in the beginning man was born from creatures of a different kind; because other creatures are soon self-supporting, but man alone needs prolonged nursing. For this reason he would not have survived if this had been his original form. . . . Living creatures came into being from moisture evaporated by the sun. Man was originally similar to another creature—that is, to a fish. . . . Fishes and men came into being in the same parents . . . and having become adequate to look after themselves, they then came forth and took the land.

The Presocratic Philosophers, ed. and trans. G. S. Kirk and J. E. Raven (Cambridge: Cambridge University Press, 1962), 141, frags. 136–37, 139–40. I have included only those statements that sound most like our present theory. Still, this does not militate against Dobzhansky's conclusion that Vico is in a sense the source of the theory, because there is little indication that Anaximander's zoogony and anthropogony have exercised any extensive, direct influence on the development of Western thought, whereas Vico clearly has. I thank James Goetsch for pointing the Anaximander fragments out to me.

It is also worth noting that these same "evolutionary" ideas reappear in Lucretius' *De Rerum Natura*, book 5, parts 3–4 (lines 769–1008). Some of his remarks even seem to indicate the idea of natural selection (see esp. lines 828–31). Lucretius then traces this "evolutionary development" into the birth and rise of civilization itself. It is not clear whether Anaximander is to be credited as the source of this, but a fairly credible line can be drawn from Anaximander to Empedocles, and from there to Epicurus and on to Lucretius. The latter's thought was then influential through the Latin rhetorical tradition, particularly by way of Cicero, and this is very likely the venue whereby evolution came into Vico's thought (since Vico was Professor of Latin Eloquence at the University of Naples). For a full discussion of Vico's influences and development, see Donald Phillip Verene, *Vico's New Art of Autobiography* (Oxford: Clarendon Press, 1992). The best and most complete account of the ancient history of evolutionary theory of which I am aware is Henry Fairfield Osborn, *From the Greeks to Darwin: An Outline of the Development of the Evolution Idea* (New York: Macmillan, 1894), see esp. 64–68. However, Osborn misses the connection with Vico and the philosophy of history that Dobzhansky recognized.

42. See Cassirer, *Symbol, Myth and Culture*, ed. Donald Phillip Verene (New Haven, Conn.: Yale University Press, 1979), 102 *ff*., and *Problem of Knowledge*, trans. Hendel and Woglum (New Haven, Conn.: Yale University Press, 1950), 217 *ff*. Much has been written about Vico's influence on the Germans, most notably Isaiah Berlin's *Vico and Herder: Two Studies in the History of Ideas* (New York: Viking, 1976), and Benedetto Croce's *The Philosophy of Giambattista Vico*, trans. R. G. Collingwood (New York: Russell and Russell, 1964). Aside from Cassirer, Vico is widely recognized by many philosophers as the originator of the philosophy of history. For example, see Friedrich Ueberweg's *History of Philosophy*, trans. G. S. Morris (New York: Scribner, Armstrong, 1874), 2:473–79. Most of Vico's major works are available in English. See esp. *The New Science*, trans. Max Fisch and T. G. Bergin (Ithaca: Cornell University Press, 1968). Mayr acknowledges Herder's role in the development of evolutionary theory, but does not go further back to Vico's influence on Herder; see Mayr, *New Philosophy*, 260. Yet Mayr is also clearly aware of Vico's relevance in the general field, since he mentions Vico in this connection in his magnum opus *The Growth of Biological Thought* (Cambridge, Mass.: Harvard University Press, 1982), 40, 311.

43. Dobzhansky, *Mankind Evolving*, 3. See Oswald Spengler, *The Decline of the West*, trans. C. F. Atkinson (New York: Alfred A. Knopf, 1926), 1:328–29; Arnold Toynbee, *A Study of History* (London: Royal Institute of International Affairs, 1954), 7:488–90. Toynbee did not mistrust science nearly as much as Spengler and Nietzsche did. See Nietzsche's famous essays "Schopenhauer as Educator" and "The Uses and Disadvantages of History for Life," in *Untimely Meditations*, trans. R. J. Hollingdale (Cambridge: Cambridge University Press, 1984). Nietzsche, Spengler, and Toynbee are not evolutionists in any ordinary sense, just as Vico is not. What they all share is in fact a cyclical conception of history. But a necessary step along the way to evolutionary thinking involved unseating the Enlightenment claims to certainty (and the corresponding corner on the knowledge market that was held by science and the philosophy of it). These four thinkers all held that historical knowledge was a condition for and superior to any knowledge of (supposedly) unchanging natural laws. This opens the door for evolutionary naturalism, which makes natural history and human history a part of the same general development, and locates the efforts of science to tell the story of the cosmos *within* that framework. For a fuller discussion of Toynbee, Spengler, and Nietzsche in this vein, see A. W. Levi, *Philosophy and the Modern World* (Bloomington: Indiana University Press, 1959), 102 *ff*. For a fuller account of the relation between Vico, science, and the rise of evolutionary thinking, see Paolo Rossi, *The Dark Abyss of Time: The History of Earth and the History of Nations from Hooke to Vico*, trans. L. G. Cochrane (Chicago: University of Chicago Press, 1984), esp. 195–200.

44. See Ernst Cassirer, *Philosophy of Symbolic Forms: The Phenomenology of Knowledge*, vol. 3, trans. Ralph Manheim (New Haven, Conn.: Yale University Press, 1955), among other places.

45. Charles Irving Lewis, "Values and Facts," in *Values and Imperatives: Studies in Ethics*, ed. John Lange (Stanford: Stanford University Press, 1969), 86–87.

46. Rorty's view is perhaps best encapsulated in Richard Rorty, *Contingency, Irony and Solidarity* (Cambridge: Cambridge University Press, 1989).

47. See Richard Rorty, *Philosophy and the Mirror of Nature* (Princeton, N.J.: Princeton University Press, 1979), esp. 313 *ff*., and his "Introduction" and "The World Well Lost" in *Consequences of Pragmatism: Essays 1972–1980* (Minneapolis: University of Minnesota Press, 1982), xiii–xlvi, 3–18.

48. For those who find this analogy offensive on account of its stereotypical gender choices, please feel free to change the genders around until the gender group you dislike is offended, and the group you favor comes out with the moral high ground. Otherwise, take it for what it is—an analogy.

49. See John Dewey, *Logic*, 81–98; and "Propositions and Warranted Assertibility," in Dewey, *The Later Works*, ed. Jo Ann Boydston (Carbondale: Southern Illinois University Press, 1988), 14:178 *ff*.

50. See Charles Irving Lewis, *Mind and the World Order* (New York: Dover, 1929, 1956), 230 *ff*.

51. Lewis, *Mind and the World Order*, 233 *ff*.

52. Ibid., 237.

53. See Asher Moore, "Lewis's Theory of the *A Priori*," in *The Philosophy of C. I. Lewis*, ed. Paul A. Schilpp (LaSalle, Ill.: Open Court, 1968), 155–99.

54. See Schilpp, ed., *The Philosophy of C. I. Lewis*, 659.

55. Ibid.

56. See Dewey, *Logic*, 35, 42–59.

57. Ibid., 142, 172 *ff*.

58. See Peirce, "The Fixation of Belief," in *Writings of C. S. Peirce*, 3:248. This claim, if accepted, eliminates all pretensions Cartesians may have to sensibly posing questions that express fundamental epistemological skepticism. "It is much easier to lie than to doubt," as Putnam remarked in his Emory lecture. If it is objected that this renders all philosophy circular, I accept this conclusion, along with Peirce, Dewey, Whitehead, James, and a host of other thinkers who understand what is implied by the historicity of evolutionary philosophy. I refer the reader to my essay

on the subject, "Concentric Circles: An Exploration of Three Concepts in Process Metaphysics," *Southwest Philosophy Review* 7, no. 1 (January 1991): 151–72.

59. This formulation of Dewey's view was suggested to me by Thomas Alexander, and it strikes me as correct.

60. The best general source for understanding the philosophical implications of cosmic evolution from a scientifically defensible viewpoint is the anthology edited by Bruce Weber, David J. Depew, and James D. Smith, *Entropy, Information and Evolution* (Cambridge, Mass.: MIT Press, 1988).

61. For example, note Dewey's statements near the end of *Human Nature and Conduct* (New York: Modern Library, 1957), 300–301. Many pragmatists accuse Dewey of flying off into wild speculation here, while other evolutionary thinkers (like Charles Hartshorne) accuse Dewey of not doing this thoroughly or often enough. See Hartshorne, *Creativity in American Philosophy* (New York: Paragon House, 1984), 92–102.

62. This chapter is a considerable expansion and adaptation of one that emerged from the weekly sessions of the Emory University Philosophy and Science Reading Group, particularly through our reading of the work of Ernst Mayr and Richard Dawkins. The group members all read this manuscript and criticized it constructively and liberally. By name, I am most indebted to David F. Steele, Harish Joshi, Aurora Isaac, and Victor Balaban. That much briefer essay appeared under the title "The Rise and Fall of Evolutionary Thinking Among American Philosophers" in *Southwest Philosophy Review* 9, no. 1 (January 1993): 135–50.

I must also express my gratitude to Professor Ernst Mayr of Harvard University for his numerous helpful suggestions, as well as to Donald P. Verene, James Goetsch, and Fred Marcus of Emory; Larry Hickman; and Thomas Alexander and Eugenia Gatens-Robinson of Southern Illinois University (Carbondale) for similar help. I also extend a special thanks to Bob Hollinger and David Depew for giving me the opportunity to expand and refine these ideas. Particularly, Professor Depew's assistance has been of great value. It has been a privilege to revise my work in light of his work, and I thank him for reading this manuscript so closely and making dozens of very helpful suggestions.

11

Rorty's Pragmatism and the Linguistic Turn

Rickard Donovan

Reflecting on the differences between contemporary pragmatism and the classical nineteenth-century version, Richard Rorty recently remarked: "My own answer to this question is that the new pragmatism differs from the old in just two respects. . . . The first is that we new pragmatists talk about language instead of experience or mind, or consciousness as the old pragmatists did. The second respect is that we have all read Kuhn, Hanson, Toulmin, and Feyerabend, and have thereby become suspicious of the term scientific method."[1]

The first point could be interpreted as Rorty's way of underscoring the contribution that analytic philosophy made to the history of pragmatism. By focusing on language rather than mind or experience, the analytic tradition was able to make a radical break with the philosophical tradition—a break that was not possible until the twentieth century.[2]

The second point reinforces the first by showing how the antimethod stance of much current philosophy of science is a happy offshoot of the contemporary concern with language. By pointing out how the history of scientific progress depended on the development of vocabularies rather than on "general methods," Kuhn and company have done much to undermine the authority of an earlier positivism. For instance, Carnap's notion of linguistic frameworks seems like a good illustration of how the emphasis on language served to undermine the epistemological assumptions built into the very notion of methodology. "The enduring residue of Carnap's 'formal mode of speech' is that we can now feel content with saying merely 'Chemical inquiry is into the behavior of what we call "molecules", paleontological inquiry is into the behavior of what we call "fossil remains", etc.' without going on to say something about what 'science' as such is about."[3]

Here we find ourselves at the heart of Rorty's antiessentialism, and it raises serious questions about his place in the pragmatic tradition. In rejecting notions like "the nature of science," "the nature of experience," and "the nature of mind" he has indeed set his new linguistified pragmatism squarely in opposition to some of the major assumptions of the epistemological tradition. However, these assumptions, many would argue, form an indispensable part of what pragmatism is all about. Thinkers like Dewey, James, Peirce, and Royce saw themselves as extending the lines of a tradition that stretched back to the classical philosophers of the seventeenth and eighteenth century. Is Rorty making a serious effort to further extend this tradition using the resources of analytic philosophy or is he really abandoning it?

As a preliminary reply Rorty might point out that there are indeed antiessentialist intuitions in the work of some of the older pragmatists, while noting that criticisms of the philosophical tradition can be found in the work of James and Dewey. He might even recognize an older ally to the contemporary critique of method in Royce's and Peirce's attempts to place the role of scientific inquiry within the larger context of intellectual culture. What Rorty sometimes calls the holistic side of traditional pragmatism—its antireductionist attitude toward science, religion, ethics, and art—is perhaps its most significant contribution to contemporary discussion.

Yet Rorty is also sensitive to the way in which these Romantic, anti-Enlightenment strains often clashed with America's need to define itself in terms of an emerging scientific and technological culture.[4] He interprets Morton White's description of the tension between "science" and "sentiment" in American philosophy in the following terms: "American philosophy has, in the course of a hundred years, swung back and forth between an attempt to raise the rest of culture to the epistemological level of the natural sciences and an attempt to level down the natural sciences to an epistemological par with art, religion and politics."[5]

I think that Rorty's version of pragmatism can be appreciated as offering a redescription and resolution of the tensions between the Enlightenment and Romantic traditions mentioned above. In this chapter I will try to show how the "swinging back and forth" between an Enlightenment and a post-Enlightenment sensibility can be reformulated in terms of Rorty's interesting claim that the criticisms of the epistemological tradition found in the work of Dewey and James could not be carried through within the confines of the philosophical vocabulary they inherited from the nineteenth century. While this point will hardly settle the question of what is alive and what is dead in pragmatism, I hope it will help make more philosophical sense out of Rorty's "strong reading" of that tradition, and show how Rorty's work has deeper ties to the larger American tradition than are generally acknowledged. I will begin by setting out two views of language found throughout Rorty's metaphilosophical speculations.

On Rorty's reading, the "the linguistic turn" can be interpreted first of all as a description of the way analytic philosophy made a substantial contribution to a more thoroughgoing pragmatism. I will begin with Morton White's discussion of the stages of analytic philosophy found in his *Toward Reunion in Philosophy*.[6] I will supplement that with some of Rorty's more recent reflections on the linguistic turn and on the early stages of analytic philosophy. Second, I will take a look at a very different view of "the ubiquity of language" that Rorty shares with Hegel and the Romantic tradition. This I feel is the larger historical context in which to appreciate Rorty as an American philosopher. I hope at least to indicate how both senses of language play a role in Rorty's efforts to reshape the older tradition of American philosophy and in his words "adapt pragmatism to a changed intellectual environment."[7]

In a very early paper entitled "Realism, Categories, and the Linguistic Turn"[8] Rorty gives us a glimpse of "two routes by which one may reach a conception of philosophy as something that lives, moves and has its being within language."[9] Rorty points out how ideal language theory and ordinary language analysis share a conviction about the authority of language but interpret that conviction differently.

In one view the fact that we can't get beyond language to some nonlinguistic basis for choice of a language is interpreted as a new version of Kantian epistemology. Just as we can't get beyond our categories of explanation to noumenal reality, so we can't get around the limits of our language to the world. In this interpretation of the linguistification of philosophy one's metaphilosophical view of language is tied up with a particular set of epistemological assumptions. This approach is vividly exemplified in C. I. Lewis's conceptual pragmatism.[10]

However, this neo-Kantian alternative does not exhaust the metaphilosophical options. There is a second route to the linguistic turn and it is through Hegel rather than Kant. In this more historicist appreciation of the ubiquity of language there is no appeal to a transcendental standpoint or to ultimate conditions of describability. The thesis that language cannot be transcended is the result of a practical decision to avoid the circularity involved in trying to defend one's metaphilosophical views about language by appealing to some neutral epistemological standard of acceptibility. In this context the thesis that language cannot be transcended is "simply a purification of the Hegelian thesis that the progress of dialectical controversy cannot be judged from a standpoint outside the controversy itself."[11]

A linguistic reformulation of this thesis would amount to the claim that linguistic frameworks or vocabularies can only be evaluated on their own terms— terms internal to the fulfillment of their own purposes. "To propose a set of categories is not to offer a description of some non-linguistic fact, but to offer a tool for getting the job done."[12] This more radical metaphilosophical perspective on language suggests a way of freeing language from the nest of epistemological perplexities that have dogged the philosophical tradition. In this early article Rorty mentions "how the difference between realistic epistemology and non-realistic epistemology becomes negligible when metaphilosophical problems are posed in this purely practical context.''[13] Later we will see how this turn from theoretical grounding to practical justification came to form a central strategy in Rorty's metaphilosophical pragmatism. It is in play in his most recent reflections on controversies in the philosophy of science and it will surface in his discussions of idealism and classical pragmatism. It is necessary first, however, to take a closer look at the theoretical, transcendentalist neo-Kantian interpretation of the linguistic turn.

In Rorty's view, the conviction that language could become the twentieth-century substitute for ''experience'' was tied up with the hope that philosophy could again become an autonomous discipline. As Rorty notes in a later article, the attempt on the part of Frege and the young Wittgenstein to make language into an *a priori* discipline with the help of the new logic was to bestow on the philosophy of language all the privileges of Kant's transcendental standpoint. Just as Kant had proposed ''conditions of experiencibility,'' a philosophy of language would provide ''conditions of describability.''[14] Referring to this project, Rorty suggests that ''what Gustav Bergmann christened 'the linguistic turn' was a rather desperate attempt to keep philosophy an armchair discipline.''[15] Morton White's analysis of the stages of analytic philosophy into the ''age of meanings,'' the ''age of words,'' and the ''age of decisions'' is a good summary of how this attempt eventually failed.

In the age of meanings, common to the young Moore and Russell, a traditional epistemological and metaphysical model remained in place. The question can be posed in terms of the problem of self-referentiality facing the new logic. If the logic of Frege and Russell is to supply the conditions for all description, how does such allegedly unconditional knowledge escape description and still qualify as knowledge? How can logic be an exception to the conditions that it lays down? Russell's revival of Platonic forms, or ''logical objects,'' is a response to this problem.[16]

Attempts to describe the status of universal meanings or logical objects soon led to the development of a set of metaphors that described the nature of ''the mind'' or ''understanding.'' The new logic required a metaphysical complement—a realm of meaning that could serve as the ''object'' of an intellectual intuition. As ''objective,'' meanings were not reducible to mere words or physical objects.

However, this revival of metaphysical realism would soon face the challenge of a new generation of philosophers whose ''prodigious concentration on language''[17] helped change the vocabulary of analytic philosophy. The age of words covers the positivistic phase of analytic philosophy, beginning with the early Wittgenstein. Combining a strong commitment to empirical science with a new seriousness about the relation between language and logic, the early positivists were able to supply philosophy with a new self-image. ''For the positivists, philosophy became a second order discipline, and philosophical talk became primarily logical talk about the talk of others.''[18] By following up on

Wittgenstein's suggestion that logic is "the incomparable essence of language," and accepting the therapeutic view that philosophical problems are posed because "the logic of our language is misunderstood," philosophers found new tools with which to reinterpret their tradition. By understanding how the so-called "perennial problems" of philosophy were relative to various conceptual frameworks, they were in a position to regard them as pseudo-problems.

As a consequence, the more philosophers became absorbed in an analysis of linguistic expressions, the more skeptical they became of the value of controversies connected with the older subject-object model of knowledge. The more they turned to an analysis of propositions, the more pointless seemed an explanation of knowledge in terms of cognitive faculties. Supplying truth conditions for sentences seemed more promising than trying to grasp "the structure of consciousness" or picturing how something called an "idea" hooked on to something called "the world." The positivists and their successors were beginning to appreciate Rorty's point that the "malleability of language is a less paradoxical notion than the malleability of nature or of objects."[19]

But the positivist account of language did not remove epistemological perplexity. Frege's famous dictum that "only in the context of a sentence do words have meaning" helped move philosophy away from Cartesian subjectivism but not from the neo-Kantian problematic of modern philosophy. As White points out, "Frege's reasons for invoking the semantic distinction between sense and denotation is his belief that it flows from and supports the epistemological distinction between the a priori and a posteriori."[20] Like the early Wittgenstein, he saw philosophy as coextensive with an investigation into the possibility of meaning.

For Frege, then, concepts are not ideas or mental representations. Yet concepts are more than linguistic expressions. They occupy an abstract realm where logical criteria predominate. While substituting linguistic meaning for the problematic of ideas, Frege's thought still provided an objective realm of meaning, a shared structure supplying a philosophical foundation for language. A theory of meaning drawn along Kantian lines was to supply truth conditions for analytic statements and factual statements. The former would conform to the logic of propositions, the latter to the controversial verifiability principle. In both cases an analysis of sentences committed the positivists to the existence of extra-linguistic entities (e.g., "propositions" and "facts").

White does a convincing job of showing how the positivists floundered in their attempts to appeal to a theory of meaning and a verifiability theory to supply truth conditions for sentences. The notions of analyticity and synonymy proved to be more difficult and mysterious than the notion of *a priori* knowledge they were supposed to illuminate. Equally troubling was the epistemological assumption that the meaning of a sentence could be reduced to knowing what sensations or "facts" would confirm or disconfirm it. On the contrary, "facts" seem to be something signified by the subject and the predicate of the sentence in question. This suggests that the only way we can have access to a "fact" is to know the meaning of the sentence that purportedly describes that "fact." But this in turn makes it difficult to see how the latter can confirm or disconfirm the former—how a "state of affairs" outside of language can determine the meaning of linguistic expressions.

Looking back at the early period of analytic philosophy and the failures of reductive analysis, it is natural that Rorty would view logical empiricism as a reactionary movement. It took one step forward and two steps backward.[21] By virtue of its concentration on language, it moved philosophy away from essentialist questions about "consciousness" and "mind" only to revert to asking essentialist questions about language. However, for Rorty's purposes the first step forward was very important. By identifying philosophy with the scientific culture and developing a sophisticated "logical analysis" of conceptual frameworks, the early positivists were in a position to put the whole metaphysical tradition on the defensive.

A good example of a positivist reading of the library of philosophy along these lines can be found in the work of Hans Reichenbach. Moreover, in Rorty's discussion of Reichenbach's views we get in turn a good sense of the positivist deposit in Rorty's metaphilosophical perspective. In *The Rise of Scientific Philosophy* Reichenbach clearly identifies the problems of philosophy with Kant's problems—for example, the nature and possibility of scientific knowledge. He characterizes philosophy before the age of science as sheer speculation wherein problems are raised without the means of resolving them. Thanks to the new logic, philosophy for the first time in its history found itself in a position to reformulate epistemological problems with the kind of precision and rigor that admit of solution. In Reichenbach's narrative, philosophy has made progress. It has advanced from speculation to science.[22]

Given these assumptions it is not surprising that Reichenbach found the tradition of post-Kantian Idealism no more than a reactionary attempt at speculative philosophy—a series of failed attempts to achieve the status of science without submitting to the rigorous discipline of scientific investigation. He saw the great systematic accounts of "experience" offered by nineteenth-century metaphysicians as nothing more than the expression of "naive generalizations and analogies." Reichenbach's positivism stands as the most thorough repudiation of philosophy as a form of super-scientific knowledge.

While recognizing how one-sided and dated this reading of the history of philosophy looks today, Rorty does, however, buy in on the positivist criticism of philosophical accounts of "experience" that try to set themselves up as rivals to the detailed causal accounts offered by other disciplines. "He (Reichenbach) was right in dismissing lots of philosophical programs as attempts to claim the status of 'science' without imitating its procedures or respecting its results."[23] Rorty shares with Reichenbach a thorough repudiation of the ideal of philosophy as a super-science, and a deep skepticism in regard to the explanatory power of large-scale philosophical theory. "Pragmatists think that any such philosophical grounding is, apart from elegance of execution, pretty much as good or as bad as the practice it purports to ground."[24]

By the mid-1950s the de-transcendentalization of analytic philosophy—what Morton White called the "age of decision"—was well under way and its affinities to the pragmatic tradition were becoming apparent. The positivist ideal of the purely cognitive or the purely descriptive, embedded in the Kantian distinctions, began to give way to the realization that there are no sharp boundaries marking off the cognitive from the normative and the emotive. By pointing to the ways in which the vocabularies of logic, science, and ethics overlap, White made contact with the holistic impulse common to James and Dewey.

By showing how legal and ethical metaphors are appropriate to linguistic behavior he was able to undermine the notion of language as sheer description—a way of representing "the nature of things." For White, terms like "analytic," "synthetic," and "meaningful" are not descriptive predicates. They are acts of linguistic legislation, performed for a certain purpose. By emphasizing phrases like "ought to be made analytic," "ought to be left undefined," "ought to be called meaningful," White moved the question of justifying knowledge from the empirical and the logical to the moral. By seeing language as something "we do" rather than a shared logical structure or a privileged set of representations, he was able to envision a "reunion in philosophy"—a synthesis of positivism and pragmatism. Linguistic decisions are to be evaluated like other sorts of decisions—in terms of how they fit into the larger context of a form of life.[25]

In short, White's analysis seemed to be pointing in the direction of a social practice account of language. By focusing on the moral context of discourse, he was paving the way for the liberation of a philosophy of language from the trappings of epistemology and the dominance of the scientific culture celebrated by Reichenbach. In a sense, the "age of decision" can be interpreted as the beginning of a more radical break with a distinctively philosophical view of language. Rorty sums up the legacy of linguistic philosophy in these terms by citing a passage from the work of Donald Davidson: "The upshot of linguistic philosophy is, I would suggest, Davidson's remark that 'there is no such thing as a language, not if a language is anything like what philosophers . . . have supposed. . . . We must give up the idea of a clearly defined shared structure which language users master and then apply to cases.' "[26] Davidson's remark can in turn be given a broader historical context by linking it up with Rorty's point that "the analytic movement in philosophy was based on a tacit agreement to pretend that Hegel had never lived."[27] This reference to Hegel brings into focus the second and most important way in which language matters to Rorty's pragmatism.

In a sense, the figure of Hegel surrounds all of Rorty's discussions of language. In the course of making some comparisons between nineteenth- and twentieth-century conceptions of philosophy, Rorty points out how nineteenth-century philosophical thought began with Romanticism's challenge to the Enlightenment's legacy, and closed out with a strong endorsement of the positive sciences.[28] As we have just seen, the twentieth century began with philosophy taking on the image of the scientific culture in the name of the new logic, and is now closing out amidst a new-found appreciation of man's historical and cultural being. Just as Hegel was present at the beginning of the nineteenth century, so we find him among our contemporaries as we close out the twentieth. An important part of that story can be found in Rorty's interpretation of the relationship of Romanticism to idealism.

The early nineteenth century's challenge to the Enlightenment took a specifically philosophical form in the unprecedented attempt on the part of the German idealists to put science in its place by offering a competing vision of experience—a vision compatible with man's most exalted capacities as a cultural and spiritual being. By combining the scientific respectability of the problematic of ideas with Kant's suggestion that science was only one of the forms of human rationality, Hegel and the idealists were encouraged in the name of philosophy to claim access to an all-inclusive vision of intellectual culture. As the all-inclusive vision of reason, philosophy was the only intellectual form of life capable of exhibiting the different forms of rationality appropriate to art, religion, and science. As such, German idealism represents the most powerful challenge to Reichenbach's thesis.

Today Reichenbach might find himself in agreement with Rorty's claim that German idealism was an overreaction to the scientism of the Enlightenment.[29] In Rorty's view, the triumph of German idealism was short-lived thanks to the Hegel of the *Phenomenology* who, in displaying the historical relativity of all expressions of the Idea, opened the possibility that so-called perennial philosophical problems might be better appreciated as expressions of specific social practices and vocabularies. In Rorty's radically historicist reading of Hegel, the possibility of moving in and out of vocabularies suggests that the problems that arise in one set of descriptions vanish when a new descriptive vocabulary takes over. "What Hegel describes as the process of spirit gradually becoming self-conscious of its intrinsic nature is better described as the process of European linguistic practices changing at a faster and faster rate."[30]

Rorty's Hegel emerges as the creator of a "new literary genre" that kept the name of science but "without the distinctive mark of science—willingness to accept a neutral vocabulary in which to state problems and make argumentation possible."[31] He thereby helped liberate Romanticism from idealism and with it the assumption of a privileged philosophical vocabulary. The Romantic intuition that truth is *made* rather than found can be preserved in the realization that vocabularies are historically contingent redescriptions of experience that make no claim to describe "the nature of the world" or express "the nature of the self" or reveal "the structure of language."

Just as logical empiricism was an important first step in separating philosophy from the metaphysical tradition, so metaphysical idealism was an important first step in liberating the literary culture from science.[32] By contributing a new historical awareness of language, Romanticism provided the next stage in the realization of a thoroughgoing pragmatism. By giving up on the notion of language as a "shared structure" and thus abandoning the quest for a privileged philosophical vocabulary, Romanticism became identified with "the thesis that what is most important for human life is not what propositions we believe but what vocabulary we use."[33] By giving up on all varieties of essentialism and celebrating the fecundity of language, the Romantics have led us straight to Rorty's metaphilosophical-literary pragmatism. "The romantic sense that everything can be changed by talking in new terms"[34] chimes nicely with the pragmatic sense that vocabularies are tools to create and accomplish various purposes. I would now like to indicate briefly how influences from the Romantic tradition and from the post-positivistic phase of analytic philosophy come together in Rorty's criticism of the older idealist and pragmatist tradition.

Just as Rorty's pragmatism in part grew out of the holistic account of language offered by Quine, Sellars, and Davidson, so traditional pragmatism, in its own day, was nourished by the holistic account of knowledge offered by Royce, Green, and Morris. In fact, the influence of idealism on pragmatism can be summarized in terms of the decisive role that the coherence theory of truth played in undermining versions of the correspondence theory common to the older empiricist and rationalist traditions. The realization that we can't compare thought or language with unmediated reality is common to attacks on epistemological doctrines of "givenness" running from Thomas Reid to T. H. Green to Wilfred Sellars. It is present in pragmatists as diverse as Royce, Quine, and Davidson. This suggests that a look at Rorty's discussion of American idealism might provide a way of comparing the kind of coherence offered by a twentieth-century version of pragmatism—a pragmatism centered around discussions of language rather than "experience" or "mind" with one that still bore ties to the nineteenth-century metaphysical tradition. In this connection I think that Rorty's reading of the American philosopher Brand Blanshard might be useful. Given the fact that Blanshard lived through the heyday of analytic philosophy and actively resisted what he saw as "that tiresome obsession with language which has done so much in our day towards making philosophy trivial,"[35] he seems a particularly good choice.

Rorty opens a discussion of Blanshard's *The Nature of Thought* by noting how Blanshard's holistic arguments against reductionist theories of meaning sound very much like Quine, Sellars, and Wittgenstein's criticism of empiricism.[36] Blanshard held that the root error of the older empiricist-rationalist tradition consisted in "the 'atomist' notion that isolated bits—images flashed on the retina, simple natures poised before the eye of reason—were by themselves capable of offering knowledge and certainty."[37] Blanshard's idealism, like Sellars's and Wittgenstein's pragmatism, seemed to be offering another version of Rorty's historicized Hegel—a radical contextualism amounting to a wholesale indictment of the Platonic and Cartesian paradigms of philosophy.

However, as Rorty's analysis goes on to show, Blanshard's holism and contextualism are not of a piece with contemporary criticisms of empiricism any more than his idealism is a natural extension of Hegel's historicist view of language and culture. As Rorty puts it, a radically historicized reading of Hegel, one that viewed philosophical problems as relative to specific philosophical vocabularies, "was too rich for the blood of such English idealists as Green and Joachim."[38] We can add that it was also too rich for American idealists like Morris and Royce. These thinkers, who were reviving Hegel in the second half of the nineteenth century, preferred the Hegel "who insisted that the world was rational through and through, because Reason (or "Spirit") alone was real."[39]

Like their forerunners, the German idealists, the American and British Hegelians were convinced that the challenge posed by the emergence of the scientific culture in the nineteenth century called for some sort of large-scale philosophical resolution. Thinkers like Royce and later Blanshard were convinced that the epistemological problems inherent in this view of the world could only be resolved through a metaphysical exploration into the ultimate conditions of self-consciousness. For them, coherence would take on the metaphysical character of a total system of ideas.

It is easy to see with Rorty how these attempts at reform remained safely within the problematic of the Cartesian tradition. They consisted in a series of attempts to resolve the paradox inherent in the "subject-object" model of knowledge. In Rorty's view this model is committed to the assumption that the very "mark of the mental" is an incorrigible relation between "the mind" and an assemblage of representations whose accuracy (relation to the external world) can be clarified only in terms of a specifically philosophical (epistemological) analysis. The latter must be prepared to meet the challenge of the skeptic—the insinuation that we have no grounds for claiming that our representations conform to anything beyond themselves.

The efforts of idealists and pragmatists to answer the skeptic took the form of efforts to unite the subject and object by redescribing the object in terms of the subject. What Lovejoy described as the great "revolts against dualisms" in the early part of the century encompassed the attempts of thinkers like Whitehead as well as James and Dewey to "redescribe the sort of stuff that is 'out there' so that it is the same stuff which is 'before our minds.' "[40] Their task was to supply an intuition of something directly present prior to and more basic than the Cartesian division into the mental and the physical. If they could show that the latter distinction was a function of a more basic "unity of experience" then the latter could bridge the gap between subject and object. The skeptic would be answered and the paradox of knowledge resolved. In all of this they held to the Cartesian assumption that knowledge consisted in having something "before the mind."

Blanshard's discussions of the "nature of thought" and of "thinking" as getting "the thing itself in some degree within the mind"[41] fall well within this framework. Rorty points out how Blanshard's defense of notions like "objective necessity," "self-evidence," and "certainty" sit uneasily with his holistic attack on the notion of meaning as "hard little nuggets" unmodifiable by context and increasing knowledge.[42]

The key to these tensions is found in the assumptions underlying the epistemological puzzles that Blanshard is struggling to resolve. By construing the relation of idea to object as the internal relation between purpose and fulfillment, Blanshard has offered his solution to the paradox of knowledge. By giving up on correspondence and embracing coherence, Blanshard can describe "the nature of thought" in terms of a complete system of ideas. "Ideas" construed as "purposes" are discovered to be implicated in more and more inclusive explanatory contexts. Blanshard's holism consists in an expansion of that circle of implication in terms of a complete system of ideas expressed as the one Absolute fulfillment of purpose. "If thought can be seen as a stage on the way to its transcendent aim or object, as that end itself in the course of becoming actual the paradox of knowledge is in principle solved."[43] The complete object of thought, the union of appearance and reality, purpose and fulfillment, can be explicated in terms of a philosophical vision beyond the terms of common sense and science.

Rorty's quarrel with Blanshard, and with the tradition he calls "Cartesian metaphysics,"[44] is over this whole representationalist view of knowledge, and the view of philosophy that supports it. From his critique of "privileged representations" in the *Mirror* to his antirepresentationalist view of science in his later writings, Rorty has argued against the assumptions underlying this entire conception of the mind.[45] The extravagant means the idealists employed to resolve the paradox of knowledge and answer the skeptic make sense only if we grant them all the assumptions built into the problematic of ideas.

On the other hand, by setting aside the metaphor of the mental eye and the paradoxes that went with it, Rorty sees philosophers of language like Wittgenstein and Sellars making possible a more effective criticism of the Cartesian tradition than was available to the older idealist-pragmatist tradition. The real break comes when we no longer think of knowledge as "getting something before the mind" and return to the common-sense view of knowledge as the ability to "say something about something." "To know the nature of something is not a matter of having it before the mind, of intuiting it, but of being able to utter a large number of true propositions about it."[46] "Reason," in this common-sense view, is not a special faculty capable of getting in touch with a special "realm of objects" or "meanings," but the capacity to give reasons—a complex form of linguistic behavior that enables us to "utter sentences with the intention of justifying the utterance of other sentences."[47] In this way we can link up Sellars's statement that "all awareness . . . is a linguistic affair"[48] with the Hegelian intuition that knowledge (as speech) has to do with the relationship between persons—relationships formed in terms of the linguistic and social practices of a historical community.

Another way of indicating the break with idealism is to make a sharp distinction between intentional and nonintentional discourse, thereby avoiding the idealist's mistake of confusing causal explanations of the origin of our beliefs with epistemic justifications of those beliefs. This is to agree with the old empiricists that "the world is out there," and with the idealist that "truth is not out there." The former includes any empirical account of the way the world impinges on the language user. "World" in this sense is not the idealist's "fulfillment of ideas" but the ordinary objects of our experience, which are not, as the idealist supposes, caused by mental acts or altered because of new descriptions.

On the other hand, as language users we only know this world under a description. The epistemic authority of our beliefs comes from the language in which we describe our experiences. As Hegel and the Romantics have taught us, these languages are themselves the expression of historical contingency. As Rorty puts it, "To say that truth is not out there is simply to say that where there are no sentences there is no truth, that sentences are elements of human languages, and that human languages are human creations."[49]

This is the difference between Blanshard's holism and holistic philosophies of language like Sellars's and Quine's. The trick is to be a coherentist without being an idealist. By taking "the linguistic turn" and investing epistemic authority in social practices—in what the linguistic community lets us say—post-positivistic analytic philosophers have undermined efforts to supply anything like a philosophical "analysis of the possibilities of knowledge." If all epistemic justification has its roots in the historical linguistic practices of a community, there is no possibility of climbing out of them and seeing how they correspond with "the object of inquiry." In Rorty's view, the second revolt against dualism, the revolt in the names of linguistic behavior, was decisive. "For the second revolt undercut the premise which the first kind of revolt shared with Descartes himself: the premise that we have intuitive knowledge, knowledge which is prelinguistic and which thus serves as a test for the adequacy of language."[50]

It is no surprise to find that Rorty's criticism of the pragmatism of James and Dewey is pretty much of a piece with his criticism of Blanshard and idealism. This is not to suggest, however, that Dewey's and James's versions of pragmatism left Cartesian assumptions intact. To describe ideas as plans of action or as tools for the accomplishment of certain purposes is to decisively undermine a spectator theory of knowledge. Dewey's wholesale criticisms of the epistemological tradition and James's "put downs" of professional philosophy fit in well with the mood of Rorty's post-philosophical pragmatism. Rorty puts the difference between idealism and pragmatism this way: "What separates the pragmatist from the idealist is the former's whole-hearted acceptance of Darwinism."[51]

Here Rorty is of course referring to the naturalizing of Hegel and the rise of evolutionary biology. Around the turn of the century, metaphors of survival and adaptability began to replace those of picturing and representing. This naturally jeopardized the idealist claim that the universe has a fixed nature, something that could be represented in thought. Reading the "linguistic turn" into the perspective of an evolving universe, one might rather say with Rorty that "The universe is just what languages describe, and there are as many languages, as many alternative descriptions, as purposes to be served by such descriptions."[52]

However, any attempt to reduce Dewey's treatment of knowledge to a form of linguistic social practice by way of Darwin runs into serious difficulties. Rorty acknowledges that in his later years Dewey attempted to put something in the place of the tradition he had criticized. He wanted to offer something along the lines of "a metaphysics of experience," or "a general theory of inquiry." By stressing the close relationship between language and logic Dewey hoped to show how "the science of logic" was rooted in the social practices of the community. On the other hand, by insisting on the connection between logic and metaphysics, he wanted to raise discussions of language to the level of epistemological and metaphysical generality. When he talked about language as social *praxis*, Dewey was closer to Hegel and Darwin. When he tried to hook up language to logic and metaphysics he was beginning to sound like Blanshard and the idealists. As Rorty puts it, "For although Darwin saved Dewey from inheriting Green's Cartesian notion of mind, he did not save him from the epistemological problematic with which Green had struggled."[53]

The same ambivalence toward the epistemological problematic and the same traces of idealism turn up in the pragmatism and radical empiricism of William James. As we have noted, his playful spoofing of the pretensions of philosophy fit in well with the metaphilosophical tone of Rorty's pragmatism. Rorty sees him in the company of Nietzsche as offering "the possibility of a freer, more romantic, more playful, form of philosophical life—a possibility that our century is still exploring."[54]

On the other hand, there is James who early on came under the influence of Royce's metaphysics and became involved in the "Battle of the Absolute." Even after James had gotten out from under the spell of Royce he still remained, as Dewey did, within the problematic of ideas. His radically temporalized and personalized account of cognition still bears reference to how an "idea works" by leading us to have the experience that the idea anticipates. Toward the end of his career he was working out his own version of a "metaphysics of experience," a way of reconciling the relation of subject and object in terms of a more primordial and inclusive account of reality.

Of course, for Rorty, this is just more "Cartesian metaphysics." As Dewey saw Royce's absolute unity of thought and will as a betrayal of the pragmatic legacy, Rorty interprets James's Radical Empiricism and his account of "pure experience" as heading in the opposite direction from his pragmatism.[55] Rorty sees the process metaphysics associated with James, Bergson, and Whitehead as of a piece with Dewcy's "metaphysics of experience." Taking a page from Hans Reichenbach, Rorty sees them all as "weakened versions of idealism— attempts to answer 'unscientifically' formulated epistemological questions about the 'relation of subject and object' by 'naive generalizations and analogies' which emphasize feeling rather than cognition."[56] They all tried to find some "realm of meaning," some privileged vocabulary beyond the range of science and common sense. They all wanted to restore philosophy to the status of a super-science. They are all legitimate targets of Reichenbach's positivist criticism.

The kind of naturalism that Rorty would like to see his version of pragmatism identified with is one that would be entirely free from the image of philosophy as a super-science. It would completely abandon the Kantian project of supplying conditions of possibility for language, as well as mind, or consciousness. It gives up on the Idealist's quest for a nonempirical knowledge of the "Self." It accepts radical contingency in the same spirit that it accepts causal explanation as the only kind of explanation. "I shall define naturalism as the view that anything might have been otherwise, that there can be no conditionless conditions."[57]

In Rorty's historicist view, our most cherished social practices, vocabularies, and institutions could have been otherwise. Through all kinds of complex causal factors they emerged in history and proceeded to make all sorts of new things possible. Scientific vocabularies not only served the purposes of prediction and control, but have helped to create those very purposes, just as poets and political thinkers helped to make the world different by creating other vocabularies.[58]

Again, to be naturalist and historicist in respect to language and culture is for Rorty to tap into what is most vital in the Romantic tradition. Creating new vocabularies creates new selves and changes the face of culture. "What the Romantics expressed as the claim that imagination rather than reason, is the central human faculty was the realization that a talent for speaking differently, rather than for arguing well, is the chief instrument of cultural change."[59] By reinterpreting the legacy of Hegel and Romanticism for American philosophy, and by bringing this tradition to bear on some of the most important developments in analytic philosophy, it seems that Rorty has gone a long way toward achieving his aim of "adapting pragmatism to a changed intellectual environment."

NOTES

1. Richard Rorty, "The Banality of Pragmatism and the Poetry of Justice," in "Symposium on the Renaissance of Pragmatism in American Legal Thought," *Southern California Law Review* 63, no. 6 (September 1990): 1911.

2. Richard Rorty, "Comments on Sleeper and Edel," *Transactions of The Charles S. Peirce Society* 21 (Winter 1985): 40–48.

3. Ibid., 43.

4. See Cornel West, *The American Evasion of Philosophy, A Genealogy of Pragmatism* (Madison: University of Wisconsin Press, 1989), Chapters 2, 3.

5. Richard Rorty, "Pragmatism Without Method," in *Philosophical Papers* (Cambridge: Cambridge University Press, 1991), 1:63.

6. Morton White, *Toward Reunion in Philosophy* (New York: Atheneum, 1963). Originally published by Harvard University Press, 1956. (Hereafter, *TRP*.)

7. Rorty, "Comments on Sleeper and Edel," 47.

8. Richard Rorty, "Realism, Categories, and the Linguistic Turn," *International Philosophical Quarterly* 2 (May 1962): 307–22.

9. Ibid., 313.

10. Ibid., 312. Rorty refers to the contribution of the neo-Kantian tradition to the growth of pragmatism in "From Language to Logic to Play," *Proceedings and Addresses of the American Philosophical Association* 59 (1986): 749. Also in Richard Rorty, "Wittgenstein, Heidegger, and the Reification of Language," *Philosophical Papers*, 11:53.

11. Rorty, "Realism, Categories, and the Linguistic Turn," 313.

12. Ibid.

13. Ibid.

14. Rorty, "Wittgenstein, Heidegger, and the Reification of Language," 53.

15. Ibid., 50.

16. *TRP*, 30–34.

17. Ibid., 10.

18. Ibid., 11.

19. Ibid., 13.

20. Ibid., 34, 35.

21. Richard Rorty, "Pragmatism, Davidson, and Truth," in *Philosophical Papers*, 1:150.

22. Hans Reichenbach, *The Rise of Scientific Philosophy* (Berkeley: University of California Press, 1951), quoted by Rorty in "Philosophy in America Today," in *Consequences of Pragmatism: Essays 1972–1980* (Minneapolis: University of Minnesota Press, 1982), 211–18. (Hereafter, *CP*.)

23. Rorty, "Philosophy in America Today," 212.

24. Richard Rorty, "Pragmatism, Relativism, and Irrationalism," in *CP*, 167.

25. *TRP*, chapter 9, 148–63.

26. Donald Davidson, "A Nice Derangement of Epitaphs," in *Truth and Interpretation: Perspectives on the Philosophy of Donald Davidson*, ed. E. LePore (Oxford: Blackwell, 1986), 446. Quoted in Rorty, "Wittgenstein, Heidegger, and the Reification of Language," 50.

27. Richard Rorty, "Epistemological Behaviorism and the De-Transcendentalization of Analytic Philosophy," in *Hermeneutics and Praxis*, ed. Robert Hollinger (South Bend, Ind.: University of Notre Dame Press, 1985), 106.

28. Rorty, "From Language to Logic to Play," 748.

29. Richard Rorty, "Non-Reductive Physicalism," in *Philosophical Papers*, 1:113.

30. Richard Rorty, *Contingency, Irony, and Solidarity* (Cambridge: Cambridge University Press, 1989), 7. (Hereafter, *CIS*.) Rorty's early reading of Hegel gave direction to his historicist reading of philosophy: "Almost as soon as I began to study philosophy, I was impressed by the way in which philosophical problems appeared, disappeared, or changed shape, as a result of new assumptions or vocabularies." Richard Rorty, *Philosophy and the Mirror of Nature* (Princeton, N.J.: Princeton University Press, 1979), xiii. There are well over a hundred references to Hegel in Rorty's work.

31. Richard Rorty, "Nineteenth-Century Idealism and Twentieth-Century Textualism," in *CP*, 147.

32. Ibid., 149.

33. Ibid., 142.

34. Ibid., 149. Rorty can legitimately be placed in the rhetorical rather than the foundationalist tradition. See Stanley Fish, "Rhetoric," in *Critical Terms for Literary Study*, ed. F. Lentricchia and T. McLaughlin (Chicago: University of Chicago Press, 1990), 203–22. See also Hilary Putnam, *Renewing Philosophy* (Cambridge, Mass.: Harvard University Press, 1992). "Relativism a la Rorty is Rhetoric," 71.

35. Brand Blanshard, *Reason and Analysis* (LaSalle, Ill.: Open Court, 1962), 267.

36. Richard Rorty, "Idealism, Holism, and the Paradox of Knowledge," in *The Philosophy of Brand Blanshard*, ed. P. A. Schilpp. (La Salle, Ill.: Open Court, 1980), 742. (Hereafter, "IHP.")

37. Ibid., 746.

38. Ibid.

39. Richard Rorty, "Relations, Internal and External," in *The Encyclopedia of Philosophy*, ed. Paul Edwards (New York: Macmillan, 1967), 7:126.

40. Richard Rorty, "Contemporary Philosophy of Mind," *Syntheses* 53 (November 1982): 329.

41. Brand Blanshard, *The Nature of Thought* (New York: Macmillan, 1939), 11, 261. Quoted by Rorty, "IHP," 742.

42. Rorty, "IHP," 746.

43. Blanshard, *The Nature of Thought*, 11, 494. Quoted in Rorty, "IHP," 757.

44. Rorty, "Contemporary Philosophy of Mind," 329.

45. Rorty, *Philosophical Papers*, vol. 1, Introduction.

46. Rorty, "Contemporary Philosophy of Mind," 331.

47. Rorty, *Mirror of Nature*, 182.

48. Quoted in Rorty, Ibid. Rorty refers to Sellars as a lost leader of pragmatism in "Transcendental Argument, Self-Reference, and Pragmatism," in *Transcendental Arguments and Science*, ed. Bieri, Horstmann, and Kruger (Dordrecht: D. Reidel, 1979). For Rorty's most thorough and incisive estimate of Wilfred Sellars's place in contemporary pragmatism see "Representation, Social Practice and Truth," in *Philosophical Papers*, 1:151–61.

49. Rorty, *CIS*, 5.

50. Rorty, "Contemporary Philosophy of Mind," 332.

51. Richard Rorty, "Just One More Species Doing Its Best," *London Review of Books* 25 (July 1991): 3.

52. Ibid., 4.

53. Rorty, "Comments on Sleeper and Edel," 40.

54. Richard Rorty, "The Pragmatist," Review of *A Stroll with William James*, by Jacques Barzun, *New Republic* 9 (May 1983), 34.

55. Ibid., 33.

56. Rorty, "Philosophy in America Today," 214.

57. Rorty, "Wittgenstein, Heidegger, and the Reification of Language," 55.

58. Rorty's reading of Hegel underscores what he deems most vital in neopragmatism as well as the direction his own work has taken. "Hegel's romantic description of how thought works is appropriate for post-Hegelian politics and literature and almost entirely inappropriate for science." Rorty, "Nineteenth-Century Idealism," 149. This is also Rorty's reading of the Emersonian legacy. "Professionalized Philosophy and Transcendentalist Culture," *CP*, 67–69.

59. Rorty, *CIS*, 7.

Part III

Pragmatism and
the Postmodern Condition

Introduction

David Depew and Robert Hollinger

By the late 1950s and early 1960s, the notion had become well entrenched that logical empiricism had given correct accounts of scientific explanation and scientific theories, and had shown why it was both to be expected and desired that laws and theories of lesser scope should be reduced to more basic ones. Attention then turned to the task of bringing the social sciences within the scope of this analysis. This time, however, resistance was encountered. Sometimes this resistance was grounded in the metaphysical notion that persons are not the kinds of beings that can, or should, be explained in terms of laws and the external forces to which law-governed objects are assumed to be subject. More frequently, however, the issue was posed in epistemological terms. Applying the methods of the natural sciences, it was said, could not be expected to yield the kind or amount of knowledge that those working in the human sciences were seeking.

Those trying to hold back the extension of the logical empiricist philosophy of science to the human sciences found a rich source of counterexamples to the unity of science program in historical explanations. Once ordinary language philosophers had convinced pragmatized positivists that explanation itself is an inherently pragmatic, or context-dependent, notion, it was pretty easy to show that the narratives by which we come to understand the past are more explanatory than any laws that could cover them, either step-by-step or as a whole. Soon American philosophers sensitive to arguments like these were finding their way to Continental philosophers, who often seemed to support their main point. That was because it turns out that something very close to an argument like this had already been fought out in German-speaking countries during the waning decades of the nineteenth century, when broadly neo-Kantian philosophers, seeking to maintain the traditional dominance of the human studies (*Geisteswissenschaften*) in their universities, resisted the rather crude reductionist materialism that had characterized apologists for science in Bismarkian Germany by proclaiming that the human sciences wield a distinctively hermeneutical or interpretive method that makes little or no use of natural laws, or even empirical regularities. The importation of this body of thought, to which thinkers as eminent as Dilthey, Rickert, Windleband, Weber, Husserl, Heidegger, and Gadamer had made contributions, was a major event in the history of American philosophy. From that period to the present, the duality between the *Naturwissenschaften* and the *Geisteswissenschaften* has been reflected in a split between "analytic" and "Continental" schools in philosophy departments.

At first, hermeneutic enthusiasts (henceforth 'hermeneuts') generally did not question the ascendancy of positivist philosophy of science within its paradigmatic sphere of application. On the contrary, a sort of compromise took hold. Positivist models were assumed to apply to the natural sciences, interpretive or hermeneutic criteria to the social sciences and humanities. It soon began to appear, however, that the hermeneuts had a better hand to play than they had expected. Among the rippling effects of Quine's argument that scientific theories are underdetermined by data, of Kuhn's *Structure of Scientific Revolutions*, and of Paul Feyerabend's even less compromising attack on the empiricist foundationalism that had been so deeply entrenched among scientists and their philosophical apologists was the perception that science itself is a hermeneutical activity. By 1970, Kuhn himself was saying so.[1] From that time until the present, the law-covered explanations of the positivist tradition have continuously lost ground to an aggressively universalizing hermeneutics, in which even the most well-established scientific theories are viewed as social constructions and products of rhetorical negotiation. Philosophers of science trying to stem this revenge of the humanities on the natural sciences have been forced to jettison large parts of the received neopositivist philosophy of science in order to defend their core commitment to the epistemic solidity of science, and to preserve bits and shards of the once persuasive notion that science can preside over society in the same way that philosophy and religion once did.

The first fruits of Richard Rorty's attempts to work out the *Consequences of Pragmatism*, the premises for which had been set forth in *Philosophy and the Mirror of Nature*, consisted in his interventions in these disputes about the natural and human sciences. "Pragmatism," Rorty wrote in the introduction to *Consequences*, "does not erect Science as an idol to fill the place once held by God. It views science as one genre of literature. . . . Physics is a way of trying to cope with various bits of the universe; ethics is a matter of trying to cope with other bits.[2] Accordingly, there is no reason why you cannot apply interpretive methods to things and laws to persons, or must think that the one method will be more productive than the other."[3]

What makes this claim pragmatic is Rorty's studious refusal to preassign different "bits of the universe" to particular "genres," as neo-Kantians and their American epigones did, or to claim, with the positivists, that only some of these genres produce real knowledge. In order even to be possible, these programs would require either an inconceivable end-run around language to naked reality in order to find out which chunks of the real map, or fail to map, onto which chunks of language; or an appeal to the old theological notion that God wrote the world in only "one language" (Newton thought it was the calculus); or at the very least antecedent prejudices, such as those that mar Quine's behaviorist pragmatism, in favor of the general utility of some languages over others for every legitimate purpose. These alternatives, Rorty says, even if they are coherent, will prejudge too many matters that should be left up to the course of inquiry itself to determine, and to the (Millean) contestation between competing views as they bear on particular problems. On this account, the usual aprioristic way of splitting the difference between the natural and human sciences is illegitimate. "The only constraints on inquiry are conversational ones," Rorty writes, "those retail constraints provided by the remarks of our fellow inquirers."[4] There is nothing "in the nature of things" that says you can't "predict and control" people as well as billiard balls, nor anything about scientific theories that belies their creative and metaphorical status. There is no categorical contrast between "representation" and "expression."[5] Nor is there any "metaphysical difference between morality and science."[6]

As he makes clear in the introductory chapter of *Contingency, Irony, and Solidarity*, Rorty's favorite arguments for this conclusion are taken from Donald Davidson's gloss on his teacher Quine's theory of language.[7] Davidson argues that Quine's notions of "stimulus meaning" and "observation sentences" are artifacts of old epistemic, skeptical worries about how languages hook onto an "external world." The skeptical doubts that such questions raise lead Quine to favor extensional, behavioral, stimulus-response "languages," from which the slippery truth-conditions of intentional or purposive action drop away as predictively and explanatorily useless. Davidson holds that Quine might more profitably have spent his time specifying the concrete truth-conditions for asserting something in particular in a language than worrying about the grand epistemic warrants that lead us to prefer one whole language and its ontology to another. This mistake derives, according to Davidson, from Quine's residual attachment to a "third dogma of empiricism" even after he had destroyed the distinction between analytic and synthetic statements (the first dogma), and its corollary, the belief that one can confirm or disconfirm sentences one at a time by reference to "sense data" (the second dogma). The third dogma is that a language is a "conceptual scheme" that orders or can be applied to an independent "content." According to Davidson, languages are not the sort of thing between which one might pick and choose to perform this or that task, or that can even be contrasted with an external given at all. The "very idea of a conceptual scheme" is incoherent. Nor is it the case that "different languages [could pose] as barriers between persons and cultures" after the fashion in which Navajo and English are portrayed in the famous, and deeply fallacious, Whorf-Sapir-Hypothesis.[8] "If a language is anything like what philosophers have supposed," Davidson says, "there is no such thing as a language."[9]

All this being so, consequences for philosophy's favorite problems begin to flow like water. From this piecemeal or meliorist perspective, it seems to Davidson that a theory of meaning, if such there be, simply is an account of the truth-conditions for sentences in a particular language.[10] Whatever that language may be, moreover, if we wish to assign a truth value of false to one or several of our sentences, or those of someone else, it is logically necessary that we must presuppose that most of the other ones we are prepared to utter under appropriate conditions, as well as most of those uttered by others, must be presumed to be true. For it is only against such a background that we can accuse someone of particular errors.[11] Given such a presupposition, it is incoherent to imagine that our words could conceivably slip wholesale off the world. On the contrary, it seems that the world (where "world" means the full range of things, events, and processes in it, including social and cultural practices) makes our beliefs the way they are by setting the truth-conditions for our statements. But in that case, the general relation between language and the external world is causal rather than referential or evidential.[12] We should not, accordingly, countenance the old philosophical doubts that Davidson thinks still linger in Quine's appeal to sensory stimulations. We should not do so for the same reasons that we should not think that representations of the world have to filter through skeptical, world-less Cartesian minds before we can be sure that there are grounds for believing anything. The only reason for ever thinking that way arose from epistemic distrust of the intentional world, a distrust strangely shared by those who would replace intentions with something more *naturwissenschaftliche*, as well as by those who would preserve intentions in a hermeneutically sealed world by denying them causal status. Now that the illusory grounds of distrust have been removed, however, by the causal tie between our beliefs and the world, the cultural world, constituted through intentions, is accorded equal standing with the physical world. Indeed, since reasons, desires, and the objects of propositional attitudes—the "folk psychological apparatus" of which Quine is so skeptical—are parts of the world so construed, and since the world causally makes our reasons to be what they are, it follows that reasons are causes.[13] Hermeneuts are not, accordingly, entitled to say that causes apply to the natural order, and that something else, called reasons, allows us to understand and conduct human affairs. That is not because there are no such things as reasons, as standard-issue behaviorism suggests. On the contrary, it is because reasons are very often the causes of our actions.

Rorty drives these arguments to a place where Davidson himself often fears to tread. Pushing Davidson's version of the linguistic turn in the direction of a number of old pragmatist themes, Rorty argues that if language is a *tool*, the uses of which are much more engaged and piecemeal than they are represented by any picture in which language is "a third thing intervening between self and reality,'' then when we translate, disagree, redescribe, or play any of a number of other ''language games,'' as Wittgenstein dubbed them, we, as *active* intelligent beings, are already always fully *in* the world. For language gives us the world through our participation in the ''forms of life'' that it constitutes. There is and can be no world behind that world, accessible to pure passive contemplation. If there is, says Rorty, it is ''a world well lost.''[14] Moreover, since there is no contrast between our constructions and the world as it might be independent of us, neither can there be, as Davidson himself admits, any principled difference between metaphorical and literal uses of language. What we mean by the literal is simply that the once living, but now routinized metaphors of yesteryear constitute our way of getting around in the world.[15] We will get around better in it, Rorty's pragmatism insists, by using fresh metaphors. We should in fact make every effort to let our conversations go wherever they go, in whatever vocabulary turns up, driven hither and yon by the life cycle of the metaphors in and through which we converse. Nothing is forbidden, in fact, except the premature and preemptive constraints on conversation that are induced by literalists, who stultify creative and purposive activity by killing off metaphors before their time.

In this way, Rorty turns Davidson's theory of metaphor into a historicist picture of constantly changing causal conditions for assigning truth values over time as discourse goes its merry way. He does so, moreover, in a way that echoes the motives that long ago drove James to pragmatism, as Nevo, Cotkin, Campbell, Gunn, and Hickman note in this volume. This does not mean that Rortyean conversations are not rule-governed or rational. Rorty does not deny that discursive communities justifiably erect whatever standards and rules they think allow the conversation to proceed properly. What is ruled out of bounds are attempts to gain unfair advantage by short-circuiting the relevant forms of discursive interaction. Inserting transcendental buckstoppers, or preassigning certain ways of talking to certain kinds of things, for example, as philosophers are prone to do, violates the very conditions under which language use is a coherent activity. If something more gradualistic and pedestrian than this seems to emerge from Davidson's own pages, Rorty suspects that is because Davidson still clings to philosophical semantics to assure us that all is right with the world as it is rather than to stimulate us to change it. Since philosophers are second only to priests in the persistence of their attempts to constrain conversations, Rorty believes that the linguistic turn, as completed by Davidson, cannot fully come into its own until it puts the philosophical discourse out of which it arose under suspicion. That, and nothing more, is what Rorty means by the ''end of philosophy.''

Rorty believes that his version of Davidson's philosophy of language has large implications for reviving the fortunes of the pragmatic tradition. Rorty, speaking on behalf of ''we Davidsonians,'' hopes to steer pragmatism away from the scientism and technologism that has hitherto tagged along with it, to link it more closely with the interpretive disciplines, and to make pragmatism testify on behalf of the ideals of political liberalism. The general schema of arguments to these effects shows Rorty arguing in a wide variety of ways that Davidsonian semantics is a good way of portraying the patterns and norms of discourse in a distinctively liberal society, and, to the extent that Davidsonian semantics is philosophically more valid than its competitors, asserting that it yields a more coherent and consistent defense of liberalism than that political and social philosophy has hitherto enjoyed. Once essentialist norms rooted in an immutable human nature and its underlying capacities are put out of play as mere constraints on discourse in the service of illegitimate power, for example, it is a good deal easier to see that nothing facilitates the individual freedom that is dearer to liberals than other goods than the recognition that we do not need permission from nature, nature's God, or society to become whatever we want to become, and to do whatever we want to do. In this connection, Rorty takes Mill as the pinnacle of the liberal democratic tradition, and reads Dewey (rather than James) as the American Mill. The distance these writers had already taken from appeals to human nature and natural rights, and their shift to utilities and purposes, is increased by Rorty's Davidsonian arguments for liberalism without foundations, "cosmopolitanism without emancipation," and "mild ethnocentricism" without conservatism. "Bourgeois liberalism," Rorty writes in *Consequences of Pragmatism*, "seems to me the best example of solidarity we have yet achieved, and Deweyan pragmatism the best articulation of it.[16] In turn, Rorty's Davidsonian arguments are proposed as the best articulation yet of Deweyan pragmatism.

The old notion that pragmatism could serve its reformist purposes well by attaching itself to the ideal of scientific progress through experimentalism is not likely to be helpful in arguing for this form of liberalism. Thus, it is not surprising to hear Rorty saying that "The rhetoric of scientific objectivity, pressed too hard and taken too seriously, has led us to people like B. F. Skinner," who have fruitlessly, and even maliciously, "attempted to be 'scientific' about our moral and political lives."[17] Accordingly, if older forms of pragmatism were self-consciously scientistic, its new devotees go out of their way to make room for the humanities and for a literature-centered, humanistic, or posthumanistic view of the world.[18] Science may be fine for helping us predict and control things and people. But in the crucially important, indeed intrinsically good, activity of self-exploration, self-creation, and self-expression, nothing is as useful as art, literature, and the interpretive skills sharpened by our encounters with them.

Kolenda interprets and endorses these Rortyean themes by turning Rorty's defense of the *humanities* into a defense of philosophical *humanism* in ways that accentuate the Romantic, expressivist side of his thought and downplay Rorty's commitment to physicalist naturalism. Kolenda's humanistic Rorty predicates the primacy of the hermeneutical disciplines over the natural sciences on a strongly Kantian ontology of freedom of the will and a rather thin phenomenalism about science. Kolenda's Rorty is, in fact, something of an existentialist without the *angst.* "Just as it is an error to think of the world as manifesting certain persistent structures prior to and independent of our attempts to describe them," Kolenda writes, "so it is an error to see ourselves as manifesting an antecedent human nature which our self-knowledge supposedly discovers."[19] That is one reading of Rorty. Magnus's Rorty, by contrast, is more of a post-humanist than a humanist, and more of a postmodernist than a modernist. There is no unitary self, whether discovered or homemade. There is only a continuously made, unmade, and remade text about something we call ourselves. Nor, says Magnus, is there a "generic distinction between *Natur- und Geisteswissenschaften,*" or more generally "any inherent division of labor among disciplines." A posthumanist pragmatism is, in these respects, postmodern precisely because it gives up these dualities with no regrets, and gives up as well any hopes for a deep foundation of the self. By incorporating elements from acknowledged postmodern masters like Foucault, Lyotard, and Derrida, Rorty presents himself as a postmodern pragmatist who hopes to commend the American version of the "Conversation of the West" to those who are willing to give up the notion that our project will ever be grounded in anything other than our commitment to continue it, and who are ready to believe that the liberal values into which we have happily evolved by means of conversation will in the future be deepened precisely by making our reasons for clinging to them shallower.

Whether it is conceived as modernist or postmodernist, humanist or posthumanist, the patent desire of postmodern pragmatists to pry pragmatism loose from traces of science-worship is easy enough to understand. The rise of positivized pragmatism in the 1950s and 1960s reignited old debates about Dewey's "pragmatic acquiescence" for the simple reason that many of those who identified themselves as pragmatists in those decades favored precisely this sort of top-down social control. In the earlier period, Walter Lippmann, in coming reluctantly to the view that democratic consent to geopolitically realistic and economically progressive policies must be manufactured from above, felt that he had to adjure the faith of a pragmatist. For in Lippmann's day, "pragmatism" was a term still heavily tilted toward the democratic, participatory, and populist faith of Dewey that Lippmann was explicitly renouncing. The transformation of the pragmatist tradition by its encounter with the positivist tradition, however, made it possible, by the 1950s, for those advocating managerial and technical control to think of themselves as pragmatists. This significant shift occurred in and through the context of the Cold War, when advocates of "piecemeal social engineering" could appear as defenders of liberal democracy against the holistic, and hence distinctly nonpragmatic, social engineering of dogmatic Marxists and other totalitarians. It was in this context that Daniel Bell could plausibly enough think of himself as a liberal, a democrat, and a pragmatist precisely when he was insisting that the worst thing that could possibly befall a democracy is to have too ideologically charged a spectrum of social discourse. Bell, as well as Sidney Hook, was then free to portray Dewey as an end-of-ideology liberal too,

whose belief in technology and the managerial revolution was intended to license scientific intervention in the liberal free market just enough to guarantee
a steady output of consumer goods, so that liberalism's true goods, political
choice and personal freedom, could be maximized on a material base strong
enough to prevent outbreaks of disruptive ideology from left to right.[20]

Some people were uncomfortable with this portrait of Dewey and his legacy.
In the 1960s, accordingly, efforts were made to rescue the praxical, democratic,
communitarian side of Dewey from scientist and technologistic distortions that
had rather anachronistically been thrust upon him. This was done with the means
of persuasion at hand. Dewey was construed as a hermeneutic humanist rather
than a scientistic technocrat. This tendency is observable in Richard Bernstein's
efforts to link Dewey with such heroes of the European hermeneutical tradition
as Heidegger, Gadamer, Habermas, and Arendt, all of whom want to restore the
primacy and autonomy of Aristotelian practical reason (*phronesis*) against its
displacement by technical conceptions of rationality, and who argue that practical reason is genuine and genuinely effective only when it is embedded deeply
within, and rises out of, a hermeneutically thick appropriation of living cultural
traditions.[21] Bernstein's assimilation of Dewey to Gadamer, Arendt, and Habermas links him to the later twentieth-century Hegelian revival, which decapitates
Hegel's system by dropping the notion of Absolute Spirit and allowing Hegel's
ideas to restabilize themselves around his powerful theory of social and political
Sittlichkeit or solidarity. In reconstructing Dewey's account of democracy
against this background theory, Bernstein picks up a genuine aspect of Dewey's
thought, the aspect that derives from his self-consciously post-Hegelian democratic communitarianism. In the process, however, Bernstein makes Dewey tacitly favor a division of labor between the *Naturwissenschaften* and the
Geisteswissenschaften that Dewey himself would undoubtedly have recognized
as a new sort of dualism, and that makes Dewey less naturalistic than he was.
(Bernstein professes to be no less relieved than Rorty that Dewey wished he
had written *Experience and Culture* rather than *Experience and Nature*.[22]) By
using the categories of the European hermeneutic tradition, and its critique of
mass society, moreover, Bernstein makes Dewey into a cultural conservative,
albeit one who escapes the usual consequences of conservatism because he
thinks of American culture as deeply democratic.

Is this the real Dewey, or merely a 1960s-style *geisteswissenschaftliche* reaction to 1950s-style positivism? It is certainly the case that Dewey's criticism
of Marxist politics requires one to defend the claim that Dewey's deep belief
in democratic culture and tradition was also a belief in radical criticism, deep
reform, and commitment to extend participatory democracy to every sphere of
life, including the economic. (Robert Westbrook has demonstrated that Dewey
was consistently all these things in *John Dewey and American Democracy*.) An
interpretation like Bernstein's also requires clarification of Dewey's naturalism,
hopefully in ways that retain something of his biocentric vision. Finally, if we

are to see Dewey as a radical communitarian democrat, we should not be able to find in him anything like a Cold War managerial liberal.

It is natural that we should look to Rorty's Dewey to meet these challenges. Indeed, it is quite profitable to see Rorty's interpretation of Dewey as a response both to Bell's reading and to Bernstein's. Not everyone, however, has found Rorty's way of steering between these technocratic and communitarian poles helpful or convincing. The pole star of Rorty's work is liberalism, and especially its hallmark commitment to the idea that people should be free to do whatever they please, and become whatever they want, if they don't hurt anyone. Rorty uses Davidsonian arguments to back up, even if not to "ground," his liberalism. Only a liberal society can keep the path of inquiry open and the encouragement to invent and disseminate new languages alive in ways that put the brakes on transcendentally contaminated schemes and other constraints on discourse. To be a liberal, however, is not necessarily to be a thoroughgoing democrat. If Bernstein's Dewey, like Westbrook's, is thoroughly democratic, it is because his Dewey was a post-Hegelian communitarian, and in that sense precisely *not* a philosophical liberal. In liberalism, for example, there is no requirement that every private person be a politically engaged citizen as well. Nor is there any sense that constraints on the market, even among those liberals who believe that constrained markets foster the overall aims of liberalism, can be justified precisely because they allow political man to flourish in a way that is easily undermined by the vulgarity, egocentrism and consumerism of *homo economicus*. To say that would be to step on the individual's liberal right to do whatever he wants. The Hegelian Dewey, however, does not take this view. The Rortyean Dewey does. Indeed, some of Rorty's best commentators, including Nancy Fraser and, in this volume, Isaac Nevo, become acutely anxious when they find Rorty arguing for precisely the opposite view. Not only is it not required that each person be a *citoyen*, but it is, on the contrary, highly desirable that the entire political realm be a sphere relegated to the technical, instrumentalistic rationality of experts and managers so that intrinsic goods can flourish in the sphere of personal privacy.[23]

Rorty apparently assumes, with neo-Burkean, anti-Rousseauian Michael Oakshott—whose notion of the "conversation of mankind" Rorty appropriates—that whenever the public sphere is regarded as a site for the expression of abstract rationality and highly charged discursive practices, it will necessarily and inevitably become a scene of disaster, in which the utopian visions of poets and revolutionaries are allowed to inflate into cognitive and normative domination over society. Rorty's counterproposal is that all such dreaming and scheming should be pushed back into the realm of privacy, where it is to constitute a realm of intrinsic goods that is to be facilitated and fostered by the wholly instrumental rationality and piecemeal social engineering of a public sphere that is "beyond ideology." This is to interpret the pragmatic ideal, however, after the fashion of Cold War positivists, for whom the scientifically informed control of experience is tantamount to a defense of rule by a body of skilled experts, who, in a dangerous, complex, and tragic world act as surrogates for a population whose role is largely restricted to happily consuming the "utilities" that the new class is supposed to maximize by its managerial and technical efficiency. Rorty seems to think that the technocrats are doing a pretty good job, and will do a better job when they give up their scientism. Humanists should concur in this arrangement because the "piecemeal social engineering" that has come out of the positivized pragmatic tradition has, in spite of scientistic excesses that need correction, more often led to a net increase in good (i.e., less cruelty) than the grand schemes of metaphysical humanism. Fraser and Nevo call attention to the resultant gap between Rorty's Romantic and technocratic sides.

On no possible interpretation, however, can Dewey be construed as treating democratic culture as one in which the private expressive life is to thrive at the expense of the public life of shared learning, making, and governing. What is more seriously doubtful, however, is whether Rorty's refusal to regard the public sphere as a site for the realization of intrinsic goods is consistent with the deepest impulses of pragmatism itself, and its continuity as a tradition over time. A purely instrumental conception of the public and social, that is to say, will fail to embody, and to teach, the *moral* conceptions that are required for individuals to sustain their commitment to the aims of democratic society even under Rorty's conception of it. By the same token, sustaining the *common* life of a society in which the moral ideals of democracy are actually realized is itself an *intrinsically* good action, and not just a matter of instrumentally effective social engineering.

Rorty's version of pragmatism incorporates the ideas of Max Weber and Daniel Bell more than the ideas of Dewey. As Nancy Fraser and Isaac Nevo demonstrate, Rorty bifurcates the private and the public, privatizes values, and defends a thin conception of democracy that amounts to piecemeal social engineering imbued with an abstract Christian ethos of love. Further, he defends Daniel Bell's end of ideology thesis, itself a variation on Weber's mixture of private romanticism and *Realpolitik*, which was Weber's defeatest response to the iron cage. For Rorty and Bell, the public sphere necessary for Deweyan democracy vanishes.

The reader should contrast these Weberian views with those of Gunn and West, whose essays in this volume draw, respectively, on the American literary and religious traditions, to revitalize Dewey's notion of democratic culture and to avoid the Weber-Bell-Rorty combination of private romaticism with social engineering. Gunn draws upon Dewey's *Art and Experience*, while West's essay is infused with the spirit of Dewey's *The Public and Its Problems*, *Liberalism and Social Action*, and *A Common Faith*. The question that remains to be addressed is whether viable versions of postmodernist pragmatism can build upon the democratic ideas of Dewey and avoid what Rorty preserves from cold war liberalism.

NOTES

1. In the important postscript to the second edition of his 1962 book, Kuhn says that he had been a hermeneut all along, rather in the sense of Moliere's bourgeois gentleman, who discovers he has been speaking prose all his life. See T. S. Kuhn, *The Structure of Scientific Revolutions*, 2nd ed. (Chicago: University of Chicago Press, 1970).

2. Richard Rorty, *Consequences of Pragmatism: Essays 1972–1980* (Minneapolis: University of Minnesota Press, 1982), xliii.

3. Richard Rorty, "Method, Social Science, and Social Hope," in *Consequences*, 191–210. See also Richard Rorty, "A Reply to Dreyfus and Taylor," *Review of Metaphysics* 24 (1980): 39–55.

4. Richard Rorty, "Pragmatism, Relativism, Irrationalism," in *Consequences*, 165.

5. Richard Rorty, *Contingency, Irony, and Solidarity* (Cambridge: Cambridge University Press, 1989), 11.

6. Rorty "Pragmatism, Relativism, Irrationalism, 163.

7. Rorty says that Davidson's argument is "a transcendental argument to end all transcendental arguments" in "Transcendental Arguments, Self-Reference and Pragmatism," in *Transcendental Arguments and Science*, ed. P. Bieri, R. Horstmann, and L. Kruger (Dordrecht: D. Reidel, 1979), 78. In the Introduction to *Contingency*, he seems to give a more pragmatic defense of Davidson's semantics.

8. Rorty, *Contingency*, 14.

9. Donald Davidson, "A Nice Derangement of Epitaphs," in *Truth and Interpretation: Perspectives on the Philosophy of Donald Davidson*, ed. E. Lepore (Oxford: Oxford University Press, 1986), 446.

10. Donald Davidson, "A Coherence Theory of Truth and Knowledge," in Lepore, ed., *Truth and Interpretation*, 319.

11. Ibid.

12. Davidson, "A Coherence Theory," 314–18. Davidson aims this claim against Quine's form of behaviorism: "Quine makes interpretation depend on patterns of sensory stimulation, while I make it depend on the external *events* and *objects* the sentence is interpreted as being about."

13. Donald Davidson, "Reasons, Actions and Causes," in Davidson, *Essays on Actions and Events* (Oxford: Oxford University Press, 1980), 31–49.

14. Richard Rorty, "The World Well Lost," in *Consequences*, 3–18.

15. Davidson, "Derangement," 433–46.

16. Richard Rorty, "Method, Social Science, and Social Hope," in *Consequences*, 207.

17. Richard Rorty, "Solidarity and Objectivity," in J. Rajchman and C. West, *Post-Analytic Philosophy* (New York: Columbia University Press, 1985), 16.

18. Konstantin Kolenda, *Rorty's Humanistic Pragmatism: Philosophy Democratized* (Gainesville: University Presses of Florida, 1990), 14.

19. On this period in pragmatism's genealogy, see Cornel West, *The American Evasion of Philosophy: A Genealogy of Pragmatism* (Madison: University of Wisconsin Press, 1989).

20. R. Bernstein, *Praxis and Action* (Philadelphia: University of Pennsylvania Press, 1983). See also R. Bernstein, "Dewey, Democracy: The Task Ahead of Us," in Rajchman and West, *Post-Analytic Philosophy*, 48–58.

21. For an able treatment of this criticism of Rorty, see Nancy Fraser, "Solidarity or Singularity: Richard Rorty Between Romanticism and Technocracy," in *Reading Rorty*, ed. A. Malachowski (Cambridge: Basil Blackwell, 1990), 303–21.

22. Larry A. Hickman, *John Dewey's Pragmatic Technology* (Bloomington: Indiana University Press, 1990) argues vigorously against interpreting Dewey as a scientistic technocrat.

23. See Rorty, *Contingency*, 92–95.

12

American Pragmatism and the Humanist Tradition

Konstantin Kolenda

THE PRIVATE/PUBLIC DISTINCTION

To understand a tradition is to examine its origins and its present state. Starting at the beginning, we see a tradition as it was in its infancy; looking at its present shape, we can notice how it became transformed. As Aristotle noted, we learn what a thing is by watching what it becomes. Following this clue, we may get a better sense of what humanism is by examining its present form and then considering the forces that helped to shape it.

The humanist tradition is very much alive in the version recently articulated in Richard Rorty's pragmatism. That version includes a recommendation that we make a firm distinction between the private and the public components of human lives.[1] Rorty's reasons for this recommendation are complex and are connected with his broad criticism of the epistemological bias in our entire philosophical tradition. By exposing the incoherence of the idea that thought and language mirror or correspond to reality, he has alerted us to the importance of human interests and creative thought in constructing our concepts of reality.

Rorty's critique of epistemology reaches deep into our intellectual past. He suspects that "foundational" philosophical doctrines that purported to announce *the* truth about reality were in fact ingenious imaginative constructs of the human mind. Each of them provided a perspective from which some important phenomena could be usefully or illuminatingly viewed, but none of them lived up to the (impossible) dream of capturing "the thing-in-itself" or reality as such. The purported disclosures about the essence of reality or of human nature were also given practical applications: they were often thought to provide a foundation for social and political structures. Since many of such "foundational" beliefs comported well with desirable human goals, philosophical doctrines—in religious or metaphysical garb—greatly benefited humanity's efforts to organize its social structures around the ideals of justice, equality, and respect for human dignity. Thus, Plato's vision of Forms helped him to defend the moral and political ideals of *The Republic*; Augustine's projection of the City of God aided in formulating the ordering and the values of the Middle Ages; and Locke's proclamation of natural rights, enthusiastically embraced by the Enlightenment, helped to bring into existence modern liberal democracies. But it is also the case that the appeal to metaphysical or religious foundations often proved oppressive and inimical to human freedom, especially the freedom to question the believability of doctrines and arguments on which political structures were based. Thus Plato was perceived by the critics of his metaphysics as an enemy of the open society, the medieval order was criticized for its authoritarianism, and the liberal democracies were blamed for spawning possessive and narcissistic individualism.

This is where Rorty's advocacy of separating the private from the public comes in. He recommends such a separation because by making it we can avoid a premature and unwarranted application of philosophical ideas to political action. Such ideas may provide plausible pictures of how the world may be viewed, but they can become problematic when one expects them to deliver practical answers on public issues. Rorty finds this to be clearly the case with regard to philosophies formulated by Nietzsche and Heidegger. Neither of them has anything helpful to say about social and political issues. In fairness to Nietzsche, it should be noted that he regarded his writings as aiming only at individuals, as an aid to their own personal reflection.[2] The intensely debated question about Heidegger's work is whether he thought of his philosophy, especially of such key concepts as Being and Dasein, as having political consequences. Are they to be understood as having been formulated in the light of his idiosyncratic views about the political and cultural circumstances of his place and time, or are these views separable from, and do they not essentially affect, his philosophical ruminations? With regard to this question, Rorty thinks that, although a brilliant philosopher, in political matters Heidegger was a "Schwarzwald redneck."[3]

What is problematic and dangerous about a carryover from private reflection to public application is that it tempts the proponents to regard their political views as expressing the Truth about Reality As Such, that they are universally valid for all times and places. The danger consists in the tacit claim that the particular practical application has the *authority* of Reality Itself. This danger is avoided if one views philosophical reflection as experiments in thought. The results of such experiments may be cherished for providing perspectives that look attractive and illuminating, but they may have no plausible implications for social or political action. The capacity of philosophy to produce intellectual delight was well expressed by the British philosopher F.C.S. Schiller, who called himself a "humanistic pragmatist." "Does not every page of every philosophic history teem with illustrations that a philosophic system is a unique and personal achievement of which not even the servilest discipleship can transfuse the full flavor into another's soul? Why should we therefore blind ourselves to the invincible individuality of philosophy, and deny each other the precious right to behold reality at the peculiar angle whence he sees it?"[4] Philosophical reflection may provide us with a "final vocabulary" in terms of which we are inclined to formulate our "ultimate" views, believing them to be better, more convincing than all other alternatives. But a private satisfaction derived from such reflective conclusions does not necessarily guarantee that they will be equally convincing to others, especially to those with a different cultural, social, and intellectual history. It is, therefore, questionable and unwarranted to recommend the creation of institutions and the initiation of public action in terms of such privately held "ultimate" views.

The vocabularies in which people prefer to describe themselves will no doubt appear important to them; they are likely to resist someone else's redescriptions of them, that is, redescriptions couched in other "final vocabularies." Because one has projected so much of one's experience into one's self-image, an alternative vocabulary, devised by someone else, with a different cultural and intellectual background, may look humiliating. As Rorty puts it, people do not like to be redescribed. "They want to be taken on their own terms—taken seriously just as they are and just as they talk."[5] To be told that the language they speak is optional has something potentially cruel about it. It is a mark of humaneness not to indulge in cruelty and humiliation. That is why Rorty recommends a separation of the private sphere from the public; that recommendation is motivated by a respect for people's desire to formulate for themselves the beliefs that make sense to them. That respect always constituted an important part of the humanistic ideal.

THE HUMANISM OF PRAGMATISM

The private/public distinction is congenial to pragmatism because it suspects that the project to discover the Essential Nature of Reality is an incoherent dream. The originality of American pragmatists lies in their attempts to articulate plausible alternatives to all forms of essentialism or foundationalism. In these projects, the crucial pragmatic move is to connect the concept of knowledge to the concepts of human action, expectation, and prediction. Having abandoned the project of *copying* reality, pragmatism brings to the fore the notion of *coping*, because that notion conjoins knowledge, action, and hope.[6] The key motivating thought is the assumption that the only way in which the nature of things is accessible to us is through their effects on our perceptions and subsequent behavior, including its linguistic components. It is not surprising, therefore, that our concepts reflect our human interests. Echoing the leitmotif of American pragmatism, Ludwig Wittgenstein declared: "Concepts lead us to make investigations; are the expression of our interest and direct our interest."[7]

To connect knowledge with human capacities and interests is not to demote knowledge from some allegedly superior, humanity-transcending status; on the contrary, it is to acknowledge and exploit its inescapably anthropomorphic origins and goals. When language acquires a shareable and communicable use, the speakers are entitled to claim access to knowledge governing the particular realm of phenomena captured in that language. This realistic understanding of what language consists of undercuts the delusive dream of "perennial philosophy" to create a "supervocabulary" transcending human experience. The delusion is tellingly captured in Wittgenstein's comment on his own failed attempt to attain, in his early philosophy, a "crystalline purity" of language. "We have got on to slippery ice where there is no friction and so in a certain sense the conditions are ideal, but also, just because of that, we are unable to walk. We want to walk: so we need *friction*. Back to the rough ground!"[8]

Dewey's instrumentalism views knowledge as arising from the organism's interaction with the environment. The function of intelligence for him is "not that of copying the objects of the environment, but rather a taking account of the way in which more effective and more profitable relations with these objects may be established in the future."[9] Propositions are not something merely entertained by the mind; they enter effectively into reconstructing and transforming the objective situation: "the proposition is itself a factor in the completion of the situation, in carrying it forward to its conclusion." Dewey does not deny that there is a causal element in our sensations and perceptions, but the meaning of what is "given" to us in experience can be captured only in the way it is "taken," that is, in articulating by means of language further connections to which it calls attention.

Dewey's view is a development of the pragmatic theory of his predecessor, William James. James also emphasized that in our contact with "fixed elements of reality," "we still have a certain freedom in our dealings with them." There is no denying *that* sensations are beyond our control, "but *which* we attend to, note, and make emphatic in our conclusions depends on our own interests. . . . What we say about reality thus depends on the perspective into which we throw it. The *that* of it is its own; but the *what* depends on the *which*; and the which depends on *us*. Both the sensational and the relational parts of reality are dumb; they say absolutely nothing about themselves. We it is who must speak for them."[10] James makes this point in the context of agreeing with F.C.S. Schiller, who equated pragmatism with humanism by claiming that the world is essentially what we make it. James puts this point a bit more cautiously: "Human motives sharpen all our questions, human satisfactions lurk in all our answers, all our formulas have a human twist."[11] But both agree that reality is "plastic," that what we say about it has been "peptonized and cooked for our consumption" by previous human thinking.[12] "Our nouns and adjectives are all humanized heirlooms, and in the theories we build them into, the inner order and arrangement is wholly dictated by human considerations, intellectual consistency being one of them."[13]

James and Dewey acknowledged their indebtedness to Charles Sanders Peirce as the initiator of the pragmatic analysis of meaning. That analysis received a succinct formulation in Peirce's famous "pragmatic maxim": "Consider what effects which might conceivably have practical bearings, we conceive the object of our conception to have. Then, our conception of these effects is the whole of our conception of the object."[14] Peirce believed this maxim to be but a special case of his theory of signs. Every word is a sign to be interpreted in terms of other signs; its meaning is its interpretation, and there are no "incognizables," that is, uninterpretable, intuitively and directly grasped signs. What a sign or a word means is shown in the linguistic practice of a community. "All thinking is in signs," he declared, and he argued that interpretation of signs shows how language enters and organizes human practice. As constant interpreters of signs, human beings are themselves signs. "The word or sign which man uses *is* man himself," and that's why "my language is the sum total of myself."[15] These Peircian claims come close to Wittgenstein's later observation that language is a form of life. That form cannot be other than human, but Peirce did not think that the imputation of anthropocentrism can be taken as criticism, because knowledge *is* a human form of coping with experience. If there is an alternative to that form, its description would require a specification of that alternative. We admit this to be the case when, in trying to envisage such forms, either in religion or in science fiction, we unavoidably humanize or anthropomorphize them.[16]

Does the private/public distinction enter the thought of classical pragmatists? It does so in an emphatic way, even though, not surprisingly, the emphasis is in each case different. Dewey regarded individuals as reconstructive centers of society, and his recommended reforms aimed at enlarging opportunities for the flourishing of individuals. One of his key objections to the economic arrangements of his time was that they tended to bring into existence "the lost individual." Using this phrase as a chapter title in his book, *Individualism Old and New*, he complained that "the development of a civilization that is outwardly corporate—or rapidly becoming so—has been accompanied by a submergence of the individual."[17] Believing that business cannot avoid being involved in some form of socialism, he distinguished between capitalistic and public socialism. He faulted the former for being motivated by pecuniary profit and wanting to keep individualism alive in order to serve its own ends, but he endorsed the latter for wanting to remake society so that it may "serve the growth of a new type of individual."[18]

Dewey was skeptical of "any all-embracing system or program,"[19] because it would make it impossible to develop integrated individuality. "For individuality is inexpugnable and it is of its nature to assert itself. The first move in recovery of an integrated individual is accordingly with the individual himself. In whatever occupation he finds himself, he is himself and no other, and he lives in situations that are in some respect flexible and plastic.''[20] The constantly changing conditions require selective choices that have to be continually made and remade, requiring a distinctly felt preferential bias in reacting to the impacts of the world. Responsible individuals will keep any program of ends and methods from becoming fixed and rigid. In embracing what he called "liberal humanism" Dewey was prepared to make use of a slogan made famous by Voltaire, a champion of Enlightenment humanism. "To gain an integrated individuality, each of us needs to cultivate his own garden. But there is no fence about this garden: it is no sharply marked-off enclosure. Our garden is the world, in the angle at which it touches our own manner of being. By accepting the corporate and industrial world in which we live, and by thus fulfilling the precondition for interaction with it, we, who are parts of the moving present, create ourselves as we create an unknown future.''[21]

Since Dewey directed his philosophically persuasive powers to the circumstances of his time—the need to create democratically structured conditions for the advancement of the individual in a corporation-dominated society—it is not surprising that he focused on the public dimension of life. That focus was nevertheless balanced by his writings on art and religion, in which he recognized the central importance of "consummatory" experiences and the desirability of reflection on the ideal possibilities of humanity. These themes, explored in *Art as Experience* and in *A Common Faith*, clearly express the spirit of the humanistic tradition. Writing in a different historical and intellectual context, William James put a greater emphasis on the private, personal dimension. Concerned that modern science and its burgeoning technological applications appeared to have a materialistic bias, thus undercutting "tender-minded" needs of the human spirit, James endeavored to make his pragmatism serve the individual right (or will) to shape a personal perspective, religious or philosophical. This explains his desire to represent human aspirations as possibly connected to higher powers, even though that connection had to be sought in *varieties* of religious experience, the credibility of which is a private matter and is to be judged by individuals themselves.

James believed that morality is strengthened, its mood becomes more "strenuous," when it is seen as expressing the will of God, admittedly unascertainable and vague. Whether God exists or not, however, is not of great importance to a pragmatist. What is important is to form "an ethical republic here below." " 'The religion of humanity' affords a basis for ethics as well as theism does.''[22] A religious belief simply provides "a pretext for living hard, and getting out of the game of existence its keenest possibilities of zest.''[23] James encourages individuals to formulate their own private conceptions of what significance human existence may ultimately have, using as the only measure of the belief's validity its consequences for living. A genuine pragmatist "is willing to pay with his own person, if need be, for the realization of the ideals which he frames.''[24] The type of religion James's pragmatism advocates can be, as he says, pluralistic or merely melioristic. "But whether you will finally put up with that type of religion or not is a question that only you yourself can decide."[25]

James's claim that "religion is susceptible of reasoned defence" flows from his general pragmatic epistemology, according to which knowledge is transactional in character. Although an object of knowledge is numerically distinct from its knower, "if the talker be a humanist, he must also see this distance-interval concretely and pragmatically, and confess it to consist of other intervening experiences—of possible ones, at all events, if not actual."[26] A plausible way of interpreting this claim would be to treat "intervening experiences" as statable in further propositions applicable to the object in question, thus indicating that our access to reality is never unmediated but requires linguistic articulation. Such an interpretation comports well with what James says about his notion of God. "I myself read humanism theistically and pluralistically." He views God not as an "absolute all-experiencer, but simply the experiencer of widest actual conscious span."[27] This view is distinctly humanistic inasmuch as it does not embrace supernaturalism. Consider what James says in *The Varieties of Religious Experience* about "the higher part" of a believing individual: "He becomes conscious that this higher part is conterminous and continuous with a MORE of the same quality, which is operative in the universe outside of him, and which he can keep in working touch with, and in a fashion get on board of and save himself when all his lower being has gone to pieces in the wreck."[28] Notice that the MORE does not exist apart from the universe but is "operative" in it. As Dewey later argued in *A Common Faith*, the locus of this MORE may be found in the operation of human ideals, which always transcend what is actual, without requiring a supernatural status.

A pragmatic interpretation of ideals acknowledges their connection with will and freedom. To be more than wishes or inclinations, ideas must appeal to the free exercise of will. "The *fons et origo* of all reality, whether from the absolute or the practical point of view, is thus subjective, is ourselves. But, as thinkers with emotional reaction, we give what seems to us a still higher degree of reality to whatever things we select and turn to *with a will*."[29] In elaborating his Pragmatic Rule, according to which the truth of an idea is determined by the difference it makes in experience, James sometimes gives it a highly individualistic interpretation, allowing that difference to be applicable only to "some possible person's history."[30] He also claims that where a situation is objectively indeterminate, a person's free choice can determine the outcome, thus *making* some possibility true. This is the way James proposes to solve some metaphysical questions, for instance, whether it is rational to believe in the freedom of the will. One must ask oneself how the belief fits into one's experience, whether it makes that experience more satisfactory. According to James, nothing in the universe can deny a person the right to believe under such conditions.

This highly individualistic note in James's pragmatic humanism bothered his mentor C. S. Peirce. Like Dewey after him, Peirce thought of truth as determinable by a *community* of inquirers; truth is a matter for public, not private, determination. Some scholars argue that Peirce's philosophy lacks the principle of individuation or that the notion of the individual was for him at least a serious embarrassment.[31] He does say explicitly that individuals are but cells in a social organism.[32] But Peirce's position is more complex than such occasional pronouncements seem to indicate. It emerges more fully when we take with equal seriousness other components of his philosophical system.

That system is undergirded by, and always presupposes, his phenomenological doctrine of the categories: Firstness, Secondness, and Thirdness. The use of signs or language is a manifestation of Thirdness, but any *actual* manifestation of Thirdness (Secondness) has also a certain *spontaneous* character (Firstness). One consequence of this is that to intellectual activity three kinds of norms are applicable: logical, ethical, and aesthetic. In problematic situations especially, a reflection on all applicable norms is required. Since in Peirce's system aesthetics is understood as applicable not just to art but to anything that is "admirable in itself," the really creative and innovating moments of inquiry require the highest degree of self-control; the individual engaged in an investigation is responsible for its outcome. Peirce insisted on supplementing the traditional forms of reasoning—deduction and induction—by a third form, which he called abduction or hypothesis. "An Abduction is Originary in respect to being the only kind of argument that starts a new idea."[33] It is a "process of forming an explanatory hypothesis."[34] Hypothesis-formation is an indispensable step in making intellectual progress. Hypotheses are "guesses at the riddle" or leaps of the mind, not determined by the already available data. Since their background is already intellectual, namely, the inquirer's grasp of all applicable laws, rules, and principles (Thirdness), the formation of new hypotheses, by means of which science advances, is an instance of rationality in operation (Thirdness of Thirdness).[35]

Given this general view about the way our beliefs are formed, it is not surprising that Peirce, like James, has his own private brand of religion. For him, the notion of God is a supreme guess at the riddle, and he produces a "neglected argument" for God's reality understood as the locus of the convergence of truth, goodness, and beauty as envisaged by a "muser" while surveying all already established knowledge about the universe. Here is Peirce's account of his religious experience: "in the Pure Play of Musement the idea of God's reality will be sure sooner or later to be found an attractive fancy, which the Muser will develop in various ways. The more he ponders it, the more it will find response in every part of his mind, for its beauty, for its supplying an ideal of life, and for its thoroughly satisfactory explanation of his whole threefold environment."[36] This autobiographical confession would deserve inclusion in James's *Varieties*. It purportedly represents Peirce's boldest, most comprehensive hypothesis, and it leaves room for less comprehensive, limited original hypotheses or abductions that may be produced by individual inquirers into still unexplored areas of human experience. All of Peirce's philosophy is a ringing endorsement of and propaganda for such a humanistic and admittedly anthropomorphic endeavor, to be spearheaded by individuals and subsequently subjected to confirmation by the community.

THE HUMANISM OF MODERNISM

Ralph Waldo Emerson is often recognized as a precursor of pragmatism. John Dewey proclaimed him to be the Philosopher of Democracy and credited him with "restoring to the common man that which in the name of religion, of philosophy, of art, and of morality has been embezzled from the common store and appropriated to sectarian and class use."[37] Oliver Wendell Holmes called Emerson's essay, *The American Scholar*, a "National Intellectual Declaration of Independence." That famous essay celebrated "the new importance given to the single person" and struck another blow for humanism by declaring the world, in comparison with humanity, to be nothing; "in yourself is the law of all nature," "in yourself slumbers the whole of Reason; it is for you to know all, it is for you to dare all."[38] Most recently, Cornel West argued that Emerson prefigured the dominant themes of pragmatism: individuality, idealism, voluntarism, optimism, amelioration, and experimentation. In all his writings and sermons Emerson aimed to promote self-reliance, "vast-flowing vigor," and personal fulfillment. As West puts it, "the aim of Emersonian provocation is to subjectify and humanize unique individuals."[39]

The forward-looking and optimistic thrust of pragmatism is also prefigured in the ideals of the Enlightenment that provided the foundation for American democracy. It is no accident that pursuit of happiness appears alongside life and liberty in the Declaration of Independence. As historians have noted, happiness was the obsession of the Age of Enlightenment. That age is the culmination of the process that, beginning with the Renaissance, turned humanity away from its preoccupation with the ecclesiastically supervised supernatural and directed it toward the multiple task of explaining and exploring nature for the benefit of ever-improving human generations. "From *this* earth stem my joys," proclaims Goethe's Faust, a quintessential Renaissance man. Goethe echoes and amplifies the sentiment expressed by Pico della Mirandola, who, writing in the fifteenth century, still wanted to preserve allegiance to the supernatural, while shifting attention to the liberation of human powers. "We have set thee at the world's center that thou mayest from thence more easily observe whatever is in the world and mayest fashion thyself in whatever shape thou shalt prefer."[40]

Humanism as a broad tendency, a set of presuppositions that assigns to human beings a special position in the scheme of things, is clearly at work in American pragmatism. Its intellectual sources, derived from the Enlightenment thinking and from modern science, are in debt to the Renaissance and also to *its* ancient classical sources. The word "humanism" came into general use only in the nineteenth century but is applicable to intellectual and cultural developments that took place in previous eras. A teacher of classical languages and literatures in Renaissance Italy was described as *umanista* (contrasted with *legista*, who taught law), and what we today call "the humanities" stood for a group of subjects: grammar, rhetoric, history, literature, and moral philosophy. The inspiration for these studies came from the rediscovery (rebirth, revival) of Greek and Latin texts; Plato's complete works were translated for the first time, and Aristotle's philosophy was studied in more accurate versions than those available during the Middle Ages.

The unashamedly humanistic flavor of classical writings had a tremendous impact on Renaissance scholars. Here, one felt no weight of the supernatural pressing at all points on the human mind, demanding homage and allegiance. Humanity was seen as the center of interest—distinct human capacities, talents, worries, problems, possibilities. It has been said that medieval man philosophized on his knees, but the new studies dared man to stand up and to rise to full stature. Instead of devotional Church Latin, the medium of expression was the people's own language—Italian, French, German, English. Poetical lyrical self-expression gained momentum, affecting all areas of life. New painting showed great interest in human form. Even while depicting religious scenes. Michelangelo celebrated the human body, investing it with intrinsic value and dignity. The details of daily life—food, clothing, musical instruments, nature, and landscape—domestic and exotic—were lovingly examined in painting and poetry. The imagination was stirred by stories brought home by the discoverers of new lands and continents, enlarging the scope of human possibilities in the customs and the natural environments of strange, remote peoples.

The humanist mode of thinking deepened and enlarged its tradition with the advent of eighteenth-century thinkers. They include French *philosophes*—Voltaire, Diderot, Rousseau, and other European and American figures—Hume, Bentham, Lessing, Kant, Franklin, and Jefferson. Not always agreeing with each other, these modern thinkers nevertheless formed a family united in support of such values as freedom, equality, tolerance, secularism, and cosmopolitanism. They championed untrammeled use of the mind and wanted it to be put to use in social and political reform as well, encouraging individual creativity and exalting the active over contemplative life. They believed in the perfectibility of human nature, innate moral sense, rational and responsible use of freedom, and the possibility of progress.

SOCRATES: THE HERO OF HUMANISM

As we have seen, modern humanistic themes are incorporated into American pragmatism. In their turn, the Renaissance, the Enlightenment, and the nineteenth- and twentieth-century "process philosophies," spearheaded by Hegel's historicism and stimulated by Darwin's theory of evolution, picked up ancient classical themes. A slogan that encapsulates all these themes was coined by Protagoras: "Man is the measure of all things." That slogan calls attention to the task that the thinkers of ancient Greece set for themselves: to make the world intelligible to the human mind and amenable to the satisfaction of human interests. The speculative and scientific ventures stemming from this project soon became cognizant of their own inherent revisability, as manifested in the ensuing rivalry and contest among concepts, principles, and doctrines existing side by side or rapidly succeeding one another. The intensity and the seeming irresolvability of proposed perspectives and theories from time to time gave rise to dispiriting moods of skepticism, sophism, and relativism.

But the Greeks also produced a thinker who believed to have discovered an effective antidote to such moods. That thinker was Socrates. He warned against what he called misology, distrust of human reason; repeatedly disappointed, people may give up on efforts to come up with credible explanations of the world and of our place in it. What Socrates envisaged and promoted was not a search for one ultimate vision valid for all times and places—a vision that had an irresistible grip on his pupil, Plato—but only an endless quest for improving one's mind through a continuing conversation with others. This is the heart of the Socratic "method." It is not a method in the sense of providing a definite set of rules of how and about what one should carry on conversations. To call this method "dialectical" is to do no more than to indicate that always a new move—contradictory, revisionary, hermeneutic, or "edifying"—could be made either by one's interlocutors or by oneself on further reflection. That the word "dialectic" in the minds of future thinkers, such as Hegel or Marx, could be transformed into the dialectic of spirit or matter or history, only testifies to its being a most general term for continuing indefinitely the process of inquiry, exploration, and interpretation. This is the most important legacy Socrates bequeathed to future philosophizing.

Socrates's interest in philosophical inquiry was primarily moral, not metaphysical. It was Plato who steered his teacher's ideas in the direction of metaphysics. Plato was the one who converted Socrates's attempts to "examine life" into a search for Reality's Own Language, which he proceeded to lodge in the World of Forms, thus giving rise to an unending wave of Platonists, religious and secular. Socrates was a humanist in the sense that he expected from philosophy help in solving human practical problems, while Plato was a metaphysician who aimed at disclosing the timeless, eternal Truth. It is plausible to view American pragmatism as a return to the Socratic project: to examine the ways in which life may be worth living, both in the public and the private arenas. The intervening centuries, of course, have accumulated a great wealth of information, knowledge, models, paradigms, techniques and methods that can be taken into account in addressing oneself to practical issues. In virtue of this accumulation alone, the intellectual enterprise and its applications have become much more complex than could be dreamt of in Socrates's time. But the shift recommended by pragmatism still honors the Socratic focus: "Know thyself." To do full justice to this project, we need to take seriously Rorty's claim that it calls for a separation between the private and the public.

Socrates himself made this separation when he insisted that he should not be punished by the state for carrying on his investigations of matters "under the earth'' or in the realm of divinities. On the contrary, he believed that such private explorations by individuals in the long run would benefit society. He insisted on the right of citizens to engage in such freely conceived and openly pursued ventures of the mind. Since participation in such activities is voluntary, the beliefs that emerge from them are arrived at by persuasion and not by force. It is precisely this freedom of the mind that constitutes the most precious possession of humanity, and Socrates dramatized its importance by the way he conducted his life and faced his death. When he pleaded with his friends not to accept any principle or any conclusion unless and until they can judge it to be best, he pointed to the same value that centuries later Jefferson wanted to preserve when he warned against a public order that would sanction the ''tyranny over the mind.'' A similar warning is contained in Peirce's injunction, ''Do not block the road to inquiry!'' and in his dismissal of merely ''vital,'' proximate topics in favor of long-range intellectual adventures. In his lecture at Harvard University, Peirce opined that fashionable, ''vitally important topics are of all truths the veriest trifles.''[41] The invitation to embark on one's own independent path is also contained in James's invocation of the right to believe when there are no objective, public criteria to adjudicate one way or another a momentous matter.

Socrates's celebrated case is a perfect example of what is at stake when the private/public distinction is pondered. Rorty advocates that we keep the two areas separate, because of the conviction that a free, unimpeded, and uncensored reflection on life makes it possible for us to redescribe some aspects of it as a result of such a reflection. Socrates is a fitting model here, for it is quite correct to say that what emerged from his conversations with his friends was a redescription of their fellow Athenians, of their beliefs and practices. The intellectual activity carried on during walks in the gardens, in the market place, or in private homes contained elements of what in our times is carried out in the educational institutions and in the media. Socrates believed that everyone benefits from keeping this activity free, the way modern democratic societies benefit from the freedom of the press and from the wide-ranging pursuits of autonomous universities.

Socrates was aware of the temptation to generalize from one area to others. He pointed out the tendency of people to regard themselves competent in all areas of life just because they are competent in one; a politician may believe himself qualified to govern people just because he is good at training horses. This is one reason why Socrates's rhetorical and argumentative skills were often perceived by important political figures as a threat to their positions. When confusions and contradictions in your statement are exposed to view, you are likely to feel humiliated. That's why Meletus was irritated when during the trial Socrates pointed out the incoherence of accusations made against him by Meletus and Anytus. Unable to distinguish between his general philosophical quest and his criticism of politicians, the Athenian court sided with the accusers. Only by failing to see the distinction could they punish him for "undermining the state," of which he was accused, self-servingly, by those who held power.

It must be admitted that the two activities—raising general questions about principles and criticizing actual performance—are sometimes difficult to keep apart. Philosophical reflection on what constitutes competence, for instance, *may* have implications for what is actually going on in the public arena. But the mere raising of the question does not amount to a *political* act of questioning the competence of those in power. Furthermore, even if Socrates were to criticize explicitly any particular politician, he would be exercising this right as a citizen of a democratic state. However, this is not, he insisted, what he was doing when he extolled the virtues of an "examined life." His "gadfly" activity, admonishing the sluggish horse to bestir itself, was directed at *everyone*. Socrates urged people to be concerned about their souls, whatever their status in public or in private life. He did so in the conviction that if *individuals* change their lives, the society as a whole will be improved. In this way Socrates defended private philosophical reflection-*cum*-conversation as an activity which, by keeping individual minds alert and open to new ideas, created favorable conditions for maintaining a healthy society. When he predicted that future generations would condemn the verdict against him, he expressed confidence that his redescriptions of desirable practices for the Athenian society would eventually find general acceptance. But his contemporaries misinterpreted his general philosophical explorations as an outright attack on the state. By not tolerating private reflection and perceiving it as inevitably undermining public order, they went down in history as enemies of philosophy and of humanism.

PRAGMATISM AND POSTMODERNISM

In turning away from essentialism and foundationalism, pragmatism anticipated the contemporary skepticism about "meta-narratives" as indispensable for orienting ourselves in the world. If modernism is seen as a succession of such "meta-narratives," then their abandonment justifies calling our age "postmodern." That label is now widely used to take note of the proliferation of deconstructive, circumventive, and interpretive strategies that acknowledge the need for inventing fresh metaphors, paradigms, and styles in all areas of intellectual and cultural activity. For some critics, this ferment has the alarming earmarks of anarchism, nihilism, or sophism. Whether these fears are justified is an open question, but since this multifaceted pluralism looks to many observers as disconcerting and bewildering, some response to it is called for.

Pragmatism proposes a solution: take the private/public distinction seriously. Since the "postmodern condition" not only affects philosophers and other intellectuals but invades all other areas of culture, the distinction should be acknowledged and respected in all of them. The question to ask in each case is: Does a given "final vocabulary" favored by an individual or a group harm or endanger or humiliate those who prefer a different vocabulary? If the answer is no, if it makes no difference to the mutually acknowledged desire to live with others in peace and harmony, the coexistence of alternative beliefs or schemes of thought is not a drawback but an advantage.

A person's final vocabulary has many sources. A few are derived from a sustained and organized reflection, utilizing the accumulated scientific, philosophical, or literary heritage. Some, embracing large numbers of people, are located in specific religious traditions and practices. Others are found in particular traditions celebrating their cultural, national, or ethnic roots. In many cases, the sources are mixed; in deciding what to think about themselves and their place in the world, people draw to some extent on fragments of all the available resources. Furthermore, the values of one's immediate cultural or religious community, initially seen as worthy of acceptance and allegiance, may undergo modifications and revisions as one becomes aware of alternatives. Viewing our planet over a span of time, a Martian would be impressed both by the great variety of final vocabularies by which human groups describe themselves and by the increasing speed with which these vocabularies have been changing in our postmodern period.

By preserving the distinction between the public and the private spheres of life, pragmatism acknowledges the right of every person to resist any "totalizing narrative" that purports to be valid for everyone because it allegedly tells the final truth about the cosmos, the world, humanity, or language. This resistance lies squarely in the humanistic tradition. Witnessing the ongoing intellectual and cultural ferment—the crisscrossing of philosophies and religions; the revisionism in political and economic doctrines; the steady stream of scientific, technological, and literary inventions—a postmodern mind may find it difficult to remain loyal to any one set of descriptions of oneself and the world. Alive to this difficulty, humanistic pragmatism relegates the enterprise of attempting a comprehensive perspective to private reflection and individual intellectual conscience.

Each self-description can be scrutinized for its public relevance, and in many instances that relevance may be nonexistent. Even when people share a wide range of self-descriptions and see themselves as "us" when contrasted with "them" (i.e., people who prefer a different set of self-descriptions), such differences may have no practical—moral or political—consequences. Sometimes, however, they *may* have such consequences, and then, of course, the "us"-"them" distinction becomes problematic. If people's private beliefs affect adversely the way they use common space, resources, and institutions, the embraced self-descriptions may be a source of trouble. Such self-descriptions can cease being private but may be seen as characterizing an entire group that perceives itself as being oppressed, mistreated, or discriminated against by those who wield power. When this happens, those who regard themselves as victims resent being described by the oppressors in the way that allegedly justifies their victimization. Understandably, they reject the description as unfair and humiliating; it does not fit their self-description. In order to preserve their private self-image, which gives them a sense of personal dignity and self-worth, they may join forces with others who share their self-descriptions and begin to regard them as publicly relevant. Thus, the distinction between the private and the public tends to evaporate; the private is absorbed into the public. Private beliefs are mobilized to serve the common cause of the group, and self-descriptions become politicized.

Political conflicts are harder to resolve when they become ideological, that is, when the focus of debate shifts from specific grievances—unequal pay for women, lack of access to education, jobs, and medical facilities for ethnic minorities—to general beliefs and attitudes of those toward whom those grievances are directed. This is where the private/public distinction would help to defuse antagonisms; instead of irrelevantly focusing on each other's private beliefs, the disputants could turn their attention to the substance of their disagreements. One of the virtues of democracy is that it encourages disputants to seek common good while respecting each other's "ultimate" commitments. If one views democracy as not dependent on any particular religious or philosophical foundation and instead regards it as favoring certain institutions and procedures, then private beliefs of citizens will not stand in the way of living up to the demands of justice and equality under the law.[42] Democracy relies on four key institutions: free elections, independent courts, an unmuzzled press, and autonomous universities. Elections ensure that all citizens and their interests are represented; independent courts see to it that the laws passed are not in conflict with the constitution guaranteeing equal rights for every citizen; the free press provides access to information of interest to the citizenry; and autonomous universities preserve accumulated knowledge and enlarge its extent.

Concerning the philosophical and religious beliefs and cultural preferences of citizens, the institutions and procedures of democracy are neutral. Although its historical origins are European, democracy does not depend on any particular religious or philosophical values, Western or Eastern. Its cosmopolitanism makes it attractive to peoples all over the world. After decades of humanly costly experimenting with the totalitarian "dictatorship of the proletariat," adherents of communism are rediscovering democracy. Its task is to ensure the citizens' safety, compliance with adopted laws, maintenance of public order, and adjudication of disputes concerning the fair way of agreeing upon common objectives. It aims at maintaining conditions under which individuals and groups can pursue their objectives.

These objectives may include a desire to live within a certain religious, ethnic, or cultural tradition. But every living tradition, if its followers are not persecuted, humiliated, or discriminated against by the state or some hostile elements in it, usually displays ferments, creative tensions, projects of reinterpretation and retextualization, revising its past and reformulating its future goals. No viable tradition is blindly proud of its heritage, nor is it unanimously agreed on what it should be like in the future. If it is at all healthy, it will have its debunkers and critics, as well as prophets and visionaries who see alternative options for further change and growth. This means that adherents of such a tradition will project different visions and desiderata, and that such visions may be in conflict with one another. None of them need to gain followers and to achieve public consensus in order to be important and personally satisfying to their originators, who will cherish their tradition precisely because, by enlisting creative participation, it makes room for self-creation. In other words, even within particular traditions there is always a need to maintain the private/public distinction.

What is special about our postmodern world is that it provides unprecedented opportunities for self-revision and self-creation, both on the part of traditions and individuals. The world has become an intellectual and cultural global village, besides being made physically accessible by burgeoning technologies. Communication and information leap across oceans and mountains, exposing people to unheard-of influences. No matter how hard a culture or a nation tries to insulate itself from those influences, it cannot keep them out altogether, because people *want* to be exposed to the new and unfamiliar, in addition to being driven by the basic desire to improve their standard of living. Modernization, although sometimes received with mixed feelings, is reaching the most remote parts of the globe. At the same time, the bringers of new ideas and techniques are not likely to remain untouched by views, values, and practices of the cultures with which they come in contact. It should not be surprising that the very phenomenon of postmodernism, intoxicated with what is new and different, is itself being conditioned by influences that are invading the European traditions from all corners of the world.

Stimuli for innovation and experimentation crisscross the world in all directions, affecting art, science, technology, and politics. Adherents of any cultural or religious tradition at least eavesdrop on this global conversation, picking up suggestions and signals as to how their final vocabularies might be changed in the light of what is being thought or argued or advocated elsewhere. (How else can the demise of the Soviet empire be explained?) Before an idea reaches a public forum of any kind, it first has to take hold of a single individual mind (Gorbachev's?), which must be given a chance to ruminate on it in private before throwing it into the common pot as a possible ingredient of public nutrition. Because the individual human mind serves as a necessary vanguard of any shared project, there are moral and pragmatic reasons for maintaining and respecting the private/public distinction. That distinction is the most important aspect of contemporary humanism.

While recalling the views of the founders of American pragmatism, I have noted that in addition to their analyses of knowledge and inquiry, each of the three thinkers—Peirce, James, and Dewey—supplemented it with a private view of how they understood religion. Following their lead, let me conclude by adding still another, also private, view as to how pragmatism and religion might merge.[43] It is significant, I believe, that most religions represent God as a being who is concerned with performing an *evaluation* of whatever transpires in the world. God is the ultimate and unfailing judge, interested in giving each thing and each being its due. Suspecting that our concept of God is made in human image, we may see in the representation of God as evaluator our own desire to arrive at the correct estimate of the value of phenomena we encounter in our individual experiences. The point of such evaluations, both in the divine and in the human case, is not just to register actions, events, and phenomena impartially and objectively, but also to acknowledge and affirm some of them as *good*. Were God not to make such affirmations, he would not be doing justice to his own creation. And we are told in the Scriptures (2 Genesis) that upon creating the world, God declared it to be very good. Similarly, if we do not engage in the process of affirming, appreciating, and celebrating instances in which our private final vocabulary seems to work, giving us new and valuable insights and flashes of understanding, possibly usable by others as well, we fail to engage in an activity we attribute to the highest being. But if that being is only the work of imagination, as I believe it to be, the function imputed to it is still admirable—and it devolves on us.

NOTES

1. Richard Rorty, *Contingency, Irony, and Solidarity*, (Cambridge: Cambridge University Press, 1989), 92–95.

2. Nietzsche has Zarathustra "speak not to the people but to companions. Zarathustra shall not become the shepherd and dog of a herd. To lure many away from the herd, for that I have come." *Thus Spoke Zarathustra*, Prologue 9, *The Portable Nietzsche*, ed. Walter Kaufmann (New York: Viking, 1954), 135.

3. Richard Rorty, "Taking Philosophy Seriously," review of *Heidegger et le Nazisme*, *New Republic*, April 11, 1988.

4. F.C.S. Schiller, *Humanistic Pragmatism*, Reuben Abel, ed. (New York: Free Press, 1966), 25. Like Rorty, Schiller does not envisage "the end of philosophy." " 'Systems' of philosophy will abound as before, and will be as various as ever. But they will probably be more brilliant in their colouring, and more attractive in their form. For they will certainly have to be put forward, and acknowledged, as works of art that bear the impress of a unique and individual soul" (p. 72).

5. Rorty, *Contingency, Irony, and Solidarity*, 89.

6. Konstantin Kolenda, *Rorty's Humanistic Pragmatism: Philosophy Democratized* (Gainesville: University Presses of Florida, 1990), 22–26.

7. Ludwig Wittgenstein, *Philosophical Investigations*, ed. and trans. E. Anscombe et al. (New York: Macmillan, 1953), Par. 570.

8. Ibid., Par. 107.

9. John Dewey, "The Logic of Judgments of Practice." *Journal of Philosophy*, 1915, reprinted in Amelie Rorty, ed., *Pragmatic Philosophy* (New York: Doubleday, 1966), 234.

10. William James, *The Writings of William James*, ed. John J. McDermott (Chicago: University of Chicago Press, 1977), 452.

11. Ibid., 451.

12. Ibid., 453.

13. Ibid., 455.

14. Charles Sanders Peirce, *Collected Papers of Charles Sanders Peirce*, 8 vols., ed. Charles Hartshorne, Paul Weiss, and Arthur W. Burks (Cambridge, Mass.: Harvard University Press, 1931–1958), 5:402.

15. Ibid., 5:314.

16. " 'Anthropomorphic' is what pretty much all conceptions are at bottom." Peirce, *Collected Papers*, 5:47. See also 5:536.

17. John Dewey, *The Later Works, 1925–1953*, vol. 11 ed. Jo Ann Boydston (Carbondale: Southern Illinois University Press, 1981–1990), 66.

18. Ibid., 80. See also Dewey's statement in "What I Believe" in *I Believe*, ed. Clifton Fadiman (New York: Simon and Schuster, 1939), 347: "I shall now wish to emphasize more than I formerly did that individuals are finally decisive factors of the nature and movement of associated life."

19. Dewey, *Later Works*, 121.

20. Ibid., 120.

21. Ibid., 122–23.

22. *The Writings of William James*, 619.

23. Ibid., 628.

24. Ibid., 471.

25. Ibid., 472.

26. Ibid., 307.

27. Ibid., 306.

28. Ibid., 755.

29. William James, *The Principles of Psychology: The Works of William James*, 2 vols. (New York: Holt, Rinehart, and Winston, 1890), 2:296–97.

30. William James, *Some Problems of Philosophy* (New York: Longmans, Green, 1911), 61.

31. This claim is discussed in my article, "Peirce on Person and Community," in *Person and Community in American Philosophy, Rice University Studies* 66, No. 4 (1980): 15–32.

32. Peirce, "Now You and I—What Are We? Mere Cells of the Social Organism," *Collected Papers*, 1:673.

33. Ibid., 2:96.

34. Ibid., 5:171.

35. See Kolenda, "Peirce on Person and Community," 21–25.

36. Peirce, *Collected Papers*, 6:465.

37. John Dewey, "Ralph Waldo Emerson," in *Character and Events* (New York: Holt Rinehart and Winston, 1929) 1:75.

38. Ralph Waldo Emerson, *The American Scholar: Selected Writings of Ralph Waldo Emerson*, ed. William H. Gilman (New York: New American Library, 1965), 240.

39. Cornel West, *The American Evasion of Philosophy: A Genealogy of Pragmatism* (Madison: University of Wisconsin Press, 1989), 27.

40. Pico della Mirandola, *On the Dignity of Man*, in *The Renaissance Philosophy of Man*, ed. Ernst Cassirer, P. O. Kristeller, and J. H. Randall, (Chicago: University of Chicago Press, 1948), 225.

41. Peirce, *Collected Papers*, 1:673.

42. The desirability of keeping democracy free of antecedent philosophical commitments is defended by Rorty in his essay "Priority of Democracy to Philosophy," in *Virginia Statute for Religious Freedom*, ed. Merrill D. Patterson and Robert C. Vaughan (Cambridge: Cambridge University Press, 1988).

43. Such a merger, resting on the claim that central religious concepts are derived from common human experience, is attempted in my *Cosmic Religion: An Autobiography of the Universe* (Prospect Heights, Ill.: Waveland Press, 1987). The disadvantages of maintaining the separation are also explored in my "Problems with Transcendence," in *God, Values, and Empiricism*, ed. Creighton Peden and Larry E. Axel (Mercer, Ga.: Mercer University Press, 1989).

13

Postmodern Pragmatism: Nietzsche, Heidegger, Derrida, and Rorty

Bernd Magnus

"When 'I raise my arm' my arm goes up. . . . What is left over if I subtract the fact that my arm goes up from the fact that I raise my arm?"
—L. Wittgenstein, *Philosophical Investigations* #621

Four decades ago a philosophical movement—"existentialism"—crossed the Atlantic Ocean from French and German shores causing widespread confusion, consternation, and anxiety among intellectuals, at least initially. Discussions, screeds, and hostile commentaries often preceded translations of the original German and French texts that were to be located in philosophic space, the very texts that were the presumed causes for concern and alarm. Condemnations often preceded commentaries. For example, a respected New York philosopher, while reviewing as late as 1962 the English-language translation of a book that had been published in Germany thirty-five years earlier, was able to write that there are three kinds of nonsense—"simple nonsense," "interesting nonsense," and "vicious nonsense"—and to assure his readers that "interesting nonsense this is not," thereby leaving it to his reader to decide whether it was simple or vicious nonsense that was under review. Sidney Hook went on, in that same *New York Times* Sunday book review, to characterize and to dismiss the book that is my object lesson here—Heidegger's *Being and Time*—as the work of a self-hating and other-hating ego.

"Existentialism" was as much reviled as it was admired four decades ago, but it was seldom understood initially. It quickly became a cultural force in this country associated in the popular mind (with equal silliness) with turtleneck sweaters and the Beat Generation.

Some of us who are interested in postmodernism are experiencing *déjà vu*. To be sure, time, context, and details are different. Nevertheless, we have once again a "foreign" import threatening to corrupt the Anglophone Way, and charges of relativism and nihilism often drown out the equally exaggerated claims of many ardent admirers who often find in the latest Parisian intellectual fashion a label to justify their discontent over real or imagined injuries as well as real or imagined shortcomings of analytical philosophy.

Given this state of affairs, the form and motivation of my recent reflections is this: I have once again lost my way.[1]

In order to begin to find my way, I have found it useful to try to restrict the concept of the "postmodern" to philosophic discourse, primarily because the term "postmodern" seems to mean quite different things in different disciplinary contexts. The use of the term in architecture or painting, for example, sheds very little light in trying to find one's philosophic way. The use of the term "postmodern" means different things in art and architecture than in literature or philosophy. For example, in architecture the concept is relatively clear. It displaces modernism in assignable ways, emerging as an oppositional force against architectural modernism.[2]

Recall, if you will, that architectural modernism had its origins in the utopian architectural theory and practice of the early decades of this century, specifically in the Bauhaus credo and practice so forcefully articulated in their 1919 manifesto, and in the work and writing of Walter Gropius, Henri Le Corbusier, and Mies van der Rohe. This trio, despite their differences, articulated and charted a unified program of revolutionary change in architecture. Henceforth, they argued, architecture would abandon all nostalgia, all pretentious adornment, and would devote itself to—indeed would celebrate—what is new. Architectural modernism delivered itself over completely and without reservation to newness. New materials, new technologies, and new modes of production made possible through the industrial revolution were glorified and celebrated. And this newness found ideological expression primarily reductively, primarily in abstract geometric simplification and concentration. Line, space, and form were to be pared to the minimum function they were to serve. Form not only followed function; function was to become beauty itself. Moreover, the high priests of architectural modernism saw the simple reduction of form to function as the *liberation* of the *internal unity* of an object, typically its geometrical unity. An architectural object was to be viewed as "an organic-entity.... as contrasted with that former insensate aggregation of parts.... one great thing instead of a quarrelling collection of so many little things,"[3] Frank Lloyd Wright wrote in 1910.

The modernists' utopian aspirations would in time give us the International Style, buildings that express the simple, geometrical intensity envisioned by Gropius and van der Rohe, as in the Chicago Civic Center's assemblage of horizontal spans, and van der Rohe's "curtain wall" construction exemplified by the Lake Shore housing units in that same city. And yet, these geometric shapes in which we have come to live and work, in which we move and have our being, ambivalently both assert and simultaneously deny their form. They claim to be only squares and boxes, only functional shapes, nothing else besides; and yet they proclaim their own geometrical perfection, their otherworldly distance from time and history, their transcendence of the weight of site and contingency. (Perhaps that is why it is becoming increasingly difficult for some of us to distinguish one medium-sized city skyline from another throughout the world.) Architectural modernism was by no means free of agendas either. Its aspirations were overtly hegemonic, as in the rhetoric of the 1919 Bauhaus manifesto, for example: "Together let us desire, conceive, and create the new structures of the future, which will embrace architecture and sculpture and painting in one unity and which will one day rise toward heaven from the hands of a million workers like the crystal symbol of a new faith." One legacy of this modernism, perhaps, is the tiny and large boxes that clutter our lives and spaces, entities we call buildings and homes. Post–World War II large urban housing projects from Amsterdam and Frankfurt to New York and Chicago are especially good illustrations.

Charles Jencks was able to write without any apparent trace of self-consciousness that "Modern Architecture died in St. Louis Missouri on July 15, 1972 at 3:32 p.m."[4] That is the date and time at which the monstrously ugly Pruit-Igoe housing project was dynamited, after millions of dollars had been spent attempting to repair the unending acts of vandalism perpetrated upon it by its own inhabitants. To Jencks, this act of resistance and rebellion on the part of the projects' inhabitants marks the death of architectural modernism. Razing, dynamiting the project, is therefore to be read as modernism's gesture of preemptive capitulation and violent self-immolation.

Postmodern architecture begins parasitically, begins by taking the form of a critique of modernism. Above all it begins with a critique of the conception of the self-sufficient space that modernist architecture aspired to fill. There *is* no such nonsignifying context, no ahistorical geometric space in which we move and have our being, it is argued. Postmodern architecture therefore begins with a refusal of modernist univocity. Borrowing from Saussure and semiotics generally, buildings are conceived as signs that signify, structures that refer beyond themselves while simultaneously referring *to* themselves as well. The language of architecture is not a language of archetypal forms, but a play of identity and difference, of identity *as* difference, of identity *in* difference, a domain in which structural elements derive their meaning from their relationship of contrast and similarity to other elements.

In the work of Robert Venturi and Denise Scott-Brown, for example, the referential function of the environment is retrieved and stressed, as in Venturi's *Learning from Las Vegas*, in which he urges architects to try to recover the sense in which buildings are read and translated by contexts, as in Las Vegas's forest of painted and illuminated roadside signs, which are at once literal and emblematic:

The emerging order of the Strip is a complex order. It is not the easy, rigid order of the urban project or the fashionable "total design" of the megastructure. . . . the order of the strip *includes*; it includes at all levels. . . . It is not an order dominated by the expert and made easy for the eye. The moving eye in the moving body must work to pick out and interpret a variety of changing, juxtaposed orders.[5]

The retrieval of the signifying function of architecture also entails an openness to the past, to the iconography of history, and this is perhaps the most distinctively recognizable feature of postmodern architecture (e.g., in UC Irvine's "barn" simulation and in its "postmodern anthology" generally, which contrasts and incorporates stylistic elements of the earlier 1960s style (neo-penal?) perimeter buildings, or in Des Moines's new skyscraper which comments upon and incorporates elements from Des Moines's own past, from its capitol building). Postmodern architecture frequently engages and retrieves previous historical styles and techniques. Typically, its retrieval becomes disguised commentary, as in the use of collapsing tubes to mimic Doric and Corinthian columns, as in Irvine's Housing Administration Services Building, or as in Philip Johnson's A.T. & T. Building in New York City, which humanizes the traditional skyscraper steel-and-glass-box look by giving it the shape of a grandfather clock, topping it off with a Chippendale broken pediment. Sometimes the retrieval becomes a direct revival, a wholesale historical simulation, as in the J. Paul Getty Museum in Malibu, California, which is an exact recreation of the Villa of the Papyri at Herculaneum.

To sum up, then, postmodernism in architecture can be understood, as a first approximation, as a set of reformulations of and resistances to architectural modernism. The modernist principle of abstraction, of geometric purity and simplicity, is displaced by multivocity and pluralism, by renewed interest in buildings as signs and signifiers, interest in their referential potential and resources. The modernist's aspiration to buildings that are timeless in an important sense is itself read by postmodernists as an iconography that privileges the brave new world of science and technology, an aspiration that glorifies uncritically the industrial revolution of which it is itself a quintessential expression. And this aspiration to timelessness is displaced by a direct and self-conscious openness to and engagement with history.[6]

If the meaning of "postmodern" is relatively clear in architecture, the concept becomes murkier and more contested in other domains, sometimes leading to dismissive characterizations such as the one offered by Charles Newman, a remark that dismisses postmodernism *tout court* as "a band of vainglorious contemporary artists following the circus elephants of Modernism with snow shovels."[7]

Despite this sobering reminder, I want to suggest a first approach to the problem of postmodernism in *philosophy* specifically, an approach that is indifferent to the more standard Lyotard-Jameson-Baudrillard trio, an approach that is in fact indifferent to the analytic/Continental split.[8] Let me begin this suggestion with what amounts to conceptual Morse Code.

I think it can be said that there exists a cluster of concepts loosely associated with postmodern *philosophy*. These include (1) its putative anti- (or post-) epistemological standpoint; (2) its antiessentialism; (3) its antirealism; (4) its antifoundationalism; (5) its opposition to transcendental arguments and transcendental standpoints; (6) its rejection of the picture of knowledge as accurate representation; (7) its rejection of truth as correspondence to reality; (8) its rejection of canonical descriptions; (9) its rejection of final vocabularies; and (10) its suspicion of grand narratives, or metanarratives. These are some of the things postmodern philosophy is "against." Postmodernism also (11) opposes characterizing this menu of oppositions as "relativism," "skepticism" or "nihilism" and (12) it rejects as "the metaphysics of presence" the traditional, putatively impossible dream of a complete, unique, and closed explanatory system, an explanatory system typically fueled by (13) binary oppositions. "Posties" loathe binarisms. In addition, and on the "positive" side, one often finds the following themes: (14) its critique of the notion of the neutrality and sovereignty of "reason"—including insistence on its pervasively gendered, historical, and ethnocentric character; (15) its conception of the "social construction" of word-world mappings; (16) its tendency to embrace historicism; (17) its critique of the ultimate status of a contrast between epistemology on the one hand, and the sociology of knowledge on the other; (18) its dissolution of the notion of the autonomous, rational subject; (19) its insistence on the artifactual status of divisions of labor in knowledge acquisition and production; and (20) its ambivalence about the Enlightenment and its ideology.[9]

This long list of twenty family-resembling traits needs to be fleshed out, of course.[10] And having struggled to find a modest list of candidate features that would help to illuminate the philosophical expressions of postmodernism, I have found it equally important *not* to treat these features either as necessary or sufficient conditions for the correct application of the concept "postmodern philosophy." They are family resemblance features at best. In fact, this turns out to be a somewhat unhelpful list, in the end, precisely because of the very length of the list itself. Postmodernists don't all subscribe to every element of this party platform. And, in addition, this list simply lets too much in. After all, there have even been unreconstructed "positivists" who are antirealists about the status of abstract objects, are typically antiessentialist, and have little use for transcendental arguments (although they may have a weakness for truth as correspondence, for foundationalism, and for the possibility of final, canonical vocabularies). And positivists certainly rejected metaphysics, just as posties do, and have tended to reject the notion of an autonomous moral and rational subject as well.

But the deeper failure of the search for necessary and sufficient conditions in this case—which was my initial approach—appears to have been my odd motivating belief that postmodernism must have something like a philosophic essence, that the term must name something like a natural kind which can be isolated and defined. It slowly dawned on me that what might be more helpful in getting my bearings was something like a genealogical narrative—an account of conceptual connections, of elective affinities—from which the family resemblance among "postmodern" thinkers might begin to emerge.

The genealogy I propose to trace is selective. It focuses primarily (but not exclusively) on four philosophers: Friedrich Nietzsche, Martin Heidegger, Jacques Derrida, and Richard Rorty.[11] What I hope to accomplish is to offer a genealogical account of the changed self-image of philosophy that emerges from the writings of these four thinkers, and to trace some of the implications of this altered self-image for other sectors of intellectual culture as well. This proposed genealogy may therefore be usefully construed instead as a quasi-narrative, a conversation in which the themes, plot, and filial connections among writers are established by Nietzsche. Put differently, Nietzsche is what the authors under consideration have in common either directly, as in the case of Heidegger and Derrida, or indirectly through the mediation of one of these heroes or father figures, as in the case of Rorty. Sometimes, to be sure, the influence is both direct and indirect at the same time.

NIETZSCHE

Nietzsche commentators disagree about most aspects of his thinking—as one would expect—especially about what an *Übermensch* is supposed to be, what eternal recurrence asserts, whether he had developed or had intended to formulate a full-blown theory of the will to power, as well as what his perspectivism may be said to assert. These are disagreements concerning the substance, goal, and success of Nietzsche's attempted transvaluation of all values. On the other hand, there is considerably less disagreement about identifying the deconstructive aspect of his work, the sense in which he sought to disentangle Western metaphysics, Christianity, and morality in order to display what he took to be their reactive decadence. Put crudely and misleadingly, there is considerably less disagreement concerning the negative, deconstructive side of Nietzsche's thinking than there is about the positive, reconstructive side.

These, then, are the two faces of Nietzsche that are recognized by virtually all critics. One looks at our past and vivisects our common cultural heritage at its roots; the other seems to be turned toward the future, suggesting visions of possible new forms of Western life. The negative, deconstructive, backward-glancing Nietzsche is the face that is more easily recognized by his commentators and his critics. But when one tries to examine in detail Nietzsche's positive, reconstructive face, one is beset by an immediate difficulty. For this other, future-directed face turns out to be not one portrait but at least two possible ones. One sketch of Nietzsche's positive face portrays his remarks about truth, knowledge, superhumanity, eternal recurrence, and will to power as his answers to perennial, textbook philosophical problems: as his theory of knowledge, his moral philosophy, and his ontology. On this reading of his reconstructive side, Nietzsche seems to be shattering the foundations of past theories as one demolishes false idols, in order to erect his own, better phoenix from their ashes. The alternative rendering of this reconstructive side of Nietzsche rejects the positive/negative dichotomy itself and depicts him instead as attempting to liberate us precisely from the felt need to provide theories of knowledge, or moral theories, or ontologies. The first, reconstructive portrait assimilates Nietzsche's project to the great tradition of "the metaphysics of presence"—to the tradition epitomized by Plato, Descartes, and Kant. The alternative portrait sees the negative, deconstructive side of Nietzsche as already *constructive*, in the therapeutic manner of the later Wittgenstein, late Heidegger, Derrida, Rorty, and Foucault. And this postmodern reading reads critics who try to find a positive teaching in Nietzsche's writings as seekers for a sublime Ann Landers.[12]

What is at the bottom of these conflicting portraits, it seems to me, is an unarticulated difference scarcely recognized among Nietzsche scholars, not to say philosophers generally. It is the difference between those who believe that one is paying him a compliment by reading Nietzsche as "a philosopher" who gives Kantian-style answers to textbook questions, and those who view that characterization as depreciating his more broadly "therapeutic" achievement.

A nice illustration of this bifurcated state of affairs is what seems to be occurring in discussions of Nietzsche's perspectivism. What seems to be occurring among Nietzsche scholars is not only a difference of detail—a difference about how to construe Nietzsche's remarks about "knowledge," "truth," "correspondence" and "perspective"—but a metaphilosophical split about the *point* of Nietzsche's perspectivism. For many commentators, Nietzsche's perspectivism is, roughly, his theory of knowledge. It wants to assert four distinguishable claims: (1) no accurate representation of the world as it is in itself is possible; (2) there is nothing to which our theories stand in the required correspondence relation to enable us to say that they are true or false; (3) no method of understanding our world—the sciences, logic, or moral theory—enjoys a privileged epistemic status; and (4) human needs always help to "constitute" the world for us. Nietzsche tends to run (1)–(4) together; often he confuses them. But the most serious difficulty for Nietzsche's perspectivism lies elsewhere: the self-reference problem. Are we to understand his many naturalistic and historical theses as accurate representations of the world as it is in itself, as corresponding to any facts of the matter, as privileged perspectives, ones that are conditioned by no need whatsoever? If we are, then Nietzsche's perspectivism is self-contradictory in all four versions mentioned. But that is just to say that the theories Nietzsche offered either are not to be taken perspectivally—in which case his perspectivism must be abandoned—or that they are only perspectives, in which case they may not be true and may be superseded. To say that they may not be true, however, is just to say that what he maintains may be "false."

But how can he then maintain that there is nothing to which our theories stand in the required correspondence relation to enable us to determine whether they are true or false? Further, in saying that there is no truth did Nietzsche mean to say something true? If he told the truth, then what he said was false, for there had to be a truth to be told for him to say, truly, that there is no truth, if what he said is false, on the other hand, then it is false to assert that there is no truth. But then at least something is true in an unmitigated sense. Similarly, if every great philosophy is really only "the personal confession of its author and a kind of involuntary and unconscious memoir" (BGE 6), then what is Nietzsche himself confessing? What is his involuntary and unconscious memoir *really* about? Perhaps the best way to understand his perspectivism, then, is to construe it in a neo-Kantian way, as providing a transcendental standpoint in which putative "facts" about human needs and human neurophysiology play a role not unlike that of Kant's categories and forms of intuition. Think of it as the empirical turn gone transcendental! In admittedly quite different ways, this seems to be an orientation common to the work of Danto,[13] Wilcox,[14] Clark,[15] and Schacht;[16] or perhaps it is a framework toward which their work points.

There is another, second, and quite different way to construe Nietzsche's perspectivist remarks: Nietzsche's "perspectivism" is not a *theory* of anything, and it is most certainly not a *theory* of knowledge. To say that there are only interpretations (or perspectives) is just to rename all the old facts "interpretation." Similarly, to say that "truth" is "error" is not to offer a theory of truth so much as it is to rename it. The point of the renaming is to help us set aside the vocabulary of accurate representation that still holds us in its Platonic thrall. So Nietzsche's tropes concerning "truth" and "error," "fact" and "interpretation" are best understood as rhetorical devices to help the reader understand and confront the widely shared intuition that there must be something like a final truth about reality as such, which it is the goal of philosophy to disclose. The reader's own penchant for the God's-eye-view is surfaced and called into question. Indeed, a theory of knowledge is not something Nietzsche has; the yearning for its possession is what his tropes parody. Knowledge is the sort of thing about which one ought to have a theory primarily when the Platonically inspired God's-eye-view has seduced us, primarily when we construe knowledge on the analogy of vision—the mind's eye seeing the way things really are—primarily when we see philosophy as culture's referee, allowing or barring moves made elsewhere in culture that claim to be items of knowledge. Yet this is precisely the picture of philosophy and inquiry Nietzsche urges ought to be set aside. Put oversimply, "knowledge" and "truth" are compliments paid to successful discourse, as Rorty and others have suggested. To give an account of such success is always to say why this specific item is "true" or "known"— for example, the superiority of the heliocentric over the geocentric account of planetary motion. There can be explanations and illustrations of successful discourse on a case by case basis, illustrations and explanations of the relative attractions of various competing concrete proposals; but there is no way to slide

an unwobbling pivot between "theory" and "reality" that will register an unmediated fit between word and world. There can only be a misconceived "theory
of" successful discourse, in this view. Despite admitted differences, enormous
ones, this seems to be a useful way of capturing an orientation suggested by the
work of Alderman,[17] Derrida,[18] Nehamas,[19] Deleuze,[20] Strong,[21] Shapiro,[22] and
Rorty,[23] for example.

The case of the "will to power" is equally messy, but for different reasons.
These are primarily textual[24] and conceptual. Even if there exists a doctrine, one
that can be unpacked "analytically" as a psychological principle, how is it to
be grasped ontologically, as discarded notes from the *Nachlass* seem to suggest?
How is the will to power to be understood as an assertion of the way things
are, rather than as a figure for the self in quest of self, a self in transformation?
In the end, the will to power may well reduce to the view that if one must do
metaphysics—and perhaps Nietzsche's final recommendation is that this comfort
is better given up—then one buys the picture of language as accurate representation, of theory as correspondence to facts; one buys the ultimate and decidable
purchase of mapping metaphors along with the correspondence theory of truth.
To mitigate the force of that picture, think of Nietzsche's remarks concerning
will to power as recommending that we think, instead, of "things" as events
and as families of events. In such a view, the paradox is that a world of only
wills, only events, is necessarily formless and formed at the same time. Formless, because wills conceived as events are form-giving while possessed of no
fixed or inherent structure of their own, apart from their contextual articulation,
apart from what Nietzsche called their "interpretation." Formed, because wills
conceived as families of events are always acting upon one another, are always
imposing form upon one another. The paradox is intractable. If we are no longer
to think of "wills" as "things," we can form no clear mental image of them.
They elude representational thinking. Insofar as we do form a clear mental
image, a representation, the formless antecedent eludes us. We invariably picture
an entity that has already been formed, structured. We grasp only an "interpretation." Consequently, will to power is the general characterization of this action
of will upon will, in which form is imposed by will upon will, that is, by event
upon event, in which there is visible only the articulation which we call "the
world." Grasping things as events *simpliciter* is counterintuitive, to be sure, for
it requires that we abandon the notion that events consist of items, that they are
constituted by the interaction of things. Indeed, propositional language fails us
here, for we are asked to grasp the world as a family of events constituted by
and consisting of no-thing in particular, a "world" of relations without relata.
This difficulty in stating Nietzsche's position is not restricted to his discussion
of the will to power. It is a recurring problem in making Nietzsche's argument
plain, that in order to state his position or argument one must resort to a vocabulary whose use often depends upon the very contrasts he sought to displace
or set aside.

I have characterized this feature of Nietzsche's central themes elsewhere as the "self-consuming" character of his concepts, categories, and tropes.[25] A self-consuming concept is one that requires as a condition of its intelligibility (or even its possibility) the very contrast it wishes to set aside or would have us set aside. The notion of will to power as relation(s) without relata is self-consuming in the sense specified, as may be the notion of invoking the analogy between seeing and knowing, which Nietzsche's perspectivism explicitly does, in order to set aside the dominating visual metaphorics of traditional epistemology. The notions of eternal recurrence and the ideal life may also be usefully viewed—as a preliminary approximation—as self-consuming concepts.

Nietzsche's presentation of eternal recurrence is central to his philosophic project. It is the generating thought of his *Zarathustra*, the thought that most divides commentators.[26] It is unarguably the subject of two of Zarathustra's speeches—"On the Vision and the Riddle" and "The Convalescent"—and is fully rehearsed in *The Gay Science* under the heading "*Das Grösste Schwergewicht.*" That entry (#341) concludes by asking its interlocutors two questions framed as one:

If this thought (of eternal recurrence) were to gain possession of you, it would transform you, as you are, or perhaps crush you. The question in each and every thing, "Do you want this once more and innumerable times more?" would weigh upon your actions as the greatest stress. Or how well disposed would you have to become to life and to yourself to *crave nothing more fervently (um nach nichts mehr zu verlangen)* than this ultimate eternal confirmation and seal?

In Nietzsche's various published writings in which we are invited to think through the notion of eternal recurrence, we are asked the question "How well disposed would one have to become to oneself and to life to crave nothing more fervently than the infinite repetition, without alteration, of each and every moment?" Nietzsche invites his reader to imagine a finite number of possible states of the universe, each destined to recur eternally, and asks his reader's reaction to this imagined state of affairs. Presumably most presons should find such a thought shattering because they should always find it possible to prefer the eternal repetition of their lives in an edited version rather than to crave nothing more fervently than the recurrence of each of its horrors. Only a superhuman being (an *Übermensch*) could accept recurrence without emendation, evasion, or self-deception, a being whose distance from conventional humanity is greater than the distance between man and beast, Nietzsche tells us in the Prologue to *Thus Spoke Zarathustra.*

But what sort of creature would desire the unaltered repetition of its exact life, would prefer each and every moment of its life just as it is, and would prefer this to any alternative possibility it could imagine? What sort of attitude is suggested by a person, a quester, who could regard his or her life as Leibniz's God regarded the world: the best of all possible worlds?

One way to approach this question would be to argue that to want each moment unconditionally is to want it for its own sake, not because of something else or as a means to something else. When Aristotle is said to argue, for example, that happiness is the highest good, he argues that it alone is wanted unconditionally, is wanted for its own sake. On this view, health and medicine are not wanted for their own sakes but because they promote happiness, they are desired as means to ends, are desired in order to achieve happiness. Even pleasure is not the highest good for Aristotle, just because it is pursued not only for its own sake but as a means of achieving happiness. It is not wanted simply and only for its own sake. In this reading of Nietzsche's eternal recurrence each moment must be wanted for its own sake, as Aristotle thought happiness was wanted, neither because of something else nor as a means to something else.

To make the enormity of this task more transparent and more vivid, imagine or recall for one moment the most entirely satisfactory sexual experience of your life, the moment in which you preferred your beloved to any possible alternative beloveds, a moment in which you also urgently preferred to be the lover you were just then. Imagine further that, upon reflection, you would welcome the eternal recurrence of that experience, just as it is, without addition, subtraction, or remainder. Let us say of this unconditionally cherished sexual ecstasy—real or imagined, it does not matter which—that you desired it for its own sake. Now also imagine, in contrast, the moment of your deepest despair, or the searing pain of your most unfulfilled longing, or the shattering blow of your most ruinous humiliation, or the self-deceptive acid of your most secret envy. Finally, if you can, imagine having just the same attitude toward the cataloged moments of your greatest anguish that you were asked to imagine of your most cherished sexual ecstasy or fantasy. Just *that* is what Nietzsche's eternal recurrence requires of each and every moment wanted for its own sake, it seems to me, and just *that* is what turns this requirement itself into a self-consuming human impossibility, a conceptual and existential oxymoron. It ought to give pause to those who think that Nietzsche's thought of eternal recurrence taught us to "celebrate" each moment: *carpe diem.*

If the notion of a self-consuming concept is to be of use in understanding Nietzsche's remarks concerning the will to power, eternal recurrence, the ascetic ideal, and the *Übermensch*, then it should also be of use in motivating the sense in which these central themes in Nietzsche generate one version of an old question: Is Nietzsche playing the same philosophical game with different rules or is it now a different game? Is Nietzsche offering new critiques of the tradition, followed by substantive epistemic, moral, and ontological theories on which the critiques depend, or is he suggesting that we cease to speak this way?

For postmodernists, perhaps Nietzsche's critiques just *are* the new game, as they are for Foucault, who follows him in this. As in psychotherapy, the negative act of being deprived of something—say, a cherished neurosis—just *is* the gift-giving virtue.

On the assumption that a coherent yet sufficiently nuanced account of Nietzsche's postmodern enterprise can emerge by pursuing this line of thought, I turn to Martin Heidegger, for whom Nietzsche brings Western metaphysics to its end.

HEIDEGGER

It has become a cliché to say of Heidegger that he is "the thinker of Being (*Sein*)," just as it has become a cliché to observe that the preposition in the phrase "thought of Being" really does intend to leave open the question whether Being is the object of Heidegger's thought or whether Being thinks through Heidegger, becomes articulate through him—whether Heidegger's thought-path was Being's own thought.[27]

Heidegger's initial project, in *Being and Time*, was designed to reawaken the question, What is the sense of the Being (*Sein*) of beings (*Seiendes*)? This thrust toward what he called a fundamental ontology required a "recapitulation and destruction" of the history of ontology. Today we would have called it a "deconstruction" of metaphysics, without violating Heidegger's sense in the least. Heidegger's critique of metaphysics is directed at "metaphysics" in a narrow sense, the sense in which it constitutes a certain way Being has been understood since Plato, a way that is synonymous with the history of Western philosophy. It is this narrower sense of metaphysics Heidegger originally sought to overcome precisely in the name of a fundamental ontology that finds its roots in an order metaphysics—that of the pre-Socratic philosophers. In effect, Heidegger's initial endeavor to reawaken the allegedly lost sense of Being was an attempt to recall traditional metaphysics from its obliviousness to its own origins, the thought of Being. He was persuaded initially that the traditional categorial treatment of Being failed to articulate clearly what is meant for a thing "to be" in general. The tradition that informed an account of "Being" was inherently defective, according to the early Heidegger. He argued that the criteria that sustained an approach to Being—undefinability, universality, and self-evidence—are not simply inadequate but are themselves the result of an inadequate account of Being, *viz.* the narrow sense of metaphysics. The criteria are allegedly derived from the success of discursive speech in application to beings, to entities. According to this view, categorial inquiry since Plato enjoys considerable success in eliciting the sense of beings, the ontic, but misapplies its energies in treating Being in the categorial mode, through discursive thought. "Plato," "philosophy," "metaphysics," "the metaphysics of presence" as presence, all signify the same event: "Since Plato, thinking about the Being of beings becomes 'philosophy.' ... The 'philosophy' first begun with Plato hereafter possesses the characteristic of that which is later called 'metaphysics.' ... Even the word 'metaphysics' is already molded in Plato's presentation."[28] The unity of philosophy as Platonic metaphysics conditions its possible forms up to Nietzsche, after which its inner logic is exhausted, after which philosophy comes to its end in the triumph of calculative thinking:

Throughout the whole history of philosophy, Plato's thinking remains decisive in changing forms. Metaphysics is Platonism. Nietzsche characterizes his philosophy as reversed
Platonism. With the reversal of metaphysics . . . the most extreme possibility of philosophy is attained. It has entered its final stage. To the extent that philosophical thinking
is still attempted, it manages only to attain an epigonal renaissance and variations of that
renaissance.[29]

   As is known widely, Heidegger's narrative tried to show that philosophic
discourse, since Plato, assumes an unanalyzed conception of truth as correctness,
that is, a correspondence between a statement and a state-of-affairs. Before Plato
truth, *alétheia*, meant disclosure; being-in-a-state-of-uncovering. Truth, according to Heidegger, originally meant wresting from concealment. *Létho, lanthano*,
originally suggested covering-up, hoarding, concealing, disguising, forgetting.
The alphaprivative in *alétheia*, consequently, was said to uncover, unconceal;
to bring into the light. Heidegger maintained that truth, in the epistemological
sense—*adequatio intellectus et rei*—while applicable to ontic discourse, to talk
about things, is incapable of grasping Being, the emergence within which things
come to be. Ontic discourse about Being has characterized the history of philosophy as metaphysics. Truth devolves, historically, from *alétheia* (pre-
Platonic), to *orthotes* (the "correct" discourse about things), to *adequatio
intellectus et rei* (medieval period), to certitude (Descartes), to error (Nietzsche).
The revelatory essence of truth is allegedly subservient to correct speech, in
Plato. "Correctness" then evolves its own career; from medieval correspondence to Cartesian self-evidence, in which mathematical certainty serves as paradigm of truth, to Nietzsche's extraordinary claim that truth is the sort of error,
the sort of falsification of fluid becoming, without which human beings could
not live.
   As a consequence of the sharpening of truth in the epistemological sense,
Being devolves from *Anwesenheit*, the pre-Platonic presence of emergence, to
Idea (Plato), to transcendence (God), to "will" (modern period). Heidegger
maintains, I need only add briefly, that Being appears as will in the entire post-
Cartesian period, not only in Nietzsche.
   Philosophy, as Heidegger reads it, is the failed attempt to make Being *qua
physis* become word. "Failed" because thinking must make Being present, must
represent it to make it available for discursive speech. "Representation," "intuition," "perception," "idea," "the directly evident" are so many palimpsests
that efface Being.
   A seductive feature of Heidegger's work is the persuasiveness with which it
reverses our everyday understanding of what is basic and what is derivative.
Being as *physis* (*Anwesenheit, Ereignis*—coming to be, arising, being born) is
primary; *ousia* (presence, that which is present, that which stands) is said to be
derivative. With that linguistic archeology alone Heidegger implicitly condemns
philosophy to representational thinking. Truth as *alétheia* is primary, we are
told; correspondence is derivative. "To be" in a world in a spatial, geographic

sense is said to be parasitic upon being-in-the-world as being-at home; theoretical understanding is not our primary access to the real but emerges only after *Dasein* divests itself of all concernful dealings; our average everyday mode of being in the world is said to be a dispersal of ourselves away from ourselves, a glossing over of the voice of conscience; anxious being-towards-death is said to be the condition of authenticity. The list of Heidegger's reversals of primordial and founded, basic and derived, host and parasite could go on and on.

I have myself gone on at such self-indulgent length first about Nietzsche and now about Heidegger because this now puts me in a position to say something about one thrust of this postmodern genealogy. For one problem that emerges clearly from Nietzsche as from Heidegger is the claim that, in some sense or other, philosophy has come to an end, that what remains of it is but "an epigonal renaissance and variations of that renaissance." That philosophy has ended is asserted not only by Heidegger, we should recall, but is often thought to be asserted by Derrida and Rorty as well.

The claim that philosophy has come to an end can be understood in a narrow or wide sense, much as Nietzsche's recording of the fact that God is dead can be understood in a wide or narrow sense. In its narrow sense, God's death could be said to be of interest primarily to theologians and believers. In its wider sense, however, it announced an event of world historical importance. Similarly, to say that philosophy has come to an end is not to say (only) that philosophers no longer have pride of place in culture. But what, exactly, does it assert and imply? Derrida may be of indirect help here.

DERRIDA

There are more than ordinary obstacles to locating Derrida in interpretive space. That is because it is a part of Derrida's substantive strategy to call into question the notion that thinkers can either be neatly located or paired-off in conceptual space, to challenge the view that they represent "philosophical positions" (what Nietzsche called "a dance of bloodless categories"), to call into question the unstated but powerful assumption that there exists over and above one's interpretive practices a neutral ideal space that one's categories of reflection merely exemplify, a kingdom of Platonic natural kinds never tiring of yet another instantiation. Further still, Derrida's writings often suggest that the seemingly innocuous task of paraphrasing a thinker, or of attempting to characterize his or her work, is itself part and parcel of "the metaphysics of presence," that one's critical procedures that may seem natural—even necessary and inevitable—are instead optional products of a specific institutionalized vocabulary, of a specific form of life. His writings suggest that the tasks of paraphrase and characterization of philosophical views are themselves the optional products of vocabulary choice.[30] Once chosen, one's critical practices may come to feel natural, even inevitable; they carry in their wake the unspoken conviction that one's most fundamental interpretive strategies and categories are inevitable for any rational inquirer, that they derive this power from their essential correctness, from their correspondence to the way things (or texts) are in themselves. One begins to feel as if there were a fact of the matter about which vocabulary, taken as a whole, is the right one. In this way, an optional vocabulary hides its origins from itself, Derrida's writings seem to insist. If Nietzsche's work resists paraphrase, and Heidegger's work suggests that paraphrase must purchase its success by obscuring the matter of thought—descending to chatter, to idle talk (*Gerede*)—Derrida's writings may be read as extended reflections on the impossibility of paraphrase and characterization. They may alternatively be read as an extended performance in which the received categories of literary and philosophical reflection are successively called into question. And yet—or perhaps "therefore"—the most neutral and apparently uncontroversial characterization of the conceptual space Derrida occupies can be made problematic, as is illustrated by his own remarks on the term "deconstruction":

the word "deconstruction" has always bothered me. . . . When I made use of this word . . . I had the impression that it was a word among others, a secondary word in the text which would fade or which in any case would assume a non-dominant place in a system. For me, it was a word in a chain with many words. . . . as well as with a whole elaboration which is not limited only to a lexicon, if you will. It so happens that this word which I had only written once or twice . . . all of a sudden jumped out of the text and was seized by others who have since determined its fate in the manner you well know. . . . For me "deconstruction" was not at all the first or the last word, and certainly not a password or slogan for anything that was to follow.[31]

Derrida's reluctance notwithstanding, one may usefully begin by relating his texts not only to those he explicitly discusses but to those he assumes have shaped his interlocutors' vocabulary as well. Saussure is one such absent presence, a consideration that is not without significance, since the movement from rigorous phenomenology in the Husserlian manner—with its stress on a perceptual vocabulary—to structuralism and semiology is mediated through Saussure. In contrast, Anglophone philosophy of language and German hermeneutics remained relatively untouched by Saussure, at least initially. Accordingly, Derrida's vocabulary shifted after 1967 from terms such as consciousness, intentional object, intentional act, and intuition of essences to the language of sign, signifier, and signified.

Saussure's *Course of General Linguistics* had claimed that "in language there are only differences without positive terms,"[32] an insight that strikes at the heart of the representational picture of language apparently acquired with mothers' milk. Indeed, as Saussure observed, "there are only differences. Even more important, a difference generally implies positive terms between which the difference is set up."[33] Yet just that is what is being set aside, displaced. How to think of language nonrepresentationally—how to think of difference without presupposing identity—mirrors Nietzsche's difficulty of thinking of "world" as will to power, thinking of "things" as families of events, as consisting *of* and constituted *by* no-thing in particular, thinking "things" as relations without re-lata.

Saussure's implicit challenge to referential semantics chimes well with J. L. Austin's generative thought—to which Derrida frequently attends—that lan-guage, which was typically treated as descriptive and hence as the medium for bringing thoughts into correspondence with facts, might as usefully be regarded as a performative instrument and as the vehicle of a kind of action. So Austin is lauded (in *Différance*) for combating what he called "the descriptive fallacy," for having exploded the concept of communication as a purely semiotic, lin-guistic, or symbolic concept. Nevertheless, the concept that is exploded is re-quired to detonate the charge. Hence, argues Derrida, performativity is parasitic on descriptivity after all.

Consider the standard example: When I say "I promise," I am not describing anything; I am doing something, promising consisting in saying "I promise." However, I have in effect just said "I promise" without making any promise at all, merely showing instead with which instrument of language it is done. Thinking primarily of stage actors, Austin dismisses such citational cases as themselves parasitic. But Derrida insists that if an action is to consist in saying something, then there must be a rule that transforms the saying into doing; and the rule must *cite* the expression: therefore, no citation, no performance. This oversimple example of "deconstruction" can be understood as a demonstration that a thesis actually requires as one of its conditions the very thing it means to reject; and precisely this is a recurrent feature of Derrida's work.[34]

This self-deconstructing parasitology, this mutual dependence of action upon citation and citation upon action (or speech upon "writing"), is but a single instance of a broader tendency: Derrida's general transformation of our sense of the stability and autonomy of the world itself into a textual exigency, as if self and world were themselves inscriptions.

Within the received view, within what Heidegger had called "the ontotheolog-ical tradition," Derrida invites us to think of the dream of philosophy as inhabited by three unwobbling pivots, consisting of (1) the world (or becoming, appearance, *hyle, res extensa*, object, phenomena, etc.), (2) the philosopher (or subject, person, observer, theorist), and (3) the in-principle correct account of the world, Reality's Own Vocabulary. Nietzsche had argued that point three is a function of a self-deceptive will to power. And Heidegger had agreed with Nietzsche that no dis-course can be reality's canonical self-description. Philosophers cannot play the role of Charlie McCarthy for Reality's Edgar Bergen. However, this now places Derrida in a position to say that "there is nothing outside the text," that notions of truth, meaning, and reference only make sense when the dream of philosophy— the ternary "metaphysics of presence"—is assumed, only when there exists something *more* than interpretations, only when the word/world connection can be stitched together again: but we "cannot legitimately transgress the text toward something other than it, toward the referent (a reality that is metaphysical, historical, psychobiographical, etc.) or toward a signifier outside the text whose content could take place, could have taken place outside of language, that is to say, in the sense that we give here to that word, text.''[35]

Put differently, Derrida is able to thematize the end of philosophy, conceived as the theory of accuracy of representation, as an event within writing, by recognizing that its dream of three unwobbling pivots applies to reading and writing as well. For think now of a book as a ternary relation between (1) a text (an inscription), (2) a reader, and (3) the meaning of the text (the in-principle correct interpretation, the Text's Own Self-Description). Invoking Saussure's linguistic insight and Nietzsche's perspectivism, Derrida is able to say that the meaning of the text is undecidable, that there can be no such thing as the univocal, canonical, absolute meaning of a text. Even divine inscriptions require optional encodings. Indeed, under the pressure of Nietzsche's perspectivism, all we are left with is ''the text'' and texts ''about'' texts. ''The idea of the book,'' in contrast,

is the idea of a totality, finite or infinite, of the signifier; this totality of the signifier cannot be a totality, unless a totality constituted by the signified preexists it, supervises its inscriptions and its signs, and is independent of it in its ideality. The idea of the book, which always refers to a natural totality, is profoundly alien to the sense of writing. . . . If I distinguish the text from the book, I shall say that the destruction of the book as it is now under way in all domains, denudes the surface of the text.[36]

This somewhat oblique entry into Derrida manages to underscore the claim that we are left with a Nietzschean domain of intertextuality only, a perspectival space, a domain in which no spectator standpoint is available to distinguish the conceptual from the literary, a domain in which literal speech is understood as dead metaphor, metaphors we have forgotten were metaphors, desiccated poetry, a framework in which philosophy is (just) one more literary genre.

Nietzsche here as elsewhere anticipated Derrida when he wrote—in answer to the question, What is truth?

a mobile army of metaphors, metonymes, and anthropomorphisms—in short a sum of human relations, which have been enhanced, transposed and embellished poetically and rhetorically and which after long use seem final, canonical, and obligatory to a people; truths are illusions about which one has forgotten that this is what they are; metaphors which are worn out and without sensuous power; coins which have lost their pictures and now matter only as metal, no longer as coins.[37]

Derrida has in common with Heidegger and Nietzsche the view that the history of philosophy is a narrative of presence, closure, and totality—the dream of a unique, complete, and closed explanatory system—fueled by binary oppositions. Each agrees, in his own way, that the dream at the heart of philosophy begins paradigmatically with Plato. And just as Heidegger absorbs Nietzsche into the history of philosophy as the closure of nihilism rather than its confrontational overcoming, as Nietzsche would have it, Derrida's strong misreading (his misprision) absorbs Heidegger within the metaphysics of presence too. Heidegger's magic inscription—*Sein*—betrays his vestigial yearning for unmediated vision (perhaps better: for unmediated hearing) beyond intertextual discourses: "There will be no unique name, even if it were the name of Being. And we must think this without *nostalgia*, that is, outside of the myth of a purely maternal or paternal language, a lost native country of thought. On the contrary, we must *affirm* this in the sense in which Nietzsche puts affirmation into play, in a certain laughter and a certain step of the dance."[38]

One can therefore characterize Derrida's relation to Heidegger hyperbolically as castration of the father-figure and a reassertion of the grandfather Nietzsche—reassertion of a perspectivism that is not a concealed yearning to be more than perspectivism itself—or as patricide. And just as Heidegger reverses our ordinary work-a-day conception of the relation between primordial and founded, basic and derived, host and parasite, Derrida also applies this tool, whether it be in suggesting the priority of writing over speech-acts, the metaphorical over the literal, *bricolage* over engineering, or signifier over signified. But unlike Heidegger, and crucially I think, Derrida's reversals are not offered to establish or to argue that the derivative *is* primordial. Derrida's reversals always appear to be strategic, concerned to reverse the dominance relation between opposed concepts, as in the male/female reversal in *Spurs*, to annul the privileging of presence itself. Heidegger's profound linguistic and archaeological suggestions of origins remain, for Derrida, necessarily part and parcel of the metaphysics of presence.[39]

RORTY

Richard Rorty can be read as continuing the theme that, somehow, philosophy has come to an end. Anyone concerned to situate Rorty in postmodern space, therefore, will first have to explicate and assess Rorty's "deconstruction" of analytic philosophy. *Philosophy and the Mirror of Nature* tells that story interestingly and well; *Consequences of Pragmatism* sheds light on how Rorty got there and suggests where to go from there. *Contingency, Irony, and Solidarity* is also of help in situating Rorty in postmodern conceptual space, not only in its explicit discussions of Nietzsche, Heidegger, and Derrida, but in its discussions of the contingency of language, the contingency of selfhood, and of a liberal community. Its treatment of connections between irony and theory, cruelty and solidarity discloses a more robust and nuanced voice than is sometimes heard in Rorty's two earlier books.

Two immediate concerns for any critic will be whether Rorty's attempted deconstruction of analytic philosophy succeeds—whether his analyses are compelling—and whether his historical narrative (derived from Heidegger and Foucault) is persuasive.[40] Finally, while the implications of Derrida's work may remain unclear, the consequences of Rorty's "end of philosophy" theme seem a bit more clear. To wax exegetical for the last time:

1. We are urged to give up the view that "philosophical problems" arise naturally upon reflection. Instead, philosophy names no natural kind, no activity intrinsic to our species, but is a historic, principally Western achievement.

2. Giving up #1 entails giving up the view that there is a fixed, permanent philosophical agenda, a set of problems that defines philosophy, a common paradigm that transcends natural languages, dictions, frameworks, idioms, distinctions, and interests. We are asked to give up the textbook picture of philosophy as a United Nations translation service in which the living converse with the honored dead.

3. We are asked to give up the notion of an inherent division of labor among disciplines, a division that marks philosophy neatly off from literature or the arts and sciences, and the sciences from the arts. We are asked instead to view philosophy as a cultural genre—a voice in "the conversation of mankind," in Oakeshott's phrase borrowed by Rorty—and to give up altogether the generic distinction between *Natur-* and *Geisteswissenschaften*, between the natural and human sciences.

4. If there is no metahistorical philosophical agenda, we are also asked to recognize that there are no final solutions to putative philosophical questions. Rather, in philosophy as elsewhere in culture, interests ebb and flow, topics of conversation change. For example, philosophers trained in analytic circles three or four decades ago were worried about the problem of the counterfactual conditional, the nature of analyticity, and the emotive meaning of ethical terms. Some of their European counterparts were at the same time concerned about the death of phenomenology in its existential incarnations, the proper definition of existentialism, and whether a pure domain of apodictic noemata could be grasped. The debates have shifted; scarcely anyone is concerned with such issues today. Philosophical issues are not solved, it would appear; we simply—perhaps not "simply"—change the subject.

5. If there are no final solutions to philosophical questions, then we must also come to see that there is no final vocabulary—no ultimate principles, distinctions, insights, and descriptions—that defines rationality in virtue of its privileged attachment to reality, no vocabulary that is reality's own potential canonical self-description.

6. Finally, we are advised to be cautious about the generality and use of mirroring metaphors that have shaped our common representational vocabulary—instituted by Plato and codified by Descartes—which lead us to think of philosophy chiefly in representational terms. Talk of correctness of representation may usefully be replaced with talk about what we are warranted, are justified in asserting, for example.[41]

Foundationalists will be inclined to think that giving up the six items I have just enumerated is equivalent to giving up philosophy itself. For it is surely to admit that there is no distinct, permanent *Fach* that is philosophy's own, that there is no univocal philosophic method—what we today call argument analysis, for example, resembles "rhetoric" in the classical quadrivium—and that no answers to putative philosophical problems have withstood the test of time. But it is certainly fair to ask what is left after God's-eye-view assumptions have been displaced.

The end of the God's-eye-view involves, paradoxically, the end of "the end of philosophy"; this may require, in Rorty's terms, a post-Philosophical culture, one in which philosophy understands itself as the interpretation, integration, and self-reflection of the arts and sciences. Or, put in Hegel's terms, post-Philosophical philosophy may be construed as its own time reflected in thought, not in the sense that its own age is the object of reflection but that we see its age through its work—just as most of us have come to understand the Greeks essentially through Plato's and Aristotle's eyes. Philosophy in a post-Philosophical culture will be characterized—in Sellars's unhelpful phrase—as seeing how things, in the widest possible sense of the term, hang together, in the widest possible sense of the term.[42] In such a culture the notion of corresponding to some brute *Ding an sich* will have lost its force. There will be no constraints on philosophical inquiry save conversational ones, shaped by our shared need to cope.

Rorty's new pragmatism is often regarded as "relativistic." A reply available to him is just to say that the charge of relativism in one, straightforward philosophical sense is parasitic upon a set of metaphors he is trying to set aside— truth as correspondence, language as picture, literature as mimetic. It is not the case that a postmodern pragmatist cannot distinguish between knowledge and opinion; for to say that something is a matter of opinion, for a postmodern pragmatist, is just to say that disagreement with the relevant community's current consensus on a given topic does not defeat membership in that community. To say that something is knowledge is to say that such disagreement *is* incompatible with membership in that community.

Without denigrating the achievements of science or philosophy, therefore, Rorty can be read as wishing to liberate our thinking from its bondage to a specific picture of inquiry, to surface and set aside a set of metaphors designed to establish scientific investigation as the paradigmatic human activity, and to set aside the resulting picture of philosophy as *the* theory of representation. Conceived as representing representation, philosophy tends to carve up inquiry into disciplines that represent reality accurately, less accurately, or not at all. So conceived, epistemology—or its successor discipline, philosophy of language— functions as arbiter of representational claims, as culture's referee, and regards as permanent the division between our scientific and our literary culture. From Rorty's perspective, in contrast, science is "the vocabulary which is handy in predicting and controlling nature"[43] not a discourse privileged by capturing Nature's Own Vocabulary. Consensus may be easier to achieve in physics than in art criticism, to be sure, but that advantage is due to the fact that in the one case discourse is "conducted within an agreed-upon set of conventions about what counts as a relevant contribution, what counts as answering a question, what counts as having a good argument for that answer or a good criticism of it."[44] There is no deeper representational moral to derive here.

The postmodern genealogy I have just sketched hastily looks like skepticism, relativism, or nihilism to those who have not taken the postmodern turn, a turn that Nietzsche announced with the death of God. Such foundationalists think that vocabularies—taken as a whole—are either true or false in virtue of their representational accuracy, in virtue of their correspondence to the way things are independent of our descriptions of them. Moreover, such a genealogy frequently sounds suspiciously like an invitation to reactionary politics to its critics as well.[45]

Let me step back for a moment, therefore, and remind myself of Rorty's own earliest struggles with foundationalism in morality and politics, as exemplified by his 1979 Presidential Address to the Eastern Division of the American Philosophical Association, reprinted in *Consequences of Pragmatism*. In that essay—entitled "Pragmatism, Relativism, Irrationalism"—Rorty identifies the issues as follows: "The real and passionate opposition is over the question of whether loyalty to our fellow-humans presupposes that there is something permanent and unhistorical which explains *why* we should continue to converse in the manner of Socrates. . . . whether one can be a pragmatist without being an irrationalist, without abandoning one's loyalty to Socrates."[46] This question is given force, Rorty thought in 1979, because

> the sullen resentment which sins against Socrates, which withdraws from conversation and community, has recently become articulate. . . . Our tyrants and bandits are more hateful than those of earlier times because . . . they pose as intellectuals. Our tyrants and bandits write philosophy in the morning and torture in the afternoon; our bandits alternately read Hölderlin and bomb people into bloody scraps. So our culture clings, more than ever, to the hope of the Enlightenment, the hope that drove Kant to make philosophy formal and rigorous and professional. We hope that by forming the *right* conceptions of reason, of science, of thought, of knowledge, of morality, the conceptions which express their *essence*, we shall have a shield against irrationalist resentment and hatred. Pragmatists tell us that this hope is vain. On their view, the Socratic virtues—willingness to talk, to listen to other people, to weigh the consequences of our actions upon other people—are *simply* moral virtues. They cannot be inculcated nor fortified by theoretical research into essences.[47]

The difference in the importance postmodern pragmatists, foundationalists, and lapsed foundationalists attach to philosophy in general and to critical social theory in particular is striking, as is well illustrated in a recent exchange between Rorty and Thomas McCarthy, in *Critical Inquiry*.[48]

In that piece McCarthy argues for the importance of developing concepts of "reason, truth and justice, that, while no longer pretending to a God's-eye point of view, retain something of their regulative force,"[49] as Putnam, Apel and Habermas have done. Specifically, the regulative force of traditional philosophical categories and tropes provides a "moment of unconditionality that opens us up to criticism from other points of view,"[50] without which radical social critique seems impossible. In this context, argues McCarthy, " 'truth'. . . . functions as an 'idea of reason' with respect to which we can criticize not only particular claims within our language but the very standards of truth we have inherited."[51]

Rorty replies, predictably perhaps, that what makes criticism possible is not a philosophical reflection on its enabling conditions but "concrete alternative suggestions—suggestions about how to redescribe what we are talking about"— as in Galileo's redescriptions of the Aristotelian universe, Marx's redescriptions of nineteenth-century life, Heidegger's redescriptions of the West as a whole, Dickens's redescriptions of chancery law, Rabelais's redescriptions of monasteries, and Virginia Woolf's redescriptions of women writing. It is "fresh descriptions . . . new suggestions of things to say, sentences to consider, vocabularies to employ (that) do the work."[52] From this perspective, McCarthy's "moment of unconditionality" is an item that does no work at all, "a wheel that can be turned though nothing else moves with it," in Wittgenstein's phrase, "not part of the mechanism." Indeed, Rorty's suggestion is that "when we look for regulative ideals, we stick to freedom and forget about truth and rationality. We can safely do this because, whatever else truth may be, it is something we are more likely to get as a result of free and open encounters than anything else. Whatever else rationality may be, it is something that obtains when persuasion is substituted for force. . . . If we take care of political and cultural freedom, truth and rationality will take care of themselves."[53]

   In the sort of post-Philosophical culture Rorty imagines, it will come to seem odd to think that the tasks of social criticism must be grounded in some sort of transcendental argument in order to get off the ground, as if philosophy were methodology police. For

that the middle class of the United States, as of South Africa, is unwilling to pay the taxes necesarry to give poor blacks a decent education and a chance in life seems to me a fact we need no fancier theoretical notions than "greed," "selfishness," and "racial prejudice" to explain. That successive American presidents have ordered or allowed the CIA to make it as difficult as possible to depose Latin American oligarchies seems another such well-known fact, whose explanation is to be found on the level of details about Anaconda Copper in Washington's corridors of power. When I am told that to appreciate the significance of these facts I need a deeper understanding of, for example, the discourse of power characteristic of late capitalism, I am incredulous.[54]

Me too.

CONCLUSION

   I began this chapter with an epigram from Wittgenstein on which I want to reflect in order to bring these remarks to a close. Wittgenstein's remark, remember, consists of the following conundrum[55]: "When 'I raise my arm' my arm goes up. . . . What is left over if I subtract the fact that my arm goes up from the fact that I raise my arm?" The central point of Wittgenstein's question is to mark the difference between an action and a mere bodily movement, to bring to the surface our shared preconception that there is in fact a difference to be drawn between an action and a bodily movement. One might be inclined to say that the mere (bodily movement) fact that my arm goes up when 'I raise my arm' neither captures nor exhausts the intentional character of the act, that presumed further fact that distinguishes my free *action* from a twitch or a post-hypnotic reaction, from a mere bodily movement, in short.

Wittgenstein's purposes aside, I want to conclude by generalizing his question as follows: If from our current vocabulary we could subtract our current vocabulary,[56] what, if anything, remains left over? And I want to suggest that there are three standard prereflective as well as philosophical responses to this question:

1. *Whether it is the right vocabulary* (i.e., whether our current self and world descriptions—taken as a whole—are correct, are true in an unqualified, correspondence sense; whether what we claim to know *is* knowledge; whether our morality is the right one; and whether our sense of the ideal life is the correct perception and description of it);

2. *Nothing remains left over—acknowledged with nostalgia, regret, or a sense of loss*;

3. *Nothing remains left over—acknowledged without nostalgia, regret, or a sense of loss.*

The third reaction seems to me to be the paradigmatic, philosophically postmodern response and a clue to its defining disposition, the disposition glimpsed in the writings of Nietzsche, Heidegger, Derrida, and Rorty.

If the card-carrying foundationalist's reaction is captured in the first response to my question, because he or she regards himself or herself (and theories generally) as playing the role of Charlie McCarthy to ''reality's'' Edgar Bergen, then those who respond in the second way can be characterized as lapsed foundationalists. Lapsed foundationalists accept one version or another of ''historicism,'' but worry that with the death of God—that is, with the recognition of the mortality and contingency of all final vocabularies—everything may be lost. Like Kierkegaard, and like Dostoevski's Ivan in *The Brothers Karamazov* (and like metaphysical realists generally), foundationalists often tend to believe that if there is no ''God,'' then everything is permitted. Yet they often do not believe that there is a ''God''—that is, a trope and concept for the single in-principle correct account of the way the world is as it is in itself—and this fact distinguishes them from our first respondents (the card-carrying foundationalists) for whom all descriptions actually or potentially either represent or fail to represent their object as it is in itself. So our lapsed foundationalists feel a keen sense of loss when belief in unconditional foundations, nonhistorical groundings, transcendental arguments, essences, and natural kinds is given up. Some worry about ''relativism'' and ''nihilism.'' Others want to destroy any established order on the (mistaken) belief that without a privileged attachment to reality all vocabularies are arbitrary: All optional vocabularies are arbitrary power/knowledge webs, in this view. Foucault sometimes seems to talk this way. Still other lapsed (realist) foundationalists, such as Heidegger, while arguing for the contingency and mortality of vocabularies, want their writings desperately to point toward unmediated visions of Being, to achieve a transparency in which Being has become word.

The third response, in contrast, is (or ought to be) Richard Rorty's.

It would be a mistake, however, to consider postmodern philosophy as having "discovered" the (philosophical) fact that vocabularies are optional, contingent, and mortal. Worse still it would be self-referentially incoherent to produce a transcendental argument to dispose of the possibility of transcendental arguments. Rather, answer number three, above, is best understood as the postmodernists drawing a moral from the history of our own philosophical practice. Crudely put, the presumption of the history of philosophy counts against the foundationalist precisely because there is not now nor has there ever been a canonical consensus on *any* "philosophical" question. And if we can be said to have had knowledge (*qua* certainty) only when we have had apodictically justified true belief, then we have *never* known anything.

Perhaps, then, we have been in the grip of a misleading picture of knowledge and inquiry all along. After all, if no agreement on a final vocabulary has yet been achieved, how long ought one to wait before giving up the picture of inquiry as the search for the ultimate vocabulary? Having waited 2,500 years, shall we change the subject only after 3,000 (failed) years? 10,000? I call this "the presumption-creating argument." It should not be construed as a species of skepticism or nihilism. Rather, it is a recommendation that we give up the notion of philosophy as the theory of accurate representation.

The force of the above point can be put another way. Since Plato parted company from the wise persons (*sophoi*) of his day, knowledge and opinion, truth and persuasion, logic and rhetoric, have gone their separate ways. The Platonic demotion of "rhetoric" was purchased with a primissory note, however. That promissory note was this: among all the competing self and world descriptions one and only one could be picked out as the vocabulary reality would itself choose to describe itself, if it could. Given the history of philosophy as the history of failed attempts to become reality's Charlie McCarthy, it should be argued that Plato should now be viewed instead as the first and most successful sophist, as the most persuasive rhetor. If the knowledge/opinion, truth/persuasion binary oppositions are parasitic upon cashing Plato's promissory note—which remains uncashed—then perhaps we can do all that needs to be done without invoking the metaphorics of final vocabularies and ultimate resting points.

Richard Rorty once suggested, in *Consequences of Pragmatism*, that James and Dewey will be found at the end of the road Derrida and Foucault have travelled. I have been arguing here that Rorty's postmodern pragmatism is the end of the road we are all travelling, a road whose starting point began with the inscription "God is dead."[57]

NOTES

1. I do not mean to suggest that my confusions are a result of the fact that the phenomenon has received inadequate attention or discussion in print or elsewhere. On the contrary, the literature on postmodernism has become extensive—a virtual cottage industry—and the expression has been invoked in connection with everything from philosophy and art to cornflakes and movies. MTV, one notes, has even had its own postmodern program. For useful, representative discussions and bibliographies, see especially Linda Hutcheon, *A Poetics of Postmodernism* (New York: Routledge, 1988); Henry A. Giroux, ed., *Postmodernism, Feminism, and Cultural Politics* (Albany: State University of New York Press, 1991); Linda J. Nicholson, ed., *Feminism/Postmodernism* (New York: Routledge, 1990); Steven Connor, *Postmodernist Culture* (Cambridge: Basil Blackwell, 1989); and Christopher Norris, *What's Wrong with Postmodernism* (Baltimore, Md.: Johns Hopkins University Press, 1990).

2. This, too, is an oversimplification, of course. (At a 1990 conference on postmodern architecture, sponsored by the UCHRI, for example, a ninety-three-page bibliography was distributed to participants). Nevertheless, that postmodern architecture is attempting to "post" modern architecture, to displace, dislodge, or replace it, is reasonably uncontroversial. In contrast, it is not at all clear what postmodern philosophy is trying to displace, dislodge, or replace. Sometimes it looks as if it is the history of modern philosophy—its framework and its categories—that is to be overcome, as in Rorty (at least in *Philosophy and the Mirror of Nature*, if not later) and Foucault. But that would be too thin a time-slice for Nietzsche, Heidegger, or Derrida, for whom the career of philosophy since the fifteenth century seems simply to be an intensification of tendencies already diagnosed in Plato. From that angle of vision, it is the entire metaphysical tradition that is to be displaced or set aside, to be "posted"—with the peculiar consequence that philosophical modernism may be as old as philosophy itself, from this point of view.

3. Walter Gropius, *The New Architecture and the Bauhaus* (London: Faber and Faber, 1965), 82.

4. Charles Jencks, *The Language of Post-Modern Architecture*, 4th ed. (London: Academy Editions, 1984), 9.

5. Robert Venturi, *Learning from Las Vegas* (Cambridge, Mass.: MIT Press, 1962), 135–36. Must one add that this citation is used to illustrate a point, not to endorse Las Vegas's Strip architecture?

6. This simplification is subject to the cautions mentioned in note 2, above.

7. Charles Newman, *The Post-Modern Aura: The Act of Fiction in an Age of Inflation* (Evanston, Ill.: Northwestern University Press, 1985), 17.

8. Lyotard, Jameson, and Baudrillard are not discussed here, nor are other candidates, Foucault or Irigaray, for example. These exclusions are almost entirely pedagogical, for I think the specifically philosophical points that are to be made can be put in sharper relief by developing the genealogy traced here, rather than alternative trajectories and inflections. But I could be as mistaken about this as I have been (and may still be) about other substantive matters.

9. For bibliographical details see my *Postmodern Postures: Nietzsche, Heidegger, Derrida, and Rorty* (New York: Routledge, forthcoming).

10. A more adequate discussion of these points is undertaken in my *Postmodern Postures*, forthcoming. Briefly, these twenty suggestions derive from considerations that include (but are not limited to) some of the following items: the growing opposition to the spectator theory of knowledge, in Europe and in the English-speaking world (in Anglophone philosophy this took the early form of Dewey's [and pragmatism's] opposition to positivism, early Kuhn's redescription of scientific practice, and Wittgenstein's insistence on the language-game character of representation); critiques of "the myth of the given" from Sellars to Davidson and Quine; the emergence of epistemology naturalized; the putative description-dependent character of data, tethered to the theory dependence of descriptions (in Kuhn, Sellars, Quine, and Fine—perhaps in all constructivists in the philosophy of science). One thinks of Neurath's marvelous contrast/analogy of conceiving "philosophy" either

as building a secure foundation as one would for a house or rebuilding it in the manner of a wooden ship at sea on a long voyage.

In Europe, think of Heidegger's and Derrida's attacks on Husserl's residual Cartesianism; their rejection of essential descriptions (*Wesensanschauungen*) in Husserl's sense; Saussure's and structuralism's attack on the autonomy and coherence of a transcendental signified standing over against a self-transparent subject; Derrida's deconstructing the metaphysics of presence; Foucault's redescriptions of epistemes; the convergence in the philosophy of science between Latour et al. and social constructivists—for example, Traweek and Pickering; the attack on the language of enabling conditions, as reflected in worries about the purchase of necessary and sufficient condition talk on both sides of the Atlantic; Lyotard's many interventions, particularly those against grand narratives; and think of the many, virtually universal challenges to "moral philosophy" as it has been understood traditionally in the West, not only in German and French philosophy, but recently in the reevaluation of "the morality of principles" in the work of MacIntyre, B. Williams, M. Nussbaum, and J. McDowell.

Above all, perhaps, think of the challenges of feminist theory, and gender theory generally (on both sides of the Atlantic, once again), to the conception of "reason" itself as it has functioned in the shared philosophical tradition—as a conception that, it is often argued, is (en)gendered, patriarchal, homophobic, and deeply optional (as in Nancy Fraser's work, for example).

11. Allan Megill discusses many of the same thinkers in his *Prophets of Extremity: Nietzsche, Heidegger, Foucault, Derrida* (Berkeley: University of California Press, 1984), but his treatment is at right angles to mine. Perhaps this is merely a function of the differing disciplinary perspectives that inflect and inform our respective approaches.

12. Compare this contrast with Steven Taubeneck's "Translator's Afterword" titled "Nietzsche in North America: Walter Kaufmann and After" in Ernst Behler, ed., *Confrontations: Derrida/Heidegger/Nietzsche* (Stanford: Stanford University Press, 1991): "Danto, Magnus, and Schacht, each with his own suggestions, offer principles different from Kaufmann's as alternative bases for understanding Nietzsche. Nehamas and Krell highlight to differing extents the roles of Nietzsche's many styles. Bloom, among those who use Nietzsche for other arguments, retains the humanistic-anthropological emphasis and adds a critique of the politics; Rorty downplays the politics and drops the belief in a foundational human nature" (p. 176).

13. Arthur C. Danto, *Nietzsche as Philosopher* (New York: Macmillan, 1965).

14. John T. Wilcox, *Truth and Value in Nietzsche* (Ann Arbor: University of Michigan Press, 1974).

15. Maudemarie Clark, *Nietzsche on Truth and Philosophy* (New York: Cambridge University Press, 1990).

16. Richard Schacht, *Nietzsche* (London: Routledge and Kegan Paul, 1983).

17. Harold Alderman, *Nietzsche's Gift* (Miami: Ohio University Press, 1977).

18. Jacques Derrida, *Spurs* (Chicago: University of Chicago Press, 1979) and *Otobiography: The Ear of the Other* (New York: Schocken Books, 1985).

19. Alexander Nehamas, *Nietzsche: Life as Literature* (Cambridge, Mass.: Harvard University Press, 1985).

20. Gilles Deleuze, *Nietzsche et la philosophie* (Presses Universitaires de France, 1962), translated by Hugh Tomlinson as *Nietzsche and Philosophy* (New York: Columbia University Press, 1983).

21. Tracy B. Strong, *Friedrich Nietzsche and the Politics of Transfiguration* (Berkeley: University of California Press, 1975).

22. Gary Shapiro, *Nietzschean Narratives* (Bloomington: Indiana University Press, 1989) and *Alcyone: Nietzsche on Gifts, Noise, and Women* (Albany: State University of New York Press, 1991).

23. Richard Rorty, *Contingency, Irony, and Solidarity* (Cambridge: Cambridge University Press, 1989).

24. For discussion of the textural difficulties see my "The Use and Abuse of *The Will to Power*"

in *Reading Nietzsche*, ed. R. C. Solomon and K. Higgins (New York: Oxford University Press, 1988).

25. See especially chapter 1 of *Nietzsche's Case: Philosophy as/and Literature* by Bernd Magnus, Jean-Pierre Mileur and Stanley Stewart (New York: Routledge, in press).

26. For discussion, see ibid., and my "Deconstruction Site: The Problem of 'Style' in Nietzsche's Philosophy," *Philosophical Topics* 19 (Fall 1991): 215–45.

27. For a discussion of Heidegger's pragmatism, see Mark Okrent, *Heidegger's Pragmatism* (Ithaca, N.Y.: Cornell University Press, 1988). For a discussion of Heidegger's politics—a topic that is not considered in this brief gloss—see Tom Rockmore, *On Heidegger's Nazism and Philosophy* (Berkeley: University of California Press, 1992).

28. Martin Heidegger, *Platons Lehre von der Wahrheit*, (Bern: Francke Verlag, 1947), 49.

29. Martin Heidegger, *On Time and Being*, trans. Joan Stambaugh (New York: Harper and Row, 1972), 62.

30. I am aware of the fact that much of what I have now said appears to undermine itself, for to characterize Derrida's work as resisting characterization just *is* to characterize it; and to assert that his writing may be read as a generalization of this point, a challenge to the familiar procedure of paraphrasing and characterizing philosophical writers and their writings, simply deepens the appearance of oddity.

31. Jacques Derrida, *Otobiography: The Ear of the Other* (New York: Schocken Books, 1985), 86–88.

32. Ferdinand de Saussure, *Course of General Linguistics* (New York: McGraw Hill, 1966).

33. Ibid.

34. Most of Derrida's "deconstructions" can be read as instances of this same gesture enacted and reenacted in different settings. I selected the example above simply because of a prescribed economy—it took only a paragraph or two to characterize. In a similar vein, Derrida's much-discussed reversal of the priority of writing over speech—his overcoming of Saussurean "phonocentrism"—can be read with profit as a strategic move, one in which it is pointed out that one would not be able to recognize sounds as meaningful phonemes unless "traces" of intelligibility had already been "inscribed" (i.e., "written") in the psyche—as in Plato's theory of recollection.

35. Jacques Derrida, *Of Grammatology* (Baltimore: Johns Hopkins University Press, 1974), 17–18.

36. Ibid.

37. KGW III 2, 375–75: "On Truth and Lies in the Non-Moral Sense." This entire discussion, in Nietzsche's as well as in Derrida's case, seems in some respects to prefigure Donald Davidson's work on the literal/metaphorical contrast. To think of literal speech as a platform built up out of dead metaphors, to think of it as one would a coral reef composed of dead organisms, chimes well with Nietzsche's and Derrida's suggestions. This may also help to explain why Rorty much prefers the contrast between the familiar and unfamiliar to the literal/metaphorical contrast. See, for example, Rorty's *Contingency, Irony, and Solidarity*, chapter 1 and his "Deconstruction and Circumvention."

38. Jacques Derrida, "Différance," in *Margins of Philosophy* (Chicago: University of Chicago Press, 1982), 27.

39. It makes no difference to the coherence of the argument whether "origins" is understood by Heidegger and his commentators chronologically, causally, ontologically, or phenomenologically. "Origins" itself is the problem.

40. These are two tall orders, neither one of which is undertaken here. For a discussion, however, see Magnus, *Postmodern Postures*.

41. All of this is alarmingly fast, too glib, I know. For a discussion, see the promissory note mentioned in note 40, above.

42. Rorty and others have sometimes been understood as proclaiming the end of philosophy departments—and the functions they serve—when they have been understood to argue for "the end of philosophy." These are distinguishable and distinct issues, however. For discussion, see my

"The End of 'The End of Philosophy,' " in *Hermeneutics and Deconstruction*, ed. H. Silverman and D. Ihde (Albany: State University of New York Press, 1985).

43. Richard Rorty, *Consequences of Pragmatism* (Minneapolis: University of Minnesota Press, 1982), 140.

44. Richard Rorty, *Philosophy and the Mirror of Nature* (Princeton, N.J.: Princeton University Press, 1979), 320.

45. For a thoughtful discussion and criticism of Rorty's views from a sympathetically disposed perspective, that of "democratic-socialist-feminist-pragmatism," see Nancy Fraser, *Unruly Practices: Power, Discourse, and Gender in Contemporary Social Theory* (Minneapolis: University of Minnesota Press, 1989). For a defense of Rorty's political correctness, see Konstantin Kolenda, *Rorty's Humanistic Pragmatism: Philosophy Democratized* (Gainesville: University Presses of Florida, 1990).

46. Rorty, *Consequences of Pragmatism*, 171.

47. Ibid., 171–72.

48. Thomas McCarthy, "Private Irony and Public Decency: Richard Rorty's New Pragmatism," *Critical Inquiry* 16 (Spring 1990): 355–70.

49. Ibid., 367.

50. Ibid., 370.

51. Ibid., 369.

52. Ibid., 634.

53. Ibid., 635.

54. Ibid., 642.

55. *Philosophical Investigations* #621.

56. I take the term "vocabulary" in the widest sense, as the best available current self and world descriptions; the principles, distinctions, theories, and arguments that tell us what we *can* know, what we *do* know, how we *ought to* live, and what we *may* hope for.

This is similar but not identical to Rorty's use of the concept of a "final vocabulary" in *Contingency, Irony, and Solidarity*: "All human beings carry about a set of words which they employ to justify their actions, their beliefs, and their lives. These are the words in which we formulate praise of our friends and contempt for our enemies, our long-term projects, our deepest self-doubts and our highest hopes. . . . I shall call these words a person's 'final vocabulary.' It is 'final' in the sense that if doubt is cast on the worth of these words, their user has no noncircular argumentative recourse. Those words are as far as he can go with language; beyond them there is only helpless passivity or a resort to force."

57. An earlier version of this chapter was read in September 1990 at the Catholic University in Louvain, Belgium, at the Conference of the Society for the Study of the History of European ideas. I am grateful to the conference organizers for their kind invitation, especially Ezra and Sasha Talmor, and Elliot Levine. A subsequent version was read as the plenary address of the Iowa Philosophical Society, in November 1990. I am grateful to the Iowa Philosophical Society, especially to Jack Worley and Joseph Cummins, for inviting me to deliver this address.

14

Richard Rorty's Romantic Pragmatism

Isaac Nevo

In recent articles, Rorty contrasts the viewpoint he calls "scientism," which he takes to be characteristic of philosophy's main traditions from Plato to Kant, with an antitheoretical attitude in philosophy shared by pragmatists and Heideggerian postmodernists.[1] Scientism, Rorty explains, is the metaphilosophical doctrine that conceives of philosophy as a theoretical domain and advocates the acceptance of science as a model for philosophical theorizing. Scientism, he believes, is to be detected equally in the works of rationalists and empiricists, phenomenologists and positivists, Kantians and Hegelians. Theoretical differences between these schools of thought are merely of secondary importance.

Philosophers in these various traditions are subject to what, following Wittgenstein, one may call a "craving for theory." They project standards of objectivity suitable to the narrow domain of science onto other fields of intellectual activity. For this reason, traditional philosophers tend to postulate a neutral and independent viewpoint, in relation to which the distinction between reality and all appearances could be drawn, and from which judgment about reality could be rendered. In opposing this tradition, pragmatists and Heideggerians argue that there is no discourse-transcendent viewpoint from which the Platonic, Cartesian, or Kantian projects could be launched. This claim, according to Rorty, constitutes not merely a rejection of the scientistic philosophical tradition, but a rejection of this tradition precisely on grounds of its scientism. Pragmatists such as Davidson and Heideggerians such as Derrida share the rejection of scientism as their philosophical common ground.

A few quotes from Rorty should give the flavor of these moves. On the scientistic view, "Philosophy is modeled on science and is relatively remote from both art and politics'' (SMP: 13). This is the view shared by Husserl and Carnap, who ''shared the traditional Platonic hope to ascend to a point of view from which the interconnections between everything could be seen'' (SMP: 15). In opposition to this scientistic view, ''Heidegger turns away from the scientist to the poet,'' while ''pragmatists such as Dewey turn away from the theoretical scientist to the engineers and the social workers'' (SMP: 13). Heideggerians take philosophy to be ''a series of poetic achievements'' (SMP: 13). For pragmatists, philosophy is better seen as a ''bag of tools'' (SMP: 13), to be utilized or discarded as need arises. Both share a ''deep distrust of the visual metaphors that link Husserl to Plato and Descartes'' (SMP: 15). In so using scientism as his theme, Rorty redescribes the history of philosophy in particularly bold strokes. Details, one can appreciate, are not his primary focus.

But there are also some important differences that Rorty acknowledges between pragmatists and Heideggerians. For all their common rejection of scientism, ''Heidegger's and Dewey's conceptions of philosophy are nevertheless very different. Their common opposition to foundationalism and to visual metaphors took radically different forms'' (SMP: 15). Although both pragmatists and Heideggerians deny that there is any discourse-transcendent viewpoint, pragmatists try to supplant philosophy's scientistic descriptions of intellectual activity with descriptions more conducive to social reform, while Heideggerians prefer descriptions and vocabularies more amenable to poetic self-expression. According to Rorty, however, these differences, while undeniable, are practical rather than philosophical in nature. The different reactions pragmatists and Heideggerians have taken toward the philosophical tradition come down to different preferences as to which ''vocabulary'' should replace the prevailing scientistic one. In this context a ''vocabulary'' should be understood as an inseparable, holistic mixture of language and belief. Since reality does not come equipped with its own ''objective'' description, preferences in the choice of vocabularies cannot be given an objective basis. Neither the pragmatist nor the Heideggerian can claim any greater objectivity to the descriptions they prefer. The pragmatist takes philosophy for a bag of tools, the Heideggerian for a poetic achievement, but this difference is merely a practical difference about which vocabulary to adopt once the scientistic vocabularies of traditional philosophy have been discarded.

The practical differences between pragmatists and Heideggerians arise, in Rorty's view, from a difference in political orientation. Heidegger and Dewey differ in their attitude to the legacy of the French revolution, a legacy Rorty characterizes as the political attempt to secure ''the greatest happiness to the greatest number'' (SMP: 24). Dewey accepts this legacy as strongly as Heidegger rejects it. The pragmatist is a progressive. For him, foundational philosophy, in its demand for objective justification, is a major roadblock on the way of liberal social engineering. The Heideggerian, by contrast, is a classical conservative. To his mind, scientistic philosophy is a threat to received national culture, to its identity and integrity. Philosophically, both agree that there are no discourse-transcendent truths, but their postfoundationalist preferences are determined by their respective political orientations. For Rorty, the political difference between liberals and classical conservatives, between those who would extend the "legacy" of the French Revolution further and those who would roll it back, does not depend on some prior philosophical difference about human nature or natural rights. Apparent philosophical differences such as those between pragmatists and Heideggerians are, at bottom, just political.

We may summarize Rorty's redescription of the history of philosophy as the conjunction of three theses, one of which (no. 3, below) is of a philosophical nature. The remaining two (nos. 1 and 2) are more in the nature of historical appraisals. These theses are as follows:

1. The Western philosophical tradition is fundamentally scientistic. It is built around the acceptance of philosophy as a theoretical domain, governed by the methods and principles of natural science. Epistemological foundationalism and metaphysical dualism are merely consequences of this scientistic stance.

2. The rejection of scientism is the common philosophical ground shared by pragmatist and Heideggerian philosophers, who reject any claim to a discourse-transcendent reason, or reality. Thus, pragmatists and Heideggerians not only reject the same traditions, but they reject them for the same reasons.

3. Differences in orientation between pragmatists and Heideggerians are political in nature. There are no philosophical issues remaining to be settled between proponents of these two schools.

On the basis of these theses, Rorty attempts a reconciliation of pragmatist and Heideggerian views. He envisions a poeticization of pragmatism that transcends political differences, as well as the differences between the continental tradition in philosophy and the analytic, or Anglo-American tradition. The crux of Rorty's proposal is that the differences in question can be split by prioritizing the preference for poetic self-redescription in matters belonging to the private sphere of interest, while accepting the pragmatist emphasis on social utility insofar as public interests are at stake. After all, once scientism has been rejected there can be no expectation of uniqueness in the selection of vocabularies and descriptions by which intellectual affairs are to be conducted. Any residual conflict between alternative proposals can in principle be resolved by "territorial," or political, compromises. An explicitly political resolution of the pragmatist/Heideggerian divide is preferable to the use of "Aesopian philosophical language," for again, "The difference between Heidegger's and Dewey's ways of rejecting scientism is political rather than methodological or metaphysical" (SMP: 28).

Rorty has been taken to task for the seemingly absolute distinction he draws between the private and public spheres of interest. Writing from a feminist perspective, hence a perspective that basically approves of "the legacy of the French Revolution," Nancy Fraser warns against too complacent an acceptance of the distinction between the private and the public, "lest we see our theory go the way of our housework.''[2] Fraser's worry is that no room is left, in Rorty's scheme, for radical social criticism that is not formulated in terms of utility and social engineering. In radical social criticism, social and political demands are made in the name of utopian redefinitions of society and humanity. By Rorty's lights, utopian criticism confuses the private sphere of interest, where self-redefinition is of great value, with the public domain, where it constitutes a totalitarian threat. But Rorty's account presupposes a distinction between the private and the public that is hard to sustain. It is unlikely that people who disagree over the legacy of the French Revolution are likely to agree on what belongs to the public and what is just a private affair. The private/public distinction is as much in need of context as any other. Taking Rorty's compromise to be on shaky ground, Fraser concludes that Rorty's whole work is "stalemated" between contrary, pragmatic versus Romantic pressures. At different times one of these tendencies asserts itself over the other, but no decisive view emerges in his writings, which alternately advocate both social engineering and poetic nihilism.

These observations may well be true. But by focusing on politics alone, however, they may yield Rorty too much ground. The philosophical underpinnings of Rorty's "poetic" pragmatism, which I have summarized as theses 1–3 above, are in dire need of critical scrutiny. If there is a stalemate between pragmatic and Heideggerian pressures in Rorty's writings, it is, I shall argue, a stalemate between contrary *philosophical* views, not merely between postphilosophical, cultural, or political orientations.

In this chapter, I argue against all three of Rorty's underlying theses. Beginning with Rorty's metaphilosophical thesis (no. 3) that no philosophical issues arise in the pragmatist-Heideggerian divide, I argue that, although the choice of postfoundationalist "vocabularies" cannot be governed by anything like a foundation, not all vocabularies are equally suited for the purpose of articulating, explaining, or defending the naturalist perspective of the scientific enterprise. The matter of coming to terms with the scientific enterprise is a fundamental philosophical issue, regardless of whether there is an *a priori* foundation for that enterprise or not. The failure of the foundationalist attempt to reach what Rorty and Putnam call the "God's-eye view" is not necessarily the failure of philosophical enquiry as such, which may continue, as Quine would have it, in a naturalized, holistic manner. The viability of naturalized philosophical enquiry is not independent of the choice of postfoundationalist "vocabularies." In particular, it is not independent of the difference between the vocabularies of pragmatists and Heideggerians. This is so in spite of the fact that a naturalized philosophical enquiry admits of no *a priori* ground, or foundation.

Pragmatism, I argue, is first and foremost a form of philosophical naturalism. What the pragmatist is pragmatic about is primarily the question of justifying the scientific enterprise. The pragmatist responds to the failure of foundationalism by relativizing the justification of science to the (holistic) perspectives of the practicing scientist. The Heideggerian, on the other hand, or more generally, the Romantic, responds to the failure of foundationalism differently. Rather than relativizing theoretical justification to some contingent viewpoint, he takes a generally antitheoretical attitude, postulating an antithesis between explicable order and inexplicable change. Rather than holism, the Heideggerian employs what I wish to call a Romantic-dichotomous view, which maintains such distinctions as those between order and chaos, logic and temporality, or reason and culture. The difference between holistic pragmatism and Romantic-dichotomous Heideggerianism is, I argue, philosophical, despite the fact that it cannot be resolved by means of *a priori*, foundational reasoning.

In *Philosophy and the Mirror of Nature*, Rorty criticizes Quine for the mere contingency of his naturalism.[3] Given the holism of "Two Dogmas of Empiricism," Quine's preference for physicalism, for extensional languages, and for the "special" indeterminacy of translation is according to Rorty purely an aesthetic preference. There can be no objective justification of these preferences that does not invoke the untenable distinctions Quine has rejected. Rorty believes that it would have been more consistent on Quine's part to accept a plurality of descriptive languages, including some that are intensional, rather than a hierarchy of an extensional notation to limn the structure of reality and an intentional idiom suitable for practical purposes only. This criticism, however, is hardly available for an antifoundationalist such as Rorty. In the absence of a neutral foundation, Quine's naturalistic preferences serve to provide a contingent basis for epistemology. It shows that the failure of foundationalism is not necessarily the end of all philosophical theorizing. Indeed, the failure of foundationalism is sufficient for Rorty's antitheoretical approach to philosophy, only on the assumption that philosophical theorizing is necessarily foundational. The latter assumption is not available to Rorty as an advocate of contingency. Consequently, his argument against Quine fails to provide a bridge from naturalism to Heideggerian Romanticism. A philosophical difference remains in this context that is well worth exploring.

Given the untenability of the metaphilosophical thesis here recorded as no. 3, Rorty's more historical theses (nos. 1 and 2) concerning the scientism of Western philosophy as a whole and the sharing of an antiscientistic approach by pragmatists and Heideggerians look questionable. To take scientism rather than dualism or foundationalism as the common focus of antifoundationalist criticism in philosophy is already a decisive shift in the direction of Heideggerian and Romantic thinking. Thesis no. 2, which contains this description, is not likely to be accepted by most pragmatists, who have no objection to scientific philosophy as such. The pragmatist objects to the scientific model in philosophy only when this model is employed within the dualistic assumption that the subject matter of philosophy constitutes a higher, more than empirical, sphere of truths. There is, however, no pragmatist objection to the scientific model in philosophy when the employment of this model is divorced from such traditional assumptions. Thesis no. 1 is similarly skewed. In no way can scientism, that is, the acceptance of science as a model for philosophical enquiry, be taken as the unequivocal core of Western philosophical tradition, even in its modern period. The contrary is more likely true. In its dualism, modern foundationalist philosophy betrays more suspicion toward natural science than it does scientistic craving for its model. Foundational philosophy constitutes a refusal to accept natural science on its own terms, that is, without additional justification from sources of authority that stand entirely outside its province. Taken in its historical context, modern philosophy looks less like a craving for science that allows no exceptions, and more like a sustained effort to put "roadblocks" in the way of scientific enquiry in the service of the Christian, prescientific view of things. In this case, too, Rorty's view seems to be tilted in the direction of Romanticism. Modern philosophy deployed the rhetoric of "theory," or "reason," to delimit the scientific perspective, which it could not directly oppose, so as to leave room for principles of the prescientific worldview that were elevated for this purpose to the status of superempirical "foundations." It takes a Romantic-Heideggerian perspective to consider such ambivalence as the mark of uncompromising "scientism."

I now return to thesis no. 3 in order to cast doubt on the claim that no philosophical issues arise in the debate between pragmatists and Heideggerians, and that the issues separating them are merely political in nature. In Rorty's view, once "scientism" has been rejected, on whatever grounds, all distinctively philosophical considerations have been dismissed. The choice of alternative vocabularies is now a practical, not a philosophical matter. These points are made, sharply and succinctly, in texts such as the following:

In what precedes I have sketched what I take to be the central meta-philosophical disagreements of recent times. On my account there are two basic lines of division: one between the scientism common to Husserl and positivism, and the other between two reactions to this scientism. The first reaction—Heidegger's—is dictated by a tacit and unarguable rejection of the project of the French Revolution, and of the idea that everything, including philosophy, is an instrument for the achievement of the greatest happiness of the greatest number. The second—Dewey's—is dictated by an equally tacit and unarguable acceptance of that project and that idea. (SMP: 24)

The political preferences attributed to Heidegger and Dewey respectively cannot be argued from first principles. There is no permanent neutral matrix from which to begin. From this point Rorty concludes that no philosophical issues arise in the debate. For philosophy, so Rorty assumes, is inextricably interwoven with the defunct scientistic model of first principles and Cartesian starting points. It follows that one has to resort to nonphilosophical considerations in order to articulate the acknowledged differences between Heidegger and Dewey. Hence, we get Rorty's historical talk about the French Revolution.

To establish this point, Rorty discusses the status of metaphor in Davidson and in Heidegger. The aim of his discussion is to show that there are no substantial differences between these philosophers on the subject of metaphor. This does not, perhaps, suffice to establish his point in its full generality, but it is an important case. The status of metaphor, and more generally, the status of what we may call the literary as distinguished from the scientific point of view, has always been an important bone of contention between positivists and Romantics. If by the time we get to Davidson and Heidegger no such difference survives, then Rorty's point about the political nature of the pragmatist/Heideggerian cleavage will have been supported to a significant degree. In other words, if on the subject of metaphor no philosophical differences remain between pragmatists and Heideggerians, this must be so because the positivist attempt to isolate the cognitive domain by means of the verification principle, and to relegate the literary and the metaphorical to the noncognitive, has been entirely superceded.

Rorty fails, however, to establish his point. In fact, his discussion of metaphor shows how far he has strayed from Davidson's holistic account of language in his quest for a common ground with Heidegger and the Romantic tradition. In essence, Rorty reads into Davidson's holistic conception of metaphor a Romantic dichotomy between reason and inspiration as sources of belief and belief revision, a reading almost diametrically opposed to Davidson's own. This reading obscures the difference between a holistic critique of positivism as an ill-conceived model of the cognitive domain, on the one hand, and the Romantic insurrection against the cognitive as such, which tacitly accepts the positivist account of it, on the other. The point comes out most clearly in Rorty's account of metaphor.

In Davidson's view, there are no metaphorical meanings over and above the literal meanings of words. The distinction between literal and metaphorical meaning, Davidson might have said, is an untenable dualism, a metaphysical article of faith. In short, Davidson does to "metaphorical" what Quine did to "synonymous" or "analytic"; he relativizes the distinction within a holistic scheme.

"Metaphor," Davidson contends, "belongs exclusively to the domain of use."[4] Use in this context is the practice of revising belief in accommodating recalcitrant experience or theory change; the use of language and the determination of belief are not determinately demarcated. Thus, an account of metaphor as belonging exclusively to the domain of use is an account of metaphor as a by-product of belief revision. In Davidson's holistic conception, the process of belief revision is governed by the need to harmonize the often conflicting demands of theory and experience within a logically coherent scheme. The fundamental principle at work here is that experience by itself does not suffice to determine belief, because any experience can be accommodated by conflicting belief systems by means of internal revisions within them. In the process of revision, statements held false gradually come to be seen as true, at first "metaphorically." Later, as things settle around the particular belief revision, the metaphor "dies" and the belief in question is taken for a literal truth. This view requires, as Rorty notes, that no distinction between belief change and meaning change should be accepted, and that meaning in general should be identified with use.

Rorty is, no doubt, correct in his assessment that this Quinean-Davidsonian view of language is "the best current expression of the pragmatist attempt to break with the philosophical tradition" (SMP: 18). This is so because the holistic conception of scientific method, which determines these views, leaves no room for the absolute distinctions upon which the dualism of traditional philosophy could be made to rest. Distinctions in truth category (necessary versus contingent), in epistemic category (*a priori* versus *a posteriori*), or in semantic category (analytic versus synthetic) all become "contextualized," or relativized to the underdetermined perspective of a particular belief reviser, the busy sailor adrift in Neurat's boat, to use Quine's image, whose task it is to bring his belief system into coherence while taking into account the conflicting demands of theory and experience.

So much for Davidson's account of metaphor and the pragmatic perspective it is made to serve. Consider now the Heideggerian gloss that Rorty puts on this account. While for Davidson, as we saw above, metaphor is a *by-product* of holistic belief revision processes, that is, processes governed by both experience and logic, for Rorty, metaphor is a further *source* of belief revision, over and above perception and inference. More specifically, he reads Davidson's view as implying that metaphor is "a third source of beliefs," and a "third motive for reweaving our networks of beliefs and desires" (SMP: 16). Thus, in Rorty's account, there are three independent sources of belief revision, of which metaphor, or the intellectual interest in redescription for its own sake, is one, with perception and inference being the others. This doctrine may sound similar to Davidson's, but it is really diametrically opposed to it. In Davidson's account, perception and inference are sufficient sources of belief revision, and the account of metaphor requires no other. This is so because the resulting theories, or belief systems, are taken by Davidson to be underdetermined. According to Rorty, however, this very limitation of possible belief revision represents what he calls, after Heidegger, "the mathematical attitude," namely the acceptance of a pre-existent matrix of possibilities within which revision is to take place. The importance of this difference cannot be overestimated. In Rorty's argument, restricting belief revision to the resources of perception and inference can only be motivated by a belief that perception and inference suffice to determine a unique "logical space." On this ground, Rorty attributes to Davidson an acceptance of metaphor as another source of belief revision. But this fails to take into account that a restriction of belief revision to the sources of perception and inference may be a way of advocating underdetermination of theory, rather than a determinacy of logical space. Contrary to what Rorty is saying, one may restrict belief revision to inference and perception, admitting the underdetermination of the resulting belief system, without having to admit a unique system or logical space. Indeed, this is, in all probability, Davidson's view. The attribution of a "third source" doctrine to him is groundless.

Rorty's underlying argument can be summed up as the following hypothetical syllogism:

(P_1) Belief revision is restricted to perception and inference *only if* the resulting belief systems are uniquely determined by these sources.

(P_2) Belief systems are uniquely determined *only if* there is a preexistent logical space in which every determinate belief is located.

Therefore:

(C) Belief revision is restricted to perception and inference, *only if* there is a preexistent logical space in which every determinate belief is located.

Since on grounds of holism, Davidson would no doubt reject the belief in a preexistent logical space, one may safely conclude that given the conclusion (C), Davidson would also reject its antecedent, namely, the claim that belief revision is restricted to just the effects of perception and inference. Hence, the third source doctrine that Rorty attributes to Davidson. However, the doctrine of holism, or more specifically, the doctrine of the underdetermination of belief revision, precludes the first premise, too. Restriction of belief revision to the effects of perception and inference does not materially imply the unique determinacy of the resulting belief system.

For Davidson, "metaphor works on the same linguistic tracks that the plainest sentences do."[5] These tracks are perception and inference, namely, the need to bring belief systems into coherence under the conflicting pressures of experience and theory. Given the thesis of holism and its consequences, for example, the underdetermination of theory, no other sources of belief need be accepted. This point is usually made against notions of pure analysis, or truths of reason, as putative sources of belief, but it is equally true of metaphor or inspiration. Rorty does not seem to accept this. Losing sight of his own holism, he says: "Such a conception of language [namely, the one that allows only inference and perception as sources of belief revision] accords with the idea that the point of philosophy is what Husserl took it to be: to map out all possible logical space, to make explicit our implicit grasp of the realm of possibility" (SMP: 16). But in truth, confining belief revision to just perception and inference has no such consequences. For the pragmatist, perception and inference are the exclusive determinants of belief and belief revision, because for him no system of belief, no theory of the world, can claim to be uniquely supported by the evidence. Multiple systems are possible which are not equivalent to one another, and therefore the confinement of belief revision to inference and perception, excluding analysis, reason, or metaphor, leads to no rigid conception of logical space.

So in place of a holistic conception of metaphor, which relativizes metaphorical "meaning" to belief revision under the conflicting pressures of perception and inference, Rorty offers a dichotomy of different kinds of "sources" of belief revision. Perception and inference govern belief revision from within "logical space," while metaphor induces revision as a "voice" from outside any such space. Rorty's characterization of this dichotomy should leave little doubt that it is conceived after the fundamental Romantic cleavage between Apollonian order and Dionysian disruption. In Rorty's language:

A metaphor is, so to speak, a voice from outside logical space, rather than an empirical filling up of a portion of that space, or a logical philosophical clarification of the structure of that space. It is a call to change one's language and one's life, rather than a proposal about how to systematize them. (SMP:17)

All the elements of Romanticism are at work here: change versus systematicity, life versus theory, logic versus temporality. These antitheses have nothing to do with Davidson or with pragmatism. They constitute the imposition of Romantic doctrine on the critical devices of pragmatism. Contrary to Rorty's claims, moreover, these impositions fly in the face of deep-lying philosophical differences.

Rorty's account of metaphor fails to establish the point Rorty is trying to make, namely, that no philosophical difference appears in the debate between pragmatists and Heideggerians. The difference, we saw, comes up as the difference between Davidson's construal of metaphor as a function of use, or belief revision, which proceeds on the normal "linguistic tracks," on the one hand, and Rorty's account of metaphor as an independent "source" of, or motive for, belief revision, over and above the normal tracks of inference and perception, on the other. This difference is no minor variation on Davidson's theme. Rorty's version glosses over the fundamental philosophical difference between holistic and Romantic-dichotomous criticism of foundational philosophy. Davidson's holistic approach is a critique of foundational philosophy as an inadequate conception of the *scientific enterprise*, a conception that places too stringent demands on its epistemological justification, and carries over in the formulation of these demands metaphysical dogmas that preserve the notion of a higher, extrascientific and more than merely natural court of appeal to which science could be referred. Rorty's account of metaphor, however, echoes a very different line of criticism. In his Romantic-dichotomous criticism, foundationalist strictures are not challenged on grounds of their epistemological inadequacy with respect to the scientific enterprise. Rather, the scientific enterprise itself, along with its traditional epistemological justifications, are claimed to be inadequate for capturing some principle of inexplicable change, or flux, which is further claimed as an equal determinant of "our life," or our culture. Rorty's account of metaphor is an instance of the latter, Romantic-dichotomous approach. Rorty obscures its super-natural dimension by trying to assimilate it to Davidson's holistic account. But for all of Rorty's rhetoric, there could be no greater difference in philosophy between relativizing the order of the universe to the perspectives of a practicing scientist—Neurath's busy sailor, to use Quine's image again—and postulating a principle of dis-order, or chaos, of which our life and our poetry are to be models. Both these claims can be expressed by the anti-dualist slogan that there is no single order in the universe, no unique theory of the world that is true and objective. But beyond this common target, pragmatism and Romanticism could not be farther apart.

For the pragmatist, the failure of uniqueness in world systems and scientific theories is no vice. The pragmatist is willing to acquiesce in the perspectives of the practicing scientist, even though no unique view, or theory of the world, is thereby determined, provided that the practicing scientist in question operates within a recognizable scientific tradition allowing at most for conservative extensions in this direction or that. In this, the pragmatist is a naturalist. For him, there is no higher reality to which the practicing scientist could be held accountable. Even the matter of justifying the practice of science has to be handled within that practice, in continuity with the relevant theories in neighboring sciences. The pragmatist neither calls into question the viability of science, nor does he dismiss philosophy, along with some of its traditional questions, on grounds of this naturalism. For the pragmatist, philosophy does not have a separate subject matter, or *fach*, as Rorty calls it, which is discontinuous with that of the natural sciences. But it doesn't follow that it has no subject matter at all. Philosophy is continuous with the sciences and its subject matter is continuous with theirs. For the pragmatist, in short, philosophy survives as a theoretical domain, though one that is part of the natural sciences, not one that is prior to science with its own kind of truth. In objecting to the untenable dualisms of the foundationalist tradition, the pragmatist objects to the inadequacies of foundationalism as an account of science and philosophy, not to science and philosophy as such, which he seeks to continue "without the dogmas."

None of this is acceptable to Heideggerian Romantics or to postmodernists. For them it is the scientific tradition, not merely its foundationalist justification, that has been exhausted and deconstructed by the failure of uniqueness and determinacy in science. More specifically, it is the failure of such categories as truth, logic, and identity, which seem to have the requirement of uniqueness built into them, and which govern all theoretical thinking, scientific and philosophical. This failure in uniqueness of vision, or theory, is therefore a celebration of the poetic, or the tragic, or the intertextual, or any other image that may be offered as a model of the inexplicable. For the Romantic, inexplicability in the service of the temporal is no vice. On the contrary, it is a mark of the freedom gained from scientism, from the expectations that things would make sense under the unsatisfiable categories of truth and logic.

Elements of this view are not hard to find in the works of Rorty's heroes: Nietzsche, Heidegger, Derrida, and others. Heidegger, we know, takes "temporality," in a suitably primordial sense to the term, to constitute the "transcendental horizon for the question of Being." Temporality, in other words, is the condition that makes the question (and the questioning, that is, *Dasein*) possible. Primordial temporality differs from more ordinary notions of time by being incompatible with identity across time. It is the flux. Primordial temporality cannot be stepped twice into.[6] Similarly, Nietzsche believes logic to be a falsification, to spring from a will other than the will to truth, because the notion of form on which it depends presupposes the illusory notion of identity across time.[7] From Derrida we learn both that "iterability" is the essential mark of writing, that is, the possibility of grafting the written sign in contexts beyond the control of its author, and that iterability is not an identity-preserving operation. "Iterability alters!" we learn, so it is difference, rather, that constitutes the transcendental horizon of writing, which cannot therefore be grasped by stable structures or meanings.[8] These philosophers are the advocates of a dichotomous view of logic and time; of the belief that logic, science, or reason merely project unstable orders, or structures, beyond which a different, deconstructive perspective is to be gained, which is better modeled by Heraclitus's diver than by Neurath's sailor. All three of these philosophers are, of course, aware of the perspectival status of the dichotomies they employ, for which they can claim no privileged objectivity. But their view remains dichotomous, rather than holistic, despite its perspectival status. The failure of epistemology-centered philosophy is, for them, the failure of *objectivity*, not only of the dualist attempt to base it on *a priori* truth.

We may put these differences in a historical perspective by taking a brief look at the other components of Rorty's view, namely theses nos. 1 and 2, above. We found that the differences between pragmatists and Heideggerians are indeed clearly philosophical, and not merely political in nature. What now of Rorty's historical scheme, which portrays the philosophical tradition, Carnap, Husserl, and all, as a fundamentally scientistic enterprise (thesis no. 1), and the opposition to this scientism as the common core of the pragmatist and Heideggerian proposals (thesis no. 2). The questions to ask are: (a) How much justice is there in Rorty's account of mainstream philosophy as a scientistic craving for theory, a craving that induces philosophers to believe in, or postulate, a God's-eye view from which to distinguish between reality and mere appearances? and (b) Is it really the case that both pragmatist and Heideggerian critiques of such a perspective are also critiques of scientism, or a craving for theory, that Rorty postulates? I conclude with a few observations about these matters.

Rorty's account of scientism is, in essence, a "craving analysis." Philosophers in the Plato-Kant tradition are confused about the distinction between reality and appearances because they are obsessed with theory, or theoretical reasoning, and they extend its demands to questions and issues that cannot be handled theoretically. The question: "Why be moral?" or "How do things, in the most general sense of the term, hang together, in the most general sense of the term?" do not give rise to theories, but to attitudes, and it is only the cravings of philosophers, their disquietudes, that commit them to the fruitless task of trying to formulate theories that would answer these questions. Such theories are bound to fail, and even in their most successful, they do not address the philosophical disquietude that has brought them up.

"Craving analyses" of philosophical confusions are, however, problematic, and Rorty's analysis is no exception. They raise the question whether the confusions under consideration (realism, dualism, the God's-eye view) are really due to some universal craving, or whether such cravings themselves are due to a more particular confusion. In our case, the question is whether the dualist confusions of the Plato-Kant sequence are due to an unhistorical craving for theory, or whether there is some better, perhaps more historical explanation of these confusions, that would also serve to explain the cravings, if they are to be detected at all. I believe that in the case of scientism and dualism there is such an explanation to be offered.

Two views can be distinguished in this context. On the one hand, there is Rorty's view, which is also Wittgenstein's, that philosophers suffer from intellectual cravings, of which their metaphysical doctrines, dualism, realism, and so forth, are the symptoms. The alternative view is that dualism, rather than being a symptom, was for many philosophers the remedy to a conflict they could not resolve, namely, the conflict between a scientific perspective they could not deny, and a Christian perspective they could not give up. Rather than being a symptom of some philosophical craving, dualism, or foundationalism, offered the hope of splitting the difference between these general systems. Science could be put into question without rejecting it altogether. Foundations could be demanded into which elements of the prescientific view of things could be incorporated. The Christian narrative of creation and redemption could be reconceived as providing foundational presuppositions for the scientific enterprise. Thus, the attempt to put metaphysics on the ''secure path of science,'' which Rorty sees as a deep scientistic craving, was more an attempt to delimit the scope of science, to place it under metaphysical questioning and subject it to various demands that could not be satisfied within the scientific enterprise. In this account, historically the more faithful account, no strange cravings need be attributed to philosophers, but only the reasonable concern for the integrity of their culture, given the challenge of science. Their dualism, or foundationalism, need not be viewed as a neurotic symptom, but merely as an attempted compromise between conflicting cultural pressures. Overall, I believe, this picture is by far the healthier one.

Pragmatism and Romanticism, of which Heidegger's thought is an instance, can be seen, in light of this view, as conflicting resolutions of the ambivalences of foundational philosophy. For the pragmatist, foundational philosophy carries over too much of the prescientific picture of the world. The Romantic objection, on the other hand, is that foundational philosophy concedes too much to science and to the scientific enterprise. Rorty's account of foundationalism as scientism is an expression of the latter view. But for this reason it is a description the pragmatist need not endorse.

NOTES

1. See in particular Richard Rorty, ''Philosophy as Science, as Metaphor, and as Politics,'' in *The Institution of Philosophy*, ed. A. Cohen and M. Dascal (La Salle, Ill.: Open Court, 1989)

(henceforward SMP). See also Rorty, *Philosophy and the Mirror of Nature* (Princeton, N.J.: Princeton University Press, and Oxford: Basil Blackwell, 1980), and Rorty, *Consequences of Pragmatism* (Minneapolis: University of Minnesota Press, 1982), especially ''Introduction: Pragmatism and Philosophy,'' and ''Pragmatism, Relativism and Irrationalism.''

2. Nancy Fraser, ''Solidarity or Singularity? Richard Rorty Between Romanticism and Technocracy, in *Reading Rorty*, ed. Alan Malachowski (Cambridge: Basil Blackwell, 1990). For the feminist warning quoted above, see p. 313.

3. Richard Rorty, *Philosophy and the Mirror of Nature* (Princeton, N.J.: Princeton University Press, 1980), ch. 4.

4. Donald Davidson, *Enquiries into Truth and Interpretation* (Oxford: Clarendon Press, 1984), 246.

5. Ibid., 259.

6. See Martin Heidegger, *Being and Time* (New York: Harper and Row, 1962). The themes quoted above constitute the declared purpose of ''Part One'' of Heidegger's Magnum Opus, which is the only part he ever completed.

7. See, for example, Nietzsche's remarks on logic, Fredrich Nietzsche, *The Will to Power*, trans. Anthony M. Ludovici, vol. 2 (New York: Russell and Russell, 1964), 28.

8. Jacques Derrida, ''Signature, Event, Context,'' in Derrida, *Margins of Philosophy*, trans. Alan Bass (Chicago: University of Chicago Press, 1982).

15

Pragmatism, Democracy, and the Imagination: Rethinking the Deweyan Legacy

Giles Gunn

If the recent revival of pragmatism has taught us anything other than that fact that pragmatism has long since lost its American coloration and can now be found, as Hans Joas has pointed out, inflecting the work of thinkers as philosophically and politically diverse as Emile Durkheim, Jurgen Habermas, Karl-Otto Apel, Max Scheler, and Martin Heidegger, or, as I would add, Pierre Bourdieu and Michael Oakeshott, it has made it plain that the relationship between democracy and the imagination is far from obvious.[1] Indeed, in the writings of most of pragmatism's more prominent reinterpreters, the arts play at best a diagnostic role and the imagination serves a largely personal function. While the arts reveal the seeds of cruelty within ourselves or disclose pain and suffering in places we would never have thought to look for them, the labors of the imagination are focused chiefly, so one influential pragmatist argument goes, on projects of self- rather than social renovation. Thus the imagination may have been, and may still be, of enormous assistance in emancipating selves for possible redescription and hence in encouraging society to exchange the dream of, say, rationalizing itself for the dream of poeticizing itself, but it is largely ineffectual as an agent of social change.

Richard Rorty, to whom I am referring here—though I could just as easily have been thinking about Hilary Putnam, Cornel West, or even Richard J. Bernstein—has recently, it is true, expressed some second thoughts about the epistemological primacy of the imagination, but these have not led him, at least not yet, to change his opinion of its political efficacy. In a recent essay in the *London Review of Books*, Rorty is prepared to concede that poets like Wordsworth and Rilke may put us in touch with horizons of significance of which a Deleuze or a Foucault is simply unaware, an order of things for which we have no adequate language, but even if this order of meaning is accessible only to the imagination, he is not certain how it could or might impact our politics. Thus, on the report of Wordsworth, or Rilke, or Hölderlin, there may well be a horizon of significance of the sort that Derrida and his followers are always trying to delegitimate, a horizon that "is no more anthropocentric than it is theocentric, no more subjectivist than it is metaphysical," but Rorty is much less certain than Charles Taylor, whose *Ethics of Authenticity* he is discussing, about how to link the mysterious symbolic totality it may represent to us that we call the universe with any democratic policies we might propose for the protection of, let us say, the biosphere.[2]

Like many social thinkers both within and outside the pragmatist tradition, Rorty believes that the imaginative desire to project ourselves into modes of being other than our own will only carry us so far in the direction of social renewal because he thinks that there is a fundamental incompatibility between the languages of personal hope and the languages of public responsibility. While it is clear enough, as he says following Judith Sklar, that cruelty is the worst thing we do and solidarity the best, there is no way of satisfactorily explaining how to move from an ethics of personal authenticity to an ethics of public accountability. On the contrary, Rorty is convinced, more than twenty centuries worth of attempts to reconcile the languages of personal fulfillment with the languages of social obligation have proven that it can't be done. The only reasonable alternative, he therefore concludes, is to keep these languages as separate as possible and to live with the inevitable tension between them.

This tension situates Rorty, as it situates a good many contemporary intellectuals, somewhere between the Foucaults of this world who, as Rorty puts it, are too ironic to be liberal, and the Habermases who are too liberal to be ironic. Such people are compelled to live at the intersection of what might well be construed as the two dominant intellectual traditions of the present, postmodernist moment: between the Nietzschean-Foucauldian line, which holds that most of our social ills derive from turning private, provisional vocabularies into public, final ones, and the line that goes from Mill to Dewey to Habermas, which is always reminding us that the social goal of reducing pain and humiliation should have precedence over any need for individual reconception or renewal. The first accords the imagination a kind of epistemological and moral primacy but views its political consequences as potentially pathological; the second holds that there are things more important than personal re-creation, which presumably draw on faculties fundamentally different from the imagination.

Rorty's inability to bring these two lines of reflection into closer conversation with one another stems from his conviction that the radical metaphysical suspicions of the Nietzschean-Foucauldian line undercut the implicit metaphysical pretensions of the Mill-Dewey-Habermas line. But this is in effect to forget that Rorty's hero, John Dewey, who happens to be the only one of these three figures in the solidarity tradition who has concerned himself explicitly with metaphysics, viewed metaphysics as an ally rather than an enemy of redescription, and then went on to show—if not in *Experience and Nature*, his book of 1925 that served as the basis for Rorty's famous repudiation of Dewey's metaphysics, then in *Art as Experience*, his 1934 sequel to it—how, in a truly poetized or aestheticized universe, metaphysics of a certain sort was not inconsistent with the reconstruction of philosophy itself.

Dewey's argument, to briefly summarize it in *Art as Experience*, proceeds from the assumption that philosophy should no longer be concerned with the establishment of eternal verities but rather with the assessment of values; should no longer try to stabilize experience by determining its ultimate forms but seek to augment experience by exploring its capacities for richer fulfillment. Thus, if modern philosophy originated in an act—or, rather, a succession of acts—of metaphysical deconstruction, it could fulfill itself, Dewey was convinced, only through an act or acts of aesthetic reconceptualization. Just as modern philosophy had to relinquish "the quest for certainty," as Dewey titled his Gifford lectures of 1921, to inaugurate its new work, so the redefinition of experience as a form of the aesthetic, and the reformulation of the purpose of aesthetics as life's continuous revaluation of itself—and thus as the formal realization of its own possibilities—were necessary for modern philosophy to pursue that work constructively.

The word "aesthetic," then, marks for Dewey a difference in experience that is descriptive not of kind but only of degree. Resulting from an attempt to refine, intensify, and subtilize satisfactions that are potential to, but not always possible for, nature itself, the aesthetic is for Dewey predicated on the possibility of converting what he refers to as obstacles or impediments into instruments of further growth. Rooted in, and a more refined version of, what for Dewey is the more elemental structure of rupture and recuperation that defines the experience of nature itself, where the "live creature," as he puts it, is continually falling out of step with the march of surrounding things and then recovering step before another falling out, but always, so to speak, on slightly different footing, the aesthetic accomplishes this conversion by means of the imagination, that agency by which we create new experiences out of meanings derived from past experience.

Dewey's theory of the imagination is thus at once Romantic and pragmatist. It is Romantic insofar as it associates the imagination with processes occurring within nature, and associated particularly with the reconciliation, or at least the assimilation, of qualities that are diverse and discordant, if not disjunctive; his view of the imagination is pragmatic to the degree that it identifies the imagination with processes that nature, as it were, initiates or furthers beyond itself. Hence, Dewey can talk about works of art both as products of the imagination and as operating imaginatively. They are products of the imagination by virtue of the way they replicate in their forms the processes by which meanings from past experience are engrafted onto, and thus become enablements of, the meanings of new experience. They operate imaginatively not simply by evoking a sense of what they express but by compelling in response a like act of imaginative bridging, absorption, and performance.[3]

The aesthetic is therefore not only a dimension potential to every experience but, in Dewey's reading, the potential destiny of all experience. Thus the history of experience is in some sense coterminous with the history of art, and the history of art is essentially the record of experience's movement not toward closure or fulfillment exactly but toward realizations, or, as Dewey termed them "consummations" that, quite beyond their own satisfactions, intend as one of their effects to produce further extensions and enrichments of experience itself. From this perspective, the aesthetic represents what Dewey called "a sense for the better kind of life to be led," a life that fulfills itself not by resting in its own completions but by using those momentary completions to stimulate in response more such experiences like them.[4] Hence, life lived under the sign of the poem, in the agon of the aesthetic, is for Dewey the richest life we can live, the best life the universe understood metaphysically can yield, a life in which there are no permanent summings-up, no final culminations, but only the perpetual struggle for, and enjoyment of, new meaning.

This struggle is a result of the complementarity of the consummatory and the critical. For if the purpose of art is a continual figuration within its own forms of the possibility of creating in response to them more things like them, art is inevitably—and emphatically—in the business of assessing and reassessing values, even the value of its own consummations. But in works of art this reassessment never occurs directly but only indirectly: by submitting actual conditions and their probable consequences to the contrasting prospect of the purely plausible outcomes of merely potential experiences. Yet as Dewey went on to remark in one of the most famous sentences of *Art as Experience*, "it is by sense of possibilities opening before us that we become aware of constrictions that hem us in and of burdens that oppress."[5] This convinced Dewey "that art is more moral than moralities," since moralities merely reinforce the established order, whereas art challenges the status quo and destabilizes the established order by "keeping alive the sense of purposes that outrun evidence and of meanings that transcend indurated habit."[6] It also cemented his conviction that the crucial importance of art lies not in its meaning as an end in itself but as our chief implement for furthering culture as a whole. Only by emancipating and expanding the meanings of which experience is capable, Dewey asserted, can culture advance; and only by critically assessing the valuations of which culture is composed can the meanings potential to it, but not yet effectively realized within it, be successfully liberated. Holding that such liberation is what in the deepest sense we should mean by social reform, Dewey made the critical function of art identical with its moral and political function: "to remove prejudice, do away with the scales that keep the eye from seeing, tear away the veils due to want and custom, [and] perfect the power to perceive."[7]

This is a noble faith, but one that is currently shadowed, at least in the United States, by two kinds of intellectual suspicion. One has to do with whether the critique of values, within art or outside, is anything other than the attempt to subordinate one cultural subject position to another. The second has to do with whether cultural subject positions are ever capable of adequate comparison and contrast. Implicit in the first suspicion is the assumption that all intellectual and imaginative work is inherently political and that the politics of the imagination, no less than the politics of the intellect, ultimately reduces to a politics of identity. Implicit in the second suspicion is the presupposition that cultural subject positions, like cultures themselves, are inherently unique and thus exceptional, in which case any attempt to bring them into discursive, much less critical, relation with one another risks violating the integrity of each. If expression of the first suspicion has taken the form of what is now called political correctness, expression of the second has taken the form of what is now termed multiculturalism.

The debate about political correctness, as most everyone knows, originated over the need to impose standards for appropriate public behavior and practice in American higher education. But this controversy, to the extent that it remains a public issue, now involves much more than the regulation of campus discourse and conduct, the enforcement of affirmative action policies, or even the establishment of new guidelines for what is to be taught and how. The recent politicization of the academy, so its critics maintain (the majority of whom are from the political right and center), amounts not only to dictating, for example, what subjects are suitable for academic study but challenging the disciplinary boundaries and broader institutional hierarchies that currently define such matters. Carried to its extreme, then, the project of political correctness extends well beyond the critique, and if possible alteration, of the self-interested character of all disciplinary and pedagogical arrangements in the academy to encompass a challenge to the cartographic practices of the wider society that legitimates them.

While this means, as the proponents of political correctness claim it surely should mean, that higher education in the United States must become more accessible and accountable to a wider spectrum of Americans that in particular includes women and minorities, this does not necessarily mean, as the detractors and opponents of political correctness insist, that the American academy has now, for the first time, suddenly fallen into politics. American higher education has always been linked to politics, and specifically to the politics of class, gender, and race, since its origins as an institution was created principally for the training of white, male clergy, and it acquired the essential rudiments of its present form of politicization long before the controversy over political correctness arose, during the period following World War II when an extraordinary "marriage of convenience" was arranged between the American university system, Big Business, and the federal government. Hence, the argument that education ought to remain apolitical, disinterested, and objective sounds more than a little disingenuous to most of those on the left in this debate, especially when that argument is made by many conservative critics who are anything but apolitical, disinterested, and objective themselves.

On the other hand, these same critics on the right have an undeniable point when they variously assert that political correctness has given way at various moments and places to a new academic self-righteousness that is potentially not only antiintellectual but discriminatory in reverse. This occurs whenever the politically valid desire to protect others from the abuse of their rights under the First Amendment encourages some to imperil the rights of everyone else by legislating not only what constitutes permissible discursive practice in higher education but also how the general education curriculum should be restructured and to what end. Such arguments are often made on behalf of protecting the notion of "difference," and the notion of "difference" is then turned into an unquestioned, even unchallengeable, source of social and political legitimacy. At the geopolitical level, this leads to the absurd proposition that any people who can differentiate themselves by whatever hereditary or historical arguments from any others deserve, by that very fact, to become a nation; at the academic level, it leads to the view that anything that can define itself as "other" to the dominant ideology or group is thus rendered beyond criticism except by its own representatives.

Fractured as it may be for other reasons, however, the university is neither as divided as the reports of this controversy have made it out to appear, nor divided into the simple oppositions by which its publicists, most of whom are not members of university faculties and are thus intellectually ill-equipped to understand the subtlety of their politics, have caricatured it.[8] More of those divisions are generational, disciplinary, and methodological than political, and almost none of them pit those who want to save the humanities against those who want to destroy them. The real division in the humanities, though rarely acknowledged as such, is between two strategies for combatting their increasing marginalization in the academy, a marginalization that, of course, is simply mirrored in the wider society outside; between, specifically, those who believe that their study can clarify our understanding of the kinds of values by which the world should be organized and governed, and those who believe that their study will sharpen instead our sense of the values by which our experience of the world should be determined. The irony is that the heat produced by both these groups has shed so little light on the far graver issue of the radical break-down of American education generally, a breakdown of which the marginalization of the humanities is, at least for the present, but one symptom.

But the debate over political correctness is only one of the factors that have undercut the kind of faith Dewey possessed in the connections between art and politics, between the imagination and democracy. A second factor has been confusion surrounding the now recherché term known as *multiculturalism*. Described by the *New Republic* as "one of the most destructive and demeaning orthodoxies of our time" because of its association in certain quarters with a kind of racial or ethnic or sexual or nationalistic essentialism, multiculturalism could just as easily be viewed from another perspective as one of the only real orthodoxies we have ever actually encouraged in the United States. Known by another name as the fact—as opposed to the theory—of democratic pluralism, multiculturalism could be said to derive from the promise, going back to the founding of the nation itself, that out of many peoples and traditions the citizens of the United States could establish a society based on the protected individuality and even, where it did not jeopardize the like rights of others, the idiosyncracy of each one of its members. Insisting that the United States must now make good on its own myths and traditions of origin by acknowledging that its strength and distinctiveness as a culture depends not on bleaching out the emotional, intellectual, and moral resources of its various peoples but on encouraging their development, multiculturalism, in the minds of its advocates, turns not on the word "difference" but on the word "diversity" and translates the word "diversity" into a new call for a thousand flowers to bloom.

Serious difficulties arise for multiculturalism, its critics contend, only when diversity is politically transformed into the sole, or at least the principle, source of cultural authenticity, and then all forms of cultural authenticity are held to be equally inviolate, equally pristine. At this point, multiculturalism begins to provide the rationale for a world always on the verge of dividing along lines of prejudice, resentment, and enmity, always ready to fragment into hostile camps; or when this tragic fate can be avoided, then a world where wearing one's "differences" becomes the only way to belong. Whichever the case, multiculturalism is then quickly reduced to just another form of monoculturalism, and monoculturalism threatens to move in the direction of either one of two political extremes: where difference is essentialized, cultures begin to move in the direction of pogroms and ethnic cleansing; where difference is normalized or, as Louis Menand has suggested, "mainstreamed," cultures move in the direction of conformity and regimentation.[9] In the first scenario, difference is sacralized in behalf of a politics of what Kenneth Burke once termed "Holier Than Thou."[10] In the second, difference is swallowed up by, again to revert to Menand, the self-consuming appetites of global popular culture.

No doubt one of the more obvious reasons why multiculturalism is vulnerable to these distortions—distortions that prevent it from fulfilling its otherwise politically admirable aim to stimulate the exploration and appreciation of cultural heterogeneity wherever it is found—is because the symbolic sedimentation of cultural demarcations and differentiations goes so deep. However integral and often indispensable such differentiations and demarcations are to the organization of human life as we know it historically, they derive much of their power from what I hope it will offend no one to call their status as fictions. Cultural distinctions deserve to be called fictions at least in a limited sense not only because they often tend, when reified as some element of the cultural template, to presuppose a homogeneity or uniformity of experience that their historical development actually belies, but also in the sense that they derive their authority from assumptions that are, among other things, decidedly aesthetic. This is not to argue that such significations are any less real and legitimate—or experienced as being any less real or legitimate—because they are imaginative as well as political, figurative as well as social, metaphoric as well as economic; it is merely to assert that whatever the experiential terrain on which such artifacts, and the deep attachments they afford, are expressed, these same artifacts, and the emotional appeals with which they are identified, are cultural before they are anything else. That is, they are forms by which people make sense of the sense their experience makes to themselves, and make more valuable sense the more that sense can be expressed in figurative terms, the more it can be rendered, as it were, tropological.

To make full sense of such forms of sense-making, as we have learned in cultural studies, we need methods that are not only adept at rendering their imaginative appeals, as it were, visible to themselves, but methods that are also capable of throwing into critical relief some of the inner assumptions of the divergent constitutive ambitions that are buried within them. That is, the real question posed by multiculturalism is not how to bring such diverse forms of the imaginary into view but how to place them in mutually interrogative relations with one another, how to make them interpretively accessible and morally responsive to one another—in short, how to render them educative or instructive without, at the same time, allowing them to be either hypostatized or coopted, valorized or silenced, in the process. To accomplish this, we need interpretive theories that are not only adept, as Clifford Geertz has put it, at translating the performances and practices of one culture into the idioms of another, but that are also capable, as Renato Rosaldo has insisted, of submitting the cultural positioning of their own idioms and perspectives to the critique of the performances and practices they would translate into them. If in anthropology this amounts to something like acknowledging that the social analyst is not a *tabula rasa* but a positioned subject who must nonetheless realize, as Rosaldo puts it, "that the objects of social analysis are also analyzing subjects whose perceptions must be taken nearly as seriously as 'we' take our own," in intellectual work more broadly it means that "knowing and the known," as Dewey titled his last book, are reciprocally dependent on one another in at least two senses: not only is the known in part a construct of the knower, but the construction of the knower is in part affected by the constructedness of the known.[11]

This is the theory that Dewey, and before him James, and after him George Herbert Mead, all following up some suggestions from Charles Sanders Peirce, thought they had developed, the theory that became known as pragmatism. Originally devised as, on the one hand, a method of philosophical inquiry that associated the meaning of ideas with the effects they are calculated to produce in experience and, on the other, as a theory of truth that asserts that all beliefs, including transcendental ones, are confirmed or disconfirmed by whether or not they put us in more effective touch with the rest of our experience, pragmatism has over the years turned itself more generally into a technique for criticizing cultural values in a world without absolutes, or, to state it more accurately, in a world in which the search for absolutes has become too treacherous as well as futile to pursue. Reflection thus begins, as Frank Kermode once said about narrative, in the middest, with the cultural prejudices we already possess, but it does not have to end there.[12] If thinking cannot entirely remove those prejudices, it can nevertheless help to educate them, and possibly even encourage their revision, by showing what concrete difference they will make to the course of human experience if anyone acts on them.

Specializing, then, in the social and moral practices generated by theories, pragmatism is not interested in reducing all theories to a set of themes and then applying them in a variety of different textual contexts—all psychoanalysis is reduced to the Lacanian postulate that the unconscious is structured like a language and then critics set about looking for linguistic structures in every unconscious trace; all of Foucault is reduced to a theory of power and then critics set about proving that there are no symbolic or epistemic structures that do not attempt to subordinate one form of consciousness to another—but in placing their referents in more dialectical, if not more dialogical, engagement with one another. Viewing theories pretty much the way Emerson viewed principles, as little more than an eye to see with, pragmatism is out to resuture the connection between concept and conduct, between assumptions and action. In its comic or ''Burkean'' version, this eventuates in a form of moral bookkeeping designed to show us how to make assets of our liabilities and produces a proverbial wisdom based on the capacity to see the world's vast store of error as a potential repository of the truth. In its more elevated, or at least less proverbial, version, it results in a search for what Wallace Stevens once called ''acutest speech,'' a mode of speech dedicated neither to saying ''more than human things with human voice'' nor to saying ''human things with more/Than human voice,'' but to speaking ''humanly from the height or from the depth/Of human things.''

Pragmatism thus conceives of itself less as a new idea than as a new slant, or, to borrow some words from Owen Barfield, ''a comparatively slight readjustment of our way of looking at the things and ideas on which attention is already fixed.''[13] And in a world where attention has come to be fixed increasingly on the issue of cultural difference, pragmatism has become more preoccupied not only with demonstrating how discourses and practices once considered indifferent or inimical to one another can, when played off against each other, sometimes illumine each other's salient insights, but also with exploring ways that the salient insights respective to each may possibly be converted into the constituents of a new kind of public culture.

This is a public culture that, from a Deweyan point of view, would be ideally democratic. It should be democratic because of being premised on the belief that the best mode of living is an associated mode of living centered around what Dewey once called ''conjoint communicated experience.''[14] By this pregnant phrase, Dewey meant to underline the fact that the word ''democracy'' designates more than a political state, that it also designates a psychological and moral state, a way of life characterized by a particular form of human relationships. What distinguishes any form of human relationship that is democratic, Dewey held, is the specific sort of accountability it requires, where all who participate in it are required to refer their own actions to the actions of others and to consider the actions of others as giving point and direction to their own. If the intended result of such accountability is extended participation and mutual sympathy, its aim, as Dewey conceived it, is the fuller release of human possibilities, and its method something as simple, but also as difficult, as the substitution of consultation, negotiation, cooperation, and persuasion for coercion, intimidation, domination, and control.

In a manner that contemporary intellectual taste might find objectionable, Dewey linked this understanding of democracy with what he called ''humanism.'' While the humanism he had in mind was nothing more Eurocentric or elitist than a faith in the potentialities of human nature as such, he believed that this humanism not only lent democracy its moral character but furnished it with its moral measure. That is, democracy could be regarded as moral because it is ''based on faith in the ability of human nature to achieve freedom for individuals accompanied with respect and regard for other persons, with social stability built on cohesion rather than coercion.''[15] At the same time, democracy provided an instrument for measuring cultural institutions in moral terms because it proposed that the question to be put to every institution of cultural life—from science, ethics, and religion to education, industry, and politics—should be their effectuality in the ''release, maturing, and fruition of the potentialities of human nature.''[16] Lest this sound like Dewey was identifying democracy simply with another moralistic call-to-arms, he maintained that the sole moral significance of what he alleged to be its humanistic basis lay in the test democracy provides for social reform: ''find out how all the constituents of our existing culture are operating [he proposed] and then see to it that whenever and wherever needed they be modified in order that their working may release and fulfill the possibilities of human nature.''[17]

But what if the possibilities of human nature at any given moment were to find themselves in conflict with the constitutive institutions of culture at any given point? Indeed, what if the interests and potentialities of individuals or minorities in any given culture were come into serious, if not irreconcilable, collision with the desires of the majority? More to the point, what if people were to develop reasons for questioning the existence of anything like a universally shared human nature? Dewey's somewhat superficial view of the humanistic basis of democracy not only tends to gloss the fact that democracies often act tyrannically; it also discounts the possibility that certain values and perspectives, indeed whole mindsets, may be experienced as fundamentally incompatible, even incommensurable. If complete liberty, for example, is incompatible with complete equality, if perfect justice is irreconcilable with absolute mercy, if full truth is often inconsistent with utter kindness, how much more radically incomparable and irreconcilable are the meanings, the essential values, the life worlds, of, say, Serbs and Muslims, or Israelis and Syrians, or Zulus or Xhosas, or Armenians and Azerbaijanis, or Iraqis and Iranians, or Poles and Gypsies? In the face of such seemingly intractable culture conflicts, pragmatism is no closer to a remedy than any other liberal therapies, which in such cases as these must content themselves with the struggle to create the kind of pluralistic system advocated by Isaiah Berlin, where one tries insofar as possible to prevent situations from arising where human beings are compelled to act in ways fundamentally contrary to their deepest moral convictions.[18]

However, even if it were possible to adjudicate—without resolving—the conflicts produced by the incommensurability of various cultural beliefs, values, and perspectives, there remains the question of controlling the effects of that pervasive psychocultural process known as scapegoating where, as Kenneth Burke long ago reminded us, we transform others into sacrificial objects for the ritual unburdening of our own unwanted vices.[19] A horrific practice that is almost endemic in human history because of the effective relief it provides for the sense of ambivalence, inadequacy, and stain that attends virtually any human life, scapegoating turns cultural essentialism into a mechanism of cultural victimage by not only saddling "the other" with the unassimilated residue of one's own childhood phobias and insecurities but also rendering the cultural "other" virtually opaque to anything it might mediate from beyond itself. The question then becomes whether pragmatism offers any antidote to these dilemmas and the social and political pathologies they carry in their wake; whether it represents any technique, if not for loosening the psychocultural knots they tie us in, at least for diagnosing them and for suggesting some alternative ways that the threads of cultural meaning might be rewoven.

Though antidote is no doubt the wrong medical term to invoke in relation to a problem this resistant to treatment, pragmatism does represent a kind of therapy for combatting this disease. And like any good therapy, cultural or otherwise, it assumes that the best way of combatting the effects of the disease is by attacking the cause. If the disease itself is diagnosed as some version of cultural essentialism and exceptionalism, pragmatism assumes that its cause derives from what the cultural psychologist, like the historian of secularization, might well call the threat of loss. Assuming further that the loss threatened here is not the loss of life so much as the loss of meaning, pragmatism responds to this threat, as I have noted elsewhere, by cultivating what, in his brilliant book on "disillusionment and the social origins of psychoanalysis," the cultural psychologist Peter Homans has termed "the ability to mourn."[20] An ability that cultural essentialism and exceptionalism so often inhibits, if not destroys, and that pragmatism, like psychoanalysis, tries to encourage, both isolate the grounds of its inhibition in the self's continuous need to reconstruct itself in the image of some past that it fears has been lost to it. It then represses or sublimates that fact— partly out of anger and envy, partly out of confusion and fear—by pretending that this past can still remain effectively available, and thus present, to the self when it is imaginatively reified or, as it were, monumentalized as some form of cultural otherness. Mourning is the process by which the self can—and must— shed itself of such narcissistic attachments in order to become free to re-create itself instead out of whatever elements of the social or moral world are still sedimented historically in its own psychic life.

This is as much as to say that mourning is not, then, a process that entails a rejection of the cultural past altogether but merely a relinquishment of the attempt to compensate for the continual dissolution of the past's previous forms of historical unity and coherence by absolutizing some version of them as an adequate model for the construction of the whole of selfhood and society. Thus, for both psychoanalysis and pragmatism, psychological maturity depends on sacrificing the security of defining the self in terms of some common set of fixed symbols that once organized, or at least once were presumed to organize, much of communal life, for the sake of trying to refashion oneself out of such new forms of subjectivity and sociality as emerge from a relaxation of its constraints.

The process by which this is achieved involves for both pragmatism and psychoanalysis what might, in other terms, be described as the resolution of a crisis of representation. This crisis is precipitated by the initial movement of mourning itself, which records, in addition to the abjection of a self that has suffered the loss of an object in some sense determinative of its own sense of presence and empowerment, the apparent negation of the self's ability to compensate for such loss except by creating a representation of its own experience of that loss. This crisis is then resolved when the work of mourning succeeds in dissociating the self from its fixation on a representation memorializing only its own experience of loss so that the self can commence to reconstruct in its place a representation that memorializes instead the object that occasioned the self's sense of loss, and in a form that can be contemplated and enjoyed rather than simply suffered and withstood. The process here described is not unlike the movement Henry James once delineated in his famous essay on immortality where, in response to the question ''Is There a Life After Death?,'' he notes the way the initial experience of almost complete collapse of the power of representation is slowly reversed as the subject of bereavement is eventually (and mercifully) transformed into an object of revery or, as he says somewhere in a letter to his brother William, thinking of the death of his beloved cousin Minny Temple, translated into ''the realm of pure thought.''

Gathering up hints from Freud, Lacan, and Melanie Klein, Mitchell Breitwiesser has deftly described this arduous process as one where the initial image, or better, sense of what has been lost *to* the self, and thus of what has been lost *of* the self, is subsequently challenged by a resurgence of memories that mark the passage of the deceased's life through the mourner's world. Threatening what Lacan calls a ''second death,'' this surge of memory begs to be blocked by the nearest mechanism at hand, a mechanism that turns out, as I have said, to be a defense of that initial image the mourner has constructed of his or her own felt sense of loss.[21] This defensive strategy promises to immunize both the mourner and the mourned against further encroachments of the experience of death and also to help reverse the mourner's sense of impotence in the face of the loss of his or her object of attachment, but it also carries with it the risk of creating within the self what Nicholas Abraham and Maria Torok have called an inert area of "crypt" which then obstructs the return of further memories and thus permanently thwarts the continued work of mourning.[22]

These impediments can be removed, and the fantasies of spurious empowerment that accompany them overcome, only by "working through" the return of those resurgent memories so that the self can eventually reconstruct a different representation of the deceased that is based this time not on the self's experience of its own loss but on what Lacan calls "the unique value/valor of the dead's being."[23] In other words, if there is no return of repressed memories, the self cannot construct out of, and for, the imagination a representation of the passage that the dead has made through its world, much less one that is distinguishable from the self's image of its own grief. Hence the work of mourning cannot be fulfilled unless the dead is allowed, as Breitwiesser puts it, to die "honorably, that is, adequately assigned to being something symbolized . . . rather than a crippling defect in a survivor who would otherwise be whole."[24]

The key to this process of honoring the dead for psychoanalysis is, of course, the technique of transference. Transference creates what Freud viewed as a region somewhere between illness and real life where the patient's blockage, now manifested in a symbolic reification centered around the patient's grief rather than around the meaning of his or her loss, can become accessible to the interpretive interventions and reinterpretations of the analyst. In transference, in other words, the therapeutic relationship, takes the form of a dialogical exchange, where the story to be reconstructed is a project of the transactions between analyst and analysand as each contributes to the production of a narrative whose truth has less and less to do with its correspondence to buried fact and more and more to do with its plausibility as the model for a hypothetical future. The meaning thus produced is neither, as in literature, the result of the author nor of the reader but of their collaborative and corrective interaction, as both work on a text that simultaneously works on them, to utilize Peter Brook's helpful formulation, in the belief that the fullest measure of so-called truth will be found through the fullest possible extension of the semiotic, the imaginative, and the hermeneutic into the domain of the psychological.[25]

But if transference can be applied to the psychodynamic process of individual therapy, where it exhibits its analogies with the work of reading, it can also be applied to the psychosocial process of cross- and intercultural dialogue and appropriation, where it exhibits albeit looser analogies with the work of cultural criticism. Here, as it happens, transference finds its most obvious parallel in the historical development of psychoanalysis and pragmatism themselves, both of which were devised as attempts to respond to the loss of a felt sense of religious and cultural unity—for Freud, the liberal Judaism of *fin de siècle* Vienna; for James and Dewey, the liberal Christianity of Victorian New England—by converting the experience of lamenting its dissolution, and consequently reorganizing self-identity around an image of its passing, into an opportunity to reconstruct the self, and the self's relations with the social and historical surround, out of the interpretive activities that had to be brought into play if some other form of psychocultural organization was to take its place. Furthermore, in each case their development as forms of psychosocial inquiry and relief was made possible by, and replicated in, the "working through" of grief in the life of their respective founders. Indeed, this experience of "working through" represented a passage in those lives very similar to the one reconceptualized as the principal therapeutic paradigm of their respective theories: a passage from the encounter with the death of meaning—or at least an encounter with the fear of that death—through a countermovement designed to forestall that death by defining the self in terms of an image of its loss, to an eventual recovery of meaning, which is made possible by a liberation of the self's capacities for imaginative and interpretive reflection.

The work of mourning thus completes itself by emancipating the self from its attachments to the common culture that had previously defined it and by opening up a new emotional and intellectual space within as well as beyond the self for the creation and enjoyment of new meanings. This is a cultural space in the mind that, as Homans points out, Freud could never quite conceive, a wholly fictive space created by fantasy and its interpretation where societies, just like selves, must learn to remake themselves, and to redefine their relations with socially significant others, by narratively or figuratively, which is to say imaginatively, reconstructing their relations with the past.[26] And being unable completely to conceive this space, Freud was also hampered in understanding how it could make such narrative or figurative reconstructions of one's relations with the past possible.

The clue to that possibility is something that pragmatism has understood since the time of William James's reflections on ambulatory thinking and that D. W. Winnicott was to express in his discussion of the psychological play of children. As Winnicott put it, the space reserved in the mind for culture is a space constituted by symbols and organized for the purposes of a certain kind of passage. A transitional or, better, liminal space, it is the site where the child creates, as Winnicott termed them, "transitional objects" that are neither an image of the self (or in infancy, an image of the child's feelings of omnipotent connection with the mother), nor an image of the self's "other" (or in infancy, an image of the child's rage in losing contact with its mother) but a symbol of what the transitional object bridges: in psychopersonal terms, the distance between mother and child, in psychocultural terms, the distance between society and self. But Winnicott didn't quite put it this way because if he could discern the space reserved for culture in the mind, he couldn't quite discern, as Homans also observes, the space for mind reserved in culture. Thus he could never quite manage to see that cultural symbols generally, like transitional objects specifically, enable this distance to be traversed imaginatively, as opposed to materially, by converting an emblem of the self's feared loss of connection *with* the world into a sign of its increasingly autonomous powers of representation *in* and redescription *of* that world.

To put this somewhat differently, Winnicott did not perceive that the cultural symbol *as* transitional object assists the adult self, no less than the infant self, in moving from an absolute dependence masquerading as omnipotence to a modified autonomy based on interdependence. It does so by furnishing it with forms that permit the self to represent its relations with the social and historical surround in ways that are no longer simply infantile. For the liminality of cultural symbols breaks the hold of what might be termed interpretive infantilism by encouraging the self to repudiate the use of such forms merely to revalorize its own self-image and begin employing them instead to bridge, and hence to strengthen, its relations with all those social others in the past and the present who have achieved their own rather different balance between solidarity and independence, between belatedness and self-creation, by working through similar, or at least related, kinds of imaginative materials.

If pragmatism therefore understands self-development, both at the personal as well as at the cultural level, to depend on access to and interaction with social and historical others, it also acknowledges that this access and interaction is necessarily to a very large degree imaginative. Our relation to social and historical others occurs most often through the mediation of symbols and narratives that have become consequential for both of us in similar ways: not because they possess the same exact significance in our different cultural-historical contexts, but because they have served, and can be recognized as having served, the same, or similar, functions in our respective moral development. What we identify with through these mediations are the psychocultural processes by which other people, often so different from us in many respects, have become more interesting, and sometimes more admirable, but in any case more exemplary, for us through their ability to redraw the coordinates of their own freedom and relatedness by reinterpreting the way they can be represented symbolically; by, as it were, converting the experience of mourning from an experience of self-deprivation into an experience of self-enhancement. What we sometimes rather miraculously achieve through such symbolic mediations, and the imaginative interventions they make in our own symbolic orderings, is that fuller enlargement of ourselves that comes from recognizing, in terms and forms often so alien and even discomfiting to us, traces of that common and unending imaginative struggle for meaning that not only still marks us all as human but still marks our humanity as necessarily a collective rather than an individual achievement.

This amounts to arguing that the "the better kind of life to be led" is unequivocally democratic and that the "sense for" it is, among other things, unequivocally imaginative. This "better kind of life" is democratic because it is predicated on the assumption that the possibility of any other than a narcissistic life without ourselves requires our interaction with, and ability to appropriate some of the more salient meanings of, the moral calculus of the lives of others. "A sense for" this "better kind of life" is imaginative before it is anything else because it assumes that such interaction and appropriation are dependent on nothing so much as our capacity not only to project ourselves into forms of life different from our own but to see ourselves from the perspective of others.

NOTES

1. Hans Joas, *Pragmatism and Social Theory* (Chicago: University of Chicago Press, 1992), 2.

2. Richard Rorty, "In a Flattened World," *London Review of Books*, April 8, 1993: 3.

3. For a fuller discussion of Dewey's theory of the imagination, see Giles Gunn, *Thinking Across the American Grain: Ideology, Intellect, and the New Pragmatism* (Chicago: University of Chicago Press, 1992), 83–90.

4. John Dewey, *Experience and Nature* (1925), in Dewey, *The Later Works, 1925–1953*, ed. Jo Ann Boydston (Carbondale: Southern Illinois University Press, 1981), 1:309.

5. John Dewey, *Art as Experience* (New York: G. P. Putnam's Sons, 1934; 1980):346.

6. Ibid., 348.

7. Ibid., 347.

8. Frederick C. Crews, *The Critics Bear It Away: American Fiction and the Academy* (New York: Randon House, 1992), xv–xvi.

9. Louis Menand, "Being an American," *Times Literary Supplement*, October 30, 1992, 4.

10. Kenneth Burke, *Counter-Statement* (Berkeley: University of California Press, 1968), 183.

11. Renato Rosaldo, *Culture and Truth: The Remaking of Social Analysis* (Boston: Beacon Press, 1989), 207.

12. Frank Kermode, *The Sense of an Ending* (New York: Oxford University Press, 1967), 7.

13. Owen Barfield, *Saving the Appearances* (Middletown, Conn.: Wesleyan University Press, 1967), 11.

14. John Dewey, *Democracy and Education* (New York: Free Press, 1944), 87.

15. John Dewey, *Freedom and Culture* (New York: Capricorn Books, 1963), 162.

16. Ibid., 125.

17. Ibid., 125–26.

18. Isaiah Berlin and Ramin Jahanbegloo, *Reflections of a Historian of Ideas: Conversations with Isaiah Berlin* (New York: Charles Scribner's Sons, 1991), 143.

19. Kenneth Burke, *The Philosophy of Literary Form*, 3rd ed. (Berkeley: University of California Press, 1973), 39–46.

20. Peter Homans, *The Ability to Mourn: Disillusionment and the Social Origins of Psychoanalysis* (Chicago: University of Chicago Press, 1989). Several passages from the remaining pages of this essay are drawn from Gunn, *Thinking Across the American Grain*, 12–18.

21. Jacques Lacan, "L'eclat d'Antigone," *L'éthique de la psychanalyse*, Le séminaire, book 7 (Paris: Editions du Seuil, 1986), 302.

22. Nicholas Abraham and Maria Torok, *The Wolf Man's Magic Word: A Cryptomany* (Minneapolis: University of Minnesota Press, 1986), xiv–xxi.

23. Lacan, "L'eclat," 325.

24. Mitchell Breitwiesser, *American Puritanism and the Defense of Mourning: Religion, Grief, and Ethnology in Mary White Rowlandson's Captivity Narrative* (Madison: University of Wisconsin Press, 1990), 41.

25. Peter Brooks, "The Proffered Word," *Times Literary Supplement*, November 9, 1991, 11–12.

26. Homans, *The Ability*, 273–76.

16

Theory, Pragmatisms, and Politics

Cornel West

Pragmatism has emerged within contemporary literary criticism in relation to two fundamental issues: the role of theory and the vocation of the humanistic intellectual. The most influential pragmatic literary critics such as Stanley Fish and Frank Lentricchia are masterful mappers; that is, they clearly situate and sort out various positions in the current debate and give some idea of what is at stake. Masterful mappers in the pragmatic grain such as Richard Rorty's illuminating narratives about modern philosophy are demythologizers. To demythologize is to render contingent and provisional what is widely considered to be necessary and permanent. Yet to demythologize is not to demystify. To demystify—the primary mode of critical theory—is to lay bare the complex ways in which meaning is produced and mobilized for the maintenance of relations of domination.[1]

Demythologization is a *mapping* activity that reconstructs and redescribes forms of signification for the purpose of situating them in the dynamic flow of social practices. Demystification is a *theoretical* activity that attempts to give explanations that account for the role and function of specific social practices. Both activities presuppose and promote profound historical consciousness—that is, awareness of the fragile and fragmented character of social practices—but demythologization leaves open the crucial issues of the role of theory and the vocation of the humanistic intellectual. In sharp contrast, demystification gives theory a prominent role and the intellectual a political task. Needless to say, sophisticated demystifiers neither consider theory as an attempt ''to stand outside practice in order to govern practice from without,''[2] nor view the political task of intellectuals to be the mere articulation of a theoretical enterprise. The former assumes a rather naïve conception of theory, and the latter presupposes that theory is inherently oppositional and emancipatory. Rather, appropriate forms of demystification subsume the pragmatic lessons of demythologization, preserve a crucial role for theory as a social practice, and highlight how modes of interpretation "serve to sustain social relations which are asymmetrical with regard to the organization of power."[3]

In a renowned essay, Arthur O. Lovejoy examined the difficulty of defining the often-used yet slippery rubric "romanticism."[4] In a less well-known paper, Lovejoy put forward thirteen different varieties of "pragmatism."[5] I suggest that we map the versions of pragmatism on the current scene in reference to three major axes: namely, the levels of philosophy, theory, and politics. The philosophical level highlights various perspectives regarding epistemological foundations and ontological commitments; the theoretical level, attitudes toward the possibility for or role of theory; and the political level, the vocation of the humanistic intellectual.

All pragmatists are epistemic antifoundationalists, though not all epistemic antifoundationalists are pragmatists. To be an epistemic antifoundationalist is simply to agree with the now familiar claims that "all interpretation is value laden," "there are no unmediated facts," "there is no such thing as a neutral observation language," and so on. One may unpack these assertions in various ways, with the help of Hegel, Nietzsche, Derrida, Quine, Davidson, Goodman, Wittgenstein, or Rorty, but it means that one gives up on the notion that epistemic justification terminates in something other than social practice.

Yet not all pragmatists are ontological antirealists. To be a realist is principally to be worried about the bottomless pit of relativism. Therefore philosophical restraints and regulations are set in place to ward off an "anything goes" ontological position. Conservative pragmatists such as Charles Sanders Peirce and Hilary Putnam (in his present incarnation) put forward limiting processes and procedures to ensure that some notion of scientific objectivity (grounded in social practices) is preserved. For Peirce, this means conceiving truth as whatever results in the long run reached by the unending community of inquirers who deploy a reliable method based on deduction, induction, and, to some degree, inference to the best explanation. Putnam builds on Peirce by affirming the need for constraints yet allowing for the proliferation of methods of inquiry and styles of reasoning. Therefore, Putnam promotes two limiting processes: the long-term results of a dominant style of reasoning among inquirers who pull from accumulated modes of thinking, and the long-term results of the facts produced by this dominant style of reasoning yielded by evolving kinds of thinking.[6] In this sense, conservative pragmatists like Peirce and Putnam are "regulative realists" in that "reality" is what inquirers agree on owing to rational canons that regulate and restrain inquirers.

Moderate pragmatists such as John Dewey and William James are not worried about relativism. They are minimalist realists in order to shun the position of idealism but remain more concerned with the plurality of versions of "reality."

Like Peirce and Putnam, they put a premium on restraints and regulations, yet do so not with the intention of privileging scientific objectivity but rather with the aim of noting how different forms of rational deliberation achieve their respective goals. In this way, the notion of scientific objectivity is not rejected, it simply becomes a self-complimenting term for a particular community who excel at explaining and predicting experience. The notions of inquiry and experimentation remain crucial but only insofar as they promote self-critical and self-correcting enterprises in the varieties of human activities, be they in sciences, arts, or everyday life.

Avant-garde pragmatists such as Richard Rorty not only jettison anxieties about relativism but also adopt a thoroughgoing antirealism. Rorty's concern here is not to ensure that restraints and regulations are in place, as they always already are, but to explode these restraints and regulations for the edifying purpose of creating new vocabularies of self-description and self-creation. For Rorty, these transgressions—Kuhnian paradigm-shifts—consist of new and novel moves in the ongoing conversation of intellectuals.

For most literary critics, these philosophical differences within the pragmatist camp are mere intramural affairs with little relevance. This is so because once one adopts the epistemic antifoundationalist position, the issue of ontological realism or antirealism primarily concerns whether the language of physicists actually refers or not; that is, the terrain is confined to the philosophy of science. Yet this philosophical debate does pertain indirectly to literary critics in that the status, role, and function of restraints and regulations relate to the fundamental issues of objectivity and relativism in literary hermeneutics.

The obsessive concern with theory in literary criticism has much to do with the status, role, and function of restraints and regulations in literary interpretation after a rather widespread agreement on epistemic antifoundationalism. The unsettling impact on literary studies of Derrida, de Man, Foucault, Said, Jameson, Showalter, Baker, and others is not that relativism reigns, as old-style humanists tend to put it, but rather that disagreement reigns as to what the appropriate restraints and regulations for ascertaining the meanings of texts ought to be after epistemic antifoundationalism is accepted. To put it another way, the debate over the consequences of theory emerged not as a means of settling upon the right restraints and regulations outside of practice in a foundationalist manner, as Steven Knapp and Walter Benn Michaels misleadingly view it, but rather as a way of rendering explicit the discursive space or conversational activity now made legitimate owing to widespread acceptance of epistemic antifoundationalism. This hegemony of epistemic antifoundationalism in the literary academy has pushed critics in the direction of historicism and skepticism.

At the level of theory, there are moderate pragmatists such as Knapp and Benn Michaels who are against theory because they see the theoretical enterprise as a cover for new forms of epistemic foundationalism—as attempts to "occupy a position outside practice."[7] Unfortunately, they view theory as *grand theory* and consider practice as close reading in search of agential-inscribed intentions and thereby truncate the debate on the consequences of theory.

On the other hand, there are proponents of grand theory such as Fredric Jameson who associate pragmatism with this antitheory stance, who deny that grand theorists must locate theory outside social practice and who insist that historicist forms of demystification are preferable to limited historicist forms of demythologization. For Jameson, only grand theory of a certain sort can provide the adequate explanatory model for detecting the role and function of literary meanings in relation to larger developments and happenings in society and history.

Between these two positions lurk ultratheorists like Frank Lentricchia, Paul Bové, and Jonathan Arac who acknowledge the indispensability of theory, especially the insights of Marxists and feminists, yet who also shun the option of grand theory. Following exemplary ultratheorists—Michel Foucault and Edward Said—who move skillfully between theory and politics, Lentricchia, Bové, and Arac stand at the crossroads of history and rhetoric, at the intersection of the operations of institutional powers and the operations of linguistic figures and tropes.

All pragmatists are against grand theory, but not all pragmatists need be against theory. Lentricchia, who describes himself loosely as a "dialectical rhetorician" drawing from pragmatism,[8] must be challenged when he asserts that

to be a pragmatist is in a sense to have no theory—and having a position requires having a theory. The liberating, critical move of pragmatism against the "antecedent" is compromised by its inability—built into the position of pragmatism as such—to say clearly what it wants for the future. Though not practice for its own sake, pragmatism cannot say what practice should be aimed at without ceasing to be pragmatism, without violating its reverence for experimental method.[9]

This critique, echoing that of Randolph Bourne more than a half a century ago, holds only for certain crude versions of pragmatism that have not adequately confronted the ideological and political issue concerning the vocation of humanistic intellectuals.

This issue of vocation is a political and ideological one even though it surfaces in our time as a discourse about professionalism.

The term *vocation* is rather unpopular these days in academic circles, principally owing to the predominance of words like *profession* and *career*. Yet I suggest that recent historical investigations into the rise of professionalism and sociological inquiries into the content and character of careerism require that we rethink, revise, and retain a notion of vocation. Such a notion must not presuppose that we have an unmediated access to truth nor assume that we must preserve a pristine tradition free of ideological contamination. Rather, we live at a particular historical moment in which a serious interrogation regarding "vocations" of intellectuals and academicians in American society can contribute to *a more enabling and empowering sense of the moral and political dimensions of our functioning in the present-day academy.* To take seriously one's vocation as an intellectual is to justify in moral and political terms why one pursues a rather privileged life of the mind in a world that seems to require forms of more direct and urgent action.

Allan Bloom's bestseller, *The Closing of the American Mind*—a nostalgic and, for some, seductive depiction of the decline and decay of the highbrow, classical humanist tradition—and Russell Jacoby's provocative book, *The Last Intellectuals*—a premature requiem for left public intellectuals—are both emblematic symptoms of the crisis in vocation of contemporary intellectuals. The professionalization, specialization, and bureaucratization of academic knowledge-forms has become a kind of *deus ex machina* in discussions about the crises of purpose among the humanistic intelligentsia. Yet even these noteworthy developments along with others such as the intensified commodification of intellectuals themselves and the reification of intellectual conversation fail to capture crucial features of the lived experience of many intellectuals in the academy. If we take Bloom, Jacoby, and others at their word, the lives of many academic intellectuals are characterized by *demoralization, marginalization,* and *irrelevance.*

Demoralization results from a variety of reasons, but the primary ones consist of what Roberto Unger has called the "Downbeat Alexandrian Cynicism" of the American academy, in which the obsession with status often overshadows the preoccupation with substance, and the naked operations of power are usually masked behind a thin veil of civility. Needless to say, demoralization takes different forms among the tenured faculty than among the untenured ones, with the former often fearful of becoming mere deadwood and the latter usually mindful of being too creative (adventurous). It is important to keep in mind that most serious intellectuals today become academics by default; that is, they simply cannot pursue the life of the mind anywhere but in the academy and maintain upper-middle-class lifestyles that provide leisure time. Self-invested, hedonistic indulgence in precious moments of reading, lecturing, writing, and conversing indeed occurs alongside the demoralization of many academic intellectuals. Yet few intellectuals would justify their activity on sheer hedonistic grounds. Most would candidly acknowledge the pleasure of their intellectual work, yet cast the justification of this work on a higher moral and political ground. And it is precisely this ground that seems to be slipping away.

For example, the increasing marginalization of humanistic studies in the academy primarily due to the popularity of business schools and computer studies is depriving many intellectuals of their "higher" moral and political reasons for remaining in the academy, for they can no longer claim that they train the best and the brightest undergraduates in order to preserve the best that has been thought and known in the world, or hold to what Richard Rorty has called the "Cynical Prudential Strategy" of academic humanists, which says to American society: "You let us have your gifted children for our universities, where we will estrange them from you and keep the best ones for ourselves. In return, we will send the second-best back to keep you supplied with technology, entertainment, and soothing presidential lies.''[10]

In the past few decades, it is clear that most of the "best ones" have not gone into the humanities or politics but rather into the private sphere of quick money making, be it in business, legal, or medical enterprises. This has resulted not simply in a relative brain drain in humanistic studies but also in a sense that humanistic intellectuals are missing out on where the "real action" is. The situation is compounded by ideological dynamics; that is, those students most attracted to humanistic studies tend to be those of a slightly more left-liberal bent, in part due to a revulsion from a boring life of money making and rat racing. As a result, many students and faculty (especially younger faculty) find themselves rather adverse to a pecuniary oriented lifestyle on moral and ideological grounds yet compelled to spell out to themselves and others the *political relevance* of their academic lifestyles; and yet the sense persists that what they are doing is, in large part, irrelevant. I shall put forward my response to this situation in the form of an examination of the three major vocational models of intellectual work. I will highlight the blindness and insights, strengths and weaknesses of these models. Then I shall suggest that a more acceptable model may be on the horizon.

Before specifying what these models are, I think it instructive to mention briefly the most influential and celebrated literary theorist of our time, the late Paul de Man. In fact, his little book, *The Resistance to Theory* (1986), is an appropriate starting place for considering the complex relation of the vocational and the theoretical. Furthermore, to render invisible his enormous presence and challenge in our discussion, especially given the recent revelations of his youthful anti-Semitic writings, is to impoverish the discussion. It is always sad to discover that one of the most engaging minds of one's time succumbed years ago to one of the most pernicious prejudices of our century. Yet it only reminds us that even the finest of intellects must breathe the polluted air of any *zeitgeist*. And few escape some degree of moral asphyxiation. To use this profound moral lapse to downplay de Man's later insights is sophomoric, just as to overlook it in the name of these insights is idolatrous.

I am interested here in de Man's sense of vocation as an intellectual. I would go as far as to suggest that what separated de Man as a literary theorist from his contemporaries—besides his prodigious talent, intense discipline, and cautious scholarship—was his dogged single-mindedness regarding his conception of himself as an intellectual. To put it boldly, de Man seemed never to waver in viewing himself as a philological scholar, as one dedicated and devoted to a critical discourse that examines the rhetorical devices of language. For de Man, the vocation of the literary intellectual was to stay attuned to the multifarious operations of tropes in language, especially literary language, which are in no way reducible to religious, moral, political, or ideological quests for wholeness and harmony. His aim was to push to the limits, by means of high-powered

rigor and precision, the inherent inability to control meaning even as we inescapably quest for it. His kind of philological scholarship revealed the various
ways in which "simultaneous asymmetry" is shot through the semantic operations of language.

De Man's viewpoint is not a simple relativism in which epistemic restraints
and regulations are nonexistent, but is rather a tortuous rendering of how such
restraints and regulations ineluctably fail to contain transgressions. His perspective is not a form of idealism in that it is grounded in the material practices of
language using decentered subjects, that is, human bodies who try to generate
meanings by way of speech and texts. It is rather a version of linguistic materialism that focuses narrowly on select conditions under which meaning is both
produced and undone.

For de Man, theory is an integral part of one's vocation as an intellectual. He
paradoxically argued that theory is inescapable yet unable to sustain itself as
theory owing to its self-undermining character—a character that yields more
theory only to be resisted by means of more theory. This theoretical resistance
to theory could not but be shot through with ideology, a focus de Man was
deepening before his death.

De Man's formulations may be persuasive or unpersuasive. My aim here is
neither to explicate them nor defend them, but rather to note how a clear sense
of one's vocation shapes a project—one that seizes the imagination of a generation of critics. The loss of Paul de Man, his authorizing and legitimizing
intellectual presence, intensified the crisis of vocation among humanistic intellectuals. Some simply abandoned his challenge. Others tried to follow but found
the going too tough. Many slavishly jumped from one bandwagon to the other,
often dictated by market forces and personal inertia with little sense of how
positions enrich or impoverish the sense of what we are about, who we are, and
why we do what we do. It strikes me that much of the attraction to Foucault
and Said is due to the fact that they grapple with vocational questions as part
and parcel of their critical practice. In addition, much of the hoopla about the
new pragmatism and new historicism—even as we leave most of the formidable
challenges of de Man unmet—has to do with the hunger for vocational purpose
in the profession.

In the current and rather confused discussion about vocation and intellectual
work, three major models loom large. First, there is the *oppositional professional
intellectual* model that claims that we must do political work where we are—in
the academy. This model encompasses liberals who call for cultivating critical
sensibilities; Marxists such as Jim Merod, who promote a revolutionary trade
union of oppositional critics; and leftists such as Paul Bové, who envision an
unceasing attack on the reigning "regimes of truth" with no humanist illusions
about "truth" or "revolution." Second, there is the *professional political intellectual* model that encourages academicians to intervene into the public conversation of the nation regarding some of the most controversial issues as
citizens who bring their professional status and expertise to bear in a political

manner. The outstanding exemplar of this model is Edward Said, although people such as Catharine MacKinnon and William Julius Wilson also come to mind. The last model is that of the *oppositional intellectual groupings within the academy*, which seek to create, sustain, and expand intellectual subcultures inside the university networks, usually with little success at gaining visibility and potency in the larger culture and society. The pertinent figures here would be Fredric Jameson, Elaine Showalter, and Henry Louis Gates, Jr., namely leading Marxist, feminist, and Afro-American critics who remain thoroughly inscribed in the academy and have successfully colonized legitimate space for their oppositional agendas. Analogues can be found in the critical legal studies movement in law schools and the liberation theology subgroups in seminaries.[11]

Each of these models is regulated by a dominant theoretical orientation. The guiding spirit behind the first model is that of the late Michel Foucault. It is, I conjecture, the most attractive model for young aspiring oppositional humanistic intellectuals, although it may fade quickly in the coming years. To put it crudely, Foucault admonishes intellectuals to scrutinize the specific local contexts in which they work and highlight the complex operations of power that produce and perpetuate the kind of styles and standards, curriculum and committees, the proliferation of jargon, and the relative absence of comic high spirits in the academy. Foucault holds that different societies preserve and reproduce themselves in part by encouraging intellectuals to be unmindful of how they are socialized and acculturated into prevailing "regimes of truth"; that is, intellectuals often remain uncritical of the very culture of critical discourse they inhabit and thereby fail to inquire into why they usually remain within the parameters of what is considered "legitimate," "tactful," "civil" discourse. Furthermore, Foucault suggests that this failure leads intellectuals often to overlook the ways in which these mainstream (or malestream) discourses construct identities and constitute forms of subjectivity that devalue and degrade, harm and harass those who are viewed as other, alien, marginal, and abnormal owing to these discourses.

The basic insight of this model is that it rightly understands the academy to be an important terrain for political and ideological contestation, and because it grasps the degree to which knowledges are forms of power in societies, this model correctly views battles over the kind of knowledge produced in the academy as forms of political practice. The major shortcoming of this model is that it feeds on an excessive pessimism regarding the capacity of oppositional intellectuals to break out of the local academic context and make links with nonacademic groups and organizations. This viewpoint is echoed in Jim Merod's noteworthy text, *The Political Responsibility of the Critic*: "Right now and for the imaginable future we have no intellectual, professional, or political base for alliances between radical theorists and dispossessed people. . . . It seems, therefore, that the concrete political means to build an intellectual coalition of professional and nonprofessional groups are not available."[12]

Yet the overriding theoretical perspective of the second model, that of Edward

Said, calls this excessive pessimism into question. Motivated by the historical voluntarism of Vico, the antidogmatic sense of engagement of R. P. Blackmur, and the subversive worldliness of Antonio Gramsci, Said stands now as the towering figure among left humanistic intellectuals. Said creatively appropriates Gramsci's notions of hegemony and elaboration in light of his own ideas of filiation and affiliation. For Said, intellectuals are always already implicated in incessant battles in their own local academic contexts. Yet these contexts themselves are part of a larger process of mobilizing and manufacturing a dynamic "consent" of subaltern peoples to their subordination by means of the exercise of moral, cultural, and political leadership. Following Gramsci, Said acknowledges that neither force nor coercion is principally responsible for the widespread depoliticization and effective subordination of the populace. Instead, the particular ways of life and ways of struggle, values, and sensibilities, moods and manners, structures of seeings and structures of feelings promoted by schools, churches, radio, television, and films primarily account for the level of political and moral consciousness in our country. And intellectuals of various sorts—teachers, preachers, journalists, artists, professors—play a partisan role in this never ceasing struggle.

This model is instructive in that it leads academic intellectuals outside the academy and into the more popular magazines and mass media; and for Said, it has led to the White House (meeting with George Schultz) due to the unprecedented heroic resistance of Palestinians on the West Bank and Gaza strip against the inhumane treatments and pernicious policies of the conservative Israeli government. Such public interventions by academic intellectuals (especially that of left intellectuals) broaden the political possibilities for present-day intellectual work. The recent example of Yale's Paul Kennedy (*The Rise and Fall of the Great Powers: Economic Change and Military Conflict from 1500 to 2000*) is worth noting in this regard.

The major shortcomings of this model are, first, that the public intervention of select intellectual celebrities gives even more authority and legitimacy to their academic professions owing to the status of the expert and second, that the scope of the public intervention is usually rather narrow, that is, confined to one issue with little chance of making connections to other issues. In this way, the very way in which one is a political intellectual promotes academic respectability, careerist individualism, and a highly confined terrain of political maneuvering.

The last model—of oppositional intellectual groupings within the academy constituting vital subcultures for space and resources—accents the crucial issues of *community* and *camaraderie* in left intellectual work. Unlike conservative intellectuals who have access to well-funded think tanks, foundations, and institutes, progressive academics must gather within the liberal universities and colleges and thereby adjust their agendas to the powers that be for survival and sustenance. The grand contribution of the Frederic Jamesons, Elaine Showalters, and Henry Louis Gates, Jrs. has been to bombard the academy with texts, students, and programs that ride the tide of intellectual interest in—and political struggle influenced by—Marxism, feminism, and Afro-American studies. This model surely signifies the academization of Marxism, feminism, and black studies, with the concomitant problems this entails. Yet it also constitutes noteworthy efforts of left community-building among academics in relatively anti-Marxist, patriarchal, and racist environments, in regard to the academy and the larger American culture and society.

Yet the major challenges of this model, namely the spilling over of Marxist, feminist, and black studies into working-class, women's, and black communities, remain unmet; and without significant social motion, momentum, and ultimately movements, this situation will remain relatively the same. The crucial questions facing progressive humanistic intellectuals are how to help generate the conditions and circumstances of such social motion, momentum, and movements that move society in more democratic and free directions. How to bring more power and pressure to bear on the status quo so as to enhance the life chances of the jobless and homeless, landless and luckless, empower degraded and devalued working people, and increase the quality of life for all?

I suggest that these challenging queries can be answered through a conception of the intellectual as a critical organic catalyst. This conception requires that the intellectual function inside the academy principally in order to survive and stay attuned to the most sophisticated reflections about the past, present, and future destinies of the relevant cultures, economies, and states of our time. This conception also entails that the intellectual be grounded outside the academy: in progressive political organizations and cultural institutions of the most likely agents of social change in America, for example, those of black and brown people, organized workers, women, lesbians, and gays. This model pushes academic intellectuals beyond contestation within the academy—be it the important struggles over standards and curriculum or institutionalizing oppositional subcultures—and links this contestation with political activity in grass-roots organizations, pre-party formations, or progressive associations intent on bringing together potential agents of social change. In this sense, to be an engaged, progressive intellectual is to be a critical organic catalyst whose vocation is to fuse the best of the life of the mind from within the academy with the best of the organized forces for greater democracy and freedom from outside the academy. This model is neither a panacea for the crisis of vocation of humanistic intellectuals nor a solution to the relation of academics to grass-roots organizing. Rather, it is a candid admission that this may be simply the best one can do in the present situation, a situation that can change in the near future depending in part on what some intellectuals do.

This primacy of the vocational has much to do with pragmatism, in that pragmatism began and prospered due in part to a new conception of the vocation of the humanistic intellectual in America at the turn of the century. Although initiated by that reclusive genius, Charles Sanders Peirce, pragmatism served as a beacon for intellectuals under the leadership of William James and John Dewey. Similar to the attraction to Marxism among serious European thinkers at the time (and Third World intellectuals in our time), pragmatism gave many American intellectuals a sense of political purpose and moral orientation. At its worst, it became a mere ideological cloak for corporate liberalism and managerial social engineering which served the long-term interests of American capital; at its best, it survived as a form of cultural critique and social reform at the service of expanding the scope of democratic process and broadening the arena of individual self-development here and abroad. The story of the rise and fall of American pragmatism is a fascinating one—one that I try to tell elsewhere.[13] Yet the resurgence of pragmatism in our time will be even more impoverished and impotent if the vocational questions are jettisoned.

My own kind of pragmatism—what I call prophetic pragmatism—is closely akin to the philosophy of *praxis* put forward by Antonio Gramsci. The major difference is that my attitude toward Marxism as a grand theory is heuristic rather than dogmatic.[14] Furthermore, my focus on the theoretical development in emerging forms of oppositional thought—feminist theory, antiracist theory, gay and lesbian theory—leads me to posit or look for not an overarching synthesis but rather an articulated assemblage of analytical outlooks to further more morally principled and politically effective forms of action to ameliorate the plight of the wretched of the earth.

On the philosophical level, this means adopting the moderate pragmatic views of John Dewey. Epistemic antifoundationalism and minimalist ontological realism (in its pluralist version) proceed from taking seriously the impact of modern historical and rhetorical consciousness on truth and knowledge. "Anything goes" relativism and disenabling forms of skepticism fall by the wayside, serving only as noteworthy reminders to avoid dogmatic traps and to accept intellectual humility rather than as substantive philosophical positions.

On the level of theory, to be against theory *per se* is to be against inquiry into heuristic posits regarding the institutional and individual causes of alterable forms of human misery and human suffering, just as uncritical allegiance to grand theories can blind one from seeing and examining kinds of human oppression. Therefore I adopt strategic attitudes toward the use and deployment of theory, a position more charitable toward grand theory than are the ultratheorists and more suspicious of grand theory than are the grand theorists themselves.

Lastly, at the level of politics and ideology, I envision the intellectual as a critical organic catalyst, one who brings the most subtle and sophisticated analytical tools to bear to explain and illuminate how structures of domination and effects of individual choices in language and in nondiscursive institutions operate. The social location of this activity is the space wherein everyday affairs of ordinary people intersect with possible political mobilization and existential empowerment, for example, in churches, schools, trade unions, and movements. The moral aim and political goal of such intellectual activity are the creation of greater individual freedom in culture and broader democracy in the economy and society. In this sense, the consequences of my own intervention into the debate over the consequences of theory are understood as being explicitly though not exclusively political.

NOTES

1. John B. Thompson, *Studies in the Theory of Ideology* (Berkeley and Los Angeles: University of California Press, 1984), 5 *ff.*

2. Steven Knapp and Walter Benn Michaels, "Against Theory," *Critical Inquiry* 8, no. 4 (1982): 742.

3. Thompson, *Studies in the Theory of Ideology*, 6.

4. Arthur O. Lovejoy, "On the Discrimination of Romanticisms," *Essays in the History of Ideas* (Baltimore, Md.: John Hopkins University Press, 1948), 228–53.

5. Arthur O. Lovejoy, "The Thirteen Pragmatisms," in *The Thirteen Pragmatisms and Other Essays* (Baltimore, Md.: John Hopkins University Press, 1963), 1–29.

6. Hilary Putnam, *Reason, Truth, and History* (New York: Cambridge University Press, 1981), 103–26, 174–200. For a brief interpretation of Putnam that chimes with mine, see Ian Hacking, *Representing and Intervening: Introductory Topics in the Philosophy of Natural Science* (Cambridge: Cambridge University Press, 1983), 60.

7. Steven Knapp and Walter Benn Michaels, "A Reply to Richard Rorty: What is Pragmatism?" *Critical Inquiry* 11, no. 3 (1985): 470.

8. Frank Lentricchia, *Criticism and Social Change* (Chicago: University of Chicago Press, 1983), 34.

9. Ibid., 4.

10. Richard Rorty, Review of Allan Bloom's *The Closing of the American Mind*, *New Republic*, April 4, 1988.

11. See Cornel West, "Third Annual Brendan Brown Lecture: Reassessing the Critical Legal Studies Movement," *Loyola Law Review* 24, no. 2 (1988): 265–75; West, "Critical Legal Studies and a Liberal Critic," *Yale Law Journal* 97, no. 5 (1988): 757–71; West, "On Christian Intellectuals" and "The Crisis in Theological Education," in *Prophetic Fragments* (Grand Rapids, Mich.: Eerdmans, 1988), 273–80.

12. Jim Merod, *The Political Responsibility of the Critic* (Ithaca, N.Y.: Cornell University Press, 1988), 191, 261.

13. Cornel West, *The American Evasion of Philosophy: A Genealogy of Pragmatism* (Madison: University of Wisconsin Press, 1989).

14. For an elaboration of the differences between Gramsci's subtle version of historical materialism and my own genealogical materialism, see Cornel West, "Race and Social Theory: Towards a Genealogical Materialist Analysis," in *The Year Left 2*, ed. Mike Davis, Manning Marable, Fred Pfeil, and Michael Sprinker (London: Verso Books, 1987), 74–90. For further explication of this conception of the intellectual, see West, "The Dilemma of the Black Intellectual," *Cultural Critique* 8, no. 1 (Fall 1985): 109–24.

Select Bibliography

The following list of references is a compilation of the citations contained in the chapters and editorial introductions of this volume. No attempt at a comprehensive or systematic bibliography has been attempted here.

Abraham, Nicholas, and Maria Torok. *The Wolf Man's Magic World: A Cryptomany*. Minneapolis: University of Minnesota Press, 1986.

Alderman, Harold. *Nietzsche's Gift*. Miami: Ohio University Press, 1977.

Alexander, Thomas. *John Dewey's Theory of Art, Experience, and Nature: The Horizons of Feeling*. Albany: State University of New York Press, 1987.

Arnold, Thurman W. *The Folklore of Capitalism*. New Haven, Conn.: Yale University Press, 1937.

———. *The Symbols of Government*. New Haven, Conn.: Yale University Press, 1935.

Auxier, Randall. "Concentric Circles: An Exploration of Three Concepts in Process Metaphysics." *Southwest Philosophy Review* 7, no. 1 (January 1991): 151–72.

———. "The Rise and Fall of Evolutionary Thinking Among American Philosophers." *Southwest Philosophy Review* 9, no. 1 (January 1993): 135–50.

Ayer, A. J. *Language, Truth, and Logic*. London: Metheun, 1935.

Barfield, Owen. *Saving the Appearances*. Middletown, Conn.: Wesleyan University Press, 1967.

Beatty, J. "The Synthesis and the Synthetic Theory." In *Intergrating Scientific Disciplines*, edited by W. Bechtel. The Hague: Martinus Nijhoff, 1986.

Behler, Ernst. *Confrontations: Derrida/Heidegger/Nietzsche*. Stanford: Stanford University Press, 1991.

Bellah, Robert, et. al. *Habits of the Heart: Individualism and Commitment in American Life*. Berkeley: University of California Press, 1985.

Bergson, Henri. *Creative Evolution*. Translated by Arthur Mitchell. New York: Henry Holt, 1913.

Berlin, Isaiah, and Ramin Jahanbegloo. *Reflections of a Historian of Ideas: Conversations with Isaiah Berlin*. New York: Charles Scribner's Sons, 1991.

Blake, Casey Nelson. *Beloved Community: The Cultural Criticism of Randolph Bourne, Van Wyck Brooks, Waldo Frank, and Lewis Mumford*. Chapel Hill: University of North Carolina Press, 1990.

———. "Lewis Mumford: Values over Technique." *Democracy* 3 (Spring 1983): 125–37.

———. "The Young Intellectuals and the Culture of Personality." *American Literary History* 1, no. 3 (Fall 1989): 510–34.

Blanshard, Brand. *The Nature of Thought*. New York: Macmillan, 1939.

———. *Reason and Analysis*. LaSalle, Ill.: Open Court, 1962.

Bloom, Allan. *The Closing of the American Mind: How Higher Education Has Failed Democracy and Impoverished the Souls of Today's Students*. New York: Simon and Schuster, 1987.

Blumberg, Albert E., and Herbert Feigl. "Logical Positivism: A New Movement in European Philosophy." *Journal of Philosophy* 28 (1931): 281–93.

Boorstin Daniel J. *The Genius of American Politics*. Chicago: University of Chicago Press, 1953.

Borgmann, Albert. *Technology and the Character of Contemporary Life*. Chicago: University of Chicago Press, 1984.

Bourne, Randolph. "Trans-National America." In *The Radical Will: Randolph Bourne Selected Writings, 1911–1918*, edited by Olaf Hansen. New York: Urizen, 1977.

Brandon, R. N. "Adaptation Explanations." In *Evolution at a Crossroads*, edited by David Depew and Bruce Weber. Cambridge, Mass.: MIT Press, 1985.

Breitwiesser, Mitchell. *American Puritanism and the Defense of Mourning: Religion, Grief, and Ethnology in Mary White Rowlandson's Captivity Narrative*. Madison: University of Wisconsin Press, 1990.

Brent, Joseph. *Charles Sanders Peirce: A Life*. Bloomington: Indiana University Press, 1993.

Brick, Howard. *Daniel Bell and the Decline of Intellectual Radicalism: Social Theory and Political Reconciliation in the 1940s*. Madison: University of Wisconsin Press, 1986.

Brint, Michael, and William Weaver, eds. *Pragmatism in Law and Society*. Boulder, Co.: Westview Press, 1991.

Brooks, Peter. "The Proffered Word." *Times Literary Supplement*, November 9, 1991: 11–12.

Brooks, Van Wyck. *The Van Wyck Brooks–Lewis Mumford Letters: The Record of a Literary Friendship, 1921–1963*. Edited by Robert E. Spiller. New York: E. P. Dutton, 1970.

Bryson, Lyman. *The New Prometheans*. New York: Macmillan, 1947.

Buchler, Justus. *Philosophical Writings of Peirce*. New York: Dover Publications, 1955.

Burch, Robert. "An Unpublished Logic Paper by Josiah Royce." *Transactions of the Charles S. Peirce Society* 23, no. 2 (1987).

———. "A Transformation of Royce's View of Kant." *Transactions of the Charles S. Peirce Society* 23, no. 4 (1987).

Burke, Kenneth. *Counter-Statement*. Berkeley: University of California Press, 1968.

———. *The Philosophy of Literary Form*. 3rd ed. Berkeley: University of California Press, 1973.

Campbell, James. *The Community Reconstructs: The Meaning of Pragmatic Social Thought*. Urbana: University of Illinois Press, 1992.

———. "Democracy as Cooperative Inquiry." In *Philosophy and the Reconstruction of Culture*, edited by John J. Stuhr. Albany: State University of New York Press, 1993.

Carnap, Rudolf. "The Development of My Thinking." In *The Philosophy of Rudolf Carnap*, edited by Paul Arthur Schilpp. The Library of Living Philosophers, vol. 11. LaSalle, Ill.: Open Court, 1963.

———. "Empiricism, Semantics, and Ontology." *Revue Internationale de Philosophie* 9 (1950): 20–40. Reprinted in A. Rorty, ed. *Pragmatism*. New York: Doubleday, 1966.

Cassirer, Ernst. *Symbol, Myth, and Culture*. Edited by Donald Philip Verene. New Haven, Conn.: Yale University Press, 1979.

———. *The Problem of Knowledge*. New Haven, Conn.: Yale University Press, 1950.

Childs, John L. *American Pragmatism and Education: An Interpretation and Criticism*. New York: Macmillan, 1956.

Clark, Maudemarie. *Nietzsche on Truth and Philosophy*. New York: Cambridge University Press, 1990.

Cohen, Morris R. *Reason and Nature: An Essay on the Meaning of Scientific Method*. New York: Harcourt, Brace, 1934.

Commager, Henry Steele. *The American Mind: An Interpretation of American Thought and Character Since the 1880's*. New Haven, Conn.: Yale University Press, 1950.

Connor, Steven. *Postmodernist Culture*. Cambridge: Basil Blackwell, 1989.

Costello, Harry T. *Josiah Royce's Seminar, 1913–1914: As recorded in the Notebooks of Harry T. Costello*, edited by Grover Smith. New Brunswick, N.J.: Rutgers University Press, 1936.

Cotkin, George. "Middle-Ground Pragmatists: The Popularization of Philosophy in American Culture." *Journal of the History of Ideas*, forthcoming.

———. *William James: Public Philosopher*. Baltimore, Md.: Johns Hopkins University Press, 1990.

———. "William James and the 'Weightless' Nature of Modern Existence." *San Jose Studies* 12 (Spring 1986): 7–19.

Cremin, Lawrence A. *The Transformation of the School: Progressivism in American Education, 1876–1957*. New York: Macmillan, 1961.

Crews, Frederick C. *The Critics Bear It Away: American Fiction and the Academy*. New York: Random House, 1992.

Danto, Arthur C. *Nietzsche as Philosopher*. New York: Macmillan, 1965.

Davidson, Donald. *Enquiries into Truth and Interpretation*. Oxford: Clarendon Press, 1984.

———. "A Nice Derangment of Epitaphs." In *Truth and Interpretation: Perspectives on the Philosophy of Donald Davidson*, edited by E. Lepore. Oxford: Blackwell, 1986.

———. "On the Very Idea of a Conceptual Scheme." *Proceedings and Addresses of the American Philosophical Association* 47 (1973–74): 1–21.

Dawkins, Richard, *The Extended Phenotype*. Oxford: Oxford University Press, 1982.

Deleuze, Gilles. *Nietzsche and Philosophy*. Translated by Hugh Tomlinson. New York: Columbia University Press, 1983.

Depew, David J. "American Philosophy in the Twentieth Century." In *Encyclopedia of United States History in the Twentieth Century*, edited by S. Kutler et al. New York: Simon and Schuster, in press.

———. "The *Polis* Transfigured: Aristotle's *Politics* and Marx's *Critique of Hegel's Philosophy of Right*." In *Marx and Aristotle: Nineteenth Century Social Thought and Classical Antiquity*, edited by G. E. McCarthy. Lanham, Md.: Rowman and Littlefield, 1992.

Depew, David J., and Bruce Weber, eds. *Evolution at a Crossroads*. Cambridge, Mass.: MIT Press, 1985.

Derrida, Jacques. *Margins of Philosophy*. Translated by Alan Bass. Chicago: University of Chicago Press, 1982.

———. *Of Grammatology*. Baltimore, Md.: Johns Hopkins University Press, 1974.

———. *Otobiography: The Ear of the Other*. New York: Schocken Books, 1985.

———. *Spurs*. Chicago: University of Chicago Press, 1979.

Dewey, John. *Art as Experience*. New York: G. P. Putnam's Sons, 1934.

———. *A Common Faith*. New Haven, Conn.: Yale University Press, 1934.

———. *Democracy and Education*. New York: Free Press, 1944.

———. "The Development of American Pragmatism." (1931). In *Pragmatism: The Classic Writings*, edited by H. Standish Thayer. Indianapolis: Hackett, 1982.

———. *The Early Works 1882–1898*. 5 vols. Edited by Jo Ann Boydston. Carbondale: Southern Illinois University Press, 1969.

———. *Experience and Nature*. New York: Dover, 1958.

———. *Freedom and Culture*. New York: Capricorn Books, 1963.

———. "From Absolutism to Experimentalism." In *Contemporary American Philosophy*, edited by G. P. Adams and W. Montague. New York: Macmillan, 1930.

———. *Human Nature and Conduct*. New York: Modern Library, 1957.

———. "The Influence of Darwinism on Philosophy." In *The Influence of Darwinism on Philosophy and Other Essays in Contemporary Thought*. New York: Henry Holt, 1910.

———. *The Later Works, 1925–1953*. 17 vols. Edited by Jo Ann Boydston. Carbondale: Southern Illinois University Press, 1981–1990.

———. *Logic: The Theory of Inquiry*. New York: Henry Holt, 1938.

———. "The Logic of Judgments of Practice." *Journal of Philosophy* 12 (1915): 505–23.

———. *The Middle Works, 1899–1924*. 15 vols. Edited by Jo Ann Boydston. Carbondale: Southern Illinois University Press, 1976–1983.

———. "The Need for a Recovery of Philosophy." In John Dewey et al., *Creative Intelligence: Essays in the Pragmatic Attitude*. New York: Holt, 1917.

———. *Philosophy and Civilization*. New York: G. P. Putnam's Sons, 1931.

———. *The Public and Its Problems*. New York: Capricorn, 1929. Reprint. Chicago: Swallow Press, 1954.

———. *The Quest for Certainty: A Study of the Relation of Knowledge and Action*. New York: Putnam, 1929. Reprint. New York: Capricorn Books, 1960.

———. "Ralph Waldo Emerson." In *Character and Events*. New York: Holt, Rinehart and Winston, 1929.

———. *Reconstruction in Philosophy*. New York: Holt, 1920.

———. "Science as Subject-Matter and as Method." *Science* 36 (January 28, 1910): 127.

———. "The Short Cut to Realism Examined." *Journal of Philosophy* 7 (1910): 553–57.

———. "Theory of Valuation." *International Encyclopedia of the Unified Sciences*. Vol. 2. Chicago: University of Chicago Press, 1939.

———. "What I Believe." In *I Believe*, edited by Clifton Fadiman. New York: Simon and Schuster, 1939.

Dewey, John, and Arthur F. Bentley. *Knowing and the Known*. Boston: Beacon Press, 1949.

Dobzhansky, Theodosius. *The Biological Basis of Human Freedom*. New York: Columbia University Press, 1957.

———. *Mankind Evolving*. New Haven, Conn.: Yale University Press, 1962.

Douglas, Paul H. "The Absolute, the Experimental Method, and Horace Kallen." In *Visions and Action*, edited by Joseph Ratner, 39–55. New Brunswick, N.J.: Rutgers University Press, 1953.

Duhem, Pierre. "Logical Examination of Physical Theory." *Synthese* 83, Dordrecht, The Netherlands: Kluwer Academic Publishers, 1990.

Emerson, Ralph Waldo. *The American Scholar: Selected Writings of Ralph Waldo Emerson*. Edited by William H. Gilman. New York: New American Library, 1965.

Ezorsky, Gertrude. "Pragmatic Theory of Truth." In *Encyclopedia of Philosophy*, edited by Paul Edwards. 8 vols. New York: Macmillan, 1967, vol. 6, 427–30.

Farrell, James T. "The Faith of Lewis Mumford." In James T. Farrell, *The League of Frightened Philistines and Other Papers*. New York: Vanguard Press, 1945.

Feffer, Andrew. *The Chicago Pragmatists*. Ithaca, N.Y.: Cornell University Press, 1993.

Feigl, Herbert. "The Wiener Kreis in America." In *The Intellectual Migration: Europe and America: 1930–1960*, edited by Donald Fleming and Bernard Bailyn. Cambridge, Mass.: Harvard University Press, Belknap Press, 1969.

Feinstein, Howard M. *Becoming William James*. Ithaca, N.Y.: Cornell University Press, 1984.

Feynman, Richard. *QED: The Strange Theory of Light and Matter*. Princeton, N.J.: Princeton University Press, 1985.

Fisch, Max H. "American Pragmatism Before and After 1898." In *American Philosophy from Edwards to Quine*, edited by Robert W. Shahan and Kenneth R. Merrill, 78–110. Norman: University of Oklahoma Press, 1977.

———. "Peirce as Scientist, Mathematician, Historian, Logician, and Philosopher." In *Proceedings of the C. S. Peirce Bicentennial International Congress*, edited by Kenneth L. Ketner et al., 3–19. Texas Tech University Graduate Studies, no. 23. Lubbock: Texas Tech Press, 1981.

Fish, Stanley. "Rhetoric." In *Critical Terms for Literary Study*, edited by F. Lentricchia and T. McLaughlin, 203–22. Chicago: University of Chicago Press, 1990.

Fiske, John. *Through Nature to God*. New York: Houghton, Mifflin, 1899.

Flower, Elizabeth, and Murray G. Murphey. *A History of Philosophy in America*. 2 vols. New York: G. P. Putnam, 1977.

Forcey, Charles. *The Crossroads of Liberalism: Croly, Weyl, Lippmann, and the Progressive Era, 1900–1925*. New York: Oxford University Press, 1961.

Foucault, Michel. "The Subject and Power." In *Michel Foucault: Beyond Structuralism and Hermeneutics*, 2nd. ed. ("Afterward.") Chicago: University of Chicago Press, 1983.

Fox, Richard Wightman. "Tragedy, Responsibility, and the American Intellectual, 1925–1950." In *Lewis Mumford: Public Intellectual*, edited by Thomas P. Hughes and Agatha C. Hughes. New York: Oxford University Press, 1990, 323–37.

Frank, Waldo. "Dusk and Dawn." In *In the American Jungle, 1925–1936*. New York: Farrar and Rinehart, 1937.

Fraser, Nancy. "Solidarity or Singularity? Richard Rorty Between Romanticism and Technocracy." In *Reading Rorty*, edited by Alan Malachowski. Cambridge: Basil Blackwell, 1990, 303–21.

———. *Unruly Practices: Power, Discourse, and Gender in Contemporary Social Theory*. Minneapolis: University of Minnesota Press, 1989.

Genovese, Eugene. *Roll, Jordan, Roll: The World the Slaves Made*. New York: Pantheon, 1983.

Gigerenzer, G., et al. *The Empire of Chance: How Probability Changed Science and Everyday Life*. Cambridge: Cambridge University Press, 1989.

Gilligan, Carol. *In a Different Voice: Psychological Theory and Women's Development*. Cambridge, Mass.: Harvard University Press, 1982.

Ginsburg, Edward. "On the Logical Positivism of the Viennese Circle." *Journal of Philosophy* 29 (1932): 121–29.

Giroux, Henry A., ed. *Postmodernism, Feminism, and Cultural Politics*. Albany: State University of New York Press, 1991.

Goldman, Eric F. *Rendezvous with Destiny: A History of Modern American Reform*. New York: Vintage, 1952.

Goodman, Nelson, *Fact, Fiction, and Forecast*. 4th ed. Cambridge, Mass.: Harvard University Press, 1983.

———. *Ways of Worldmaking*. Indianapolis: Hackett, 1978.

Gouinlock, James S. "What is the Legacy of Instrumentalism? Rorty's Interpretation of Dewey." *Journal of the History of Philosophy* 28, no. 2 (April 1990): 251–69.

Gould, Steven J. *The Mismeasure of Man*. New York: Norton, 1981.

Grene, Marjorie. *Science, Ideology, and World View*. Berkeley: University of California Press, 1981.

Gropius, Walter. *The New Architecture and the Bauhaus*. London: Faber and Faber, 1965.

Guignon, Charles B., and David R. Hiley. "Biting the Bullet: Rorty on Private and Public Morality." In *Reading Rorty*, edited by Alan Malachowski. Cambridge, Mass.: Basil Blackwell, 1990.

Gunn, Giles. *Thinking Across the American Grain: Ideology, Intellect, and the New Pragmatism*. Chicago: University of Chicago Press, 1992.

Hacking, Ian. *The Emergence of Probability*. Cambridge: Cambridge University Press, 1975.

———. *Representing and Intervening: Introductory Topics in the Philosophy of Natural Science*. Cambridge: Cambridge University Press, 1983.

———. *The Taming of Chance*. Cambridge: Cambridge University Press, 1990.

Hartshorne, Charles. "Charles Peirce's 'One Contribution to Philosophy' and His Most Serious Mistake." In *Studies in the Philosophy of Charles Sanders Peirce*, second series, edited by Edward G. Moore and Richard S. Robin. Amherst: University of Massachusetts Press, 1964.

———. *Creativity in American Philosophy*. New York: Paragon House, 1984.

Hartz, Louis. *The Liberal Tradition in America: An Interpretation of American Political Thought Since the Revolution*. New York: Harcourt, 1955.

Hawking, Steven. *A Brief History of Time*. New York: Bantam, 1988.

Heidegger, Martin. *Being and Time*. New York: Harper and Row, 1962.

———. *On Time and Being*. Translated by Joan Stambaugh. New York: Harper and Row, 1988.

Heller, Thomas C., et al. *Reconstructing Individualism: Autonomy, Individuality and the Self in Western Thought*. Stanford: Stanford University Press, 1986.

Hempel, C. *Philosophy of Science*. Englewood Cliffs, N.J.: Prentice-Hall, 1966.

Hickman, Larry. *John Dewey's Pragmatic Technology*. Bloomington: Indiana University Press, 1990.

Hodgson, Shadworth. *The Metaphysics of Experience*. 4 vols. London: Longmans Green, 1898.

Hollinger, David A. *Morris R. Cohen and the Scientific Ideal*. Cambridge, Mass.: MIT Press, 1975.

―――. "Science and Anarchy: Walter Lippmann's *Drift and Mastery*." *American Quarterly* 29 (Winter 1977): 463–75.

―――. "Why Can't You Be More Like Dwight MacDonald?" *Reviews in American History* (1988): 657–62.

Homans, Peter. *The Ability to Mourn: Disillusionment and the Social Origins of Psychoanalysis*. Chicago: University of Chicago Press, 1989.

Hook, Sidney. *John Dewey: An Intellectual Portrait*. New York: John Day and Co., 1939.

―――. *The Metaphysics of Pragmatism*. La Salle, Ill.: Open Court, 1927.

―――. "Metaphysics, War, and Intellectuals." *Menorah Journal* 28 (August 1940): 327–37.

―――. "Personal Impression of Contemporary German Philosophy." *Journal of Philosophy* 27 (1930): 144–47, 158–60.

―――. "Pragmatism and the Tragic Sense of Life." In *Contemporary American Philosophy: Second Series*, edited by J. E. Smith, 170–193. In London: George Allen and Unwin, 1970.

Horkheimer, Max. *Eclipse of Reason*. 1947. Reprint. New York: Seabury Press, 1974.

Hull, David. *The Metaphysics of Evolution*. Albany: State University of New York Press, 1989.

―――. *Philosophy of Biological Science*. Englewood Cliffs, N.J.: Prentice-Hall, 1974.

―――. *Science as a Process*. Chicago: University of Chicago Press, 1988.

Hutcheon, Linda. *A Poetics of Postmodernism*. New York: Routledge, 1988.

Hume, David. *A Treatise of Human Nature*. Edited by Selby-Bigge. Oxford: Oxford University Press, 1978.

Jaki, Stanley L. "History as Science and Science in History." *Intercollegiate Review* 29, no. 1 (Fall 1993): 20–27.

James, William. "The Chicago School." In William James, *Collected Essays and Reviews*. Cambridge, Mass.: Harvard University Press, 1906.

―――. *Essays, Comments, and Reviews*. Cambridge, Mass.: Harvard University Press, 1987.

―――. "G. Papini and the Pragmatist Movement in Italy." *Journal of Philosophy, Psychology, and Scientific Methods* 3 (June 21, 1906): 337–41.

―――. *The Letters of William James*. 2 vols. Edited by Henry James, Jr. Boston: Atlantic Monthly Press, 1920.

―――. *The Meaning of Truth: A Sequel to "Pragmatism."* New York: Longmans, 1909.

―――. "The Moral Equivalent of War." In *Essays in Religion and Morality*. Cambridge, Mass.: Harvard University Press, 1982.

―――. "On a Certain Blindness in Human Beings." In *Talks to Teachers on Psychology*. Cambridge, Mass.: Harvard University Press, 1983.

―――. "Philosophical Conceptions and Practical Results." In William James, *Collected Essays and Reviews*. New York: Holt, 1920.

―――. "A Plea for Psychology as a 'Natural Science.' " In *Essays in Psychology: The Works of William James*. Cambridge, Mass.: Harvard University Press, 1983.

―――. *Pragmatism: A New Name for Some Old Ways of Thinking*. Cambridge, Mass.: Harvard University Press, 1975.

―――. *The Principles of Psychology: The Works of William James*. 2 vols. New York: Holt, Rinehart, and Winston, 1890.

―――. *Some Problems of Philosophy*. New York: Longmans, Green, 1911.

―――. *The Varieties of Religious Experience*. Cambridge, Mass.: Harvard University Press, 1985.

―――. "What Pragmatism Means." In *Pragmatism*, edited by Bruce Kuklick. Indianapolis: Hackett, 1981.

―――. *The Will to Believe and Other Essays in Popular Philosophy*. New York: Holt, 1897. Reprint. Cambridge, Mass.: Harvard University Press, 1979.

―――. *The Writings of William James*. Edited by John J. McDermott. New York: Random House, 1967.

Jencks, Charles. *The Language of Post-Modern Architecture*. 4th ed. London: Academy Editions, 1984.

Joas, Hans. *Pragmatism and Social Theory*. Chicago: University of Chicago Press, 1992.

Kallen, Horace M. ''John Dewey and the Spirit of Pragmatism.'' In *John Dewey, Philosopher of Science and Freedom*, edited by Sidney Hook, 3–46. New York: Holt, 1950.

———. ''Pragmatism.'' In *Encyclopedia of the Social Sciences*, edited by Edwin R. A. Seligman and Alvin Johnson, vol. 12, 307–11. 15 vols. New York: Macmillan, 1930–1935.

Kallen, Horace M., ed. *The Philosophy of William James: Drawn from His Work*. New York: Holt, 1925.

Kermode, Frank. *The Sense of an Ending*. New York: Oxford University Press, 1967.

Ketner, Kenneth Laine. ''Introduction'' (to selections of C. S. Peirce). In *Classical American Philosophy*, edited by John J. Stuhr. Oxford: Oxford University Press, 1987.

Klepp, L. S. ''Every Man a Philosopher-King.'' *New York Times Magazine*, Dec. 2, 1990, 117–18.

Kloppenberg, James T. ''Objectivity and Historicism: A Century of American Historical Writing.'' *American Historical Review* 94 (1989): 1011–30.

———. *Uncertain Victory: Social Democracy and Progressivism in European and American Thought, 1870–1920*. New York: Oxford University Press, 1987.

Knapp, Steven, and Walter Benn Michaels. ''Against Theory.'' *Critical Inquiry* 8, no. 4 (1982): 11–31.

———. ''A Reply to Richard Rorty: What is Pragmatism?'' *Critical Inquiry* 11, no. 3 (1985): 139–41.

Kneale, William, and Martha Kneale. *The Development of Logic*. Oxford: Clarendon Press, 1984.

Kolenda, Konstantin. *Cosmic Religion: An Autobiography of the Universe*. Prospect Heights, Ill.: Waveland Press, 1987.

———. ''Peirce on Person and Community.'' In *Person and Community in American Philosophy, Rice University Studies* 66, no. 4 (1980): 15–32.

———. ''Problems with Transcendence.'' In *God, Values, and Empiricism*, edited by Creighton Peden and Larry E. Axel. Mercer, Ga.: Mercer University Press, 1989.

———. *Rorty's Humanistic Pragmatism: Philosophy Democratized*. Gainesville: University Presses of Florida, 1990.

Krüger, L., L. Daston, and M. Heidelberger. *The Probabilistic Revolution*. 2 vols. Cambridge, Mass.: MIT Press, 1987.

Kuklick, Bruce. ''The Changing Character of Philosophizing in America.'' *Philosophical Forum* 10 (1978): 4–13.

———. *Churchmen and Philosophers: From Jonathan Edwards to John Dewey*. New Haven, Conn.: Yale University Press, 1977.

———. ''The Emergence of the Humanities.'' *South Atlantic Quarterly* 89 (1990): 195–206.

———. *Josiah Royce: An Intellectual Biography*. Indianapolis: Hackett, 1972.

———. ''The Professionalization of the Humanities.'' In *Applying the Humanities*, edited by A. Caplan, et al., 41–54. New York: Plenum Press, 1985.

———. *The Rise of American Philosophy: Cambridge, Massachusetts, 1860–1930*. New Haven, Conn.: Yale University Press, 1977.

Lears, T. Jackson. ''From Salvation to Self-Realization: Advertising and the Therapeutic Roots of the Consumer Culture, 1880–1930.'' In *The Culture of Consumption*, edited by Richard Wightman Fox and T. Jackson Lears, 1–38. New York: Pantheon, 1983.

Leland, Dorothy. ''Rorty on the Moral Concern of Philosophy: A Critique from a Feminist Point of View.'' *Praxis International* 8 (October 1988): 273–83.

Lentricchia, Frank. *Criticism and Social Change*. Chicago: University of Chicago Press, 1983.

Levi, A. W. *Philosophy and the Modern World*. Bloomington: Indiana University Press, 1959.

Levins, Richard, and Richard Lewontin. *The Dialectical Biologist*. Cambridge, Mass.: Harvard University Press, 1985.

Lewis, Clarence Irving. ''Experience and Meaning.'' In *Collected Papers of Clarence Irving Lewis*, edited by John D. Goheen and John L. Mothershead, Jr. Stanford: Stanford University Press, 1970.

———. "Logical Positivism and Pragmatism." In *Collected Papers of Clarence Irving Lewis*, edited by John D. Goheen and John L. Mothershead, Jr. Stanford: Stanford University Press, 1970.

Lewis, Sinclair. *Arrowsmith*. New York: Signet, 1925.

Lippmann, Walter. *Drift and Mastery: An Attempt to Diagnose the Current Unrest*. New York: Macmillan, 1914.

———. "An Open Mind: William James." *Everybody's Magazine* 23 (December 1910): 800–801.

Liszka, Jakob. "Community in C. S. Peirce: Science as a Means and as an End." *Transactions of the Charles S. Peirce Society* 14 (Fall 1978): 305–21.

Lovejoy, Arthur O. "On the Discrimination of Romanticisms." *Essays in the History of Ideas*. Baltimore, Md.: Johns Hopkins University Press, 1948: 228–53.

———. "Progress in Philosophical Inquiry." *Philosophical Review* 26 (1917): 538–44.

———. "The Thirteen Pragmatisms." In Lovejoy, *The Thirteen Pragmatisms and Other Essays*. Baltimore, Md.: Johns Hopkins University Press, 1963: 1–29.

MacIntyre, Alasdair. *After Virtue: A Study in Moral Theory*. 2nd ed. South Bend, Ind.: University of Notre Dame Press, 1984.

Magnus, Bernd. "The End of 'The End of Philosophy.' " In *Hermeneutics and Deconstruction*, edited by H. Silverman and D. Ihde. Albany: State University of New York, 1985.

———. *Postmodern Postures: Nietzsche, Heidegger, Derrida, and Rorty*. New York: Routledge, forthcoming.

———. "The Use and Abuse of *The Will to Power*." In *Reading Nietzsche*, edited by R. C. Solomon and K. Higgins. New York: Oxford University Press, 1988.

Magnus, Bernd, Jean-Pierre Mileur, and Stanley Stewart. *Nietzsche's Case: Philosophy as/and Literature*. New York: Routledge, 1993.

Mansbridge, Jane J. *Beyond Adversary Democracy*. Rev. ed. Chicago: University of Chicago Press, 1983.

Marcuse, Herbert. *One-Dimensional Man*. Boston: Beacon Press, 1964.

Margolis, Joseph. *Pragmatism Without Foundations*. Oxford: Basil Blackwell, 1986.

Mayr, Ernst. *The Growth of Biological Thought*. Cambridge, Mass.: Harvard University Press, 1982.

———. "How Biology Differs from the Physical Sciences." In *Evolution at a Crossroads*, edited by David Depew and Bruce Weber, 43–63. Cambridge, Mass.: MIT Press, 1985.

———. *Towards a New Philosophy of Biology*. Cambridge, Mass.: Harvard University Press, 1988.

McDermott, John J. *Streams of Experience*. Amherst: University of Massachusetts Press, 1986.

Mead, George Herbert. *Mind, Self, and Society from the Standpoint of a Social Behaviorist*. Edited by Charles W. Morris. Chicago: University of Chicago Press, 1934.

———. "National-Mindedness and International-Mindedness." *International Journal of Ethics* 39, no. 4 (July 1929): 385–407.

———. "Scientific Method and the Individual Thinker." In *Selected Writings*, edited by Andrew J. Reck. Chicago: University of Chicago Press, 1981, 248–66.

Megill, Allan. *Prophets of Extremity*. Berkeley: University of California Press, 1984.

Menand, Louis. "Being an American." *Times Library Supplement*, October 3, 1992.

Merod, Jim. *The Political Responsibility of the Critic*. Ithaca, N.Y.: Cornell University Press, 1988.

Mills, C. Wright. *Sociology and Pragmatism*. New York: Oxford University Press, 1966.

———, ed. *The Marxists*. New York: Dell, 1962.

Moore, Asher. "Lewis's Theory of the *A Priori*." In *The Philosophy of C. I. Lewis*, edited by Paul A. Schilpp, 155–99. LaSalle, Ill.: Open Court, 1968.

Morris, Charles W. *Logical Positivism, Pragmatism, and Scientific Empiricism*. Paris: Hermann et Cie., 1937.

———. *Pragmatic Movement in American Philosophy*. New York: Braziller, 1959.

Morris, George S. *Kant's Critique of Pure Reason*. Chicago: S. C. Griggs, 1886.

Mumford, Lewis. "A Challenge to American Intellectuals." *Modern Quarterly* 5 (Winter 1930–31): 407–21.

————. *The Conduct of Life*. New York: Harcourt, Brace & Co., 1951.

————. "The Emergence of a Past." *New Republic* 45 (November 25, 1925).

————. Foreword to *Planned Society Yesterday, Today, Tomorrow: A Symposium by Thirty-Five Economists, Sociologists, and Statesmen*, by Findlay MacKenzie, ed. New York: Prentice-Hall, 1937.

————. *Herman Melville*. New York: The Literary Life, 1929.

————. *The Myth of the Machine, Vol. 2: The Pentagon of Power*. New York: Harcourt, Brace, Jovanovich, 1970.

————. "Patriotism and Its Consequences." *The Dial* 66 (April 19, 1919): 406–7.

————. "A Search for the True Community." In *The Menorah Treasury: Harvest of Half a Century*, edited by Leo W. Schwartz. Philadelphia: Jewish Publication Society of America, 1964.

————. *Technics and Civilization*. New York: Harcourt, Brace, & World, 1962.

————. "Toward an Organic Humanism." In *The Critique of Humanism: A Symposium*, edited by C. Hartley Grattan. New York: Brewer and Warren, 1930.

————. "What I Believe." *Forum* 84 (November 1930): 263–68.

Murphey, Murray G. *The Development of Peirce's Philosophy*. Cambridge, Mass.: Harvard University Press, 1961.

Murphey, Murray, and Elizabeth Flower. *A History of Philosophy in America*. 2 vols. New York: G. P. Putnam, 1977.

Myers, Gerald. *William James: His Life and Thought*. New Haven, Conn.: Yale University Press, 1986.

Nagel, Ernest. "The Eighth International Congress of Philosophy." *Journal of Philosophy* 31 (1934): 591–92.

————. "Impressions and Appraisals of Analytic Philosophy in Europe." *Journal of Philosophy* 33 (1936): 6–7, 9–10, 29–30.

Nehemas, Alexander. *Nietzsche: Life as Literature*. Cambridge, Mass.: Harvard University Press, 1985.

Nelson, H. "Officeholding and Powerwielding." *Law and Society Review* 10 (Winter 1976): 188–233.

Nicholson, Linda J., ed. *Feminism/Postmodernism*. New York: Routledge, 1990.

Niebuhr, Reinhold. *Moral Man and Immoral Society*. New York: Charles Scribner's Sons, 1932.

Nietzsche, Friedrich. *Thus Spoke Zarathustra. The Portable Nietzsche*, edited by Walter Kaufmann. New York: Viking, 1954.

————. *Untimely Meditations*. New York: Cambridge University Press, 1984.

Noble, David F. *America by Design*. New York: Alfred Knopf, 1979.

Norris, Christopher. *What's Wrong With Postmodernism*. Baltimore, Md.: Johns Hopkins University Press, 1990.

Okrent, Mark. *Heidegger's Pragmatism*. Ithaca, N.Y.: Cornell University Press, 1988.

Paringer, William Andrew. *John Dewey and the Paradox of Liberal Reform*. Albany: State University of New York Press, 1990.

Peirce, Charles Sanders. *Collected Papers of Charles Sanders Peirce*. 8 vols. Edited by Charles Hartshorne, Paul Weiss, and Arthur W. Burks. Cambridge, Mass.: Harvard University Press, 1931–1958.

————. "How To Make Our Ideas Clear." (1878) In *Pragmatism: The Classic Writings*, edited by H. Standish Thayer. Indianapolis: Hackett, 1982.

————. "Pragmatic and Pragmatism." (1902) In *Pragmatism: The Classic Writings*, edited by H. Standish Thayer, 79–100. Indianapolis: Hackett, 1982.

————. "What Pragmatism Is." In *Pragmatism: The Classic Writings*, edited by H. Standish Thayer. Indianapolis: Hackett, 1982.

————. "Why I Am a Pragmatist." Cited in Philip Weiner, *Evolution and the Founders of Pragmatism*. Cambridge, Mass.: Harvard University Press, 1949.

————. *The Writings of Charles S. Peirce: A Chronological Edition*. 3 vols. Vol. 1 (1857–1866), edited by Max H. Fisch, 1982; vol. 2 (1857–1871), edited by Edward C. Moore, 1984; vol.

3 (1872–1878), edited by Christian J. W. Kloesel, 1986. Bloomington: Indiana University Press.

Perry, Ralph Barton. *The Thought and Character of William James.* Boston: Little, Brown, 1935.

Poirier, Richard. *Poetry and Pragmatism.* Cambridge, Mass.: Harvard University Press, 1992.

Porter, Theodore M. *The Rise of Statistical Thinking: 1820–1900.* Princeton, N.J.: Princeton University Press, 1951.

Pratt, James B. "The Twelfth Annual Meeting of the American Philosophical Association." *Journal of Philosophy* 10 (1913): 91–92.

Prigogine, Ilya, and Isabelle Stengers. *Order Out of Chaos: Man's New Dialogue with Nature.* New York: Bantam Books, 1984.

Pritchett, Henry S. "Science (1857–1907)." *Atlantic Monthly*, November 1907, 613–25.

Putnam, Hilary. *The Many Faces of Realism.* LaSalle, Ill.: Open Court, 1987.

———. *Realism and Reason.* Cambridge: Cambridge University Press, 1983.

———. *Reason, Truth, and History.* New York: Cambridge University Press, 1981.

———. *Renewing Philosophy.* Cambridge, Mass.: Harvard University Press, 1992.

Putnam, Hilary, and Ruth Anna Putnam. "William James's Ideas." *Raritan* 8 (Winter 1989), 27–44.

Quine, Willard van Orman. "Five Milestones of Empiricism." In *Theories and Things.* Cambridge, Mass.: Harvard University Press, 1981.

———. *Ontological Relativity and Other Essays.* New York: Columbia University Press, 1969.

———. "The Pragmatist's Place in Empiricism." In *Pragmatism: Its Sources and Prospects*, edited by R. J. Mulvaney and P. M. Zeltner. Columbia: University of South Carolina Press, 1981.

———. "Two Dogmas of Empiricism." In *From A Logical Point of View.* Cambridge, Mass.: Harvard University Press, 1951.

———. *Word and Object.* Cambridge, Mass.: MIT Press, 1960.

Rajchman, John, and Cornel West, eds. *Post-Analytic Philosophy.* New York: Columbia University Press, 1985.

Randall, John Herman. "Epilogue: The Nature of Naturalism." In *Naturalism and the Human Spirit*, edited by Y. H. Krikorian. New York: Columbia University Press, 1944.

Ratner, Joseph. "Introduction to John Dewey's Philosophy." In *Intelligence in the Modern World: John Dewey's Philosophy*, edited by Joseph Ratner. New York: Random House, 1939.

Ratner, Sidney, ed. *Vision and Action: Essays in Honor of Horace M. Kallen on His 70th Birthday.* New Brunswick, N.J.: Rutgers University Press, 1953.

Rawls, John. *A Theory of Justice.* Cambridge, Mass.: Harvard University Press, 1971.

Ree, Jonathan. "Timely Meditations." *Radical Philosophy* 55 (Summer 1990): 31–39.

Reichenbach, Hans. "Logistic Empiricism in Germany and the Present State of Its Problems." *Journal of Philosophy* 33 (1936): 141–52.

———. *The Rise of Scientific Philosophy.* Berkeley: University of California Press, 1951.

Rescher, Nicholas. *Peirce's Philosophy of Science: Critical Studies in His Philosophy of Induction and Scientific Method.* South Bend, Ind.: University of Notre Dame Press, 1978.

Richards, Robert. *Darwin and the Emergence of Evolutionary Theories of Mind and Behavior.* Chicago: University of Chicago Press, 1988.

Rockmore, Tom. *On Heidegger's Nazism and Philosophy.* Berkeley: University of California Press, 1992.

Rorty, Richard. "The Banality of Pragmatism and the Poetry of Justice." In *Pragmatism in Law and Society*, edited by Michael Brint and William Weaver. Boulder, Co.: Westview Press, 1991.

———. "Comments on Sleeper and Edel." *Transactions of the Charles S. Peirce Society* 21 (Winter 1985): 40–48.

———. *Consequences of Pragmatism: Essays 1972–1980.* Minneapolis: University of Minnesota Press, 1982.

———. "Contemporary Philosophy of Mind." *Syntheses* 53 (November 1982): 323–48.

———. *Contingency, Irony, and Solidarity.* Cambridge: Cambridge University Press, 1989.

————. "Dewey's Metaphysics." In Rorty, *Consequences of Pragmatism*. Minneapolis: University of Minnesota Press, 1982.

————. "Epistemological Behaviorism and the De-Transcendentalization of Analytic Philosophy." In *Hermeneutics and Praxis*, edited by Robert Hollinger, 89–121. South Bend, Ind.: University of Notre Dame Press, 1985.

————. "Foucault/Dewey/Nietzsche." *Raritan* 9 (Spring 1990): 1–8.

————. "From Language to Logic to Play." *Proceedings and Addresses of the American Philosophical Association* 59 (1986): 740–52.

————. "Idealism, Holism, and the Paradox of Knowledge." In *The Philosophy of Brand Blanshard*, edited by P. A. Schilpp. LaSalle, Ill.: Open Court, 1990.

————. "In a Flattened World." *London Review of Books*, April 8, 1993.

————. "Just One More Species Doing Its Best." *London Review of Books* 25 (July 1991): 3.

————. "Love and Money." *Common Knowledge* 1 (Spring 1991): 12–16.

————. *Philosophy and the Mirror of Nature*. Princeton, N.J.: Princeton University Press, 1979.

————. "Philosophy as Science, as Metaphor, and as Politics." In *The Institution of Philosophy*, edited by A. Cohen and M. Dascal. La Salle, Ill.: Open Court, 1989.

————. "Postmodernist Bourgeois Liberalism." *Journal of Philosophy* 80 (October 1983): 583–89.

————. "Pragmatism Without Method." In *Sidney Hook: Philosopher of Democracy and Humanism*, edited by Paul Kurtz. Buffalo, N.Y.: Prometheus Books, 1983.

————. "Priority of Democracy to Philosophy." In *Reading Rorty*, edited by Alan Malachowski, 279–302. Cambridge: Blackwell, 1990.

————. "Realism, Categories, and the Linguistic Turn." *International Philosophical Quarterly* 2 (May 1962): 307–22.

————. "Relations, Internal and External." In *The Encyclopedia of Philosophy*. 8 vols. Edited by Paul Edwards. New York: Macmillan, 1967, vol. 7.

————. "A Reply to Dreyfus and Taylor." *Review of Metaphysics* 24 (1980): 39–55.

————. "Taking Philosophy Seriously," review of *Heiddeger et le Nazisme*. *New Republic*, April 11, 1988.

————. "That Old Time Philosophy." *New Republic*, April 4, 1988.

————. "Transcendental Arguments, Self-Reference, and Pragmatism." In *Transcendental Arguments and Science*, edited by P. Bieri, R. Horstmann, and L. Kruger. Dordrecht: D. Reidel, 1979.

————. "Trotsky and the Wild Orchids." In *Wild Orchids and Trotsky*, edited by Mark Edmundson. New York: Penguin Books, 1993, 29–50.

————. "Two Cheers for the Cultural Left." *South Atlantic Quarterly* 89 (Winter 1990).

————, ed. *The Linguistic Turn*. Chicago: University of Chicago Press, 1967.

Rosaldo, Renato. *Culture and Truth: The Remaking of Social Analysis*. Boston: Beacon Press, 1989.

Ross, Dorothy. *The Origins of American Social Science*. Cambridge: Cambridge University Press, 1991.

Rossi, Paolo. *The Dark Abyss of Time*. Chicago: University of Chicago Press, 1984.

Royce, Josiah "The Problem of Truth." In *Basic Writings of Josiah Royce*, vol. 2, edited by J. McDermott. Chicago: University of Chicago Press, 1980.

Ruckert, Egbert Darnell. *The Chicago Pragmatists*. Minneapolis: University of Minnesota Press, 1959.

Ruse, Michael. *The Philosophy of Biology*. London: Hutchinson, 1973.

Russell, Bertrand. "Dewey's New Logic." In *The Philosophy of John Dewey*, edited by Paul Arthur Schilpp. Evanston, Ill.: Open Court, 1939, 143–56.

————. *Mysticism and Logic and Other Essays*. New York: Doubleday, 1917.

————. "Pragmatism." *Edinburgh Review* 209 (1909): 363–68.

Saussure, Ferdinand de. *Course in General Linguistics*. New York: McGraw Hill, 1966.

Schacht, Richard. *Nietzsche*. London: Routledge and Kegan Paul, 1983.

Schapiro, Meyer. "Looking Forward to Looking Backward." *Partisan Review* 5 (July 1938): 12–24.

Schiller, F.C.S. *Humanistic Pragmatism*. Edited by Reuben Abel. New York: Free Press, 1966.

Schilpp, Paul Arthur, ed. *The Philosophy of Rudolph Carnap*. LaSalle, Ill.: Open Court, 1963.

———. *The Philosophy of C. I. Lewis*. LaSalle, Ill.: Open Court, 1960.

Schrader, G. "The Influence of Continental Philosophy on the Contemporary American Scene: A Summons to Autonomy." In *Aspects of Contemporary American Philosophy*, edited by Franklin H. Donnell, Jr. Wurzburg: Physica-Verlag, 1965.

Sellars, R. W. "Realism, Naturalism, and Humanism." In *Contemporary American Philosophy*, vol. 2, edited by G. P. Adams and W. Montague. New York: Macmillan, 1930.

Selznick, Philip. *The Moral Commonwealth*. Berkeley: University of California Press, 1992.

Shapiro, Gary. *Alcyone: Nietzsche on Gifts, Noise, and Women*. Albany: State University of New York Press, 1991.

———. *Nietzschean Narratives*. Bloomington: Indiana University Press, 1989.

Sleeper, Ralph W. *The Necessity of Pragmatism: John Dewey's Conception of Philosophy*. New Haven, Conn.: Yale University Press, 1986.

Smith, John E. *Purpose and Thought: The Meaning of Pragmatism*. New Haven, Conn.: Yale University Press, 1978.

———. *Themes in American Philosophy*. New York: Harper and Row, 1970.

Smith, L. *Behaviorism and Logical Positivism*. Stanford: Stanford University Press, 1986.

Sober, Elliot. *The Nature of Selection: Evolutionary Theory in Philosophical Focus*. Cambridge, Mass.: MIT Press, 1984.

Sommerville, John. "The Social Ideas of the Wiener Kreis's International Congress." *Journal of Philosophy* 33 (1936).

Stout, Jeffrey. "Liberal Society and the Language of Morals." *Soundings* 69 (Spring-Summer 1986): 32–59.

Strong, Tracy B. *Friedrich Nietzsche and the Politics of Transfiguration*. Berkeley: University of California Press, 1975.

Stuhr, John J. "Dewey's Reconstruction of Metaphysics." *Transactions of the Charles S. Peirce Society* 28 (Spring 1992): 161–76.

Susman, Carl, ed. *Planning the Fourth Migration: The Neglected Vision of the Regional Planning Association of America*. Cambridge, Mass.: MIT Press, 1976.

Susman, Warren. " 'Personality' and the Making of Twentieth-Century American Culture." In *Culture as History*, edited by Warren Susman, 271–85. New York: Pantheon, 1984.

Taubeneck, Ernst. "Nietzsche in North America: Walter Kaufman and After." In *Confrontations: Derrida/Heidegger/Nietzsche*, edited by Ernst Behler. Stanford: Stanford University Press, 1991.

Thayer, H. Standish. *Meaning and Action: A Critical History of Pragmatism*. Indianapolis: Bobbs-Merrill, 1970.

———. "Pragmatism: A Reinterpretation of the Origins and Consequences." In *Pragmatism: Its Sources and Prospects*, edited by R. J. Mulvaney and P. M. Zeltner. Columbia: University of South Carolina Press, 1981.

Thompson, John B. *Studies in the Theory of Ideology*. Berkeley and Los Angeles: University of California Press, 1984.

Thoreau, Henry David. *Faith in a Seed and Other Natural History Writings*. Edited by Bradley P. Dean. Washington, D.C.: Island Press, 1993.

Tufts, James Hayden. *Selected Writings of James Hayden Tufts*. Edited by James Campbell. Carbondale: Southern Illinois University Press, 1992.

Tugwell, R. G. *The Brains Trust*. New York: Macmillan, 1968.

Venturi, Robert. *Learning from Las Vegas*. Cambridge, Mass.: MIT Press, 1962.

Vico, Giambattista. *The New Science*. Translated by M. Fisch and T. G. Bergin. Ithaca, N.Y.: Cornell University Press, 1968.

Wald, Alan. *The New York Intellectuals: The Rise and Decline of the Anti-Stalinist Left from the 1930s to the 1980s*. Chapel Hill: University of North Carolina Press, 1987.

Watson, John B. *Behaviorism.* New York: People's Institute, 1925.

Weber, Bruce, David J. Depew, and James D. Smith, eds. *Entropy, Information and Evolution.* Cambridge, Mass.: MIT Press, 1988.

West, Cornel. *The American Evasion of Philosophy: A Genealogy of Pragmatism.* Madison: University of Wisconsin Press, 1989.

———. "Critical Legal Studies and a Liberal Critic." *Yale Law Journal* 97, no. 5 (1988): 757–71.

———. "The Dilemma of the Black Intellectual." *Cultural Critique* 8, no. 1 (Fall 1985): 109–24.

———. *Prophetic Fragments.* Grand Rapids, Mich.: Eerdmans, 1988.

Westbrook, Robert. *John Dewey and American Democracy.* Ithaca, N.Y.: Cornell University Press, 1991.

———. "Lewis Mumford, John Dewey, and the 'Pragmatic Acquiescence.' " In *Lewis Mumford: Public Intellectual,* edited by Thomas P. Hughes and Agatha C. Hughes, 301–22. New York: Oxford University Press, 1990.

White, G. Edward. "The Rise and Fall of Justice Holmes." *University of Chicago Law Review* (Fall 1971): 51–77.

White, Morton, *Social Thought in America: The Revolt Against Formalism.* New York: Columbia University Press, 1949.

———. *Toward Reunion in Philosophy.* Cambridge, Mass.: Harvard University Press, 1956.

Whitehead, Alfred North. *Adventures of Ideas.* New York: Macmillan, 1933.

Wiebe, Robert H. *The Search for Order, 1877–1920.* New York: Hill and Wang, 1967.

Wiener, Philip. *Evolution and the Founders of Pragmatism.* Cambridge, Mass.: Harvard University Press, 1949.

Wilcox, John T. *Truth and Value in Nietzsche.* Ann Arbor: University of Michigan Press, 1974.

Wild, John. *The Radical Empiricism of William James.* Garden City, N.Y.: Doubleday, 1969.

Williams, Mary B. "The Logical Status of the Theory of Natural Selection and Other Evolutionary Controversies." In *The Methodological Unity of Science,* edited by M. Bunge. Dordrecht: Reidel, 1973.

Wills, Gary. *Nixon Agonistes.* New York: Simon and Schuster, 1969.

Wilson, Daniel J. *Science, Community, and the Transformation of American Philosophy, 1860–1930.* Chicago: University of Chicago Press, 1990.

Wilson, E. O. *Sociobiology: The New Synthesis.* Cambridge, Mass.: Harvard University Press, 1975.

Wilson, R. Jackson. "Charles Sanders Peirce: The Community of Inquiry." In R. Jackson Wilson, *In Quest of Community: Social Philosophy in the United States, 1860–1920.* New York: Oxford University Press, 1968, 32–59.

Wimsatt, William. "Teleology and the Logical Status of Function Statements." *Studies in the History and Philosophy of Science* 3 (1972): 1–80.

Winner, Langdon. *Autonomous Technology.* Cambridge, Mass.: MIT Press, 1977.

Wittgenstein, Ludwig. *Philosophical Investigations.* Edited and translated by E. Anscombe, et al. New York: Macmillan, 1953.

Woodbridge, Frederick W. *Mind and Nature.* New York: Columbia University Press, 1940.

Index

Contributors

RANDALL AUXIER is Chair of the Philosophy Department at Oklahoma City University. He took his Ph.D. at Emory University in 1992. Aside from evolutionary theory and pragmatism, he publishes most in the areas of process philosophy/theory, post-Kantian continental philosophy, and the philosophy of history and culture. He was awarded the Greenlee Prize by the Society for the Advancement of American Philosophy in 1990, and an NEH Fellowship in 1993.

CASEY NELSON BLAKE is Associate Professor of History at Indiana University and the author of *Beloved Community: The Cultural Criticism of Randolph Bourne, Van Wyck Brooks, Waldo Frank, and Lewis Mumford* (1990), as well as many articles and reviews. He is currently working on a book on the politics of public art in twentieth-century America.

JAMES CAMPBELL was educated at Temple University and the State University of New York at Stony Brook and is currently Professor of Philosophy at the University of Toledo. He spent the academic year 1990–91 as Fulbright Lecturer in American Culture and Literature at the University of Innsbruck. He is the editor of *Selected Writings of James Hayden Tufts* and author of *The Community Reconstructs: The Meaning of Pragmatic Social Thought.*

GEORGE COTKIN is Professor of History at California Polytechnic State University, San Luis Obispo, California. He is the author of *William James, Public Philosopher* (1990) and *Reluctant Modernism: American Thought and Culture*

(1992). His essays have appeared in such journals as the *Journal of the History of Ideas*, *American Studies*, and *Reviews in American History*. He has received a National Endowment for the Humanities Fellowship and served as Senior Fulbright Scholar at the University of Rome in 1994. He is currently writing a cultural history of existentialism in America.

DAVID DEPEW is Professor of Philosophy, California State University at Fullerton. He is most recently the author of "Philosophy of America in the Twentieth Century," in the *Encyclopedia of United States History in the Twentieth Century*, and, with Bruce Weber, *Darwinism Evolving: Systems Dynamics and the Genealogy of Natural Selection*.

RICKARD DONOVAN has been a long-time student of pragmatism and an active member of the Society for the Advancement of American Philosophy (SSAP). His articles and reviews on classical and contemporary pragmatism have appeared in *The Transactions of the Charles S. Peirce Society*, *International Philosophical Quarterly*, *Cross Currents*, and *Thought*. He is currently Chair of the Philosophy Department at Iona College.

GILES GUNN, Professor and Chair of the Department of English at the University of California, Santa Barbara, has written and edited a number of books, among them *The Culture of Criticism and the Criticism of Culture*; *Thinking Across the American Grain: Ideology, Intellect, and the New Pragmatism*, and, most recently, with Stephen Greenblatt, *Redrawing the Boundaries: The Transformation of English and American Literary Studies*.

LARRY A. HICKMAN is Director of the Center for Dewey Studies and Professor of Philosophy at Southern Illinois University at Carbondale. He is the author of *John Dewey's Pragmatic Technology* (1990) and *Modern Theories of Higher Predicates* (1980). He has also published essays on film theory and criticism, medical ethics, and Texas culture.

DAVID A. HOLLINGER is Professor of History at the University of California, Berkeley. He is the author of *Morris R. Cohen and the Scientific Ideal* (1975), and *In the American Province: Studies in the History and Historiography of Ideas* (1985), and is coeditor, with Charles Capper, of *The American Intellectual Tradition* (2d ed., 1993.) He is a frequent contributor to *New Literary History*, *American Quarterly*, and *American Historical Review*. His recent essays include "Postethnic America," *Contention* (1992), and "The 'Tough-Minded' Justice Holmes, Jewish Intellectuals, The Making of An American Icon," in *The Legacy of Oliver Wendell Holmes, Jr.* (ed. Robert W. Gordon, 1992).

ROBERT HOLLINGER is Associate Professor of Philosophy at Iowa State University. He is currently completing a book-length manuscript: *The Dark*

Side of Liberalism: Elitism vs. Democracy. He is the author of *Postmodernism and the Social Sciences.* His interest in Dewey's pragmatism is connected with the goal of developing a postmodernist defense of participatory democracy.

KONSTANTIN KOLENDA (1923–1991) was Professor and Chair of the Philosophy Department at Rice University for many years. He was the author of numerous articles and books on a wide variety of topics, including *Rorty's Humanistic Pragmatism: Philosophy Democratized.* Konnie was also a regular contributor to *The Humanist* (''Philosopher's Column'') and served as President of the Southwestern Philosophical Society in 1965.

BRUCE KUKLICK is Killebrew Professor of History at the University of Pennsylvania. He has written on the history of theology and philosophy in America, and is now at work on a study of the emergence of the ancient near east as an academic field in the United States.

BERND MAGNUS is Professor of Philosophy and Director of the Center for Ideas and Society at the University of California, Riverside. His publications include *Heidegger's Metahistory of Philosophy, Nietzsche's Existential Imperative, Nietzsche's Case: Philosophy as/and Literature* (with Stanley Stewart and Jean-Pierre Mileur), and numerous articles. He is currently completing the Nietzsche volume in the *Cambridge Companions to Philosophy* series with Kathleen Higgins, as well as *Postmodern Postures: A Philosophical Analysis and Genealogy,* from which his contribution to this collection is drawn.

ISAAC NEVO teaches in the Department of Philosophy at Ben-Gurion University of the Negev in Israel. He has previously taught at California State University, Fullerton, and at the University of California at Santa Barbara, where in 1988 he received his Ph.D. in Philosophy. Dr. Nevo is currently working on a book concerning the distinction between holistic and dichotomous strategies in contemporary criticism of modern philosophy. His published work includes articles on Wittgenstein, Derrida, Rorty, pragmatism, and the postmodern debate.

RALPH W. SLEEPER (1925–1993) was Professor of Philosophy at Queens College in New York for many years. Most recently, he had been teaching at the University of New Hampshire. Ralph also was a visiting scholar at Cambridge University on two separate occasions. He was the author of many important works on American philosophy. His book, *The Necessity of Pragmatism* (1986) is generally regarded as one of the most important books about Dewey ever written.

CORNEL WEST is Professor of Religious Studies and Chair of the Afro-American Studies Program at Princeton University. Hailed as one of the two most influential Afro-American scholars active today, and as the most important American theologian since Reinhold Niebhur, West has recently gained prominence as a public intellectual. He is the author of many books and articles on a wide range of topics. Among his recent works are *The Ethics of Marxism* (1992), *The American Evasion of Philosophy: A Genealogy of Pragmatism* (1989), *Race Matters* (1993), and *Keeping The Faith: Philosophy and Race in America* (1993). Professor West moved to Harvard in 1994, where he became a Professor in the African-American Studies Department and the Harvard Divinity School.

DANIEL J. WILSON is Associate Professor of History at Muhlenberg College, Allentown, Pennsylvania. His research has focused on the impact of science and professionalization on philosophy in the United States in the late nineteenth and early twentieth century. His most recent book on the subject was *Science, Community, and the Transformation of American Philosophy, 1860–1930* (1990).